Lenin's Terror

CW00968571

This book explores the development of Lenin's thinking on violence throughout his career, from the last years of the Tsarist regime in Russia through to the 1920s and the New Economic Policy, and provides an important assessment of the significance of ideological factors for understanding Soviet state violence as directed by the Bolshevik leadership during its first years in power. It highlights the impact of the First World War, in particular its place in Bolshevik discourse as a source of legitimating Soviet state violence after 1917, and explains the evolution of Bolshevik dictatorship over the half decade during which Lenin led the revolutionary state. It examines the militant nature of the Leninist worldview, Lenin's conception of the revolutionary state, the evolution of his understanding of 'dictatorship of the proletariat' and his version of 'just war'. The book argues that ideology can be considered primarily important for our understanding of the violent and dictatorial nature of the early Soviet state, at least when focused on the party elite, but it is also clear that ideology cannot be understood in a contextual vacuum. The oppressive nature of Tsarist rule, the bloodiness of the First World War and the vulnerability of the early Soviet state as it struggled to survive against foreign and domestic opponents were of crucial significance. The book sets Lenin's thinking on violence within the wider context of a violent world.

James Ryan is a Government of Ireland Postdoctoral CARA Mobility Research Fellow in the Humanities and Social Sciences, based at the Department of History, University of Warwick, UK and School of History, University College Cork, Ireland.

Routledge Contemporary Russia and Eastern Europe Series

Lenin's Terror

The ideological origins of early Soviet state violence

James Ryan

LONDON AND NEW YORK

First published 2012
by Routledge
2 Park Square, Milton Park, Abingdon, Oxfordshire OX14 4RN

Simultaneously published in the USA and Canada
by Routledge
711 Third Avenue, New York, NY 10017

First issued in paperback 2014

*Routledge is an imprint of the Taylor & Francis Group, an informa
business*

British Library Cataloguing in Publication Data
A catalogue record for this book is available from the British Library

Library of Congress Cataloging in Publication Data
Ryan, James, 1985-
Lenin's terror : the ideological origins of early Soviet state violence /
James Ryan.
    pages ; cm. – (Routledge contemporary Russia and Eastern Europe series ; 36)
    ISBN 978-0-415-67396-9 (hardback) – ISBN 978-0-203-11576-3 (ebook)
    1. Lenin, Vladimir Il'ich, 1870-1924. 2. Violence–Political aspects–Soviet
Union. 3. State-sponsored terrorism–Soviet Union. 4. Soviet Union–
History–Revolution, 1917-1921. I. Title. II. Series: Routledge
contemporary Russia and Eastern Europe series ; 36.
    DK254.L46R89 2012
    947.084'1–dc23
                                2011051857

ISBN 978-0-415-67396-9 (hbk)
ISBN 978-1-138-81568-1 (pbk)
ISBN 978-0-203-11576-3 (ebk)

Typeset in Times New Roman
by Saxon Graphics Ltd, Derby

Contents

Acknowledgements

This book began as a doctoral dissertation at University College Cork, and since its inception I have incurred many debts of gratitude. Funding was provided initially by the Faculty of Arts at UCC, and later by the Irish Research Council for the Humanities and Social Sciences. My editor at Routledge, Peter Sowden and his team have been encouraging and most helpful from the outset. I am grateful to the two anonymous reviewers who provided essential guidance.

The academic enterprise is by nature a collaborative endeavor and, as the endnotes attest, I have made extensive use of the works of a considerable number of scholars. More particularly, Geoff Roberts has been my teacher, doctoral supervisor and mentor for a decade. He is always generous with his time, his library and with dispensing his extensive knowledge and wisdom. His input was especially valuable and appreciated during the process of converting the dissertation into book format. I could not have wished to be taught by a finer scholar. I have also benefited from discussions and correspondence with Chris Read, Ron Suny, Erik van Ree, Lars Lih, Judith Devlin, Matt Rendle and Sarah Badcock, amongst others. The annual conferences of the Study Group on the Russian Revolution, in particular, have been excellent sounding-boards for the first drafts of some of the chapters, as well as extremely enjoyable gatherings. Of course full responsibility for the errors remaining in the book is entirely my own.

The School of History at UCC has provided a wonderful home for the conduct of research, and my many friends and colleagues there and in the university more generally have provided invaluable support. In particular, I want to thank some of my closest friends who have been with me nearly every step of the way: Sarah-Anne Buckley, Gregory Foley, John Borgonovo, Susan Grant, Barbara O'Donoghue and Ruth Canning. Greg read early drafts of all the chapters and provided much-appreciated editorial advice. The staff at the inter-library loan desk in the Boole Library UCC, were very efficient in finding almost any source in Russian I requested. The staff at the Russian State Archive for Social-Political History (RGASPI), the State Archive of the Russian Federation (GARF), the Russian State Library and the State Public Historical Library in Moscow were helpful and tolerant of my Russian communication skills. The library of the School of Slavonic and East European Studies in London proved an invaluable depository, and my thanks to the friendly and helpful staff there.

Most importantly, I want to thank my family, my mother Mary, brother John and sister Marie. Their love and support have been constant, and as a close-knit family this has been the most important source of support and of my inspiration. They even tolerated me when I returned home to write up the Ph.D. This book is dedicated to them and to the memory of my late father, John (Jackie), who did not live to see us go to university but would have been very proud of us.

James Ryan
Cork
September 2011

Note: Chapter 2 was previously published as the journal article '"Revolution is War": The Development of the Thought of V. I. Lenin on Violence, 1899–1907', *Slavonic and East European Review*, vol. 89, No. 2, pp. 248–73, and is reproduced with kind permission of Deputy Editor Dr Barbara Wyllie.

Note on style

The system of transliteration used in this book is the Library of Congress style, with certain exceptions. I have chosen to use 'Bolsheviks' rather than 'Bol'sheviki', 'Trotsky' rather than 'Trotskii' and 'Zinoviev' rather than 'Zinov'ev'. I have chosen to continue to refer usually to 'Bolsheviks' rather than 'Communists' after March 1918. Dates used correspond to the calendar in use in Russia at the time. The Gregorian calendar, adopted in Russia in March 1918, was 13 days ahead of the Julian calendar in the twentieth century.

Introduction
Ideology and violence

The imagination and the spiritual strength of Shakespeare's evildoers
stopped short at a dozen corpses. Because they had no ideology.[1]
(Aleksandr Solzhenitsyn, *The Gulag Archipelago*)

This book provides a comprehensive and systematic narrative study of V.I.
Lenin's thinking on political violence from his early writings in the 1890s until his
retirement from active politics in 1923. This topic is important for understanding
Lenin the man and theorist as well as the nature of the Soviet state that came into
existence in Russia at the close of 1917. It places Lenin's ideas firmly within their
Russian and European historical contexts, and delineates narratively the interactive
relationship between ideas and circumstances/events. It is also a study of Lenin's
practice as leader of the Soviet state and Bolshevik (Communist) party after 1917,
that is, his direct advocacy of and actual directives for the use of violence. These
were certainly not always implemented, at least in the manner urged, and in any
case violence usually occurred 'from below' whether Lenin advocated it or not.[2]
Bolshevik rule was not firmly established across Soviet-controlled territory for
quite some time after the October Revolution of 1917, and in fact much of the
state and state-sponsored violence that occurred in early Soviet Russia took place
without Lenin's (prior) knowledge. The Bolshevik Party and Soviet state were
much more than Lenin. He was not a dictator in the sense that all his
recommendations were accepted and implemented, nor in that his colleagues did
not at times sharply disagree with him. However, he was the leading and most
influential figure in Party and state, and while at the helm of power policies largely
bore his imprint.

How and why did Lenin and his Party, committed to a vision of a 'beautiful
future' of peaceful prosperity for humanity as a whole, visit a violent dictatorship
upon the Russian people? To what extent did their system of ideas and beliefs
contribute to this, what were these ideas and beliefs, and does the world that they
were reacting to bear some measure of responsibility for the Soviet political
system? These are some of the questions that will be addressed in this book. The
principal research question posed is one of the most debated amongst scholars:
whether Soviet state violence, in this case as approved and directed from the

centre of power, was the product of ideological factors or a response to circumstances, or whether it is possible to attribute explanatory primacy to one or other in this regard.

The book focuses on the theory and practice of the leading actor of the Bolshevik Party and Soviet state, Lenin. It does not provide a comprehensive study of early Soviet state and state-sponsored violence. It does not examine why 'ordinary' people or regular 'state agents' – local Cheka (political police) forces or Red army units and partisans – engaged in violent practices, violence that was certainly not simply 'political' or ideological in nature. Hence the ideology in question is 'high ideology' rather than how it was understood 'on the ground'. Nonetheless the role of the state and its leadership was crucial. Joshua Sanborn points out that, though violence reached endemic levels in Russia after the collapse of the autocracy in 1917, the Bolshevik state did not so much attempt to curtail such violence engendered by the brutalization of the First World War as 'deploy an ideology of violence that was conducive to the further escalation of uncontrolled carnage.'[3]

The Soviet regime proved to be one of history's most repressive and violent experiments in social engineering. For almost all of its existence the Soviet state ruled its people with an iron fist, but widespread state violence and terror were by no means endemic features of the system. Following Iosif Stalin's death in 1953, terror in the sense of widespread physical violence ceased to characterize the mechanics of Soviet power. The bulk of Soviet state violence was committed during the 25-year rule of Stalin but between December 1917 and February 1922 – during the rule of his predecessor, Lenin – there were, at lowest estimates, 28,000 executions (excluding battlefield deaths) on average per year directly attributable to the Soviet state, a sharp contrast with the approximate total figure of 14,000 executed by the Russian Tsarist regime between 1866 and 1917. This figure approximates with that of the years of 'dekulakization' in the early 1930s, though it is considerably below the average of the bloodiest years of Stalinism.[4]

Scholarly and popular attention has invariably focused primarily on the phenomenon of Stalinism. The violence of Lenin's rule can appear more readily understandable as the inevitable accompaniment of the foundation of a new revolutionary state, especially amidst the destruction wrought by the World War and the brutal Russian Civil War, but Stalin deployed the worst of his terror in peacetime. Yet, if one accepts that Stalin and his colleagues' professed Leninism was genuinely important for their political practice, then Stalinism should be studied in the light of Leninism – Lenin's understanding and development of Marxian ideas that formed the ideological basis of the early Soviet system. Indeed, expertise regarding the significance of the violence of the early Soviet years is under-developed in the general body of work on Soviet, particularly Stalinist, state violence. Leninism (as distinct from Stalinism, Maoism, etc.) and Lenin's rule are highly interesting and important subjects in their own right, but the legacy of Leninism for the development of Stalinism is an important reason why a detailed study of Lenin and violence is valuable and necessary.

Lenin, and his Bolshevik colleagues such as Lev Trotsky, Nikolai Bukharin and ultimately Stalin, were to exert radical influences on the meaning, global influence, and fate of Marxism as an intellectual tradition and revolutionary movement. Though Marxists were certainly not averse to using violence, Lenin was the first and most significant Marxist theorist to dramatically elevate the role of violence as revolutionary instrument and function of the ambivalent Marxian concept of the dictatorship of the proletariat (working class). This concept became, in Lenin's theory and practice, explicitly violent and truly 'dictatorial', and led to bitter polemics between the Bolsheviks and their European and Russian Marxist critics who condemned the terror and dictatorship of Bolshevism and sought to discredit its pretensions to be recognized internationally as Marxist orthodoxy.

Some scholars have effectively sought to implicate Lenin and his comrades as the sources of the 'original sin' that led to the holocaustic consequences of the Stalin era,[5] and this attests to the importance of a full-length, balanced study of Lenin and violence. It is also interesting to consider how Lenin's ideas on revolutionary violence and terrorism differ from those of terrorists in his time and those today, but more significantly it is important to understand the often idealistic, indeed moralistic motivations and justifications for violence that unite some of today's violent practitioners with advocates of political violence of an earlier era. Understanding such motivations can help illustrate how best to circumvent the general phenomenon of political violence.

Despite the end of the Cold War Lenin is still a controversial figure, reviled by some (including on the Left) and revered by others. For historian Richard Pipes, Lenin was 'a heartless cynic' who displayed 'utter disregard for human life', and was in fact even more severe than Stalin.[6] Robert Gellately considers that Lenin was 'merciless and cruel', deservingly placed alongside Stalin and Hitler in a triumvirate of brutal twentieth-century European leaders.[7] On the other hand some left-wing thinkers advocate reviving Lenin's uncompromising revolutionary and partisan spirit to address today's global problems.[8] Most scholarly literature on Lenin is not so polarized, and there is much of a balanced and scholarly nature available. Recently some scholars have explicitly set about 'retrieving the historical Lenin', that is re-appraising him through careful examination of historical sources free from politicized stereotypes.[9]

Violence is often a source of interpretive contention and polemic when writing about significant historical figures, and this has certainly been the case with Lenin. Chris Read, one of Lenin's most recent English-language biographers, remarks that 'No aspect of Lenin's rule has generated more heat and less light in recent years than this one'.[10] Though a considerable volume of literature from Western, Soviet and post-Soviet Russian scholars deals with the subject, there is little sustained and lengthy scholarly treatment focused on this topic. To the author's knowledge, there is no full-length monograph study, at least in English.[11] This book will contribute to Lenin's biography by directly addressing the subject of his relationship with violence in a sustained, scholarly and systematic manner, and will make an especially significant contribution toward 'retrieving the historical Lenin'.

The book is largely one of intellectual history, and will draw principally on Lenin's *Collected Works* and published documents in Russian. Since the opening of the former Soviet archives some new material has come to light but nothing that undermines an interpretation based on Lenin's published works, although some of his more starkly violent pronouncements were only discovered in the archives in the 1990s. The book's principal purpose is to examine Lenin's relationship with violence, but it will also make an important contribution to understanding and explaining Soviet state violence more generally, and indeed the political violence of early twentieth century Europe more broadly. It does not provide a comprehensive portrait of Lenin. Its focus is on one dimension of his thought and political practice, the aspect of violence and repression, although the broader context of his political thought is explained. It is likely that a more comprehensive portrait of his thought and practice would make it clearer to the reader that, in light of what came after his death, in several respects Lenin pointed to a more humane Marxism. Lenin does not appear in this book as an endearing or admirable individual, but neither does he appear as an utterly cruel, reprehensible despot.

Robert Service is undoubtedly correct that 'nobody can write detachedly about Lenin.'[12] However it is possible to write balanced and scholarly history, regardless of one's personal beliefs and viewpoints. The present author sympathizes with certain of the Marxist diagnoses of the problems of the modern world and is not averse to an uncompromising approach to certain issues, but does not support the violence accompanying, or indeed some of the radical pretensions of, the Marxist–Leninist project. Some of Lenin's analyses, though often overstated, rang true at least to some extent. Certainly some of his indomitable and unflinching spirit, if not his ideas, could be useful for addressing some of today's national and global problems. Yet the practical experience of the often narrow-minded doctrinal Leninism, typically precluding compromise, agreement and conciliation, serves to remind of the possible dangers of absolutist and sometimes radically revolutionary approaches to politics.

Balanced and fair-minded history should not, however, preclude historical judgement. Was the amount of state violence employed by the Bolsheviks 'necessary' or counter-productive, reasonable or reflective of a particular entrenched assessment of circumstances? Could the early Soviet system have been considerably less violent and oppressive and survived, rendering less likely the later atrocities of Stalinism? The viewpoint expressed here is that, though the use of violence was essential for the Bolsheviks to hold onto their absolute power (apart from defeating the White forces in Civil War), the revolution could have been prosecuted in a less extremist manner such that its use would have been much diminished, a more stable socialist state could have been constructed, and twentieth-century Russian (and Eastern European) history could have taken a more humane course. Why this proved not to be tells us much about the nature of Bolshevism.

By 'judgement', then, is meant a scholarly appraisal of the reasonableness, significance and ultimate legacy of Leninist violence. The extent of Bolshevik violence and dictatorship was, paradoxically, both effective and ultimately counter-productive, for the price of survival was a bloody dictatorship that distorted the lofty ideals that animated the Bolsheviks to take power in the first place. Though the collapse of the Soviet regime was not inevitable, it was largely the product of its own structural weaknesses as established from the outset. It is probable that no reader or author can or indeed should engage with this subject without forming a moral judgement, but a scholarly approach to the subject serves to allow the reader to formulate a balanced, informed appraisal. This ultimately is the historian's purpose.

Introducing Lenin

For over 70 years the Soviet state, originally the Russian Soviet Federative Socialist Republic (RSFSR) and then the Union of Soviet Socialist Republics (USSR), commanded the attention of the world. Its first leader, Vladimir Il'ich Ul'ianov, known to history by his revolutionary pseudonym of Lenin, has been one of the most significant and influential figures of modern history, an iconic revolutionary leader absolutely and single-mindedly committed to Marxist, working-class revolution. Socialist-communist regimes professing adherence to Lenin's ideas and political legacy appeared in different parts of the world in the last century, exercising enormous influence upon the shaping of the contemporary world; it is certainly clear that Leninism 'should be seen in world-historical terms.'[13] Even without Lenin, an exclusively socialist government (probably leaning on the soviets – the democratic councils of the working people – or even exclusively soviet) would almost certainly have been formed in Russia in the late autumn of 1917, at least for an interim. However the particular socialist Soviet government that was created by his Bolshevik party would almost certainly not have come to be were it not for Lenin, and his successors continued the Soviet regime and, ironically, ultimately dismantled it by claiming Leninist legitimacy.

Lenin was born in the town on Simbirsk (now Ul'ianovsk) on the river Volga in April 1870. His father achieved the status of a member of the lower nobility, and the Ul'ianov children were brought up to value hard work and the intelligentsia ideal of public service. The young Vladimir excelled at school, but in the space of a year his world was severely affected by the deaths of his father and elder brother Aleksandr, in 1886 and 1887 respectively. His political awareness was aroused by the shock of Aleksandr's death, for he was hanged for his involvement in an attempt to assassinate Tsar Aleksandr III. Vladimir was expelled from university in Kazan but demonstrated his considerable academic talent by graduating with the equivalent of a first-class honors law degree from St Petersburg University, despite having been prevented from attending classes. He was an avid reader of classical Russian literature, and also of revolutionary works. He soon became involved with Marxist reading circles and his first book, a study of the development of capitalism in Russia, appeared in 1899. Four years previously he had been arrested in St Petersburg along with his activist revolutionary comrades and sent to Siberian exile. In exile he married Nadezhda Konstantinovna Kruspkaia, to whom he would remain married for the rest of his life, but they had no children. With the turn of the century Lenin left Russia and would only return for a brief time following the revolutionary upheaval in 1905, until the collapse of the autocracy in 1917. Establishing himself as a leading member of the émigré Russian Marxist leadership, he enthralled some and repulsed others, earning a reputation for a factionalist as the leader of the Bolshevik faction of the Russian Social-Democratic Labour Party (RSDLP). His contemporaries, whether supporters or opponents, were struck by the intensity of his political commitment. Following his return to Russia in 1917, he steered his Bolshevik Party to a seizure of power, and then steered the newly-founded Soviet state through its difficult infancy. He suffered his first stroke in May 1922, and by 1923 he had retired from active politics. He died in January 1924 at the age of 53.

Compared to two recent Western biographies, Lenin appears in this work as more disposed to violence and brutality and ideologically-driven in this regard than he does in Chris Read's excellent account of his life, but less inclined to violence and less influenced by the Russian terrorist tradition than Robert Service argues. He was usually an uncompromising politician who at times displayed brutal traits and an apparently shocking lack of concern for the human consequences of his violent and repressive injunctions. However his brutal correspondences as leader of the Soviet state were not products of a pathological cruelty. He was a man of high ideals, however misguided, who devoted his life to a vision of a better future for humanity, though this at times is overshadowed by his unscrupulous pronouncements. He cannot be considered a humanitarian despite his deep commitment to an ostensibly humanitarian vision.

Ideological primacy

The argument of this book is that ideology provides the primary explanatory framework for understanding state violence as instructed 'from above' in Soviet Russia under Lenin's leadership, and indeed for understanding Lenin's conceptualization and advocacy of violence as a whole. However the book rejects, as most scholars have for at least two decades, the idea that explanation should be sought in either ideology or circumstances, and it rejects the simplistic ideological causation and determinism (i.e. a neat cause and effect relationship between ideas and actions) that scholarship on Soviet history has been prone to adopt. The assertion of the primacy of ideology in explaining early Soviet state violence as approved and directed 'from above' is argued within the framework of more sophisticated post-revisionist understandings of Soviet history, understandings that have restored the importance of ideology without privileging it or even asserting its primacy. The argument is that the primacy of ideology can be asserted in explaining certain aspects of Soviet history (certainly not Soviet history in total) – in this case violence as approved and directed by the leading actors of the early Soviet state – without re-invoking the traditional ideology-versus-circumstances dichotomy.[14] Indeed, the factors leading to violence and terror (both state and social) in revolutionary Russia especially from 1917 were complex. These included the particular Russian process of modernization since the end of the nineteenth century and the 'shock' of the First World War in a largely peasant country. Russia was reeling from what was the bloodiest war in history until then and the consequent material-economic and psychological dislocation, including a general brutalization and accustoming to violence and death. Russia, possessing a particularly underdeveloped civil society, experienced a collapse of empire and breakdown in state and economic order; armed civil war and foreign intervention; and armed popular resistance to the new Soviet state. The Bolsheviks provided an ideology of revolutionary eschatology (in the secularized Marxist sense of historical progression toward the 'salvation' of humanity in communist society) and a 'high-modernist' ideological vision of 'scientific' social transformation, with a willingness to utilize violence to this end.[15] However, though unique in respects, Russia's experience was part of a general culture of unprecedented violent upheaval witnessed in many parts of inter-war Europe.[16] One of the most welcome and valuable trends in recent scholarship has been to place the Soviet experience within a broader European intellectual and practical context, arguing that the Soviet system was based not on a specific ideology alone but also reflected a broader Russian and European modernist political 'ecosystem'.[17]

This book seeks not to discover the primary *causal* factor(s) of Bolshevik and early Soviet state violence as such, but rather to contribute a more complex *explanation* of such violent practices as approved and directed 'from above'. Ideological primacy in this sense suggests that the beliefs of and understandings arising from Lenin's Marxist ideology as it developed in response to events provided the principal orientation for and justification of his, and the Bolshevik leadership's, violent practices (apart from regular combat warfare). It does not mean or imply that ideology in itself simply caused the practice of violence. It would be simplistic to suggest that the idea of ideological primacy means that circumstances and events were merely of secondary significance; ideologies are not removed from the environments in which they arise and develop. This is particularly relevant when considering the place and function of violence in the Marxist analysis; according to Maurice Merleau-Ponty, an apologist of 'progressive' violence in a Marxist sense, insofar as violence was conceived as 'necessity' it was 'justified not on its own terms but by the context of a violent world.'[18] In this sense, Lenin's ideas on violence were not simply inscribed in the meanings of the Marxist concepts of 'dictatorship of the proletariat' and 'class struggle', but were developed and justified within the context of a reactionary and at times brutal Tsarist political system, and especially within the context of the First World War and the subsequent Civil War. The world war legitimized for the Bolsheviks both the necessity of socialist revolution in Russia in 1917, and the 'revolutionary' state violence that followed.

The Bolsheviks faced a life-and-death struggle for survival in a brutal civil war, and needed to mobilize an often reluctant, even hostile populace in conditions of desperate privation. Politicians and military commanders have typically condoned and advocated various forms of violence and brutality during exceptional times – the Bolsheviks did not invent terror. The reason for according ideology primacy for explaining the *general* phenomenon of Soviet state violence as directed from above, through a study of Lenin, is due to the particulars of this ideology and how it helped structure and translate into political practice. Bolshevism possessed a strongly eschatological, apocalyptic vision of revolution as a life-and-death struggle for the salvation of humanity from the brutalities of capitalism, especially in its imperialist stage, prescribing and justifying 'revolutionary violence' broadly conceived to negate 'reactionary violence.' It was usually uncompromising, and events were processed through a largely absolutist ideological prism. The Bolsheviks in power were not merely reacting in a rational and calculated, though often brutal fashion, to circumstances and events, to the considerable problems they faced and the need to keep hold of their tenuous reins of power. Bolshevik perceptions, reactions and solutions were fundamentally informed by this eschatological and politically Manichean vision, and indeed contributed to the creation of hostile circumstances.

Driven by a high-minded Salvationist vision, the story of the early years of Bolshevik rule is partly one of tragedy. Reality proved much more reluctant to conform to theory than the Bolsheviks expected, and the Russian people found that a socialist revolution brought them not relief from the sufferings of war but renewed suffering and hardships, under a new form of autocratic rule. The heralded 'dictatorship of the proletariat and poor peasants', in many respects, turned into a dictatorship over the masses. However this was also a tragedy very much of the Bolsheviks' own making. Lenin had envisaged considerable coercion and at least some violence, for the Bolshevik project had pretensions to transform, 'cleanse' and purify society through class struggle and proletarian dictatorship, and Bolshevism was inherently disposed to political absolutism. The decision to deploy violence resulted from the choices made by particular individuals at particular times, confronted with particular circumstances. The fact that violence was also utilized by the Bolsheviks' opponents, or that most thorough-going revolutions and civil wars have witnessed terror, does not mean that Bolshevik violence can be explained simply as a consequence of the revolutionary process or the immense socio-economic dislocation of the time. The Bolsheviks, acting on the basis of theoretical appraisals, made certain choices that often intensified socio-political conflicts and resulted in the large-scale application of violence, whereas less abrasive choices were often possible.[19]

The manner in which the Bolsheviks undertook their revolution and went about ordering society anew along the principles of class warfare (though without much actual violence) before any significantly dangerous opposition to their stronghold of power was encountered was significant. They demonstrated a categorization of the body politic and willingness to place the state against significant sections of its society, seeking a highly politicized, class-antagonistic approach to the extreme difficulties that would have confronted any Russian government in 1917/8. Revolution itself was war, Lenin had maintained since 1905, and before taking power he had concluded that a proletarian state would be an instrument of 'violence' directed against the deposed bourgeoisie and their more pervasive cultural legacies, though 'violence' in this sense had a broad meaning similar to his concept of civil war. Lenin had noted on the eve of the October Revolution that a bloody civil war was a distinct possibility but that the revolution was essential in any case, though it appears that he held out considerable hope that a proletarian revolution in the twentieth century would be more straightforward and less bloody than any major revolution in history.

The Bolsheviks came to power with no clear 'blueprint' as such for employing physical violence. There was not widespread state violence until well into 1918. Initially mild in their punishments, Lenin and hardline Bolsheviks from December 1917 and into 1918 adopted a more violent and coercive rhetoric to confront the enormous problems that they faced. These problems stemmed primarily not from counter-revolution but from economic and social dislocation and what the Bolsheviks identified as the cultural backwardness of the Russian people. The widespread spiral of terror was then fuelled by the beginning of frontal civil war in those areas economically necessary for the survival of the country. However the principal phase of the Civil War was initially the consequence of Bolshevik extremism: the exclusion of the Right Socialist-Revolutionaries, a party with a predominantly peasant support base in a predominantly peasant country, from meaningful participation in political life. Civil war would likely have been inevitable in Russia sooner or later, considering the opposition of the 'Whites' not only to Bolshevism but to socialism, and especially if a socialist government took the step of extracting Russia from the World War, as the Bolsheviks did. Yet the effective establishment of a one-party dictatorship aggravated tensions between state and society under circumstances of economic and political crisis. Bolshevik dictatorial rule and the suppression of strikes, uprisings and other socialist parties were not consequences of the White threat – though this threat certainly helped Bolshevik leaders to justify these measures – and they continued and in some respects intensified after the White challenge.

Lenin revealed a particular propensity to resort to violence and the rhetoric of class conflict in response to the difficulties encountered. His rhetoric was explicitly confrontational and socially-divisive along class lines. He usually rejected recommendations from outside the Party, and from relative moderates within, to seek a less confrontational and violent approach. Violent Bolshevik campaigns during the Civil War, furthermore, were designed not merely to repress enemies but to excise socially dangerous elements in the process of forging a new healthy society.[20] With the relative normalization of Soviet life after the Civil War, terror (on a reduced and less bloody scale) and totalitarian dictatorial impulses persisted into peacetime, and the coercive function of the state as an instrument for economic and social transformation was clearly recognized. Though certainly Bolshevik thought and mechanism of rule had quite naturally become 'militarized' by the Civil War, more significant perhaps is how the experience of the Civil War and foreign intervention was incorporated into the Bolshevik metanarrative, becoming the state's 'formative experience'. Bolshevik practices continued to be reasoned and justified within a Manichean and eschatological language; despite the change in course inaugurated from 1921 with the New Economic Policy (NEP), the Bolsheviks remained recognizably 'Bolshevik'. Neil Harding explains that 'the unforeseen and the calamitous had to be presented as parts of an intelligible process',[21] rendered intelligible by reference to the ideological framework that provided meaning for their life's work.

Some scholars believe that historians of the Soviet regime should concentrate on the notion of ideology as discourse, reasoning that 'Ideology's power lies at the level of communicative action and cannot be reduced to its role in constituting beliefs.'[22] It was respect for conventions, rather than the strength of ideological belief, that mattered in Soviet politics.[23] However the original 'Old' Bolsheviks were intense Marxist believers. For the Bolshevik leadership the beliefs and tenets of revolutionary Marxism were crucial guiding points, not least during the early years of Soviet power when the Soviet Republic's existence itself was never considered secure from internal and external enemies.

Violence and ideology

It is important to clarify what is understood here by the concepts of 'violence' and 'ideology'. The usual definition of violence is that it is the infliction of physical harm or damage on a person.[24] Some scholars, such as Slavoj Žižek differentiates between 'subjective' acts of overt violence and more obscure 'objective' violence embedded into political, social, and economic structures, and the symbolism of language.[25] Indeed Lenin did not confine his use and understanding of the term violence (*nasilie* in Russian) to the existence or infliction of physical force causing bodily harm.[26] He and the Bolsheviks understood violence inflicted by a proletarian state, as one Russian historian puts it, as 'a system of political, military, economic and ideological measures of force and repression on the side of the advanced [...] class relative to the exploiting, reactionary classes'.[27] Lenin understood the very existence of the state as an instrument of violence, directed against some class and possessing organized armed force at its disposal. His understanding of proletarian state violence (he used both terms 'violence' and 'coercion' in this regard) against class enemies did not necessarily or simply mean the infliction of physical harm; it also included the removal of political, social and economic privileges and rights. In short it signified the deployment of state power, of proletarian revolutionary force, against the bourgeoisie and their 'hangers-on'. Lenin's very language was often considerably 'violent', employing such words as 'crush', 'smash', 'break', 'annihilation', and permeated with notions of enmity and struggle, without necessarily prescribing physical force.

Whereas coercion is 'the activity of causing people to do something against their will', and is not always 'violent',[28] it seems reasonable to posit that some acts of clearly arbitrary repression/coercion committed by a state, though not overtly 'violent', can be considered lesser forms of state violence.[29] Examples in this context include the arrest and incarceration of peaceful opposition socialists or striking workers, or the incarceration of workers in forced labour camps for labour 'indiscipline' at a time of scarcity and starvation. However the predominant understanding of 'violence' adopted here is that of physical force causing harm and especially death, the 'absolute violence.'[30] Violence, as Hannah Arendt noted, is by nature instrumental, it is a means to an end. Hence the importance for its practitioners to justify its use 'through the end it pursues.'[31] Whatever the external influences and pressures on its use, the decision to use violence, at least political violence, is always one that reveals certain ethical values and attitudes (and absence of others) on the part of its advocates and practitioners. Indeed more generally it can be argued that morals and ethics 'lie at the core of revolutionary commitment.'[32]

Ideology is a more complex concept, and one that has not been subjected to much elucidation in the literature on Soviet history. Political ideologies are 'more or less coherent set(s) of ideas that provide the basis for organized political action, whether this is intended to preserve, modify or overthrow the existing system of power.'[33] Given that we are thinking beings, and that we seek to make sense of the world by ordering it through mental categories, it should be clear that ideas (and ideologies) typically play important roles in determining behaviour. Ideologies embody claims to uncover truth, offering explanatory accounts of the existing world (particular 'worldviews'), descriptions of the desired future, and explanations of how political change 'can and should be brought about.'[34] Ideologies function by structuring what one thinks and how one acts through the language of a particular discourse. The problem traditionally with much Soviet-related literature has been the assumption that ideology, understood as canonized doctrine, provides a neat 'blueprint' for action. However as scholars of political ideologies (and of Soviet history) now stress, there is a constant interaction between ideas/ideologies, and other factors and events.

Michael Freeden has provided a framework for understanding both the ideational integrity of ideologies, and the input of other factors. Stressing that groups employ ideologies to 'construct an understanding' of the political world and act on that understanding, he considers that it is these 'conscious perceptions, and conscious and unconscious conceptions' of political actors that are 'a major, *if indeterminate* [emphasis added], cause of human conduct', and it is 'at that level that ideologies operate.'[35] Political conduct, then, usually results to a large extent from the meanings that an ideology provides for interpreting the world and events in order to prescribe a certain course of action; ideologies do not simplistically dictate actions but direct how political actors make choices and discard others through their reasoning process.[36] In the early Soviet context as Graeme Gill has explained, what might be termed this 'interpretive–structural' function of ideology can be understood thus:

> The ideology's provision of a general orientation towards policy questions was not a mechanistic process. The leaders did not perceive a problem and then go to some 'holy book' to seek the solution. The ideology was built in from the outset, an intrinsic part of the initial perception and understanding of the problem at hand. Rather than being an external factor, the ideology constituted the framework or set of categories through which the Bolsheviks sought to understand the world about them. The most important aspect of this was class analysis.[37]

It should be clear to the reader by the end of this book that ideology was a critical factor that structured Lenin's outlook and practices. Discourses function by allowing certain things and discouraging/impeding certain others from being said;[38] an ideology's set of ideas are rooted within certain discursive parameters dictated by the essential elements of what compose a particular ideology. Yet one should not overlook the fact that political actors can certainly utilize an ideology much more instrumentally, namely to justify actions taken for a variety of other reasons.[39] Lenin and the Bolsheviks, as sufficiently pragmatic and responsive politicians, did not always act simply according to ideological prescriptions, but as highly theoretical politicians they did attempt to relate their actions to an ideological justification.

Ideologies develop and are transmitted mainly through their discursive languages, and through cultural and individual human agencies. Ideologies are distinct belief systems but also products of their time and place; their elements, Freeden explains, are 'shaped by [...] culture: temporally and spatially bound social practices, institutional patterns, ethical systems'.[40] Hence one can understand the rise and practice of Bolshevism in terms of the discursive interpretation of Marx's thought mediated through the political culture of autocratic (absolutist) Russia – which facilitated an absolutist revolutionary politics and an undemocratic new regime after 1917 – and the circumstances of early twentieth-century Europe. Marxism as a set of ideas was quite vague regarding practical prescriptions, and required mediation through these cultural, institutional, and indeed broader intellectual patterns. Individual human agency is also crucial for understanding how ideologies are formulated, received and function; individuals internalize an ideology, make their own sense of it, and contribute to it. Ideologies shape and are shaped by individual personalities.

The ideology, Freeden continues, must 'conceive of, assimilate, and attempt to shape "real-world" events. Through it a practice or institution or event is integrated into the macro-structure of the ideology.'[41] In other words, the question whether ideology or circumstance provides explanation for political actions is a gross over-simplification, for ideologies interact with these other factors, 'including the exigencies of economic development and state-building, institutional frameworks and international relations'.[42] The core and essential beliefs, the doctrines, of Marxism–Leninism include the belief that the proletariat must accede to power and establish its rule as the 'dictatorship of the proletariat' until attainment of communism, that advanced capitalist society must split into two opposing class entities, proletariat and bourgeoisie, and that the triumph of the proletariat is historically necessary. However, specific 'action programmes' and indeed understandings of how these core concepts would operate in practice, such as the roles of violent and non-violent means in the dictatorship of the proletariat, were open to debate and led to bitter disputes between Marxists especially after 1917. These differences were the products of differing personal interpretations of the meanings of these concepts and the appropriate responses to particular events and circumstances, and differing political cultures and circumstances.

Ideologies are not uniform but can be 'loose or rigid, deliberate or unintended'.[43] Giovanni Sartori notes that 'The greater the centrality of the belief elements designating *ends*, the more a belief system will elicit normative, goal-oriented, if not futuristic or even chiliastic responses and behaviour.' Sartori also highlights the importance of understanding ideological functioning with reference to the emotive, affective (and, more generally, attitudinal) basis of political action. He notes that ideas themselves were 'not necessarily conducive to an active involvement', but that the stronger the emotional convictions of political actors in and associated with their beliefs, the more likely that ideology would be converted into political practice.[44] Lenin and his Bolshevik colleagues certainly displayed considerable fervency in and emotional commitment to their convictions, and enmity, indeed hatred, towards doubters and opponents.

Lenin, as Alain Besançon observes, 'committed himself to an ideology that imposed a vision of the world'.[45] Bolshevism/Leninism, it is argued here, was a rigid, absolutist ideology that strongly conditioned its adherents to perceive the world and events in certain ways and to act in certain ways, often to the exclusion of other view-points or effective disregard of contrary evidence. Leninism revolved around such doctrinal and teleological elements as the necessity of sharp class struggle; the impossibility of any seriously compromised 'middle course' towards communism (despite adopting NEP); and the goal of creating a world free from violence and oppression. However it was a complex ideology, as it was also somewhat flexible and Lenin was quite innovative a theorist. He even rejected the notion that Marxism was a dogma. His worldview was Marxist in an absolutist sense, but not impermeable to rational accommodation of the real world. Lenin explicitly incorporated changing realities into his belief-system and discourse, and he consistently recognized the need to mold tactics according to given circumstances. He recognized the need to 'retreat' in 1921 because ideas had proved utopian in the face of reality and concessions to capitalism were required, despite the difficulty convincing many Bolsheviks that this was justifiable. Yet this 'retreat' was strongly informed by ideological constructions and did not lead to a fundamental reappraisal of the structure of his thought.

For the most part, the 'real world' was incorporated into the ideology in such a way as to strengthen certain pre-existing convictions. For example, the First World War reinforced and heightened Lenin's conviction that war and violence were necessarily inscribed in the structure of capitalism – reaching its apotheosis in its latest historical metamorphosis of imperialism – and that historical development proceeded dialectically, thereby convincing him of the immediate necessity of socialist revolutions. Events are crucially important in their own right in explaining Bolshevik practices, but how these events were incorporated into the ideological structure is just as important.[46]

Though interest in the ideas of Marxism–Leninism has persisted,[47] since the collapse of the Soviet Union the trend in the historiography of Soviet Russia more generally has been 'to explore ideas through the study of a wide variety of discourses', not simply Marxism–Leninism, and attention has moved 'from the Soviet leadership to society as a whole.'[48] There is much, however, that a more traditional approach focused on leadership ideas can still yield in understanding the Soviet regime.

The dominant Western interpretation of Soviet repressions during the Cold War, the 'totalitarian' or liberal-intentionalist approach, argued that the 'totalitarian' Soviet regime resulted from a Bolshevik 'blueprint': the product of ideology and/or a particularly authoritarian–violent Russian culture. Terror was practiced from the outset of the regime, and Stalinism was largely a consequence of this.[49] The burden of blame lies with the Idea of Bolshevism. The times or circumstances might be discussed, but considered mainly external 'context.'[50] One variant of this approach has been to explicitly or implicitly highlight the supposedly deviant personalities/psychologies of Bolshevik leaders and practitioners of violence; one historian argues that Soviet state violence owed a great deal to a particular 'terrorist pathology' that existed amongst insurgents in Tsarist Russia.[51]

Other scholars have emphasized that widespread violent terror as policy was only gradually implemented after the revolution,[52] and that the Bolsheviks really did not come to power with a definite plan for governance.[53] 'Revisionist' historiography of the 1960s and 1970s challenged the totalitarian model and the primacy of ideas, arguing that the Bolsheviks were governing primarily in response to social and economic factors, and/or that that the ruling party was not a uniform body of thought. In the late 1980s Ronald Grigor Suny recommended an approach that 'sees ideology as both shaped by the political and social context in which it emerges and operates and shaping that context in some way',[54] and indeed the largely post-revisionist scholarly consensus today acknowledges that both ideas and circumstances played crucially important roles in the creation of the Soviet system. In accordance with a general trend in the discipline of history, as Steve Smith notes, there is now greater engagement in studies of Soviet history 'with issues of meaning and interpretation' rather than 'structure and determinacy' (whether of doctrinal beliefs or socio-economic factors),[55] and this book is broadly in line with this trend.

There has been some work specifically focused on the topic of Lenin/Leninism and violence. Joan Witte has written a useful lengthy article on the topic, though she depicts too clear a connection between his pre-revolutionary violent rhetoric and his post-1917 violent practice. She also contends that he was personally 'addicted to' violence, selecting the violent option at 'nearly every decision point'.[56] Nonetheless Witte makes the important observation that Lenin developed 'tortured theoretical justifications' for his decisions to deploy violence.[57] Eckard Bolsinger's stimulating comparative intellectual study of Lenin and Carl Schmitt, an apologist of the Nazi regime in Germany, usefully counters the notion of violence as an essential component of the Leninist political mindset and strategy. However, as a work of political theory it explicitly rejects a diachronic approach that would historically contextualize Lenin's ideas as they developed. Concerned as it is with understanding Lenin's thought within a political-realist theoretical model, it does not sufficiently analyze the motivational bases of his political thought and action. Bolsinger argues that for Lenin 'the application of violence does not result from moral rigor or fundamentalism [and] the threat and use of violence do not mean the justification of violent action in the name of highest ideals; rather they flow from an 'economy of violence'.[58] Lenin did indeed demonstrate awareness of rational calculation in the use of violence and approved of Machiavellian tactics, but he was not emotionally indifferent to its use. He considered a peaceful path to communism desirable, though probably impossible, and displayed considerable moral intensity, informed by ideology, in its advocacy. He did justify violence 'in the name of highest ideals.'

Leninist violence in context

What, if anything, was unique or particularly 'Leninist' about Lenin's thinking on and practice of violence? Considering the history of utopian movements and their modern political incarnations, the philosopher John Gray observes that 'Lenin's readiness to use terror to bring about a new world was in no sense new.'[59] Lenin as an advocate of violence certainly fits the model of an apocalyptic revolutionary. One important feature of Lenin and the Marxist tradition on violence is that violence was not considered something to be glorified in itself or championed for itself. If it could be avoided for the same ends, so much the better, though typically Lenin believed violence to be quite integral to revolutionary advance. More striking and ironic is how explicit in Lenin's (and the Bolshevik) normative conception of the purpose of revolutionary violence in Marxist theory was the very negation of violence itself, an ethical duality concerning the simultaneous condemnation and embrace of violence. The result would be attainment of true respect for the value of human life, not just the realization of a revolutionary or political goal, or a utopian society that would, as a corollary, be free of violent conflicts. Lenin can be considered a primary and most explicit just war theorist (from a non-Christian perspective). That is, in this case, the justification, at times necessity of military force to defeat the socio-economic and political bases of war and violence, in accordance with the secular messianic Marxist teleology of the realization of the salvation of humanity on earth through the actions of its most downtrodden elements.

Terrorism as a modern phenomenon began in Russia in the latter part of the nineteenth century, within the same environment that gave rise to Lenin's revolutionary ideas. It is clear that there were many similarities between Lenin's ideas and the pre-Marxist Russian revolutionary tradition that gave rise to the world's first terrorist movement. Despite their fundamental ideological differences, there are also clear similarities between Marxism–Leninism and the more recent phenomenon of radical Islam. Both involve belief in the necessity of a worldwide revolutionary wave that would wash away the iniquities of the modern world, and both possess that extremity of mindset that conceives the world in absolutist, Manichean terms, though this trait is stronger in radical Islam. However the terrorist tactics of Russian Populist revolutionaries and radical Muslims did not, and would not, find support in Leninism. Simply put, Lenin rejected acts of individual terrorism as tasks of revolutionary movements because these were considered actions apart from, and detracting from, popular mass revolutionary actions. Lenin was an advocate of popular mass insurgency rather than conspiratorial terrorist networks.

Some historians, such as Peter Waldron, argue that in essence the Bolsheviks inherited a country with an autocratic political heritage reliant on the use of repression to maintain order, and were 'simply continuing long-established political behaviour when they placed coercion at the heart of their regime and refused to institute an independent legal system'.[60] Russian society, the argument goes, 'was used to being treated this way'. By contrast other historians, such as Jonathan Daly, argue that 'late imperial Russia was fully within the ambit of European governmental practice' as by 1914 it had become more a constitutional monarchy than autocracy, with quite a secure respect for the rule of law. Hence its 'Bolshevik successor set out on a different path.'[61] It appears that Waldron exaggerates the continuities between both political systems, and that Daly exaggerates the extent to which late imperial Russia can be considered more a constitutional monarchy than an autocracy.[62]

Undoubtedly the autocratic political culture of Tsarist Russia helped shape the ideas of Russian Marxists, and certain arbitrary practices of the Tsarist state and its security apparatus, such as administrative exile, would be revived in Soviet Russia within a short time of the Bolsheviks coming to power. Tsarism left a legacy of a society without experience of established democratic traditions, thereby facilitating the establishment of another non-democratic polity. Both Tsarist and Bolshevik regimes displayed an uneasy relationship with the rule of law, whereby laws were established but quite easily circumvented or suspended.

Despite the fact that both systems were ultimately politically absolutist, there was a fundamental divide separating the nature of absolutism in both polities. Whereas the Tsarist state was backward-looking and utilized violence primarily to preserve order, traditions and privileges, the Bolshevik state was governed by an explicitly revolutionary, eschatological, Salvationist ideology encouraging social upheaval, and utilized violence to a far greater extent not simply for repression but, as already noted, for social cleansing. Tsarist autocracy had ceased to be as absolutist as the Tsar wished by the time of its collapse in 1917. Daly perceptively notes that the Tsarist state had become in effect a 'watchful state' by its end, rather than a police state. The security police was held in relatively low esteem at the highest echelons of power. It compiled enormous surveillance data on vast sections of society yet the opposition in late imperial Russia, at least the moderate and liberal opposition, possessed some avenues for publicly criticizing the government and remained relatively unmolested by the authorities.[63] In Bolshevik Russia, by contrast, the security police was a prized institution, and with considerable justification one can state that it 'stood at the very centre of Bolshevik governance and politics',[64] as the Bolsheviks explicitly theorized the state as a transitional instrument of power to suppress counter-revolution and herald a stateless society. In addition, Bolshevik Russia was unusual in a general European historical context in treating its political offenders with greater harshness than ordinary criminals,[65] at least until the 1930s. For the Bolsheviks, the former were perceived to be more consciously inveterate enemies of the new order, whereas the latter were more likely to be considered deviants as a result of material circumstances and hence more pliable to reform.

It is ideological differences and the associated removal of much of the controls on violence, within the environment of conducting a 'total revolution' in the context of a 'total war' and civil war, that account for the enormity of Bolshevik state violence relative to the last decades of the Tsarist state. Daly explains that 'the imperial Russian government did not demand compliance with any well-defined program';[66] the government did not require active social participatory support. By contrast the Bolshevik vision required highly active popular participation in political life and universal conscious acceptance of its 'rational truths', for its goal was that the state would wither away according as all citizens would be drawn into the work of administration. They did recognize the need for patience regarding the transformation of popular attitudes towards communism, while repressing the possibility of propagation of alien ideas, but at times of heightened danger or social upheaval they were not prepared to be so patient and resorted to increased violence towards certain categories of perceived enemies in the interests of security and social cleansing.

Marxism, Leninism and Stalinism

Marx and Engels bequeathed an ambiguous legacy, not a neatly systematized body of thought. Insofar as Marxist ideas became the guiding philosophy for the mass European political movements that arose towards the end of the nineteenth century, these ideas tended to be transformed in a more doctrinaire and dogmatic sense in struggles with Marxist revisionism.[67] Revisionists such as Eduard Bernstein in the German Social-Democratic Party (SPD) believed that developed capitalist states would simply evolve into socialism, considering the notion of class conflict obsolete. Revisionism was considered heresy by orthodox Marxists such as Karl Kautsky, the leading theorist of the SPD and the most influential Marxist theorist after the death of Engels. Kautsky reasoned that revisionists overlooked the fact that corresponding to the increased strength of and freedoms granted to the proletariat was the increasing strength of the bourgeois class, and the increased repressive capacity of the bourgeois state. Hence Kautsky believed that social revolution could not take place through 'peaceful' evolution but only through class struggle, and that a revolutionary conquest of power by the proletariat was necessary for the achievement of socialism. The proletariat in power would then face intense opposition and would need to utilize the state to dismantle the capitalist system.[68]

By the end of their lives Marx and Engels came to believe that socialist revolutions could take place through 'peaceful' constitutional as opposed to forceful means in the most advanced democracies. By the turn of the twentieth century Kautsky believed that a 'peaceful' revolution, without intense class struggle leading to the revolutionary attainment of power by the proletariat, would no longer be possible even in England.[69] However, it did appear to European Marxists generally that the revolutionary process could take place relatively peacefully from within the existing system, or by forcing reforms (such as through mass strikes) of the existing political structures to allow such a revolutionary social transformation. Kautsky believed that the socialist revolution would be 'much less of a sudden uprising against the authorities than a long drawn out *civil war*, if one does not necessarily join to these last words the idea of actual slaughter and battles.'[70] He could not give a definitive answer to the question of the role of physical violence in a proletarian revolution, though he was convinced that peaceful methods – 'economic legislative and moral pressure' – would predominate to a far greater extent than during the great 'bourgeois' revolutions previously. Russia, still to undergo its 'bourgeois-democratic' revolution for basic freedoms, he considered the 'only exception to this rule.'[71] Indeed, as remarked in the introduction to a recent Russian collection of some of Lenin's writings, on the soil of autocratic, repressive Russia 'Marxism acquires [sic] peculiar characteristics; in particular, though Lenin does not mention this peculiarity, the theme of violence strengthens in the Russian variant of Marxist theory.'[72] Lenin and the Russian Marxists could certainly find in the writings of Marx and Engels much to support a more violent approach to revolution. For example, writing under the influence of the revolutionary upheaval in Europe in 1848, Marx wrote that the 'cannibalism of the counter-revolution' would 'convince the nations that there is only one way in which the murderous death agonies of the old society and the bloody birth throes of the new society can be shortened [...] and that is revolutionary terror.'[73]

What, then, of Lenin's Marxist credentials? Marx's ideas were primarily a product of and aimed at the circumstances of the more industrialized Western Europe, not the relative backwardness of the Russian Empire, and he accepted that there could be different roads to socialism in a country such as Russia.[74] The basis of Russian Marxism, beginning with Lenin's mentor Georgii Plekhanov, was that capitalism had already arrived in Russia and hence would not follow a uniquely Slavic route to a socialist society. In his later years Engels had reasoned that the prospects of a particular communitarian society in Russia based on the peasant commune had passed.[75] Russia had begun a process of massive industrialization in the last years of the nineteenth century, accompanied by the rise of an industrial proletariat, though by 1917 remained a predominantly peasant society.

Lenin was certainly a fervent believer and a single-minded Marxist revolutionary whose thought developed in an absolutist, doctrinaire and yet innovative sense. He stretched the parameters of Marxist orthodoxy and inserted some significant innovations and revisions. By the end of his life, following the experience of holding power, it was clear that the regime he founded had distorted Marx's (and to a large extent Lenin's own pre-revolutionary) intentions. Lenin's was a Russianized Marxism, developed with Russian circumstances in mind, an especially politics-centred Marxism, and possessed of an absolutist mindset that some scholars attribute to a particular Russian moral–intellectual tradition.[76] Yet it can be argued that Marxism lent itself to this absolutizing process. The notion of an absolutist Marxism here refers simply to the fact that Lenin was absolutely and fundamentally convinced of its ascribed 'truths', its doctrines and outlook, through which he understood the world and sought to change it, frequently blinding him to or rejecting other or at least more subtle interpretations. Lenin's credentials as a conscious adherent of European Marxist orthodoxy before 1914, as it developed under the authority of the SPD and Kautsky, has been most convincingly demonstrated by historian Lars Lih.[77] What really distinguished Lenin and Leninism as a strand of Marxism, Lih notes, was the intensity of the emotional commitment to the liberationist vision and the leadership role of the revolutionary vanguard of the proletariat.

Shortly after the Bolsheviks assumed power in Russia, Lenin and Kautsky published very different accounts of the meaning of the Marxian concept the 'dictatorship of the proletariat', attesting to the gulf that had developed by then between 'communists' and 'social-democrats'. Kautsky was an advocate of the dictatorship of the proletariat as the attainment of power by the proletariat as a sociological majority, but proletarian rule through fully democratic, parliamentary means. Lenin had hinted at something different as early as 1906 – a class dictatorship as distinct from a democratic republic – but his divergence from orthodox Marxism on this point only became apparent just before the October Revolution. Indeed, it appears that no major theoretical divergences from the views of 'orthodoxy' characterized Lenin's thinking before the split in the socialist Second International in 1914. Moira Donald notes that even during 1905, when Lenin advanced his most innovative ideas thus far, Kautsky 'formulated views closer to those of the Bolsheviks' than the Mensheviks.[78]

Lenin and the Bolsheviks would ultimately break decisively with the thrust of the Erfurt Programme adopted by the SPD in 1891 by ensuring a new form of (supposedly class) oppression as the dictatorship of the proletariat. Yet in advocating a state so firmly directed against the deposed bourgeoisie they were providing an extreme institutional expression to the logic of the Programme that the working class alone could lead the emancipation of humanity, as all other classes had stakes in the continuation of the existing order. Indeed, Marx had written that 'every revolutionary struggle is directed against a class, which till then has been in power.'[79] In any case the effect of Leninism as it stood by the third decade of the twentieth century was that the link between proletarian dictatorship and violence appeared really quite inseparable. Robert Mayer has traced this development to Lenin's thinking during the first decade of the century, even arguing that Plekhanov, unlike Lenin, had clearly decoupled violence/ suppression and proletarian dictatorship as necessarily linked.[80] Taken as a whole Lenin's thought had not consistently made such a link necessary. Besides, an academic rhetorical exercise in cutting any necessary link between dictatorship and violent state suppression[81] does not remove the possibility of dictatorship requiring some level of violence, and this was the understanding of Plekhanov and Kautsky as 'orthodox' social-democrats.

With the outbreak of the World War, Lenin and those on the extreme revolutionary left in European social-democracy broke with the Second International, believing themselves to be the true Marxists. Lenin adopted a highly 'dialectical' interpretation that the time for socialist revolutions had become imperative under imperialism, that the conditions for socialism had certainly matured, and emphasized the importance of the subjective factor of revolutionary action in historical advance. More generally, Lenin's wartime and subsequent thought demonstrated how attempts to adjust Marxism to changing realities (and the failure of the expected revolutions in more developed countries) could serve to distort the original conception. He argued that imperialism and the acquisition of 'superprofits' in imperialist countries served to 'buy off' the organized labour movement and stave off socialist revolutions. The revolutionary impulse would, then, come initially from those more economically backward countries, such as Russia, and those exploited by imperialism. The result was the imposition of a Marxist worldview on relatively primitive economies. 'To cement the commitment of populations only partially industrialized', James Gregor notes, Marxist–Leninists would 'invoke collective sentiment and discipline' akin to that 'enjoined by totalitarians everywhere' in the last century.[82]

One of the most contested issues in the literature on Soviet history has been the extent to which Lenin/Leninism was responsible for the later development of Stalinism. This requires a complex approach. The understanding put forward in this book is that Stalinism certainly did not result inevitably from Leninism, but was one potential result under the given circumstances. David Priestland's recent study of inter-war Soviet Russia usefully argues that Leninism and Stalinism were not homogeneous polities but displayed alternating shifts between 'revivalist' policies that resulted in heightened social conflicts and violence, and 'technicist' policies that reduced these. The Great Terror of 1937–8 was neither the culmination of an inexorable Stalinist, let alone Leninist logic, nor the result of a fundamental break with the past. Certainly the contention that Lenin was 'complicit' in that which made Stalinism possible appears judicious.[83] Not only did the principal instruments and forms of state terror appear during Lenin's tenure, but despite his efforts to ensure greater control over party leaders at the very end of his life, he ensured that there could be little or no meaningful control over the absolute power of the party itself. Stalin, as Party General Secretary, was enabled to dominate state policy once he managed to dominate the Party.

Stalinist violence did display considerable divergences from Leninist violence. Both the Leninist and Stalinist regimes employed mass violence and terror against widespread sections of their societies, including their fundamental constituencies – workers and 'toiling' peasants – and not simply to repress real or perceived enemies but to engineer a new society. They did so, however, under largely different circumstances, the former principally during a brutal armed struggle with domestic and foreign forces for control of the country, the latter at a time of relative peace and security before the Second World War. The attempt to definitively impose socialism and socialist methods and relations of production through the murderous state policy of forcible agricultural collectivization and de-kulakization in the late 1920s and early 1930s would surely have horrified Lenin, for his conviction (most especially in his last writings) was that collectivized agriculture could not be imposed by force. The planned, quota-fuelled executions and deportations of suspect population categories that constituted the mass purges of the late 1930s, including terror against the ruling party itself, represented a level, form and intention of state violence altogether quite different from the general experience of Leninist rule. However it is not true, as contended by

Lenin's most recent biographer Lars Lih, that on the point of utilizing violence to effect a change in 'production relations' the 'record could not be clearer' that there was a 'radical discontinuity' between Lenin and Stalin.[84] State violence in the countryside during the Civil War and subsequent years was not simply a response to desperate economic and military circumstances. This violence was imbued with an eschatological purpose, couched in terms of a 'last, desperate struggle' with the enemy, such as the 'kulak', and served not just to pacify a rebellious countryside but to excise it of harmful elements and transform the economic and social landscape. When he believed the Civil War to be at an end, Lenin reflected in 1920 that 'we realized that we could not emerge from the old society without resorting to compulsion as far as the backward section of the proletariat was concerned.'[85]

Stalinist violence exhibited a greater level of systematic, planned extermination and terror than did Leninist violence. This was often directed against entire ethnicities or sections thereof due to perceived security threats posed by them, including forced deportations immediately before, during and after the Second World War.[86] The Lenin years also witnessed instances of systematic violence against suspect population groups as a whole, principally Cossacks in 1919–20. Overall, though, the case for considering the Soviet regime guilty of genocide is stronger for the Stalinist than the Leninist era, though it is certainly a debatable issue whether or not genocide should be broadly applied to describe Stalinist terror.[87]

One significant difference between the respective regimes of Lenin and Stalin, and Maoist China, was that alone of the three, Lenin's regime genuinely acknowledged the existence of catastrophic famine and earnestly endeavoured to combat the famine of 1921–2. It did also cynically exploit it for some political reasons, most notably to attack organized religion, and created difficulties for the American Relief Administration that saved millions. In addition, Lenin did not preside over a regime whose instruments of repression and terror were turned against its own leadership, as did Stalin and Mao. This fact has often been adduced by way of distinguishing Lenin's rule from Stalin's, but the distinction is actually quite relative considering that Lenin had no compunction against terror directed against his former party comrades, the Mensheviks.

However the language, means, and to a lesser but nonetheless very significant extent the logic of Stalinist violence, bore clear resemblance to that of Leninist violence especially during the Civil War period, the formative period for the development of a particularly militarized Soviet political culture and siege mentality.[88] Lenin and his colleagues had enshrined terror and Party dictatorship within the Soviet system, accompanied by a distinct lack of scruple regarding the violation of elementary human rights. Stalinist repressive policies were distinctly possible, though by no means necessarily so, under the economic crisis of the late 1920s and the deteriorating international climate into the 1930s. Language is an important factor that links the violence of the Leninist and Stalinist regimes, as well as, for example, Nazism and Communist rule in China. The official discourses of these regimes were, to a greater or lesser extent at various times, somewhat divorced from referents in reality, and utilized abstract terms the meanings of which often depended on those powerful enough to decide ('kulak' being a prime example in the Soviet case). The very language meanings in these regimes were often iconoclastic, explicitly confronting the meanings and ethical associations previously accorded certain words and concepts. This is directly related to the violence practiced by these regimes; as Rana Mitter notes regarding the Cultural Revolution in Maoist China, '"Humanist" and "compassion" could become hideous insults, "destruction" could become a term of immense praise.'[89]

That Stalinist violence did not necessarily arise out of Leninist theory and practice is clearly illustrated by NEP, introduced to release the overwhelming hostility that had built up between state and society. Lenin believed that henceforth socialist transformation of the Soviet homeland would occur through a more gradual, evolutionary process. However party leaders thought that this process of substantially creating the new society, and the new Soviet citizen, would take only about a decade or two, though probably more. Bolsheviks had believed that the bourgeoisie as a class could be 'castrated', as one Bolshevik put it,[90] and their distinct characteristics removed with changes in economic production. NEP, with its revival of private enterprise, was a bitter pill for them to swallow. The fundamentally millenarian, eschatological nature of Marxism–Leninism, and the deep discontent with NEP within the Party especially at lower echelons, in addition to the structural weaknesses – the unrealistic pretensions – of the ideology, ultimately militated against the long-term survival of NEP. When circumstances suggested that NEP was not working, the Party (despite some strong opposition) moved in favour of some form of mobilizational revivalist policy that would seek to decisively confront 'kulaks', 'Nepmen' (private entrepreneurs), criminals, and potential counter-revolutionary agents.

Communism and Nazism

Finally, it will be instructive to compare the violence of Communism with that of Nazism. This comparison has usually concerned Nazism and Stalinism,[91] but this can be broadened to include Soviet state violence more generally. Stephane Courtois, lead editor of *The Black Book of Communism*, a compendium of communist crimes against humanity first published in 1997, points out that both Nazism and Communism proclaimed that a part of humanity was unworthy of existence. The difference was that Communism decided this on a class basis, Nazism on a racial model.[92] Both Nazism and Communism identified a particular race or class that would, in a social Darwinist sense, lead the struggle for the salvation of European civilization, and both identified social aliens in the process. What Courtois overlooks here is the crucially important point that Lenin, as the original leader of a socialist-communist regime, did not accept physical extermination or even physical removal as the primary means of achieving the removal of the bourgeoisie.

Soviet state violence was explicitly and primarily aimed at perceived 'class enemies', though also practiced against society as a whole and the category of 'class enemies' expanded to accommodate this.[93] This was, at least initially, primarily a category denoting socially dangerous or suspect people rather than those identified for physical extermination or physical removal, though class struggle in Soviet Russia/Soviet Union certainly entailed considerable violence and at times appeared genocidal or close to it. Communists aimed at the eventual abolition of classes, through removal of the socio-economic bases of class divisions, but within the enemy camp usually distinguished dangerous 'irreconcilables' as necessitating physical removal, despite some confusion defining and distinguishing such 'irreconcilables'.[94] Furthermore the Gulag, or Soviet labour camp system, was intended as a corrective-labour system not an extermination facility, even though many died in the camps or en-route to them. Peter Holquist has distinguished a 'sociological paradigm' for Soviet violence – as distinct from the Nazi biological-racial paradigm – centred on an assessment of an individual's past and personal disposition to Soviet power rather than on more immutable abstract categories whether racial, biological or class in a simplistic sense.[95] Through the 1930s and the supposed attainment of socialist construction, Soviet rhetoric often seemed to collapse this distinction. Broad 'enemy' and suspect population categories, including even 'former' enemies, were subjected to physical removal in some form.[96] Hence Stalinist terror was at times more approximate to Nazi terror against immutable 'biological-racial' categories, especially during the Terror of 1937–8, which can be considered a form of Soviet 'final solution' against ascribed social enemies.[97]

One of the overriding messages of *The Black Book of Communism* is that attempts to present Communism as the 'lesser evil' are morally suspect if not reprehensible according to a politically-transcendent humanitarian standard.[98] Soviet violence and the devastating consequences of Soviet policies, such as the famines of the 1930s, cannot be considered less terrible than Nazi actions because Soviet ideology was ostensibly progressive and liberationist. Indeed according to its own logic Nazism was also progressive and socially redemptive (though in a sense utterly unacceptable to most people today). Yet the fact that Soviet ideology was ostensibly more humane should not be cast aside.

The Soviet project to recreate society stood more solidly in the Enlightenment tradition of universal liberation, whereas the Nazi equivalent was focused more narrowly on the perfection of the Aryan race opposed to the contamination of the wider world, which found its natural and foremost expression in a brutal 'race war' that we know as the most destructive war in history.[99] Despite this one should not overlook the fact, as one historian vividly puts it, that the Marxist–Leninist vision of a harmonious future society entering the communist 'paradise' cannot be disassociated 'from Stalin's [and to a lesser extent Lenin's] systematic attempt to eliminate those who reached the Marxist well but refused to drink from it.'[100] The Bolsheviks, however, did not imbue violent measures with the 'metaphysical and positive significance the Nazis did to the extermination of the Jews.'[101] Indeed fascists were more inclined to consider violence an aesthetic act in itself. The atrocities of the Nazi, unlike the Soviet regime, largely took place in time of war, but war was what the Nazi regime had geared itself for. It is instructive to consider the words of the Soviet writer Il'ia Erenburg in 1943: 'We are not fascists for whom war is the apex of civilization.'[102] With regard to the ideologies and intentions of both leaderships, this author cannot but conclude that Nazism struck a more chilling depth of inhumanity than Soviet Marxism–Leninism, including Stalinism.[103] Nazism posed a greater challenge to human civilization.[104]

1 'Revolution is war'

The genesis of a militant Marxism, 1894–1907[1]

> The proletariat will learn the art of civil war, now that it has started
> the revolution. Revolution is war. Of all the wars known in history
> it is the only lawful, rightful, just, and truly great war.[2]
>
> (V.I. Lenin, 1905)

On Sunday 9 January 1905 a peaceful procession for economic and political reforms was fired upon by the Tsar's troops in St Petersburg, resulting in at least 130 deaths. In the aftermath of 'Bloody Sunday', popular confidence in the Tsar was severely tested and a wave of strikes spread across the industrial centres of the country, accompanied by unrest and revolts in the countryside and widespread, multifarious forms of violence. In 1905 alone over 3,000 government officials were killed or wounded.[3] Russia had entered a time of revolutionary upheaval.[4] For Lenin, the news arriving from Russia to his place of exile in Geneva convinced him that the time had finally arrived for the Russian empire to undergo that stage in Marxist theory known as the bourgeois-democratic revolution. That is, the overthrow of the autocracy (and by extension the monarchy), the convocation of a representative people's assembly, and the procurement of widespread civil liberties. In short, it was supposed to be Russia's 1789.

Popular unrest, including amongst the liberal-minded middle classes, had been developing across the empire and become particularly apparent in 1904 during Russia's humiliating war with Japan. The conciliatory measures that the government made only served to embolden calls for change. The Tsarist regime was ruled autocratically – that is absolutely, without constitutional and parliamentary restraint – by Tsar Nikolai (Nicholas) II, and was considered by contemporary progressive thinkers the most backward, reactionary and oppressive of European powers. It was not willing to accommodate politically the modernizing processes that Russia had entered upon since the latter part of the nineteenth century, especially since the industrialization drive begun in the late 1880s, though the peasant unrest in 1905 may well have been largely in reaction to these modernizing processes.[5] This was, as John Keep notes, a time when progressive elements of society generally 'considered that violence was a natural, justified response to a brutal and repressive autocratic regime',[6] one that seemed to many revolutionaries to offer no other way than the path of violence to achieve political reform.

This chapter examines Lenin's conceptualization of violence and its significance from his earliest Marxist writings until the beginning of 1907, by which time the revolutionary movement had subsided after 1905. During these years Lenin's ideas on violence began to take distinctive shape under the influence of the so-called 'first Russian revolution', with 'military questions', as he put it, rising to the forefront of his thought. Lenin's contribution to revolutionary violence in Russia during these years was theoretical and exhortatory rather than practical, though it appears that he was directly involved in the organization of the Bolshevik Centre responsible for overseeing robberies and expropriations.[7] His discussions of revolutionary violence were relatively scant until 1905, nor did he advocate violence as an absolutely essential means of removing autocratic rule, or as an apparently crucial component of his general revolutionary conception until then. Following Bloody Sunday, Lenin was uncompromising on the necessity of force and violence to overthrow the autocracy, and this reflected the militancy of his Marxism as a particular 'Leninism' began to take shape within the context of Tsarist Russia'.

Both major factions of the RSDLP – Bolsheviks and Mensheviks (the two groups following the 1903 division due to a dispute initially concerning party membership) – were convinced of the necessity of violence to overthrow the autocracy. Lenin and the Bolshevik leadership were however usually more cavalier regarding armed insurrection and armed activities than their Menshevik counterparts, and deeper theoretical differences between the two factions were also apparent during this time. Lenin's Marxist beliefs and the parameters of Marxist discourse he expounded were revealed from 1905 as particularly militant and militarized. He displayed an especial proclivity as a Marxist for seeking unremitting and forceful class struggle, indeed class struggle as civil warfare, rejecting a more compromising and gradualist revolutionary path. The notion of a 'militarized Marxism' refers to the development of his ideas on military matters and on the primacy of forceful class struggle in historical development. Put forward here it chronologically pre-dates but complements the notion of 'militarized socialism' in Soviet Russia during and after the Russian Civil War.[8] Lenin believed in the necessity of forming an army of the revolutionary people led by a militant party in 1905. Revolution, he declared, is war.

Marxists from Marx to Karl Kautsky had defended revolutionary force and recognized its progressive function. In the context of Tsarist Russia, where non-violent means of conducting revolutionary politics appeared foreclosed to most revolutionaries, this was especially likely to mean actual bloody violence, of employing 'revolutionary violence' to negate the 'reactionary violence' of the autocracy and its supporters. The Tsarist autocracy itself was viewed by socialists as an embodiment of violence. Despite his patient approach to revolution before 1905, during 1905 to 1906 Lenin became quite impatient about the accomplishment of the revolution. He distinguished himself as a Marxist by, amongst other things, the militancy of his conception of revolution and by the ethic of violence as a means of overcoming violence itself.

Before examining Lenin's writings, it will be useful to clarify some conceptual issues. Terrorism is systematic and calculated *political* violence,[9] usually involving homicide, and designed to instill terror in a target audience. The term 'terror' usually refers to such violence as practiced by state and state-sponsored agents, and will be employed as such in this book. The targets of violent acts provide one useful means of distinguishing between insurgent terrorism and guerrilla actions; as Boaz Ganor explains, the 'guerrilla fighter's targets are military ones, while the terrorist deliberately targets civilians.'[10] In this regard, Lenin and the Russian Social-Democrats are to be understood more accurately as advocates of 'guerrilla actions' rather than 'terrorism', though the distinction between 'terrorism' and 'guerrilla actions' in Lenin's conception was not always clear-cut. Guerrilla units and their actions more closely approximate regular military operations at a time of mass upheaval than terrorist actions designed to destabilize a regime at a time of relative social calm, and are more appropriate for violence of a mass character. Whereas individual acts of terrorism in Tsarist Russia were primarily designed to destabilize the autocracy, to instill 'terror', arouse the masses, and ultimately lead to overthrow of the autocracy, Lenin wished for a mass violence designed to topple the autocracy in a more direct assault or series of assaults.

Lenin and terrorism

By early adulthood, Lenin had become a convinced Marxist theoretician, adopting the tenets of Marxism as laid down by Marx and Engels, Plekhanov in the Russian Emancipation of Labour Group, and Kautsky in the SPD. His early Marxist writings were designed to expose the theoretical fallacies of the Populist revolutionary tradition, unperturbed as he was that Russia's relative socio-economic backwardness as compared with central and western European countries might suggest that Russia was destined to follow a different developmental path. The 'Narodniks [Populists]', he declared, 'simply cannot grasp the point that "capital" is a certain relation between people, a relation which remains the same whether the categories under comparison are at a higher or a lower level of development.'[11] He was confident that, with the aid of agitation and propaganda, the working class would attain to full class consciousness – awareness of its true class interests – and he wrote of the fusion of the elemental worker movement with intellectual socialism, of the unity of proletariat and party. The workers would be tasked with spreading this awareness to the rural poor, together forming the vast majority of Russia's population. He was convinced that the theoretical correctness of Marxism, indeed the truths of Marxism, would eventually become clear to and be accepted by all socialists – that is, that Marxism was rational, scientific socialism, and any other theoretical revolutionary orientation would ultimately prove fallacious.[12]

Though he derided the Populists for their 'childish morality', Lenin made clear that scientific analysis of the proletariat's historical destiny did not preclude the moral assertion that 'the class struggle of the organized proletariat [...] will deliver humanity from the evils which now oppress it.'[13] The conditions of peasants and especially workers in late imperial Russia were indeed atrocious. The latter, the focus of Marxist propaganda and for Lenin the only truly reliable revolutionary class, worked about 11 hours a day for low pay, lived in unsanitary conditions, and were treated disrespectfully by employers – in effect as industrial soldiers without the right to challenge their conditions. Lenin thought that the workers' hatred and vengeance directed against their employers were necessary first steps in their realization of the need to struggle against the autocracy and the capitalist class to achieve their emancipation.[14] He called for a unified front of all Russian democratic forces against the autocracy but insisted on strict organizational and conceptual distinctions between the proletariat and the rest of society, including the less reliable peasant poor.[15]

Lenin as a Russian revolutionary could not ignore the issue of terrorism.[16] Before and after the establishment of a Russian Marxist movement there existed a terrorist wing of Russian revolutionaries. David Allen Newell notes that 'While others were undergoing a period of intellectual maturation, Lenin spoke out early and decisively against Lavrov, Mikhailovskii [Populists] and many of their ideas [...] viewed as conducive to the promotion of the terrorist struggle.'[17] Lenin's first important reference to terrorism came in a draft of the Party programme written at the end of 1899.[18] He reasoned that 'terror is *not* advisable as a means of struggle at *the present moment*', that 'the Party (*as* a *party*) must renounce it (until there occurs a change of circumstances that might lead to a change of tactics) and concentrate *all its energy* on organization and the regular delivery of literature.'[19] The 1890s had witnessed industrial strikes and some limited concessions for the proletariat from the regime. Encouraged by this, Social-Democrats believed it necessary to work to raise workers' political awareness, exposing in the process the impossibility of meaningful reforms co-existing with the persistence of the autocracy, and the necessity of providing organization to the elemental working class movement.

In 1901 Lenin presented 'the established views of Russian Social Democracy' on terrorism thus: 'In principle we have never rejected, and cannot reject, terror. Terror is one of the forms of military action that may be perfectly suitable and even essential for the Party at a definite juncture in the battle, given a definite state of the troops and the existence of definite conditions.'[20] Violence ('military action') was not presented as an absolute requirement for toppling the autocracy; indeed, he remarked that the autocracy would probably collapse itself under the weight of various pressures upon it.[21] In previous years he had not discounted the possibility that a 'smashing blow' could be delivered to autocratic rule through mass political strikes.[22] Violence could be successful when performed by a mass revolutionary movement, but the problem with terrorism was that it was:

... by no means suggested as an operation for the army in the field, an operation closely connected with and integrated into the entire system of struggle, but as an independent form of occasional attack unrelated to any *army* [emphasis added]. Without a central body and with the weakness of local revolutionary organizations, this, in fact, is all that terror can be.[23]

What Lenin had in mind then was 'terror' more akin to guerrilla actions than isolated conspiratorial killings. He called for continued emphasis upon political education and organization of the workers rather than prematurely summoning 'all available forces for the attack right now'. That is, he wanted

> the formation of a revolutionary organization capable of uniting all forces and guiding the movement in actual practice [...] an organization ready at any time to support every protest and every outbreak to be used to build up and consolidate the fighting forces suitable for the decisive struggle.[24]

Terrorism, he conceded, could 'at best' have some small role as one subsidiary method of striking a decisive blow against the autocracy. To clarify, when Lenin spoke of 'terror', he had two concepts in mind – what terrorism was and what it could become if its form changed (i.e. to 'mass terror'). He defined the term in the former sense as 'individual political assassinations',[25] but he would approve apparently guerrilla-type actions with party involvement when controlled by a centralized organization of mass popular activity and as part of wider mass popular revolutionary upheaval. He later claimed that it 'was, of course, only on grounds of expediency that we rejected individual terrorism.'[26] There was however a principled reason for rejecting that form of struggle; terrorism as a party tactic would have led to 'the danger of rupturing the contact between the revolutionary organizations and the disunited masses of the discontented', contact which alone would be 'the sole guarantee of our success.'[27] What is revealed here is Lenin's support for Marx's dictum that 'the emancipation of the working classes is to be achieved by the working classes themselves.' The previous year, he had advanced his own interpretation of this, that without party direction the working-class movement would 'inevitably become bourgeois' and betrays this principle. Lenin certainly had 'faith' in the revolutionary potential of the Russian masses – his principal worry was the unpreparedness of the Party to keep ahead of the mass movement – but they required leadership, organization and theoretical direction.

In 1901 the Socialist-Revolutionary Party (SR) was formed, a party that continued to practice terrorism. Lenin believed the SRs theoretically bankrupt as neo-Populists who had not fully embraced Marxism.[28] The SRs advocated terrorism 'with the closet possible connection with the mass struggle',[29] but Lenin maintained that terrorism at that time was still based upon 'an utter failure to understand the mass movement and a lack of faith in it.' The SRs constituted a distinct threat to the Social Democrats' constituency (though it had a largely peasant support base) and conception of how revolution should develop, due to fears that the encouragement of excessive 'spontaneity' of some sections of the masses would lead to premature actions. Lenin's advocacy of mass violence with the involvement of revolutionaries was now more forthrightly expressed:

> Without in the least denying violence and terrorism in principle, we demanded work for the preparation of such forms of violence as were calculated to bring about the direct participation of the masses and which guaranteed that

participation [...] the working people are literally straining to go into action [...] we shall fuse the militant organization of revolutionaries and the mass heroism of the Russian proletariat into a single whole![30]

This was a clearer indication that he believed that the decisive assault on autocracy would be bloody, and he suggested that popular organization would quite naturally lead to armed insurrection. He was an advocate of revolutionaries' involvement in violence at an opportune moment in support of a mass upheaval, and believed that a properly organized movement of the proletariat and revolutionaries would succeed in overthrowing the regime. Until then, the Party could not 'make' revolution itself, since the masses, as he put it, 'are still not ours, and [...], unfortunately, do not yet ask us, or rarely ask us, when and how to launch their military operations.'[31] Convinced that conditions under Tsarist autocracy provided sufficient 'excitation' for mass action without the additional stimulus of terrorist acts, his reasoning was that the 'socialist consciousness' of the working masses was the only guarantee of victory. Yet only a 'centralized, militant organization' that consistently carried out a Social-Democratic policy could 'safeguard the movement against making thoughtless attacks and prepare attacks that hold out the promise of success.'[32]

Regarding Lenin's early conception of the dictatorship of the proletariat, he did not associate revolutionary dictatorship with the use of violence at this time (before 1905), but he implied that some form of coercion would characterize dictatorship. In 1902 he wrote that: 'The recognition of the necessity for the *dictatorship* of the proletariat is *most closely and inseparably* bound up with the thesis of the *Communist Manifesto* that the proletariat *alone* is a really revolutionary class.' The necessity of such dictatorship was ensured by the unreliability of the support of the petty bourgeoisie (including the peasantry) for the proletariat:

If we really knew *positively* that the petty bourgeoisie will support the proletariat in the accomplishment of its, the proletariat's, revolution it would be pointless to speak of a 'dictatorship', for we would then be fully guaranteed so overwhelming a majority that we could get on very well without a dictatorship (as the "critics" [i.e. revisionists] would have us believe). [33]

This did not necessarily imply coercion towards peasants (dictatorship could simply mean leadership) but logically it suggested some level of coercion. The peasant revolutionary spirit was conditional, Lenin noted, as peasant discontent was often reactionary, in defence of the existence of small-proprietorship. Relative to the proletariat the peasantry was not considered a reliable revolutionary stratum. Recognition of the revolutionary importance of the peasantry, allied with the proletariat, was to become a plank of Leninism, but this skepticism and wariness towards the peasantry would feature strongly in Bolshevik thought shortly after October 1917, and then with very violent consequences. It is noteworthy that Lenin believed that a 'dictatorship' might not be required should the proletariat find support from the peasants, forming an 'overwhelming majority', for Marx had only envisaged such majority rule and even towards the end of his life considered proletarian dictatorship against class enemies essential.[34] Undoubtedly, as Marx had recommended, Lenin thought that the proletariat would strive to 'win over' the peasantry following a revolution through non-coercive means.

The impact of 1905

When news reached Lenin of the events of Bloody Sunday and the general strike that subsequently broke out, he was to immediately recognize the beginning of civil war in Russia, writing that 'Rivers of blood are flowing, the civil war for freedom is blazing up.'[35] The moment had arrived, he believed, for the autocracy to be brought down by a determined and unflinching revolutionary assault, and he encouraged the people to take to arms.[36] The events of 1905 suddenly gave a prominence to military affairs and, as he put it, 'all Social-Democrats have advanced the military questions, if not to the first place, at least to one of the first places, and they are putting great stress on studying these questions and bringing them to the knowledge of the masses.'[37] Lenin was not alone; the leading Menshevik Iulii Martov wrote in the Menshevik organ *Iskra* shortly after Bloody Sunday calling for preparations for a mass popular uprising. In March, Martov wrote that 'Since 9 January we have entered into civil war, to a revolutionary epoch.'[38] Now that the masses were ripe for armed struggle, Lenin was convinced of the necessity of working out the details of a military assault – becoming an 'extremist partisan of terror'[39] – contributing articles during the next two years on how to organize guerrilla squads and even on the weapons that should be used.[40] In an oft-noted letter in October, he expressed his 'horror' that the revolutionaries 'have been talking about bombs for half a year now, without having made a single one!'[41] Of particular significance to him during the revolutionary period was the need to maintain an absolutely revolutionary attitude amongst Social-Democrats, to 'criticize half-way policies of every kind' and to maintain 'the complete intransigence of our ideology.'[42] The Party would support the revolutionary-democratic forces of society more generally but only the revolutionary proletariat would be sufficiently unwavering to ensure victory, hence the idea of proletarian 'hegemony' of the 'bourgeois' democratic revolution.[43]

Insurrection and dictatorship

Lenin's consistent instruction from January was that of the necessity of armed insurrection to overthrow the autocracy.[44] He believed that successful insurrection would probably require a number of major uprisings, involving (and interspersed with, between major uprisings) 'guerrilla warfare'. With the autocracy overthrown real civil liberties, including freedom of conscience, would be granted to all. Land reform could be accomplished (the most important element in removing the remaining vestiges of feudalism), capitalism could flourish, and thereby the class struggle between bourgeoisie and proletariat would assume centrality and its resolution through socialism hastened. Lenin reasoned that the class struggle for socialism within the camp of democratic forces opposed to autocracy would of necessity begin immediately after this revolution. The revolutionary proletariat and its party should strive to win over to the proletariat's side the non-proletarian and non-party sections of revolutionary democratic society who 'serve the cause of freedom in general without serving the specific cause of proletarian utilization of this freedom'. Otherwise they would ultimately serve 'the interests of the force that will inevitably rule when freedom is won, viz., the interests of the bourgeoisie.'[45]

The autocracy, Lenin believed, must be violently overthrown and any reforms within the framework even of a constitutional monarchy would essentially be piecemeal. 'Without an armed uprising', he wrote, a constituent assembly would be a mere 'Frankfürt talking shop'.[46] It would be only insofar as a popular insurrection would be completely successful, with the 'decisive destruction of the enemy', that a representative assembly would truly be 'a popular one'. There is no half-way, he explained, for 'He who is not for revolution is one of the Black Hundreds [violent reactionary gangs]. He who does not wish to put up with Russian freedom becoming freedom for the police to use violence [...] must arm himself and immediately get ready for battle.'[47] The government had itself made insurrection 'imperative and urgent'. Lenin was not simply stating that the proletariat should meet force with force; there was, he believed, no other alternative to force and hence it should be employed 'energetically'. He noted that the autocracy and its defenders had initiated violence in 1905, but he stated categorically that 'Major questions in the life of nations are settled only by force',[48] thereby echoing Marx and drawing on a broad historical experience of revolutions:

> The reactionary classes themselves are usually the first to resort to violence, to civil war; they are the first to 'place the bayonet on the agenda', as the Russian autocracy has been doing systematically [...] since the bayonet has really become the main point on the political agenda [...] constitutional illusions and school exercises in parliamentarism become only a screen for the bourgeois betrayal of the revolution [...].[49]

Lenin conceived revolutionary violence in an enforced and defensive but, naturally, progressive sense. The violently reactionary nature of the autocracy strengthened him, as it did all socialists, in his belief in the historical but also moral bankruptcy of Tsarism and of the moral righteousness of the revolutionary cause.

The Russian autocracy to Lenin represented the most reactionary and oppressive incarnation of a state over its society, practicing intrinsic and systemic 'violence' against the Russian people (and non-Russian inhabitants of the empire), and ready to maintain this order through force of arms. Violent insurrection and revolutionary violence of an offensive as well as defensive nature were always likely to be considered essential by Russian revolutionaries. Black Hundred gangs, reacting to the revolutionary events and waves of popular violence, targeted Jewish communities especially. Lenin remarked that 'Hitherto our government trembled at the mere thought of an uprising. It now organizes uprisings of the Black

Hundreds, and hopes to provoke a civil war.' Those democratic, non-Marxist elements of society must, he thought, be convinced of the necessity of armed struggle when they witnessed such atrocities committed by state and state-sponsored agents, for 'There is no choice, all other ways are blocked.'[50] The Black Hundred reactionary gangs were actually quite independent of the government; what is significant is Lenin's assumption that all forces and elements of the 'enemy' were one and the same. Yet there was a brutal government-approved terror from late 1905, resulting in 3,000 to –5,000 deaths,[51] and over 1,000 more executions by field courts martial in 1906–7, with many more activists arrested.[52]

Successful insurrection would install a provisional revolutionary government that would, in turn, convene a representative constituent assembly. The Bolsheviks reasoned that only a provisional revolutionary government 'as the organ of a successful uprising' could overcome any reactionary resistance, secure 'full freedom for pre-electoral agitation, [and] call a constituent assembly on the basis of a general, equal, direct and secret ballot election, capable [of bringing in] the minimum socio-economic demands of the proletariat.'[53] Lenin believed that the proletarian party should attempt to enter a provisional revolutionary government in co-operation with the 'revolutionary bourgeoisie' and work to establish what he termed a revolutionary-democratic dictatorship of the proletariat and peasantry to drive the revolution to its completion, to ensure a fully democratic republic. By contrast, a socialist revolution would require a dictatorship of the proletariat alone.

The Russian Marxist idea of the proletariat as vanguard during a 'bourgeois' democratic revolution was largely a consequence of the particularity of Russia's modernization. The state had been remarkably involved in industrialization, hence the industrial middle class was quite dependent upon the authorities and, politically, relatively timid. Despite the insignificant size of the industrial workers relative to the total population, they were in fact especially militant in Russia due to the particularly concentrated nature of Russian industrial production.[54] The Mensheviks, however, were opposed to the Party's involvement in a provisional 'bourgeois' government and the establishment of a dictatorship of workers and peasants. The Bolshevik-controlled RSDLP Congress in April to May 1905 did not provide definitive guidance on the question of involvement. The fear was that the Party would 'dissolve' in the mire of bourgeois democracy and lose revolutionary credibility. In addition, the Mensheviks feared that if power were placed in the hands of the proletarian party it could not but attempt to establish socialism at a time when Russia was not economically and socially ready for it. By contrast Lenin was convinced that it was time for offensive action 'from above'[55] – from a position of power – to secure a complete break from the trappings of the old regime, and he polemicized with the Mensheviks who maintained that the Party should remain one of 'extreme opposition.'[56] Even in the event that it proved inexpedient to enter government, it would still be necessary, he thought, to arm the people and attempt to exercise pressure on the provisional government 'from below'. He was most insistent however that the coming revolution could not yet undermine 'the foundations of capitalism', and he disagreed with Trotsky's idea of establishing a 'workers' democracy' leading immediately to socialism.

Whereas the Mensheviks feared that the bourgeois parties would 'recoil' from a truly progressive path due to Social-Democratic radicalism,[57] Lenin feared that without social-democratic participation a fully democratic republic could not be guaranteed, or that the monarchy might return in one way or another. The provisional government could be 'nothing else but the revolutionary dictatorship of the proletariat and the peasantry', and he suggested that it would last for 'months',[58] during which time it could well serve as a beacon for revolutions in the West. Menshevik leaders did not renounce the necessity of the Party to advance (*dvigat'*) the revolution's development from outside the government. In fact, they even observed that Russian Social-Democracy could attain power on its 'own initiative' and hold onto it in the event that revolution spread to the advanced countries of the West. This eventuality would (as the Bolsheviks also believed) remove the 'limited historical boundaries' of the Russian revolution,[59] accelerating its progress towards socialism, but they adopted a more passive approach, waiting to see if circumstances would allow power to fall into socialist hands depending on international revolutions.

The dictatorship would, then, serve both to protect the revolution against counter-revolution and secure a fully democratic republic that would implement the proletariat's minimum demands (as opposed to the 'maximum' socialist demands), and indeed the democratic demands of society as a whole. In Lenin's most important pamphlet of the revolutionary period, he expounded upon the concept of democratic dictatorship and clearly indicated that his understanding was that it would exercise a defensive, coercive and violent function to protect the revolution and hence allow for further development of the revolutionary process. 'The workers', he observed, 'are striving to crush the reactionary forces without mercy, i.e., to set up the revolutionary-democratic dictatorship of the proletariat and the peasantry',[60] and he was clear that this would be 'precisely a dictatorship, i.e. it must inevitably rely on military force.'[61] The apparent centrality of coercion and even violence in Lenin's notion of dictatorship (though of the proletariat and revolutionary bourgeoisie) in 1905 represented a shift from his previous pronouncements on the subject, few though they were,[62] or perhaps more accurately a clarification with the march of events in Russia. His ideas on dictatorship, which received full expression only after October 1917, were taking distinctive shape. The divergence with Kautsky's conception of a probably non-violent dictatorship is clear, but due to the particular Russian circumstances that Lenin was thinking of and the need to establish a dictatorship for democracy, not for socialism utilizing an already established parliamentary system. Indeed Kautsky seemed to endorse the notion of a dictatorship of the proletariat and peasantry, that the Russian 'bourgeois-democratic' revolution would not be bourgeois in a traditional sense, and he recognized the revolutionary potential of the Russian peasantry.[63] In so far as the proletariat was this leading force, he seemed to imply acknowledgement that a limited form of proletarian dictatorship was in force, but the Russian proletariat was not yet strong enough to move towards socialism.[64]

Lenin referred to Marx's writings at the time of the defeated revolution in Germany in 1848 in order to insist on the necessity of a democratic dictatorship of the proletariat and revolutionary bourgeoisie, polemicizing with the Menshevik A. S. Martynov who had accused him of advocating a premature Jacobin-style proletarian power seizure, but he opposed the 'vulgar bourgeois' conception of dictatorship as 'annulment of all liberties and guarantees of democracy.' He quoted Marx in his assertion that 'Every provisional organization of the state after a revolution requires a dictatorship, and an energetic one at that', referring to the folly of entertaining 'illusions' of a constitutional settlement of the revolutionary crisis that would afford reactionary elements the opportunity of retaking state control and even 'ventur[ing] upon open struggle.'[65] The provisional revolutionary government would be called upon to 'mercilessly crush the counter-revolution',[66] for, he believed, a desperate counter-revolutionary struggle would ensue against a revolutionary government. In an unpublished sketch in June to July 1905, Lenin pictured the 'Frantic resistance of evil forces. Civil war *in full sweep – annihilation of tsarism'.*[67]

In this regard Lenin rejected the Menshevik idea that a provisional government, arising either through a direct popular uprising or popular pressure leading to governmental organization of a constituent assembly, should regulate the 'mutual struggle between antagonistic classes' in the course of emancipation.[68] He believed that the Mensheviks were fudging the question of conquering a truly democratic republic and failing to understand that the essential task of a provisional government would be to crush the inevitable counter-revolution of monarchists and 'big bourgeoisie', and be prepared for struggle even against the bourgeoisie generally if they attempted to undermine the gains of the proletariat.[69] The Bolsheviks – the 'Jacobins of contemporary Social-Democracy' – wished the proletariat and revolutionary bourgeoisie to 'settle accounts with tsarism' in the 'plebian way' as Marx had described the French Revolution, though Lenin noted that this was merely an analogy and that he was not advocating Jacobin means (the Terror) of doing this.[70] He wanted the first revolution accomplished as quickly as possible in order to 'prepare the ground for the second step.'[71]

'Revolutions', Lenin declared,

> are festivals of the oppressed and exploited [...]. We shall be traitors to and betrayers of the revolution if we do not use this festive energy of the masses and their revolutionary ardour to wage a ruthless and self-sacrificing struggle for the direct and decisive path.[72]

The purpose of 'democratic dictatorship', as noted, was not only to destroy and suppress but to facilitate full implementation of the democratic minimum programme by ensuring complete democratic freedoms. The point is that Lenin believed that violence would inevitably result from a successful revolution and he clearly envisaged that violence and coercion would be central to the dictatorship's functioning. Yet milder compulsive forms by the revolutionary people towards the bourgeoisie generally would also be central to dictatorship's functioning.[73]

Lenin's ideas on dictatorship were imbued with a generic meaning not restricted to the particularities of a Russian democratic revolution. It was precisely to his

1905 pamphlet, *Two Tactics of Social-Democracy*, and to his 1906 pamphlet *The Victory of the Cadets and the Workers' Party*, that he would refer in 1920 in defence of dictatorship, noting that though conceived during a democratic revolution, 1905 was the first time the question of revolutionary dictatorship had been raised in practice for Marxist revolutionaries.[74] Lenin's views on proletarian dictatorship as expressed in the latter work could have been uttered during the Civil War in 1918: 'Please note once and for all, all you Kadet gentlemen, that dictatorship means unlimited power, based on force, and not on law. In civil war, any victorious power can only be a dictatorship.'[75] However Lenin was not advocating unbridled revolutionary anarchism. Gregory Varhall notes that 'While this [sentence] could be interpreted in either of two ways – the dictatorship knows no laws or the dictatorship does not find its legal basis in constitutional succession – the latter is more probably Lenin's intent.'[76] Lenin's statement should be understood in the context of his polemic against the Kadets (liberals), who, he pointed out, were suffering from the aforementioned 'constitutional illusions' in thinking that they could succeed in convening a truly representative Constituent Assembly simply by means of participation in the Duma (parliament) reluctantly granted by the Tsar in late 1905.

In fact, as Varhall continues, Lenin qualified the anarchism of the above statement elsewhere in the pamphlet; the revolutionary dictatorship would be based on the authority of the mass of the people. What Lenin intended by dictatorship resting on force was not just or principally the application of force and violence against counter-revolutionaries but the legitimate force of popular organization and popular authority: 'What was the power based on, then? It was based on the mass of the people.'[77] Dictatorship, Lenin wrote in 1906, would exist without any artificial legal restrictions regardless of by whom established but rest on a 'new revolutionary law', on the authority of the people, such as the institutional authority of the new popular soviet organizations that had arisen in 1905. Those frightened by the word 'dictatorship', he continued, were accustomed to conceiving it in terms of a military, police dictatorship of a minority over the people, but a revolutionary dictatorship would be entirely different. It would be exercised by the people without a special police apparatus and hence radically democratic (Lenin was here providing a foretaste of his 1917 work on the state, *The State and Revolution*). Nonetheless the majority could not exercise its dictatorship over the minority without resorting to force against the 'tyrants armed with the weapons and instruments of power', for the new authority would not 'drop from the skies' but arise in the struggle against the old.

The conception of dictatorship as essentially unrestricted rule would ultimately prove detrimental to democracy in Russia after 1917, when proletarian dictatorship became synonymous with party dictatorship over society. Lenin's vision was an evidently uneasy combination of centralism and revolutionary tutelage by the most advanced revolutionary elements, and local initiative and radical popular democracy.[78] Interestingly, Lenin noted that the workers' soviets were in embryo a 'new revolutionary power' and government, rudimentary instruments of the dictatorship of the revolutionary elements of the people.[79] He thought that dictatorship would naturally be exercised initially by the 'revolutionary people' and their party, not the 'entire people' amongst whom there were sections not suitable as yet to conducting the revolutionary struggle. Conceiving the soviets that arose in October 1905 as a potentially new form of revolutionary government and dictatorship, perhaps exercising a 'dual power' function alongside a provisional government and constituent assembly, Lenin was possibly moving already towards suggesting what he would in 1917: that a revolutionary dictatorship at a higher stage would not actually take the form of a democratic republic. This would be one of his most significant revisions of Marxist orthodoxy.

Forms of revolutionary violence

Broadly speaking the phenomenon of unrest in late imperial Russia, and violence by forces of revolution, reaction and state, can be explained by the process of economic and social modernization unaccompanied by adequate political liberalization and necessary social reforms,[80] intensified by the effects of Russia's disastrous war with Japan and Bloody Sunday. The regime hesitated about how to react, mixing concessions with obstinacy and repressions, thus emboldening and radicalizing both movements for change and opposition to change. How, then, did Lenin respond in 1905 to 1906 regarding the forms of revolutionary violence appropriate to overthrow the regime? In a speech at the Third Party Congress in April 1905, Lenin advocated – as had Plekhanov in February[81] – 'temporary military agreements' with the SRs 'for the purposes of combating the autocracy', without affecting 'the integrity and purity of its [the RSDLP's] proletarian tactics and principles.'[82] During the Congress Lenin penned an unsubmitted draft that, in view of the 'mood of the working-class masses', advocated the use of 'acts of terror' committed by armed squads as 'live military training' in preparation for a mass uprising.[83] These would include 'attacks by armed squads on the police and on troops during public meetings, or on prisons, government offices, etc.' The Party Central Committee and local party authorities would 'determine the limits of such actions and the most convenient occasions for them [...] avoiding a useless expenditure of effort on petty acts of terror.'

Lenin's advocacy of such acts of violence resulted from the mass revolutionary upheaval witnessed in 1905, and as part of preparing a broader, co-ordinated mass assault on the autocracy aimed at its removal. The targets of such attacks were to be, in the main, combatants on the side of the government – the police (and informers within revolutionary ranks) and troops – in addition to government buildings. In September he learned of an incident in a Riga prison whereby two prison warders were killed and three seriously wounded when a large group of people broke into the prison to release two political prisoners. He greeted the news with some satisfaction, noting that 'military operations *together with the people* are now commencing.'[84] This sort of violence Lenin understood as minor 'separate' acts in a civil war rather than traditional acts of terrorism during periods of relative social order. He considered it would be 'mass terror' in the sense that 'workers or unemployed persons' would be the primary practitioners.[85] These military units, trained, educated and supplied with the help of the Party, would comprise tens or even 'several dozen' persons, and workers would join them 'in hundreds'.[86]

Lenin's position on terrorism was in essence consistent with his pre-revolutionary stance. In an article in the Bolshevik paper *Vperëd* in late February 1905 he acknowledged that SR calls to fuse terrorism and the mass movement were what Social-Democrats had been urging all along, but he condemned the assassination by an SR terrorist of Grand Duke Sergei, the Governor-General of Moscow. Rather he advocated that these revolutionaries 'should submerge among the masses *in actual fact*, that is, exert their selfless energies in real inseparable connection with the insurgent masses, and proceed with them in the literal, not figurative, symbolical, sense of the word.'[87] Indeed the RSDLP as a whole worked to attract considerable mass support and membership during 1905. The task of the Russian revolutionaries was to provide leadership to the mass movement that lacked organization and leadership, and he took inspiration from the initial popular 'terrorism of the great French Revolution' which, he quoted Plekhanov, 'was exceedingly instructive for the Russian revolutionary.'[88]

The resultant violence would no longer be 'terrorism' as such, Lenin thought, but something different: guerrilla warfare. 'Fortunately', he observed, 'the time has passed when revolution was "made" by individual revolutionary terrorism, because the people were not revolutionary. The bomb has ceased to be the weapon of the solitary "bomb thrower", and is becoming *an essential weapon of the people*.'[89] Guerrilla operations were to be regarded as superior to terrorism, as acts of civil war.[90] The guerrilla bands were to form units of a revolutionary army, to be engaged in 'military operations'. Nevertheless Bolshevik terrorist acts in practice did not necessarily reflect Lenin's ideal of a fusion between individual and mass terror in an organized, controlled revolutionary army.[91] The Party was to recognize 'mass terror and incorporate it into its tactics, organizing it and controlling it', but Lenin realized the necessity of 'eliminating and ruthlessly lopping off the "hooligan" perversion of this guerrilla warfare.'[92]

In October 1905 the Tsar responded to the General Strike that month by issuing an impressive Manifesto that promised broad civic rights, including broad franchise rights for a legislative Duma. The Duma suggested that autocratic rule would come to an end, as no law could henceforth become effective without Duma approval. Following the Manifesto most workers returned to their factories, but for many on the radical Left it was a sign that further socialist measures could be wrested from employers and led to renewed workers' strikes and even continued agitation for armed uprising. Lenin welcomed the Manifesto but considered, largely correctly, that the Tsar had not capitulated but had simply retreated.[93] The Fundamental Laws of April 1906, though effectively a constitution, would negate much of the Duma's potential power and reiterate the principle of autocracy. The Bolsheviks were very active in inspiring the failed workers' uprising in Moscow in December 1905, the most important of a number of other uprisings in various regions of the empire.

In April 1906 the Fourth (Unity) Party Congress convened in Stockholm, bringing together both Bolsheviks and Mensheviks. The plans and resolutions regarding 'armed uprising' and 'guerrilla activities'[94] are instructive of both the similarities and differences that characterized their respective views on armed insurgency. Both factions were very much now agreed on the necessity of a violent uprising to overthrow the autocratic regime. For the Mensheviks, however, it was essential not to strike at an inexpedient moment; the immediate task was to conduct widespread agitation amongst the masses, including urban petty bourgeoisie, peasants and troops, to convince them of the necessity of a violent confrontation with the autocracy. The Party should limit itself to supporting existing popular armed groupings. This draft was subsequently effectively adopted by the Congress.[95] The Bolshevik draft referred to the importance of ongoing agitation and unity with troops and peasants but maintained that the uprising was 'already a stage reached by the movement'.[96] The revolutionary movement, it confidently asserted, was converting from defense to offense. Regarding the troops, Lenin's conviction was that they would be 'won over' to the revolutionary struggle in the course of battle,[97] an idea the Mensheviks also shared. In short, the Mensheviks did not accept that a successful mass uprising of revolutionary elements was immediately possible. For their part the Bolsheviks were less inclined to appeal to wider social elements outside workers, peasants and troops; and the Bolsheviks were more concerned with practical military preparations and organization as immediate tasks. The Bolshevik draft spoke of the Party actively increasing armed bands and improving existing ones, and organizing its own fighting groups.

Regarding 'guerrilla activities', the Congress also adopted the Menshevik draft. Rejecting the 'expropriations' (euphemism for bank robberies) that were being conducted in the Party's name, the Congress nevertheless accepted the 'inevitability' of 'active struggle against governmental terror and Black Hundred violence', that is defensive violence, 'side by side with preparations of the revolutionary forces for the approaching uprising.'[98] The Bolshevik resolution, by contrast, proposed that the principal purpose of such acts would be the 'destruction of the government and its military apparatus and merciless struggle with active Black Hundred organizations.'[99] This proposal also advocated unrestricted (except under Party control) expropriations of public funds. Overall Lenin was quite pleased with the resolution adopted by the Menshevik-dominated Congress, utilizing it against the Party Central Committee shortly afterwards when it repudiated 'guerrilla actions'; he had no doubt that 'active struggle' against Black Hundreds meant guerrilla actions.[100]

Lenin's August 1906 article 'Lessons of the Moscow Uprising' demonstrated the extent to which he continued to espouse armed uprising as the slogan of the day, an impatient exhortation to violence, despite the evident downturn in the revolutionary movement compared with the previous year. Condemning Plekhanov for criticizing the Uprising, he reasoned that the workers needed 'to take up arms' to induce the movement to 'free itself from the narrow limits of the peaceful strike alone', which he considered had 'spent itself as a weapon' after October. The Party's failure in December, he thought, was not providing sufficient organization and direction for the masses. Plekhanov, on the other hand, thought that the workers alone should not effect this 'bourgeois' revolution, for he was quite skeptical of the revolutionary reliability of the peasants and certainly of the bourgeoisie.[101] The Bolsheviks, also focused on the proletariat as the only steadfast revolutionary class, were convinced of the revolutionary significance of peasant unrest that would, together with workers' risings, lead to a successful overthrow of the regime. Lenin recognized that only a minority of workers had engaged in the actual December Uprising, but was convinced that the peaceful strike, which he thought could neither remove autocratic rule nor the monarchy, had to give way to the 'highest form of struggle' – an uprising – and that this was actually happening.[102] This was a crucial distinction; strikes reflected the fact that the workers were looking for major reforms from their employers and the regime, and suggested that if the regime progressed some considerable distance toward meeting these demands, it could purchase its survival as a constitutional monarchy. By contrast, Lenin believed it necessary to carry out immediate agitation amongst the masses so that they realized that 'they are entering upon an armed, bloody and desperate struggle' where there must be no fear of sacrifice, of death. 'We would be deceiving ourselves and the people', he remarked with a categorical violent logic, 'if we concealed from the masses the necessity of a desperate bloody war of extermination, as the immediate task of the coming revolutionary action',[103] and he ridiculed the idea of 'preliminary stages' to the realization of freedom.

In his pamphlet *Guerrilla Warfare*, written in September 1906, Lenin provided an insightful reflection on the place of violence in his revolutionary strategy. The Marxist should not be bound by any one form of struggle, for Marxism 'does not reject any form of struggle'. The revolutionary leaders should learn from the mass movement but also anticipate the form of struggle that the movement was 'inevitably' leading to. In Europe at that time, he explained, parliamentary struggle and the trade union movement were the principal media of struggle, whereas before it had been barricade tactics. Now, in 1906 in Russia, barricade tactics had been revived and in new forms: guerrilla warfare. Between 'big acts' of civil war in the form of mass uprisings, 'guerrilla warfare' would be an appropriate and inevitable military form for the conduct of civil war.[104] The 'clear connection' between guerrilla activities and an ensuing uprising ensured, Lenin believed, that this was not the terrorism of old. His conception of guerrilla activities between incidents of actual uprising demonstrated the diffuse nature of the conceptual difference between terrorism and guerrilla warfare. These acts would pursue 'two "different" aims: assassinations of individual chiefs and subordinates in the army and police, and confiscations of monetary funds both from the government and private persons.'[105] The barricades were to be replaced with mobile guerrilla units 'of ten, three or even two persons',[106] as opposed to the dozens comprising the military units he had envisaged in September 1905. Guerrilla methods, according to Lenin, would weaken the enemy forces in advance of an uprising, 'destroy the government, police and military machinery', fight the Black Hundred gangs, train the masses in military combat, and procure funds through robberies.[107]

David Allen Newell argues that Lenin's characterization of terrorist actions in early 1906 as 'guerrilla warfare' was misplaced because the victims, such as 'village gendarmes', were 'not of military or strategic value.'[108] Clearly, though, Lenin viewed all enforcers of the Tsar's rule as legitimate military targets, and Newell acknowledges that what is significant 'is the Bolshevik inclination to presuppose such activity [guerrilla warfare] and attempt to stimulate its further development.'[109] This was because the struggle was, according to Lenin, intensifying not declining. Marx had noted, he explained, that revolution progresses by giving rise to strong counter-revolution, that the actions of the revolutionaries would push the autocracy '*to the limit* in its resistance' and in this way, would force the revolution 'to the limit in applying the means of attack.'[110] Though the mass movement had abated somewhat relative to 1905 and the government had assumed the offensive against unrest, Lenin was encouraged by what he considered an 'intensification' of guerrilla acts such as occurred in Warsaw in August. The revolution, he believed, was about to reach, and required, 'the higher and more complex form of a prolonged civil war embracing the whole country' rather than isolated, short-lived uprisings. That is, a civil war between 'two sections of the people' – the autocracy, Black Hundreds, 'reactionary strata of the bourgeoisie', and the workers, peasants, and revolutionary strata of the bourgeoisie. Though certain 'guerrilla' actions were taking 'undesirable' forms, to Menshevik objections that guerrilla warfare disorganized the movement Lenin retorted that it was not the actions themselves but the failure of the Party to control them that led to disorganization.[111]

In August 1907 Lenin would retrospectively recognize that the 'phase of decline' of the revolutionary movement had begun in 1906.[112] This might suggest that his continued calls for guerrilla warfare throughout 1906 effectively amounted to that for which he had condemned the SRs before 1905 – adventurism without a mass popular upheaval and true mass violence. Newell reasons that 'In defense of these terrorist or guerrilla acts, it was maintained that the only alternative to them was to do nothing […]. The choice […] was […] between a return to the earlier plans for agitation, propaganda and strikes or terrorism.'[113] *Guerrilla Warfare*, for Newell, epitomized the Bolshevik 'drift' from Marxism. Yet Lenin's position appears more understandable than this. Abraham Ascher notes that 'the spirit of activism' among workers, and especially sailors, 'had not been extinguished in 1906'. The atmosphere in the country was still 'dangerously volatile' and hence 'many activists as well as government leaders expected a new explosion from below.'[114]

In August 1906 Lenin had advocated Bolshevik entry into the Second State Duma to expose this 'playing' at parliament, evidently concerned that the masses were being duped by this political concession. He recognized that the substance of the Bolshevik resolution regarding armed uprising at the Party Congress the previous spring had not yet become a reality, but he was adamant that 'we shall entirely subordinate the struggle we wage in the Duma to another form of struggle, namely, strikes, uprisings, etc.'[115] Lenin's most forthright advocacy of full-blown military civil war, then, came not at the height of the mass movement in 1905 but when it was on the retreat, convinced as he was in the necessity of a decisive 'war of extermination' between the forces of revolution and of reaction. Indeed, as he reminded readers of *Guerrilla Warfare*, 'A Marxist bases himself on the class struggle, and not social peace',[116] which was now leading to armed civil war.

By 1907 and the Fifth Party Congress in London, both factions of the Party realized that the revolutionary movement had for now dissipated. The Congress adopted Martov's draft severely criticizing the disorganizing anarchism of guerrilla actions at that time.[117] Lenin finally dropped his calls for violent struggle, including guerrilla actions, as an *immediate* tactic in 1907 (though he certainly continued to point to the necessity of violence to overthrow the autocracy until 1917) and the Bolshevik Party entered the Third State Duma. In July, at a meeting of the Bolshevik faction at the Party Conference, he repudiated 'terror' as a tactic, by which time his differences with the more 'voluntarist', Sorelian-influenced Bolsheviks (such as Aleksandr Bogdanov), who dominated the conference and insisted on continued boycott of the Duma, were apparent.[118] He declared that 'at the present time' terror was not working. The 'sole method of struggle' must be 'scientific propaganda and the State Duma as agitational tribune',[119] which he believed was evident because of the absence of a popular outburst in response to Prime Minister Stolypin's reactionary electoral law of 3 June 1907.[120]

Eschatology and ethics of civil war

One aspect of Lenin's thought that received its first really clear expression during these years was the idea of a 'just' or moral war. More than simply serving a utilitarian ethic, revolution (as a continuous process toward communism internationally) would serve the eschatological purpose of the 'deliverance' of humanity from capitalist oppression. In August 1905 Lenin wrote:

> Revolution […] is a life-and-death struggle between the old Russia, the Russia of slavery, serfdom, and autocracy, and the new, young, people's Russia, the Russia of the toiling masses, who are reaching out towards light and freedom, in order afterwards to start once again a struggle for the complete emancipation of mankind from all oppression and all exploitation.[121]

This moral, eschatological component played a crucial role in Lenin's willingness to advocate and justify extreme violent methods of struggle against an arbitrary, often brutal regime willing to defend its socially oppressive order through terror. Furthermore, he was convinced that when conditions for a full-blown civil war arose, 'In such periods a Marxist is *obliged* to take the stand of civil war. Any moral condemnation of civil war would be impermissible from the standpoint of Marxism.'[122] For Lenin the significance of 'crises and revolutions', as Eckard Bolsinger notes, lay 'in their ability to make the struggle and the constellations of class forces visible, forces that remain hidden in normal times.'[123] Civil war was, according to Lenin, an essential locomotive of history, but more likely in Russia to take the form of the 'actual bloody battles' that Kautsky had considered probably unnecessary in industrial Europe.

Lenin, and indeed the Mensheviks, instinctively labeled the events of 1905 'civil war'. This civil war would be a truly heroic act that would in turn negate itself. Lenin was a theorist of the dialectical concept of peace through violence, believing that the war to be waged by the masses in the interests of the revolution would be a war against violence itself, a 'moral' violent struggle against all violence for the true liberation of all peoples. This idea that revolutionary violence would negate violence was a basic element of the Marxist justification of violence; in 1900, for example, Plekhanov had written 'if you want peace – prepare yourself for war.'[124] Lenin's very concept of revolution in 1905 became highly militant:

> Revolution is war. Of all the wars known in history it is the only lawful, rightful, just and truly great war. This war is not waged in the selfish interests of a handful of rulers and exploiters, like any and all other wars, but in the interests of the masses of the people against the tyrants, in the interests of the toiling and exploited millions upon millions *against despotism and violence*.[125]

In addition:

> Social-Democracy has never taken a sentimental view of war. It unreservedly condemns war as a bestial means of settling conflicts in human society. But Social-Democracy knows that so long as society is divided into classes, so long as there is exploitation of man by man, wars are inevitable. This exploitation cannot be destroyed without war, and war is always and everywhere begun by the exploiters themselves, by the ruling and oppressing classes [...]. And there is another kind of war – the only war that is *legitimate* in capitalist society – war against the people's oppressors and enslavement.[126]

Jacob Kipp has argued that Lenin's reading in 1914 of Carl von Clausewitz (along with his re-reading of Hegelian dialectics) resulted in his 'militarization of Marxism' and 'a substantial shift in the place of war in socialist ideology' in that the armed working-class struggle of the working class would be 'the only path towards the eventual elimination of war.'[127] What is clear from the above extracts is that the essence and justificatory basis of Lenin's concept, advanced from 1914, of converting the (imperialist) World War into civil wars to end it and defeat its basis were in fact apparent in outline as early as 1905, before his ideas on imperialism developed.

The significance of 1905

From 1905, then, the efficacy and justification of revolutionary violence were strongly developed in Lenin's thought. It will become apparent that there was a clear logic in his ideas on class warfare and violence evident in these years that would remain and be invoked when he found himself in power. This included his thinking around civil war; his commitment to persistent class struggle normally precluding peaceful compromise and the vigorous pursuit of this to its likely violent consequences; the belief that history progresses dialectically through the use of revolutionary violence to negate reactionary violence and its basis; and of the strong legitimacy and justness of such revolutionary violence. The Bolsheviks were more cavalier in his attitude to violence than the Mensheviks, but the particular militancy of his thought nonetheless reflected the context of Tsarist Russia. Though the necessity of violence was not essentially enshrined in his thinking, it became clear during the course of 1905 to 1906 that violent and strongly coercive means Lenin considered not just efficacious, but inevitable and natural accompaniments of revolutionary transformation, certainly in Russia and perhaps more generally.

Israel Getzler has argued with some accuracy that it was during 1905 that Lenin 'spelled out clearly and precisely what he understood by dictatorship',[128] though this would develop fully only after 1917. 'Democratic dictatorship' was to facilitate a fully democratic revolution in Russia but the emphasis (at least initially) would be on defense and, as Robert Mayer notes, this 'implied above all violence and repression, a regime born of insurrection and engaged in a civil war against counter-revolution.'[129] Mayer argues that in 1905 Lenin 'altered the image' of proletarian dictatorship in social-democratic theory, and dictatorship henceforth became 'a fixture of Bolshevik rhetoric'. Certainly Mayer is correct regarding the concept of a worker–peasant dictatorship before maturation of socialism, but his principal point concerns Lenin's resultant emphasis on the violent suppression associated with dictatorship. This is true considering Lenin's focused discussion of the concept dictatorship and the associated function of coercion/violence. Yet this appears more a development of the concept, with particular and explicit emphasis upon the necessity for a forceful and violent revolutionary dictatorship especially in Russia, than a distortion of the Marxian understanding of revolutionary dictatorship. Lenin certainly assiduously referred to Marx to justify his understanding. It is simplistic and incorrect to assert, as Mayer has, that Lenin made dictatorship 'synonymous' with 'lawless terror'; besides, as discussed, Lenin conceived 'revolutionary' violence in response counter-revolutionary force.

Lenin always had his mind on the 'final goal', emphasizing the Marxist distinction between the 'minimum' democratic programme and the 'maximum' socialist programme that would lead to communism. The Bolshevik peasant slogan during these years was to support the peasantry generally in effecting the democratic revolution, but then for the proletariat to support and lead the 'rural proletariat' (landless labourers and, eventually, poor peasant smallholders) against the peasant bourgeoisie, for 'We promise no harmony [...] following the victory of the *present* peasant uprising, on the contrary, we "promise" a new struggle.'[130] 'The principle of class struggle', he wrote in 1907, 'is the very foundation of all Social-Democratic teachings and of all Social-Democratic policy.'[131] However, as Abraham Ascher notes, the 'individuals who participated in the mass movements of 1905 did not believe that they were merely preparing the way for the real event at some future date.'[132]

Lenin was an absolutist. Marxism for him, reflecting the general scientific, positivist emphasis in European Marxist orthodoxy after Marx's death, was not just a convincing theoretical framework but 'truth', and there could be no tolerance of 'heresy'. 'The Marxist doctrine is omnipotent because it is true', he would write in 1913. 'It is comprehensive and harmonious, and provides men with an integral world outlook.'[133] Lenin and the Bolsheviks were possessed of a greater urgency than the Menshevik leaders to force and control events, to actively lead the emancipation of the *narod*. Lenin noted that the Mensheviks 'do not understand that the harder we [the Party] strive to take full control of the conduct of the uprising, the greater will our share in the undertaking be'. The greater that share, the less would be the influence of the non-proletarians.[134] Yet it should not be thought that the Bolsheviks, unlike the Mensheviks, lacked 'faith' in the masses to achieve their own emancipation – this would be to fundamentally misunderstand Lenin's intellectual and emotional composition. Anna Krylova has observed that 1905 clearly demonstrated to Lenin that working-class spontaneous instincts were fundamentally compatible with objective historical necessity, though spontaneity itself possessed dangers as it could be exploited by non-socialist (or incorrectly socialist) parties, and hence party leadership would still be required to help instil 'correct consciousness'.[135]

However 'Leninism' (or 'Bolshevism') as a particular Marxist ideological tendency, with a practical vision of how a revolution would proceed in Russia, was emerging.[136] Lenin's injunction to advocate revolutionary civil war to negate and overcome bourgeois violence, even perhaps full-blown wars – so crucial to his strategy from 1914 – was apparent as early as 1905. The idea of the soviets as potential forms of new revolutionary government rather than a democratic parliamentary republic was also (apparently) first hinted at during this time, as was the permissibility, indeed necessity, of the Party of the proletariat entering government and establishing a form of proletarian-directed dictatorship before socialism could be fully implemented. These were to prove perhaps the most historically consequential elements of Leninism. The full maturation of Leninism as a distinct variant of Marxism would receive its foremost impetus with the onset of war in Europe in 1914.

2 'Violence to end all violence'

Ideological purity and the Great War, 1907–1917

> The imperialist war, that is, a war for the capitalist division of spoils [...] has *begun* to turn into civil war, that is [...] a war for mankind's complete liberation from wars, from poverty of the masses, from oppression of man by man.[1]

(V.I. Lenin, 12 March, 1917)

The year 1917 witnessed two major political and social revolutions in Russia. In February a revolution erupted that led within weeks to the collapse of Tsarism. In October the Provisional Government that had replaced the autocracy was overthrown by Lenin's Bolshevik Party, seizing power in the name of the All-Russian Congress of Soviets. The Bolshevik revolution was one of the most significant events of modern history, expressly defined as heralding the culmination of human history, assimilating and superseding thousands of years of human culture and thought. The revolution arose, however, out of an even more significant event of global importance, the Great War of 1914 to 1918. The war was both context of and justification for the October Revolution.

The war, similar to the events in Russia in 1905, focused Lenin's mind once again on the general subject of violence and led to the development in particular of his ideas on civil war. It occasioned his re-examination of 'the nature of capitalist society, the function of war and, particularly, the internal situation of the socialist movement.'[2] Lenin's view was uncompromising: violent civil wars to overthrow the existing 'criminal' regimes, to bring an end to the 'criminal war', were the only means by which the peoples of Europe and their oppressed colonies would escape the brutalities of war and of imperialism as a whole. The war proved to be of enormous importance for the development of Lenin's thought, convincing him of the imperative necessity of revolution in Russia in 1917. It also led him to think that a revolution would be won and consolidated with relative ease due to the striking educational value of the imperialist slaughter for exposing the nature of the capitalist system to the working masses, and due to the existence of a new type of centralized wartime economy. This chapter will develop the idea of the dialectical duality of violence and peace in Lenin's thought (that real peace would come through violence), situating this within the context of an era that appeared to Lenin (as to others) as a civilization on the brink of destruction.[3]

Between revolution and war

In February 1907 as the Second State Duma was preparing to meet, Lenin vigorously supported the idea that the Bolsheviks would stand for election. He was still confidently predicting that the 'second wave' of revolutionary activity was imminent and inevitable.[4] He had maintained during the revolutionary upsurge that support for 'constitutional illusions' in the form of parliamentary elections under the autocracy would be harmful for the proletarian movement, and hence his initial support for boycotting the Duma. Parliamentary activity, for Lenin, was axiomatic with a downturn in the revolutionary activities of the masses, though as we have seen he soon modified this and advocated that the Bolsheviks reconsider the boycott, but was initially unable to win them over.[5] In February 1907 he was still calling for preparations for 'the most stern and extreme method of struggle conceivable – that of the armed struggle of one part of the population against the other.'[6] His belief in the imminence of revolution was due to the predicted Second Duma election results, which produced a more polarized and radical body than the First, and the evident contradiction of this against the continuation of the 'Black Hundred' regime. Yet Lenin had realized that the time for 'spontaneous' as opposed to organized activity had lapsed. The Bolsheviks would 'do all in our power to make this new struggle as little spontaneous and as conscious, consistent, and steadfast as possible', he noted, and he was confident that 'it is precisely because of its inevitability that we must not force the pace, spur or goad it on.'[7]

Lenin was not calling for an immediate, 'premature' insurrection, recognizing that this was not on the immediate agenda, but it was his belief that the autocracy would of its own accord push the workers, soldiers and 'ruined peasantry' over to armed insurrection.[8] Concerned that fellow social democrats would now concentrate exclusively on peaceful, parliamentary means of struggle, he believed that it was essential for the Bolsheviks to make use of the Duma precisely to expose the true causes of the 'revolutionary crisis' and to propagate amongst the masses the idea that the crisis of autocracy could only be resolved by force of arms. This was, he declared, a 'revolutionary, not merely a constitutional crisis',[9] and 'the Second Duma must inevitably lead to battle, to insurrection.'[10]

Following the dissolution of the Second Duma and the reactionary electoral changes of June 1907, the much more conservative Third Duma convened in November. Lenin's writings in support of Social-Democratic participation in the electoral campaign demonstrated that he had finally accepted that revolution was no longer imminent. In his lengthy pamphlet *Against Boycott* he acknowledged that the masses had not been responsive to revolutionary appeals, demonstrating an 'infatuation' with parliament.[11] Yet he was by no means prepared to settle for a long, peaceful constitutional development of the revolution, declaring with confidence: 'Does this mean [...] that the revolution is over and a "constitutional" period has set in? That there are no grounds either for expecting a new upswing or for *preparing* for it? [...] Not at all.'[12] The inherent inabilities and limitations of the Duma effectively as an appendage to the autocracy rather than a real check on it would, he believed, reconcile the masses to the necessity of overthrowing the autocracy. 'Russia', he stressed, 'cannot emerge from her present crisis in a peaceful way.'[13]

Following the ebbing of the revolutionary tide, Lenin concentrated once again on intra-party debates, including those with elements of his own Bolshevik faction. The significance of these polemics was his desire to protect revolutionary and ideological purity and his absolute belief in the guiding role of Marxist theoretical 'truths'. Marxism, he declared in *Materialism and Empirio-criticism*, his major philosophical-polemical work of this period, 'is cut from a single piece of steel, you cannot eliminate one basic premise, one essential part, without departing from objective truth, without falling a prey to a bourgeois-reactionary falsehood.'[14] It was only 'by following the *path* of Marxist theory' that 'we shall draw closer to objective truth (without ever exhausting it); but by following *any other path* we shall arrive at nothing but confusion and lies.'[15]

Interestingly, Lenin wrote some articles on the great Russian writer Lev Tolstoi following the latter's death in 1910. He acknowledged that Tolstoi's moral criticism of exploitation burned with 'emotional power' and great sincerity, but believed Tolstoi to be deeply mistaken in his outlook as a result of imbibing 'naïve' peasant tendencies, namely 'alienation from political life, their mysticism, their desire to keep aloof from the world, "non-resistance to evil."'[16] This demonstrated not only Lenin's disdain for Tolstoi's Christian convictions and his doctrine of 'non-resistance to evil' but also, once again, the clear distinction in his mind between the 'old' and the 'new', between the mass of peasants – fearful of the 'horrors' of capitalist modernization – and the concentrated urban workers destined to lead the *narod* along the only true path of revolutionary emancipation and salvation.[17]

During these intervening years of 'reaction and counter-revolution' before the outbreak of war Lenin continued to reiterate his conviction in the need, ultimately, for a violent confrontation with the autocracy to secure a republic. This was in the face of disputes within the socialist camp about the significance of the Duma and even the possibility of a constitutional path to socialism.[18] Once again, his advocacy of violence was presented as an enforced response to the inherently violent nature of the autocracy. In March 1908 he noted that 'in certain conditions the class struggle assumes the form of armed conflict and civil war; there are times when the interests of the proletariat call for ruthless extermination of its enemies in open armed clashes.'[19] Under the influence of the regime's 'counter-revolutionary repressions', he contended, 'philistine' intellectuals had cowered themselves by seeking to follow the path of '"cultured and civilized" constitutional work', whereas 'the pledge of coming successes of the revolution' in Russia lay only through means of direct struggle, whether in the form of a general strike or mass uprising.[20]

From the end of 1911 and into 1912 Russia once again began to experience considerable unrest, with a huge rise in strikes and increased governmental repressions. The Russian strike movement, Lenin noted, had reached an unprecedented scale in global terms.[21] The Lena goldfields massacre of 1912 gained particular notoriety and Lenin considered it a possible repeat of Bloody Sunday. He declared that civil war had begun once again and that, as in 1905, 'The counter-revolution *itself* started civil war by pogroms, by violence against democrats, and so on.'[22] Yet he had clearly learned to be more circumspect. The working class by itself would not be able to topple the autocracy, he made quite clear, for the support of 'the democratic peasantry and the active participation of the armed forces' were necessary for a 'timely, i.e., successful' uprising, to avoid 'premature attempts'.[23] This was in essence acknowledgement that the more restrained Menshevik position of 1906 was closer to the correct insurrectionary strategy in peasant Russia, though the situation in the country as a whole was certainly more volatile in 1906. However he encouraged more peaceful forms of revolutionary activity such as strikes and demonstrations, berating more cautious 'liquidationist' Mensheviks in the process: 'One must not resort to violence when there has been no question of it [...]. One must warn against violence. But to warn against a peaceful strike at a time when the masses are *seething*? To warn against a *demonstration*??'[24] The autocracy and its 'lackeys' in the Fourth Duma, he believed, were very rapidly creating their own downfall.

By this time it was apparent that the possibility of a European war was very real. Lenin certainly did not welcome the prospect of war, and his writings on this subject, few though they were, reveal a distinct moral indignation. He argued that the European imperialist powers were gambling 'with the lives of millions in the most cold-blooded way by inciting the peoples to a carnage for the profit of a handful of merchants and industrialists.'[25] In April 1913 he wrote a scathing criticism of the so-called 'civilized' European states that were 'engaged in a mad armaments hurdle-race [...] for all manner of weapons of destruction'.[26] What seemed most repulsive to Lenin was not so much the risk of mass slaughter as the risk of mass slaughter in the name of imperialist rivalries disguised as patriotism or national defence. Nevertheless he was not indifferent to the sufferings of millions once war broke out.

The civil war slogan, 1914 to February 1917

The war that broke out in August 1914 did not come as a shock to Lenin. What did cause him considerable dismay was the support for the war effort provided by so many of the European socialist parties in the belligerent countries, in contravention of the resolutions passed at the pre-war congresses of the Second International. This was especially because the leading theorist of the Second International, Karl Kautsky, reluctantly agreed to support the German war effort to avoid splitting the SPD.[27] R. Craig Nation has noted that 'Prior to 1914 socialism was the expression of an abstract ideal. The Great War brought an end to the movement's age of innocence.'[28] The war occasioned for socialist thinkers an imperative engagement with the nature of capitalism at that time and, consequently, the correct revolutionary strategy to pursue. Did it demonstrate that the advances made by socialist parties such as the SPD over the previous two decades were more illusory than substantial, that there could in fact be no true path to socialism from within the existing capitalist system even in advanced countries, that capitalism was now in its death throes and inherently disposed to war and destruction? Or was this war an aberration, the product of purely erroneous human volition? Should business continue as usual after the war, and socialist parties continue their struggles as before through (and for increasing) legal channels? Or was this a defining moment in history, when socialist revolutions were of immediate necessity for historical progression?

Lenin threw himself into a re-reading of Hegelian dialectics upon the outbreak of war, helping to establish his firm conviction that the war indeed signaled the death-throes of capitalism and the necessity of a revolutionary leap forward to socialism.[29] He was to prove resolute in his convictions in upholding what he regarded as the essence of revolutionary Marxism. Nation has pointed out that Lenin's wartime revolutionary strategy was one of sincere revolutionary principle, that his 'arguments were primarily concerned with elevating principle above expediency by achieving a theoretically consistent response to the European crisis.' He intended 'to repudiate the failure of the Second International [to adopt a revolutionary stance on the war]', and provide 'a radical alternative'.[30]

Lenin's response to the war was to write seven theses on the tasks of revolutionary Social-Democracy, and an assessment of the reaction of the 'social-chauvinists' who were now supporting their imperialist governments in the prosecution of the war. His reaction to the 'betrayals' of the socialist leaders was revealing: 'To the socialist it is not the horrors of war that are the hardest to endure – we are always for *"santa guerra di tutti gli oppressi per la conquista delle loro patrie!"* – but the horrors of the treachery shown by the leaders of present-day socialism, the horrors of the collapse of the present-day International.'[31] The war, he stated, was imperialist in nature; it was the product of the international rivalries for markets and colonies (for the export of finance capital) characterizing the latest (and last), imperialist stage of capitalism, and was the inevitable product of capitalism.[32] It was on this basis that Lenin castigated those socialists who justified supporting their nation's war effort and were thereby leading their workers astray, doing so by reference to Marx's support for various 'progressive bourgeois' wars in the nineteenth century.[33] Lenin declared that the time for progressive bourgeois movements amongst the European powers was over; under present-day imperialism, the socialist should not support either belligerent side but should condemn each side equally, and 'wish for the defeat of the imperialist bourgeoisie in every country.'[34]

Of the major belligerent powers the greatest opposition to the war amongst socialists was to be found in Russia, resulting in refusal to vote for war credits in the Duma. Lenin was however in an isolated position even amongst Russian Social-Democrats who shared his opposition to the war, such as the Menshevik-Internationalists, for he adopted a position of 'revolutionary defeatism'. This position, utterly unrealistic for socialist-internationalists attempting to attract mass support, stated that the defeat of Tsarist Russia 'would be the lesser evil by far' for the peoples of Russia,[35] and that socialists of each country should adopt a similar line of reasoning.[36] This was because 'Neither group of belligerents is inferior to the other in spoliation, atrocities and the boundless brutality of war.'[37] In this regard Lenin was diametrically opposed by Plekhanov who, though 'principally opposed to the war', considered it was not the time to decide 'who was right, who was guilty, and punish both'. He wanted the defeat of the aggressor – according to his conviction Germany and Austria-Hungary.[38] Lenin, by contrast, immediately called for 'a revolutionary war by the proletarians of all countries' against the 'bourgeoisie of all countries',[39] urged calls for a republican 'United States of Europe' (which slogan he retracted in 1915), and evidently conceived of offensive international revolutionary wars, not just domestic civil wars.

Upon the outbreak of war a joint Bolshevik–Menshevik declaration in the Duma demonstrated the depth of socialist opposition to the war in Russia. The declaration stated that the war resulted from the politics of conquest practiced by all belligerents and there could be no approval for the idea of national unity for the war effort. It looked forward to the workers, united internationally, taking their fate into their own hands and ensuring that the source of all violence and oppression would be removed, the implication being that a number of revolutions would bring about the end of the international rule of capital.[40] Similar sentiments were expressed in a Menshevik 'Organisational Committee' paper in October. The war, it noted, demonstrated the significance of the worker class in contemporary society. Without its active support, defence of the country would be 'inconceivable', hence the implication that if popular sentiment turned against the war it would soon terminate. However the means suggested for internal civil struggle were educational and propaganda work to expose the true nature of the war, not strikes or uprisings.[41] In December the Committee made clear that its 'battle cry' was 'peace, peace, peace' (not 'civil war'),[42] thereby revealing the generally more pacifist tendency in Menshevik thought.

The leading Menshevik–Internationalist, Iulii Martov, wrote in December 1914 that the war was above all the outcome of 'irreconcilable imperialist antagonisms' and that 'a more or less protracted, more or less agonizing new phase of the development of international capitalism has become today inevitable.' He also believed in an 'immanent connection between capitalism and militarism.' Martov depicted a picture of an oppressive and monstrous 'super-capitalism' or 'ultra-capitalism' of one imperialist monopoly, whether German or Anglo-French, that would result from 'permanent wars' and represent not progression but the retardation of revolutionary movements in those countries under its sway. Capitalism in its imperialist phase, Martov believed as did Lenin, threatened historical progress. Martov declared that the development of capitalism had created an unprecedented revolutionary situation in Europe that would convince the proletariat of the necessity of taking political power and changing the 'economic system.' He warned against both socialist refusal to oppose the War, and 'nihilism', but Mensheviks should not be afraid of providing 'grist to the mill of Leninism' by opposing the war effort.[43]

Lenin's ideas, in comparison with the non-Bolshevik Russian Social-Democrats who opposed the war, were more extreme in his prescription for ending the war though not in his diagnosis of its origins.[44] The Bolsheviks as a separate party had the advantage of greater theoretical unity than the non-Bolshevik Russian Left.[45] Lenin was adamant that opposition to the war should not be equated with pacifism. Rather, the war would provide the spark to ignite the conflagration of national civil, and international revolutionary, wars, which would be legitimate wars of liberation. The bourgeoisie of each country, through its rhetoric of national 'civil peace' and unity, was trying 'to hoodwink the proletariat and distract its attention from the only genuine war of liberation, namely, a civil war against the bourgeoisie both of its "own" and of "foreign" countries.'[46] What is noteworthy here is that Lenin's thinking had acquired a newly-found international dimension and that his strategy for revolution, to a greater extent than before, was to cross national boundaries.[47] The war had 'placed on the order of the day the slogan of socialist revolution' for the advanced European states, for it reflected capitalism's inherent contradictions and concentrated immense economic power in the hands of the state; the structure of imperialism, or finance capitalism, ensured that these societies were 'pregnant' with socialism. The task for Russia remained as before – to complete its democratic revolution and attain the 'three pillars' of a democratic republic, confiscation of the landed estates, and an eight-hour working day.[48]

In November, in an article in the Bolshevik paper *Sotsial-Democrat*, Lenin put together his thoughts on the war thus far. It was the duty of Marxists to be cognizant of historical shifts and to examine each historical epoch on its own merits. The twentieth century signaled the era of imperialism. National wars were still conceivable, given uneven levels of economic development globally, but only as conducted by those nations suffering under the yoke of various imperialist powers, such as Poland, Ireland and India. The war, he reiterated, was 'no chance happening, no "sin" as is thought by Christian priests (who are no whit behind the opportunists in preaching patriotism, humanity and peace).' It was rather 'an inevitable stage of capitalism, just as legitimate a form of the *capitalist* way of life as peace is.'[49] This was in keeping with the logic of the Marxian premise that the capitalist system would create its own downfall, that it would not be able to overcome its internal contradictions, manifest as Lenin now believed in its inherent proclivity for imperialist warfare.[50] The idea that war was an inevitable and inherent tendency of the latest phase of capitalism was challenged by Kautsky, who put forward the idea that the imperialist impulse could in fact create the possibility of a peaceful 'ultra-imperialism' in international relations in the future, i.e. a level of development of capitalism at which the capitalist powers could coexist peacefully. War, Kautsky considered, was not considered a necessary and inevitable product of capitalism.[51]

There was undoubtedly some veracity in Lenin's nonetheless exaggerated emphasis upon the 'systemic' reasons for war, but he was filtering the situation through the lens of his Marxist beliefs and coming up with his revolutionary prescriptions accordingly. If war was inherent in the capitalist-imperialist system, then, he believed, the system could only be overcome by means of war, a war against war (*voina voine*).[52] In this regard Lenin referred to Carl von Clausewitz, the nineteenth-century Prussian military theorist, whom he was reading in 1915. Clausewitz had famously written that 'war was simply the continuation of politics by other means.' Capitalist-imperialist politics would inevitably lead to further wars, and somewhat prophetically Lenin predicted that 'This war will soon be followed by others, unless there are a series of successful revolutions.'[53] The task of true socialists would be to work energetically to conduct propaganda explaining to the masses the need to convert the war into civil war, not to exhibit 'a vain yearning for the destruction of capitalism without a desperate civil war or a series of wars.'[54] Lenin sounded a note of panic, that 'Imperialism sets at hazard the fate of European culture.' The creation of socialism was supposedly a necessary historical progression but it could not be guaranteed unless revolutionary action were forthcoming to destroy imperialism and its unprecedentedly coercive state capabilities.

Lenin recognized that the war commanded considerable popular support, that 'Present-day war is a people's war',[55] and that the revolutionary crisis had not yet matured. The masses were caught up in the general mood of patriotism that had swept the continent but Lenin reminded his colleagues that 'we must not swim with the "popular" current of chauvinism'. He appeared confident in the revolutionary instinctiveness of the workers (and peasants). 'The appalling misery of the masses', he reasoned, which had been 'created by the war, cannot fail to evoke revolutionary sentiments and movements.'[56] The war would thereby tear asunder 'all veils of hypocrisy', reject 'all conventions', and deflate 'all corrupt or rotting authorities.'[57] He maintained that soldiers should not refuse to serve in the army or lay down their arms.[58] The people at home should not engage in the 'sheer nonsense' of anti-war demonstrations, for this would suggest that there could be a peaceful resolution of the national and international crises that afflicted Europe. Down with appeals for '"peace at any price"! Let us raise high the banner of civil war!'.

What, then, did Lenin mean by 'civil war'? Was this slogan merely 'a rhetorical flourish against non-revolutionary pacifism', as Robert Daniels opined, with little foresight as to the actual course of civil war in Russia?[59] It is certainly probable that Lenin did not envisage the actual ferocity of the later Russian Civil War, though this was more apparent in 1917 than in 1915. In any case European revolutions would, he believed, break out to accompany a Russian revolution so he could not have envisaged Soviet Russia's later predicament. Civil war for Lenin seems to have encompassed a broad category of meanings, from relatively mild forms of political protest up to and including actual military battles. He suggested that Europe would enter an entire period of quite fierce civil war turbulence. In early 1915, a conference of various émigré Bolshevik groups convened in Bern. There was some discordance amongst the Bolsheviks about the nature of a Russian revolution, whether bourgeois or socialist (this would persist even after the October Revolution),[60] but the Bolsheviks were agreed on the necessity for civil wars and the defeat of Tsarist Russia in the war. The conference defined civil war as:

> … an armed struggle of the proletariat against the bourgeoisie, for the expropriation of the capitalist class in the advanced countries, and for a

democratic revolution in Russia (a democratic republic, an eight-hour day, the confiscation of the landowners' estates), for a republic to be formed in the backward monarchist countries in general, etc.[61]

The slogan of civil war, propounded by the most conscious element of the worker movement, the party, would 'co-ordinate and direct' the inevitable revolutionary sentiments amongst the masses.[62] Lenin, as the Soviet historian Temkin stressed, was not an advocate of an armed putsch without mass support,[63] and as yet the war commanded the support of the Russian masses. The five 'first steps towards converting the present imperialist war into a civil war' to be adopted by Social-Democrats in belligerent countries would be to refuse to vote for war credits and resign from government; to completely renounce a 'class truce' during wartime; to organize underground organizations wherever 'constitutional liberties' were removed through declaration of martial law; to support fraternization amongst the troops in the trenches, and, finally, to support 'every kind of revolutionary mass action by the proletariat in general' (without mention here of the peasantry).[64] Once the crisis had matured, it would then be 'to our advantage to exchange ballots for bullets.'[65] In reality though, and as Lenin acknowledged, it proved extremely difficult for the Bolsheviks to conduct underground activities in the Russian Empire due to intensified police repression after the outbreak of war.[66] Once again he condemned pacifism – 'the preaching of peace in the abstract' – and extolled the 'positive significance of revolutionary wars [...] with the aim of doing away with national oppression' or defending a victorious proletariat. The Bolsheviks' moral indignation at the inhumanity of the war-mongering bourgeoisie was clear: 'At the present time the propaganda of peace unaccompanied by a call for revolutionary mass action can only sow illusions and demoralize the proletariat, *for it makes the proletariat believe that the bourgeoisie is humane.*'[67] The essentialist, 'scientific' Marxist approach to the process of history, the dialectical growing of the new society out of the old, coexisted with a more Romanticist, moralistic approach that sought to cleanse human society of its ills.

Lenin was certainly morally repulsed by the war that broke out in 1914 but he did not display the same anti-war sentiment of most socialists. His socialism was fundamentally opposed to war and envisaged a peaceful future but he was not so much anti-war in 1914 as anti-imperialist.[68] This he made particularly clear in a letter to his friend and fellow Bolshevik Inessa Armand in January 1917. There were, he pointed out, three main types of international wars: those between exploiting, imperialist nations for conquest; those between exploited and exploiting nations; and, the most 'complicated', those between 'equal' nations. Lenin opposed defending the fatherland in the imperialist war of 1914 only because in both warring camps socialist revolutions were ripe and because the war was one of plunder: 'Only therefore we are opposed to "defence of the fatherland", only therefore!!'[69]

Yet from the perspective of Lenin's increased dialectical worldview, the war represented an epochal opportunity to negate itself. Revolutionary violence would be a response to the initial violence of the government against its people. Lenin's dialectical conception of the war was clear in his remarks on Clausewitz's *On War*, evidently made in 1915.[70] Clausewitz described how, since the start of the nineteenth century, war became once again an affair 'of all the people'.[71] 'The means [of war]' had become 'lost in the energy and enthusiasm of the government and its subjects.' Lenin noted this 'NB'. In the words of the philosopher Etienne Balibar, for Lenin the war was 'not a catastrophe but a process.'[72] Involving as it did the militarization of vast masses of the people, under conditions of unprecedented technical military advancements, it provided for an unprecedented explosive situation with enormous revolutionary potential; hence the significance of Lenin's anti-pacifist stand. Bernice Rosenthal has noted that for Lenin the revolutionary violence of 1905 to 1906 provided the *narod* with 'a psychologically transforming experience.'[73] The experience of the violence of imperialist war would, Lenin was convinced, most certainly have such an effect. The worker and peasant soldiers should not renounce their weapons because, with awareness of their interests, they should use them to strike for their freedom: 'They will say to their sons: "You will be given a gun. Take it and learn the military art properly. The proletarians need this knowledge not to shoot your brothers [but] to fight the bourgeoisie of their own country."'[74]

By summer 1915 the initial popular support accorded the Tsarist government for the war effort had been waning and industrial conflict had returned to the factories.[75] Having expounded on the necessity of opposing the slogan of peace 'in general' and of any conciliation between the rule of capital and that of socialism, Lenin nonetheless warned against indifference to the growing popular sentiment for peace. 'No', he declared, 'we must make use of the desire for peace so as to explain to the masses that the benefits they expect from peace cannot be obtained without a series of revolutions', though the cessation of violence 'is our ideal.'[76] In July he wrote of civil war as '"a war against war"' that 'alone would lead to a European revolution, to the permanent peace of socialism, to the deliverance [*izbavlenie*] of humanity from the horrors, misery, savagery and brutality now prevailing.'[77] The duality of war and peace in Lenin's thought was receiving its finest airing. This signified not only the eschatological nature of his worldview, but that this worldview was informed by a moral reaction to the particular brutal juncture of European history of 1915, and the entire political, social and economic system of capitalism then in its imperialist era. Violence and brutality were, he believed, intrinsic characteristics of imperialism, hence revolutionary violence would be justified by the promise of 'the permanent peace of socialism.' History was playing on his mind – the time was approaching for the worker movement to cleanse the earth of its ills. Towards the end of the summer of 1915, he referred twice in one article to the idea of the 'salvation' (*spasenie*) of humanity 'from the horrors of the present and future wars.'[78] It was the responsibility of Social-Democrats to play a critical role in bringing about this salvation, through their revolutionary work amongst the masses. In addition, in light of the 'shameful treachery' of the erstwhile leaders of the Second International, Lenin was convinced that the lofty task of leading this international liberationist movement had devolved upon the Russian proletariat, 'through the medium of their party.'[79]

Kautsky's calls for peace, his belief in a possible 'ultra-imperialism' as well as his advocacy of disarmament, provoked Lenin's ire. He declared that, even if the imperialist governments were to proclaim disarmament (which prospect he did not take seriously) 'it would be downright treachery to the proletariat to dissuade it from taking revolutionary action, without which all promises and all fine prospects are only a mirage.'[80] Universal disarmament might bring an end to war but it would not remove the root cause of the conflict, and in any case Lenin equated the disarmament slogan with non-revolutionary socialist opportunism. Disarmament was advocated by those socialists who despaired of the horrors of war but could not accept that capitalism was preparing 'an end in horror', and that the proletariat should prepare for its legitimate revolutionary war.[81] More significantly, Lenin opposed disarmament because the dictatorship of the proletariat would itself be based on 'dictatorship', which he now defined as 'state power based directly on *violence*', and violence 'in the twentieth century [...] means neither a fist nor a club, but *troops*.'[82] In the autumn of 1916 he declared that 'Disarmament is the ideal of socialism. There will be no wars in socialist society.'[83] However, to advocate disarmament at this particular time would display 'as little Marxism [...] as there would be if we were to say: We are opposed to violence.'[84] In his proposal to the Kienthal Conference of socialists opposed to the war, he wrote that 'socialists cannot repudiate violence and wars in the interests of the majority of the population.'[85]

Lenin's theoretical analysis of the phenomenon of imperialism, which appeared in 1916 as *Imperialism, the Highest Stage of Capitalism*, drew on the earlier work of Kautsky and the Austro-Marxist Rudolf Hilferding. He reasoned that imperialism signaled that capitalism had, overall, entered its decline, its 'moribund' phase;[86] it had essentially become 'a striving towards violence and reaction.' Hence he ridiculed Kautsky's view of the prospect of a form of capitalism that would entail 'less sacrifice and suffering'. The result of Kautsky's endeavours, he charged, was 'a blunting of the most profound contradictions of the latest stage of capitalism, instead of an exposure of their depth [...] bourgeois reformism instead of Marxism.'[87] The war provided dramatic proof of what Marxism had always taught – that capitalism would bring with it greater hardships for the working people until they overthrew this system and instituted socialism, which would lead to a fully communist society. 'War', Lenin reiterated, 'does not contradict the fundamentals of private property – on the contrary, it is a direct and inevitable outcome of those fundamentals.'[88] If Lenin's Marxist economics informed his politics, his politics also informed his economics. The brutality of his times strengthened him in his beliefs, his predictions and his moral-revolutionary disposition. It was his ideological worldview and associated convictions and attitudes regarding revolutionary violence and civil war at a time of such violence that ultimately determined his conviction of the need for violent revolutions, for civil wars, to overthrow the rule of international capital. This was not, however, the only possible Marxist response to the war; Lenin had firmly established himself on the Marxist Left.

Lenin's position was also more extreme than most other international socialists who opposed the war. The Zimmerwald and Kienthal international conferences of anti-war socialists did adopt resolutions calling for greater revolutionary activism on the part of the proletariat, but despite the urgings of the Bolsheviks and Karl Liebknecht, they did not adopt Lenin's slogan of converting the imperialist war into civil war. Hence Lenin was a 'Left Zimmerwaldist', a 'minority within a minority' of European socialists.[89] In his pamphlet *Socialism and War*, written in July to August 1915, Lenin summed up his approach to war:

> Socialists have always condemned war between nations as barbarous and brutal. But our attitude towards war is fundamentally different from that of the bourgeois pacifists (supporters and advocates of peace) and of the Anarchists [...] we understand that war cannot be abolished unless classes are abolished and Socialism is created; and we also differ in that we fully regard civil wars, i.e., wars waged by the oppressed class against the oppressing class [...] as legitimate, progressive and necessary. We Marxists differ from both the pacifists and the Anarchists in that we deem it necessary historically (from the standpoint of Marx's dialectical materialism) to study each war separately. In history there have been numerous wars which, in spite of all the horrors, atrocities, distress and suffering that inevitably accompany all wars, were progressive, i.e., benefited the development of mankind by helping to destroy the exceptionally harmful and reactionary institution.[90]

The course of the socialist revolution, he declared, 'should not be regarded as a single act, but as a period of turbulent political and economic upheavals, the most intense class struggle, civil war, revolutions, and counter-revolution.'[91] Later in 1915 he envisaged a telescoping of revolutionary phases in Russia, a clear conception of 'permanent revolution'. The proletariat, following the overthrow of Tsarism, would 'at once [...] bring about the socialist revolution in alliance with the proletarians of Europe.'[92] The 'vast difference' as he understood it between the revolutionary crises in Russia in 1905 and 1915 was that the war had involved all the most advanced European countries, their respective fates were closely linked together, and hence 'no individual solution of revolutionary [problems] is possible in any single country.'[93] The Russian democratic revolution would no longer be simply a 'spark' that might ignite a revolutionary-socialist conflagration across Europe but, rather, 'an indivisible and integral part of, the socialist revolution in the West.'[94]

In 1916 Lenin devoted greater attention to what he believed would be imminent socialist revolutions. Imperialism, or monopoly capitalism as opposed to capitalist competition, was 'creating all the objective prerequisites for the achievement of socialism.'[95] Working-class organization, he thought, had been badly damaged due to socialist opportunism and popular acquiescence in defending the imperialist fatherland, but he believed a revolutionary crisis to be maturing that would restore the working-class spirit.[96]

Lenin's thinking on democracy was complex. He declared that 'socialism cannot be victorious unless it introduces complete democracy [...] the proletariat will be unable to prepare for victory over the bourgeoisie unless it wages a many-sided, consistent and revolutionary struggle for democracy.'[97] Was Lenin advocating a truly democratic republic as the form of proletarian dictatorship? He answered this in the negative a year later, reasoning that a democratic parliamentary republic would not provide the institutional means for exercising proletarian dictatorship. The dualism of Lenin's conception of democracy was expressed more explicitly in his belief that socialism:

> … can be implemented only *through* the dictatorship of the proletariat, which combines violence against the bourgeoisie, i.e., the minority of the population, with *full* development of democracy, .i.e., the genuinely equal and genuinely universal participation of the *entire* mass of the population in all *state* affairs and in all the complex problems of abolishing capitalism.[98]

That is, the bourgeoisie appeared alien to the *narod*; the 'entire mass of the population' appeared synonymous with the 'entire mass of the working people.' He continued that 'All talk of "rights" seems absurd during a war', for 'civil war, like every other, must inevitably replace rights by violence.' However violence 'in the name of the interests and rights of the majority', he explained, 'is of a different nature: it tramples on the "rights" of the exploiters, the bourgeoisie, it is *unachievable* without democratic organization of the army and the "rear"',[99] and would ultimately serve the cause of democracy. This was violence in the sense of the violation of democratic and property rights, of a state directed against a section of the population, not necessarily physical coercion. Lenin was making the case for a class-based democracy, that is, complete democratic organization for the exploited classes only, as 'civil war against the bourgeoisie is a *democratically* conducted war of the propertyless mass against the propertied minority.'[100]

Lenin reasoned that the 'labour aristocracy' – the minority of organized workers in the belligerent countries supposedly bought off with the super-profits of imperialism, and defended by 'renegade' socialists – should not be confused for what he considered, with an almost mythical quality, 'the real masses.' The duty of true socialists would be 'to go down *lower and deeper*, to the real masses […] to teach the masses to appreciate their true political interests […]'[101] Lenin, according to Balibar, 'implicitly presupposed therefore the existence of a "pure" proletarian mass, intrinsically hostile to the war, even though the turnaround of the political and trade union leaderships and the constraints of mobilization had temporarily atomized this and reduced it to impotence.'[102] The truly class conscious intelligentsia would have to reveal to the masses their own class interests for, as Lenin put it, 'it is not so much a question of the size of an organization [in terms of proletarian representation], as of the real, objective significance of its policy' that mattered. He was insistent on the necessity of bearing witness to what he believed to be the truth, even if, indeed especially because, the majority of workers were not yet cognizant of this.

Lenin's ideas on the coercion associated with the dictatorship of the proletariat were also quite revealing of his highly dialectical worldview. He noted that 'dictatorship is domination of one part of society over the rest of society, and domination, moreover, that rests directly on coercion', though 'the entire trend of development is towards [eventual] abolition of coercive domination of one part of society over another.' Such was the importance of the question of dictatorship that anyone who denied its necessity or recognized it 'only in words', Lenin insisted, should not remain a Social-Democrat.[103] He conceded that the bourgeoisie might give up power peacefully in a small country should its larger neighbors convert to socialism without need for civil war, but this was not likely. Hence Social-Democrats should enshrine civil war in their respective programmes, though Lenin reminded his readers that 'violence is, of course, alien to our ideals.'[104] For this reason, he wrote with conviction that:

> The 'social' parsons and opportunists are always ready to build dreams of future peaceful socialism. But the very thing that distinguishes them from revolutionary Social-Democrats is that they refuse to think about and reflect on the fierce class struggle and class *wars* needed to achieve that beautiful future.[105]

This was one of Lenin's most explicit declarations of revolutionary ethics, of his belief in the dialectical duality of war and peace. Intense revolutionary violence appeared necessary for the international triumph of socialism. Civil war he thought should be regarded as 'just as much a war as any other'. Furthermore he reasoned that 'He who accepts the class struggle cannot fail to accept civil wars' which 'in every class society are the natural, and under certain conditions inevitable, continuation, development and intensification of the class struggle',[106] of proletarian politics. Lenin predicted that revolutionary wars would not be confined to civil wars but would probably also extend to regular international conflicts, for victory would likely be achieved in one country first (itself an unorthodox departure in Marxist thinking) as a consequence of capitalism's uneven economic development globally,[107] thereby bringing upon it the armed force of the international bourgeoisie. 'In such cases', he reasoned, 'a war on our part would be a legitimate and just war',[108] apparently intending this in a primarily defensive sense. War would 'become impossible' only when the world bourgeoisie had been 'overthrown, finally vanquished and expropriated.'[109]

3 'History will not forgive us if we do not seize power now'

The revolutionary imperative, 1917

> The specific feature of the present situation in Russia is that the country is *passing* from the first stage of the revolution [...] to its *second stage*, which must place power in the hands of the proletariat and the poorest sections of the peasants.[1]
>
> (V.I. Lenin, *April Theses*)

The year 1917 was to prove momentous for Russia, and for Lenin personally. He began the year in exile in Switzerland, and ended it as the leader of the world's first Marxist state. He had only seven more years to live, but he would end his life as one of the central and iconic figures of the twentieth century. Lenin's writings for much of the period from February to October 1917 represent a quite distinctive shift in his views on violence from the preceding years, following the overthrow of the Tsarist autocracy. He was prepared to accept, even hope for, not only a peaceful transfer of power to the soviets that were re-established from February but even perhaps a peaceful consolidation of the revolution. By September he finally accepted that a violent overthrow of the government was required and that this risked a brutal civil war. Lenin's writings of this period provide a challenge for those who argue that his approach to violence was basically 'essentialist', that he 'eulogized' its use and never really envisaged a non-violent approach to revolution.[2] Certainly, as noted earlier, he spoke highly of the instrumental uses of violence in the interests of revolution, but violence was not desirable for itself and Lenin envisaged the possibility, however briefly and realistically, of a peaceful revolution in Russia. In any case he did not seem to envisage the extent of the violence and difficulties that would characterize the early years of Soviet rule in Russia.

'All power to the soviets'

In February to March 1917 the 'civil war' that Lenin had been urging for the previous three years began in Russia. Tensions in Russian society finally spilled over and the Tsar relinquished the throne. In the limited sense that the autocracy had been overthrown, Lenin acknowledged that the bourgeois-democratic revolution had been accomplished in Russia. In fact the resulting government was, he pointed out, unusual, as a system of 'dual power' had arisen. Political power was effectively shared between the Provisional Government formed by moderate monarchist and liberal parties in the Duma, and the embryonic form of a workers' and peasants' government, the Petrograd Soviet. In April the government would be propped up by the Mensheviks and SRs, despite the (later justified) misgivings among leading Mensheviks about entering such a government.[3] Yet Lenin maintained that the democratic revolution had not been thorough-going; Russia was not yet economically ready for complete socialism, though its revolution would, he thought, 'start' worldwide socialist revolutions.[4] The Russian proletariat had temporarily become the 'vanguard of the revolutionary proletariat of the whole world', but was not sufficiently organized or class-conscious to remain as such.[5]

Lenin's reaction to the revolution was immediately to advocate 'no support of the new government',[6] a position not initially shared by more moderate Bolsheviks in Petrograd.[7] From Switzerland, preparing for return to Russia, he dispatched a series of letters to Petrograd Bolsheviks. The rapidity of the Russian revolution, he considered, had been facilitated both by the lessons acquired by the people in 1905, and of course by the war, the 'mighty accelerator.'[8] In his first letter – the only one the Bolsheviks published in *Pravda* at the time but in edited form, as they considered some of his language too extreme – he proceeded to excoriate the new government as the product of an Anglo-French plot to ensure that the Tsarist autocracy would not conclude a separate peace with Germany. It would slaughter 'fresh millions' of Russian workers and peasants in order to continue the *imperialist* war, an interpretation that later seemed more plausible in the light of the 'April Crisis'.[9] This 'bourgeois' government was, he believed, turning against the revolutionary strivings of the masses, negotiating for a monarchist restoration, and fudging on the question of elections for a Constituent Assembly.[10] There was no explicit mention that the civil war slogan remained but there was, he believed, a need for the expansion and strengthening of a 'proletarian militia' that would replace the old police force and standing army as the 'executive organ' of the soviets, and offer 'serious resistance to the restoration of the monarchy and attempts to rescind or curtail the promised freedoms, or of firmly taking the road that will give the people bread, *peace* and freedom.'[11] He made clear that there was no question of an immediate overthrow of the government, for even if that power were overthrown, the proletariat was not sufficiently organized to *retain* power. Hence the slogan of the moment 'must be *proletarian organization*.'[12] The Soviets of Workers' Deputies were recognized as the form of revolutionary government that would replace dual power.

Lenin reasoned that 'The "revolutionary-democratic dictatorship of the proletariat and the peasantry" has *already* become a reality in Russia' in the form of the Soviet of Workers' and Soldiers' Deputies.[13] This he wrote to challenge the supposed theoretical rigidity of those 'old Bolsheviks' such as Lev Kamenev in Petrograd who appeared to him not to have grasped the significance of the novelty of Russia's situation in 1917 relative to 1905. The Petrograd Soviet was effectively sharing power with the government; such actions as the promulgation of 'Order No. 1', which allowed the garrison troops to elect their own soviets and ensured that these troops were loyal to the Soviet, were indicative of this. In this regard the dictatorship was being exercised without resort to the infliction of force. Henceforth Lenin referred to the necessity of a 'revolutionary-democratic dictatorship of the proletariat and the *poorest* peasantry [emphasis added]', a transitional stage to the full dictatorship of the proletariat, in accordance with his somewhat confusing rationale that Russia was in transition to socialism, was already passing the stage of democratic revolution, but had not yet fully completed it.[14] The difference with his position from 1905 was clear; the time had come for the proletariat, agricultural labourers (*batraki*) and poorest peasants (i.e. 'semi-proletarian' smallholders) to take power for themselves. In his *April Theses*, written as he journeyed back to Petrograd, he wrote that Russia was passing from the first to the second stage of the revolution, 'which must place power in the hands of the proletariat and the poorest sections of the peasants.'[15]

Lenin was somewhat perplexed that history had thrown up a situation whereby the *narod*, in exercising its dictatorship, was apparently ceding power voluntarily to the bourgeoisie, and he explained this as a consequence of the predominantly petty-bourgeois mentality of the Russian masses.[16] The party's task was to counteract such petty-bourgeois timidity by making a clear distinction *within* the *narod*, within the Soviet, between the 'proletarian communist' and the 'petty-bourgeois' elements, to ensure the hegemonic leadership of the former. The dictatorship of the proletariat and poorest peasantry required a differentiation between relatively well-off and relatively poor peasants, for 'The task of a proletarian leader is to clarify the difference in class interests and persuade certain sections of the petty bourgeoisie (namely, the poorest peasants) to choose between the workers and the capitalists.'[17] He was confident that the vast majority of peasants would come to the side of the workers, but overall this scenario would prove to be a misconceived sociology of rural class struggle.

Yet there could be no question of skipping historical stages and immediately inaugurating socialism in Russia, for the peasant movement had not yet 'exhausted' the democratic revolution.[18] Lenin urged such measures as land nationalization (as he had in 1905), which would both encourage capitalist development and yet facilitate socialism in the countryside, and the encouragement of large collective farms on confiscated estates organized by agricultural labourers' soviets. By October, however, he had adopted the SR policy of distributing the landed estates amongst the peasantry ('land socialization'), despite the fact that Marx had warned against measures that would serve to strengthen the petty-bourgeois proprietorial instincts of the peasants.[19] He also advocated that the Soviet introduce 'compulsory labour service' (*trudovaia povinnost'*) as a means of solving Russia's economic crisis, evidently under the influence of the wartime state's ability to mobilize society for essential industry. He believed that once labour conscription were introduced by a Soviet government and regulated by a people's militia, the people as a whole would recognize the need for 'that supreme effort necessary for averting disaster.'[20] Yet he thought that 'these reforms will be introduced only when an overwhelming majority of the people has clearly and firmly realized the practical need for them.'[21]

The civil war slogan had not disappeared. Lenin noted that the revolution in Russia merely indicated that the imperialist war had '*begun* to turn into a civil war.'[22] Once the proletariat had conquered state power, the war against Germany would be continued as a revolutionary war 'against the German – and not only the German – bourgeoisie.'[23] Yet, as mentioned, Lenin did not advocate the immediate overthrow of the government. Full power should pass into the hands of the soviets but this should be done peacefully if possible. In his *April Theses* he reasoned as follows:

> in most of the Soviets of Workers' Deputies our Party is in a minority, so far a small minority, as against a *bloc of all petty-bourgeois opportunist elements* [...] who have yielded to the influence of the bourgeoisie and spread that influence among the proletariat. The masses must be able to see that the Soviets of Workers' Deputies are the *only possible* form of revolutionary government, and that therefore our task is, as long as *this* government yields to the influence of the bourgeoisie, to present a patient, systematic, and persistent explanation of the errors of their tactics [...].[24]

Particularly significant was his fifth thesis, in which was now definitively stated that the form of proletarian rule would be the soviets and only the soviets (or equivalent lower-class organizations), since 'a return to a parliamentary republic from the soviets [...] would be a retrograde step.'[25]

The Russian people were, Lenin fervently believed, on the cusp of 'the greatest proletarian revolution in the history of mankind', the task of which was to 'rebuild the world', and the means for which had been created in the course of the most destructive war in history. The problem he thought was that 'we are afraid of ourselves. We are loathe to cast off the "dear old" soiled shirt' and trust that the soviets were capable of assuming full political leadership. The essential task of the moment was to be able to 'make the masses see the truth', Lenin declared at the Bolshevik Petrograd city conference in mid-April, with optimism about more than doubt in the potential of the *narod*. The Soviet leaders in Lenin's estimation could, in other words, be said to be the 'doubting Thomases' of the revolutionary proletarian movement, but 'it is time to cast off the soiled shirt and to put on clean linen.'[26] He was fully aware that popular opposition to the war was not yet sufficiently strong, that the workers and peasants were 'honest defencists' through their ignorance. Yet he was convinced that it would not be long before the 'truth' of their almost innate class-opposition to war would be realized and the soviets would seize power, thereby disproving Kautsky's assertion that a successful revolution would not be possible in a time of war.[27]

Upon returning to Russia in April, Lenin had actually dropped the slogan of civil war in response to his appraisal of the popular mood in Russia, and hence the need to moderate party slogans for popular consumption. This was also evidently due to the influence of more moderate members of his own party in Petrograd.[28]

The party resolved on 21 April that 'as long as the capitalists and their government cannot and dare not use force against the masses [...] at *such a moment* any thought of civil war would be naïve, senseless, preposterous [...] should violence be resorted to, the responsibility will fall on the Provisional Government and its supporters.'[29] Lenin had clarified his attitude to the civil war slogan and the overthrow of the government in an article in the Bolshevik paper *Pravda* on 9 April. Referring to this article several years later, he declared that 'When we came back to Russia in March 1917 we changed our position [on civil war] entirely.'[30] That is, despite popular disenchantment with the war, patriotic sentiment persisted and the Bolsheviks needed to be careful to avoid being branded traitors; this was especially true regarding the military forces, who would be crucial for the fate of the revolution. In this *Pravda* article Lenin argued that the government should be overthrown 'for it is an oligarchic, bourgeois, and not a people's government' but that it 'can not be "overthrown" in the ordinary way' as a consequence of its being supported by the Petrograd Soviet.[31] His vision was of a peaceful transfer of power to the soviets as a means of introducing the dictatorship of the proletariat and poorest peasantry.

In late April, at the Seventh All-Russian Conference of the Bolshevik Party, Lenin declared that 'There are no oppressors in Russia at present.'[32] Hence revolutionary violence could not be justified. His remarks on the civil war question at this conference were especially significant. 'Have we gone back on our own principles?', he asked himself:

> We were advocating the conversion of the imperialist war into a civil war, and now we are contradicting ourselves. But the first civil war in Russia has come to an end; we are now advancing towards the second war – the war between imperialism and the armed people. In this transitional period, as long as the armed force is in the hands of the soldiers, as long as Milyukov and Guchkov [leading figures in the Provisional Government] have not yet resorted to violence, this civil war, so far as we are concerned, turns into peaceful, prolonged, and patient class propaganda. To speak of civil war before people have come to realize the need for it is undoubtedly to lapse into Blanquism. We are for civil war, but only for civil war waged by a politically conscious class. He can be overthrown who is known to the people as an oppressor [...]. For the time being we withdraw that slogan [civil war], but only for the time being.[33]

Lenin's concept of 'civil war' was evidently intended here in a broad sense of pitting the 'armed people' against their class enemies and would not necessarily assume violent forms or full-blown civil war violence (that would depend on the government). Yet he was strongly suggesting what he had always maintained, that counter-revolutionary violence would be forthcoming and that revolutionary violence would therefore be required to place power in the hands of the revolutionary proletariat and poorest peasantry, and very likely would spill over into the post-revolutionary period. The very concept of revolution Lenin regarded as civil war, as he had since 1905. This civil war would he thought be fought by a class conscious of its historical significance.[34] It is worth noting also that his vision of a coming assault upon capital did not mean physical violence against individual capitalists or landowners, or even necessarily their arrest (apart from the 'biggest' capitalists). The landed estates would be turned over to the people, and he reasoned in front of an audience of peasants' deputies that 'the landowners are also citizens with equal rights whom nobody wishes to wrong; the land belongs to the entire nation, consequently it belongs also to the landowners.'[35] Nonetheless, as already noted, Lenin did not really believe that their 'equal rights' would in fact be recognized under a proletarian dictatorship, at least not while considered landowners.

In a speech at the First All-Russian Congress of Soviets of Workers' and Soldiers' Deputies in June, he declared that 'In Russia, this revolution can, by way of exception, be a peaceful one.'[36] Nowhere else was there the freedom that existed in Russia, he thought, and 'nowhere else in the world [...] can the transfer of the entire state power to the *actual* majority of the people, i.e., to the workers and poorest peasants, be achieved so easily and *so peacefully*' as in Russia.[37] In addition, as Alexander Rabinowitch notes, 'Contrary to conventional wisdom, in 1917 the Bolsheviks did not stand for a one-party dictatorship.'[38] The question of the possibility of the formation of a multi-party socialist Soviet government in the summer and autumn of 1917 is most important, for such a government would likely have resulted in a more secure socialist polity than came to exist, and a lessening of the prospects or at least the scope of subsequent civil war.[39] Lenin was confident that if the party were capable of accomplishing its task, the skilful organization of the revolutionary movement (the workers and 'nine-tenths of the peasants')[40] and use of propaganda, the self-organization of the people would follow and the restoration of a police force over the people would be impossible, for the 'armed people cannot dominate themselves.'[41]

Yet a proletarian state possessed of the capacity to deploy violence would nonetheless be necessary for the transition to full communism. It would practice 'the *strictest* order' and would '*ruthlessly* crush by force all attempts at either a tsarist or a Guchkov-bourgeois counter-revolution.'[42] Indeed in April Lenin spoke of this envisioned revolutionary dictatorship as comparable with the Paris Commune of 1871, based not on law as such and *formal* majorities but on violence (*nasilie*, or 'open force' in the English translation of the text), and that 'violence' was 'the instrument of power.'[43] Thus he echoed his 1906 pamphlet *The Victory of the Cadets* (see Chapter 2), with the meaning of 'violence' in this context the existence of a proletarian state dictatorship backed by armed force, resting on the direct will and practical force of the 'revolutionary people' and directed against the 'exploiters', without simply or necessarily connoting the application of physical armed violence.

Despite the relative patience in his revolutionary strategy, Lenin was ideologically predisposed to detect any hint of a counter-revolutionary offensive. By June he believed that this was beginning to take shape as tensions flared between the government and some soviets, most notably the Kronstadt Soviet. In particular, the government's reluctance to tackle major issues such as land reform until the convocation of a Constituent Assembly; continuing economic dislocation and hunger; and the government's commitment to the war, made for a volatile situation. Lenin initially supported a demonstration of soldiers and sailors planned for early June, but then showed restraint when it appeared that the outcome would be bloodshed. The time for peaceful protests had passed, he declared, but 'The proletariat must reply by showing maximum calmness, caution, restraint and organization.' The counter-revolutionary offensive had not yet assumed outright violent forms but if, or rather when it would, then 'We are not opposed to the use of revolutionary force in the interests of the nation's majority.'[44] Lenin, as we have just seen, had yet maintained at the Congress of Soviets that Russia was being presented with an exceptional historical possibility – a peaceful revolution – though during that same speech he announced that the Bolsheviks were in fact ready 'to take over full power at any moment' if required.[45]

Lenin's attitude was becoming increasingly belligerent towards what he considered the 'evil' of dual power. References to the French Revolution appeared in his writings. In *Pravda* he wrote that the workers and semi-proletarians would be the Jacobins of the twentieth century, in that 'they would proclaim enemies of the people the capitalists who are making thousands of millions of profits from the imperialist war.'[46] He even referred approvingly to the guillotine, though he thought the 'guillotine' would not be replicated in the twentieth century – 'to follow a good example does not mean copying it.' Rather, profits would be expropriated and, having arrested '50 to 100 large capitalists to expose their frauds', they would be released. Nonetheless, as Robert Service has noted, capital punishment would be applied to individual 'enemies of the people' for actual offenses committed.[47] Lenin concluded with admiration that the Jacobins had taken '*all* state power into their own hands'. To the question of the purpose of proletarian dictatorship – he replied categorically: 'To break the resistance of the capitalists!'[48]

All power to the Bolsheviks

Following the ambiguities of June, in early July Lenin was prompted to publicly re-consider the possibility of a peaceful revolution, which he had seemingly indicated in previous weeks, and he revived the slogan of 'armed uprising.'[49] This resulted from the unrest in the capital in the first week of July following the ill-fated decision of the coalition government to launch an offensive on the Eastern Front on 18 June. Clashes ensued between demonstrators seeking the overthrow of the government and government troops – the so-called July Days – and there was a subsequent governmental crackdown on the Bolsheviks.[50] Lenin now claimed that a virtual 'military dictatorship' was in power. During the July Days he came to oppose the more militant Bolshevik Military Organization by calling for restraint as thousands of sailors looked for leadership, but on 10 July he announced that the political situation had now resolved itself into a clear-cut struggle: 'All hopes for a peaceful development of the Russian revolution have vanished for good […] either complete victory for the military dictatorship, or victory for the workers' armed uprising.'[51] The battle lines had been drawn and Lenin dropped the slogan 'All Power to the Soviets.' The revolution, he contended, had been betrayed by the Mensheviks and Socialist-Revolutionaries, both Soviet parties in government, and he called for patient and thorough preparations for a workers' armed uprising and 'really mass, countrywide' upheaval.[52] The Mensheviks and SRs had indeed, as Rabinowitch puts it, 'actively supported [Prime Minister] Kerenskii in his attempts to disarm workers and suppress the Bolsheviks' following the July Days.[53] Counter-revolutionary sentiment and forces were gaining strength, but this does not suggest that 'counter-revolution' had actually been instituted in July. Lenin, as Chris Read succinctly notes, 'was viewing events through the prism of his earlier analyses, he was seeing events as confirmation of his predictions.'[54]

The Menshevik Raphael Abramovich argued at the All-Russian Central Executive Committee of the Soviets (VTsIK) on 3 July that if power were transferred to the soviets, as the demonstrators had been demanding, the Bolsheviks would demand that the RSDLP take full power and prematurely introduce socialism. This, the Mensheviks contended, would be against the will of the millions of peasants in a peasant country.[55] Russia was not ready for socialism, and Mensheviks would condemn the Bolsheviks after October for attempting to drive Russia beyond its given socio-economic possibilities, relying on terror and dictatorial rule to retain power. Non-Bolshevik socialists and liberals alike were fearful of a Bolshevik *coup*. The problem for moderate socialists in government, however, was that such 'restraint' in the tumultuous revolutionary year 1917 increasingly removed them from the pulse of the *narod*. Correspondingly, Lenin's overriding conviction in the counter-revolutionary nature of the government, and the 'petty-bourgeois' nature of the leading Soviet parties, militated against his desire for a 'peaceful' resolution of the political crisis. He was convinced that the Bolsheviks alone were capable of meeting popular demands for 'peace, bread and land', although Iulii Martov also briefly came out at this time in favour of a transfer of power to the soviets.[56] (Both factions of the RSDLP were as yet committed to the convocation of a democratically-elected Constituent Assembly in the near future). Lenin now suggested that after 4 July, after the Kadets had 'brought the counter-revolutionary troops to Petrograd', even the transferal of power to the soviets could not avoid civil war.[57]

Lenin did not initially succeed in winning support amongst his Bolshevik colleagues for his new stance on the 'All Power to the Soviets' slogan.[58] His new position was reiterated in his pamphlet *On Slogans*, written in mid-July. This work reads almost like a lament for what might have been, for now he stated that a 'non-peaceful and most painful course has begun.'[59] Most significantly, he reasoned that had the soviets assumed power, then the task of winning the 'petty-bourgeois' peasant mass away from the influence of the bourgeoisie and towards firm alliance with the workers and their parties would have been greatly facilitated.[60] Yet he clarified that power, if seized by the revolutionary proletariat and supported by the poorest peasants, would likely be built on the soviet model, for 'It is not a question of Soviets in general, but of combating the treachery of the *present* Soviets.'[61] The difference would be that the vacillating 'petty-bourgeois' socialist parties would be excluded. In mid-August Lenin would declare that if a repeat of July were to take place, then 'the slogan should be precisely to seize power', for the Bolsheviks, workers and soldiers alike had directly experienced governmental counter-revolution and learned that power could only be taken by sufficiently consistent and revolutionary elements.[62]

The Bolsheviks definitively approved Lenin's position at the Sixth Party (Bolshevik) Congress in late July/early August 1917. The Congress resolved that the party's support for the July events was justified and adopted Lenin's assessment that 'state power is in fact in the hands of the counter-revolutionary bourgeoisie' which had brought 'violence upon the masses […] in the presence of the complete inactivity of the central Soviet establishment.'[63] The Congress acknowledged that a peaceful transfer of power to the soviets was now impossible and that the only correct slogan would be 'to liquidate the dictatorship of the counter-revolutionary bourgeoisie', and the assumption of power by the revolutionary proletariat supported by the poorest peasantry.[64] The resolution avoided calls for immediate, premature action, urging instead that the proletariat concentrate its strength in readiness for the time when the urban and rural poor would come over to its side, and then it would seize power.[65] In addition the resolution on unity of the party (RSDLP) resolved that a 'full and irrevocable split' with the 'Menshevik-imperialists' alone was necessary, calling on all 'elements of social democracy' to break with the defencists, i.e. this was a call for a united RSDLP without the defencists.[66]

Lenin's attitude toward the possibility of peaceful revolution changed once again with fears of a counter-revolutionary coup by General Kornilov in August, for the socialist parties in government refused to serve in a new cabinet with the Kadets.[67] Alexander Rabinowitch has described the general leftward shift amongst the socialist parties occasioned by these events, and the general popular support in late August for the transfer of full state power to the soviets.[68] Lenin's change of tactic came in his article 'On Compromises', written on 1 September (OS). He argued that the new government would be formed by the Mensheviks and SRs and be 'wholly and exclusively responsible to the Soviets'; the Bolsheviks would strive for power peacefully within this structure of power. Lenin's reasoning was that:

> Now, and only now, perhaps *during only a few days* or a week or two, such a government could be set up *and consolidated* in a perfectly peaceful way [emphasis added]. In all probability it could secure the peaceful *advance* of the whole Russian revolution […]. In my opinion, the Bolsheviks, who are partisans of world revolution and revolutionary methods, may and should consent to this compromise only for the sake of the revolution's peaceful development – an opportunity that is *extremely* rare in history and *extremely* valuable, an opportunity that only occurs once in a while.[69]

However in a postscript to the article written in the following days, Lenin claimed that this opportunity had been missed as the Mensheviks and SRs proved to be unwilling to assume power as Lenin had demanded. Indeed, as he had remarked towards the end of August, he considered that civil war was an 'inevitable rather than an accidental' historical occurrence at a time of revolution.[70] Crucially VTsIK refused to abandon support for Prime Minister Kerenskii at this time, and the socialist parties accepted places in his new Directory. This government did not include Kadets (liberals) but by then the actual Petrograd Soviet had swung over to the idea of transferring all power to the soviets.[71]

Lenin's message in *On Compromises*, to make clear, had been that the Bolsheviks were ultimately striving for power for themselves, as the party of the proletariat and poorest peasants. The 'compromise' would be that the Bolsheviks would 'refrain from demanding the immediate transfer of power to the proletariat and the poorest peasants and from employing revolutionary methods of fighting for this demand', that they would rely on 'real democracy' from within the soviet structure to attain their mandate. The Mensheviks, though accepting the need for a government that would exclude the Kadets, did not quite advocate an exclusively Soviet government ('All Power to the Soviets') but, as Martov soon clarified, 'All power to democracy.'[72] Russia's political crisis was discussed at the Democratic Conference of all parties left of the Kadets in mid-September, which in fact served to demonstrate the internal divisions within the 'democracy' and the Mensheviks in particular (whose moderates feared that power to the soviets would mean Bolshevik domination).[73] The 'Pre-Parliament' established by the Conference, designed to lend increased legitimacy to the government and prepare for the transfer of power to the Constituent Assembly (election dates for which had now been set), was no more successful. Naturally all this played into the hands of Lenin and the more cohesive Bolsheviks, and seemed to corroborate his disdain for the vacillating non-Bolshevik Left.[74]

In his article 'The Russian Revolution and Civil War', published on 29 September but written early in the month (apparently before his postscript to *On Compromises*), Lenin proceeded to attack those such as the Kadets who warned of the prospect of 'rivers of blood' flowing in Russia. He clearly indicated that if power were not taken immediately by the soviets, then a civil war 'in its highest and most decisive form' would likely occur, and such revolutionary violence would be legitimated by the bloodshed of the First World War. This was because no 'rivers of blood' in a civil war could even approximate those 'seas of blood which the Russian imperialists have shed since June 19', and such a civil war 'would save the lives of hundreds of thousands of men who are now shedding their blood' in the imperialist war.[75] Civil war would possess the additional benefit of strengthening the oppressed classes, which strength could not be maximized during the course of a 'parliamentary struggle.'[76] In a discussion of the interaction between ideology/will and circumstances, an important question is the extent to which ideology can shape circumstances as well as be shaped by them.[77] In this regard there is merit in Sheila Fitzpatrick's contention that the Civil War begun in 1918 was 'not a new direction but, rather, another step in the direction indicated by the October Revolution.'[78] Lenin would lead his comrades into revolution conscious of the possibility, even inevitability, of bloody civil war in Russia if the

Bolsheviks seized power; the decisions made by the Bolsheviks, led by Lenin, certainly contributed to the creation of the circumstances in which they were to find themselves after October.

Why, though, did Lenin apparently assume that if the Mensheviks and SRs assumed power, as he was urging, revolution would not prove bloody? Would it not have been the case, as Robert Service points out, that the assumption of power even by a multi-party Soviet government would hardly have resulted in Kerenskii and his supporters retracting without a fight?[79] Indeed Lenin had implied this in April. Yet he appears to have been genuinely confident that a peaceful development of the revolution was possible, reasoning that 'a civil war begun by the bourgeoisie against such an alliance [of Bolsheviks with Mensheviks and SRs] would make civil war in Russia impossible' because the bourgeoisie would have no mass support base.[80] Lenin recognized that a Bolshevik seizure of power would appear as a coup, as effectively the first act of civil war, whereas an assumption of power by a socialist coalition would command greater authority. However the message of Lenin's communications to Bolshevik leaders later in the month was that the Bolsheviks would in fact attract widespread mass support, that the growth of popular support for the left wings of the SRs and Mensheviks would effectively mean support for a Bolshevik government, as 'A Bolshevik government *alone* will satisfy the demands of the peasants.'[81] Such support, though, was not guaranteed; it would have to be proved in practice. He had even written in October 1916 that 'Neither we nor anyone else can calculate precisely what portion of the *proletariat* is following and will follow the social-chauvinists and opportunists. This will be revealed only by the struggle [...] only by the socialist revolution [emphasis added].'[82] The task would evidently be much easier in a coalition with SRs and Mensheviks.

• By mid-September Lenin was sure of Bolshevik majorities in the Petrograd and Moscow Soviets, and a Bolshevik resolution on the composition of a new government was passed by the Petrograd Soviet. Between September 12 and 14 he dispatched two letters to the Bolshevik Central Committee from hiding in Finland, claiming that the preconditions for a Bolshevik assumption of power had been fulfilled, and that it would be 'naïve to wait for a "formal" majority for the Bolsheviks.' Besides, he believed that Petrograd and Moscow would carry the whole country with them.[83] He was convinced that it was imperative that the forthcoming Second All-Russian Congress of Soviets be presented with a *fait accompli*. Kerenskii, he argued, was going to surrender Petrograd, and 'History will not forgive us if we do not seize power now.'[84] The Soviet structure would provide the apparatus of a new revolutionary government, though it would convene a Constituent Assembly.[85] The revolution would be achieved through 'an armed uprising' in both capitals, in accordance with the mood of the masses.[86] Such an insurrection would be led by the 'advanced class', not by a conspiracy; it would rely upon 'a revolutionary upsurge of the people' and would take place when this would be 'at its height' and the ruling classes vacillating, the situation as he believed then existed.[87] Should the belligerent countries refuse the peace proposals offered by a Bolshevik government, the Bolsheviks would then become 'defencists', and in fact the 'war party par excellence.' This would occasion the removal of 'all the bread and boots from the [Russian] capitalists. We shall leave them only crusts and dress them in bast shoes. We shall send all the bread and footwear to the front',[88] thereby exacting revenge for the sending of workers and peasants to fight the imperialist war. It was not until a meeting of the Central Committee on 10 October that the Bolsheviks accepted the principle of a Bolshevik armed insurrection, but Lenin had later to give way to Trotsky's idea (Trotsky had joined the Bolsheviks in 1917) of ensuring that such an insurrection would coincide with the opening of the Second Congress of Soviets, thus presenting it as a transfer of power to the soviets. Grigorii Zinoviev and Lev Kamenev, on the other hand, were noticeably in favour of a broad socialist coalition.

Lenin, as we have seen, did not actually claim that Russia was ready yet for socialism, but he did consider Russia to be on 'the *threshold* of socialism', whereby no more rungs on the ladder needed to be scaled to attain it.[89] The introduction of state-monopoly capitalism in the course of the war had greatly facilitated the transition to socialism, he thought, for 'socialism is merely state-capitalist monopoly *which is made to serve the interests of the whole people* and [...] *ceased* to be capitalist monopoly.' Lenin's reasoning, in opposition to the Mensheviks, was that the economic basis for a transition to a higher economic system, socialism, was effectively in place in Russia due to 'the dialectics of history'. This was despite the fact that there had been no appreciable progression in the peasant economy since the revolution of 1905.

This was not a plan for the 'War Communism' that would characterize Bolshevik Civil War economics from 1918. Lenin's pre-revolutionary economic strategy did not include the nationalization of medium and small industries; his idea was that 'workers' control' and regulation would be exercised in all production industries, that there would be economic openness, but that small-scale capitalism would in fact persist under a socialist state. The Bolsheviks' economic proposals at this time, as Larisa Borisova notes, did not go beyond 'the limits of state capitalism.'[90] Lenin's pre-October economic policies appear as both radically democratic (such as 'workers' control' in factories) and yet, as was the consensus amongst economic experts at the time, cognizant of the necessity of introducing a strong political authority.[91] In his pamphlet *Can the Bolsheviks Retain State Power?*, written on 1 October, he reiterated that the state grain monopoly, bread rationing and labour conscription would be practiced by a proletarian state. The bourgeois state would be 'smashed' (see below), but when the state would be a proletarian state and 'an instrument of violence exercised by the proletariat against the bourgeoisie', then 'we shall be fully and unreservedly in favour of a strong state power and of centralism.'[92]

Lenin's rationale for socialist revolution was not just about economics but also and perhaps principally about politics; the idea of Russia's being at the stage of 'transition' to socialism was close enough in his mind to justify the political socialist revolution. It could only be through such a revolution that the peoples of Russia and Europe would extricate themselves from this and future wars. The moral-political impulse behind Lenin's revolutionary strategy in 1917 was that

'To achieve peace [...] it is necessary that political power be in the hands of *the workers and poorest peasants*, not the landlords and capitalists.'[93] Once revolutions would occur throughout the warring nations, the politico-economic basis of the imperialist war would be removed and peace would ensue, for popular patriotic support for the war was, socialist-internationalists believed, a result essentially of deceptive bourgeois chauvinism.

• Lenin's ideas on whether or not the coming revolution in Russia would be bloody were somewhat confusing and, as historian Il'ia Rat'kovskii has put it, 'in an important degree based upon a miscalculation of the strength of counter-revolution' and 'extremely vague.'[94] Lenin had noted before February that a revolution in one country would initially bring upon itself the armed force of the international bourgeoisie. How could a revolution in Russia proceed peacefully if the country were attacked from all sides? In early September he acknowledged that 'If we were alone, we should not be able to accomplish this task [revolution in Russia] peacefully.'[95] Yet he actually downplayed the prospect of immediate foreign intervention, believing that combined imperial intervention would not be practical, and that revolutions would not be long breaking out.[96] The Bolsheviks' belief in the imminence of European revolutions was 'an article of faith',[97] but in the absence of such revolutions, would they risk their own revolution to initiate a revolutionary war? Erik van Ree notes that revolutionary war became 'a dominant element' in Lenin's wartime thinking on how the 'chain-reaction' of world revolutions would be ignited,[98] but Robert Service is correct that during 1917 Lenin seemed quite coy on the subject, more inclined to consider waging revolutionary war only if forced by circumstances.[99] In early September, as we have seen, Lenin wrote that the lessons of the previous months, from April until the Kornilov incident, demonstrated that 'there is bound to be the bitterest civil war between the bourgeoisie and the proletariat' if the opportunity of the soviets assuming full power were missed, and he warned that the revolution may 'prove very difficult and bloody, and may cost the lives of tens of thousands of landowners, capitalists, and officers who sympathize with them.'[100] However on 1 October, in a letter to Bolshevik leaders he was still trying to convince of his position for a seizure of power, he concluded that the chances were 'ten-to-one' that it would be 'a bloodless victory' if power were seized by the Bolshevik-dominated Moscow and Petrograd Soviets, whether or not through insurrection, for no force would dare oppose such a government.[101] Yet in his theoretically-informed pamphlet *Can the Bolsheviks Retain State Power?*, which he completed the same day, he stated without any question that 'uncomplicated' revolutions 'never occur'. Rather, a profound revolution is 'incredibly complicated and painful, bringing about the death of the old social order and birth of the new one', and the end of 'the mode of life of tens of millions of people.' Revolution, he wrote, 'is a most intense, furious, desperate class struggle and civil war. Not a single great revolution in history has taken place without civil war.' Yet again, just a few pages later he remarked that the Kerenskii government would muster merely a 'hopeless revolt' against Soviet power, not initiate a civil war.[102] Sheila Fitzpatrick has made the point that 'As for the possibility of civil war, this did not frighten the Bolsheviks and to some extent attracted them, since they sensed that only violent confrontation with the class enemy would guarantee a true revolutionary victory.'[103] It appears that Lenin was not quite aware of what to expect. He was certainly aware that there were, as he put it, 'wolves in the forest' and that this was no reason not to venture within, but he seems to have been confident that the moral and democratic authority of the soviets – even as Bolshevik-dominated institutions – would ultimately negate any serious threat to the regime or at least ensure mass popular support in the face of such resistance. Yet in *The State and Revolution* he argued that 'desperate resistance' would be forthcoming from counter-revolutionaries.

The state and revolution

Lenin's most extensive work of this period, written up in the summer and autumn of 1917, was the aforementioned *State and Revolution*. This was his foremost treatise on the state, and as an indication of his conception of proletarian dictatorship on the eve of revolution, it is worth devoting some attention to it.[104] Lenin intended the work as a theoretical contribution to Marxist literature on the nature and role of the state, and yet one that was particularly required at the time of writing with the perceived imminence of socialist revolutions. It was also explicitly aimed at appropriating revolutionary Marxist orthodoxy from Kautsky and the 'opportunist' socialists. It is indicative of the extent to which Lenin and the Bolsheviks entered power more with assumptions and guiding principles than well-thought-out policies. Professing quite a utopian vision of communist society, it is also a work that perhaps more than any other reveals the structural problems in his thought.

The work has generated some interesting, and contrasting, scholarly interpretations, whether as a utopian tract at variance with the wider corpus of Lenin's thought,[105] or as the harbinger of a violently authoritarian Bolshevik dictatorship.[106] The latter argument has been presented most forcefully and eloquently by the political scientist A. J. Polan. Polan's thesis is that Lenin's work represents the opposite of political pluralism, whereby his understanding of the existence of a 'general will' ensured that all 'singularity must be absorbed into unity; all singularity constitutes, not a mere opposition, but a mortal threat from an unreconciled and unabsorbed Other.'[107] Polan raises an interesting methodological issue with his argument that it is only through the subsequent history of Soviet Russia/Soviet Union that the text acquires any meaning, countering the contrary idea that *State and Revolution* has been placed outside history due to its perceived irrelevance as a utopian and impractical tract.[108] Yet the danger with that is the attribution of too direct a causal, connecting link between the text and subsequent practice. It is certainly important to understand and tease out the full implications of the text as the ideas and assumptions contained within it confronted the reality of exercising power after October. The first duty of the intellectual historian however is to analyze a text in the context of the time it was written, and then as regards its wider implications, i.e. to study it historically and insert it within a narrative of ideas and responses to events. The text is valuable in itself as a historical document of Lenin's thought on the eve of October, and of the potential implications for, and disparities with, subsequent Bolshevik political practice.

Lenin did indeed advocate coercion and violence against the 'enemies' of the revolution in the work, and appears to have expressed therein, to some extent, the ideological and cultural bases in embryo of dictatorial rule. Nevertheless his spirits were high in the course of 1917. Confronted with the revolutionary enthusiasm of the people, he must have felt that the task of making revolution would be much easier and more peaceful than in 1905, and certainly less bloody than the French Revolution. Briefly put, the overriding theme of the work was the necessity to 'smash' the existing state and replace it with the direct democracy of proletarian self-rule, rather than simply utilizing the existing apparatus of state for proletarian dictatorship. In this regard Lenin was influenced by the younger Bolshevik theorist Nikolai Bukharin. There would be a 'people's militia' to suppress counter-revolutionaries and saboteurs, and all elected officials would receive no more than workmen's wages and be revocable at any time.

Lenin reasoned from the outset that the proletariat would require a violent revolution to take power. Yet he qualified this slightly – violent revolution was 'a general rule' – that is, a peaceful revolution in Russia in 1917 would, even if it were possible, be an exception to this rule.[109] He noted elsewhere in autumn 1917 that 'we shall be fully and unreservedly in favour of a strong state power and of centralism', but this seemed to conflict somewhat with his approval in *State and Revolution* of Marx's contention that 'All revolutions have perfected this [state] machine instead of smashing it.'[110] He quoted Engels that, once the proletariat assumed power, the social function of state interference would, 'in one domain after another', become superfluous and the state as such would begin to 'wither away'.[111] What Lenin really focused on was Engels's remark that 'As soon as there is no longer any social class to be held in subjection, as soon as class rule [is] removed', there would be no further need of 'a special coercive force, a state.' Later, he provided a more precise definition of the state, as 'a special organization of force [...] an organization of violence for the suppression of some class'[112] which, wielded by the proletariat, would be directed against 'inevitable and desperate' bourgeois resistance. However the existence of a proletarian state did not necessarily or simply imply overtly physical, armed violence. For example, deprivation of franchise rights for the exploiting classes would constitute a means of suppression, as later enshrined in the first Soviet Constitution.

One of the fundamental objectives of proletarian dictatorship would be 'the overthrow and complete abolition of the bourgeoisie'. Lenin intended the destruction of the bourgeoisie *as a class*, which would be achieved primarily through non-violent political and economic means, but he noted that in reality the period of transition from capitalism to communism 'is a period of an unprecedentedly violent class struggle in unprecedentedly acute forms, and, consequently, during this period the state must inevitably be a state that is democratic in a new way (for the proletariat and the propertyless in general) and dictatorial in a new way (against the bourgeoisie).'[113] This last quotation was from the small section that Lenin added to the text in December 1918. The temporary utilization of state power against the exploiters, the 'systematic use of arms by one class against another', would, Lenin considered, be necessary for the dialectical resolution of the question of the state. Wielded by the proletariat, the state would finally overcome itself. Yet Lenin remarked that this task, the suppression of the minority by the majority, would be:

> ... so easy, simple and natural a task that it will entail far less bloodshed than the suppression of the risings of slaves, serfs or wage-labourers, and it will cost mankind far less. And it is compatible with the extension of democracy to such an overwhelming majority of the population that the need for a special machine of suppression will begin to disappear.[114]

This extract captures the disparity between the text and subsequent Soviet history. Insofar as the entire people would be drawn into state functions, he thought, the state as such would effectively cease to exist. Lenin noted that a 'special apparatus' for suppression, the state, would still be necessary during the transitional period to communism but this would be a 'very simple "machine", almost without a "machine", without a special apparatus, by the simple organization of the armed people.'[115] Within weeks of the revolution precisely such a 'special apparatus' of state suppression, the Vecheka, was created, and within a few years would become institutionalized in the structure of the Soviet state. Yet its development could be considered a practical solution to a vague, unrealistic vision, and Vecheka leaders would consistently speak of the need to maintain as close a contact with the people as possible.

Lenin made clear that the state was to establish quite strict control – 'strict, iron discipline backed up by the state power of the armed workers' – over the non-proletarians (including presumably the majority peasants) and individual workers as well in order to organize large-scale production.[116] Certainly the proletarian state, like any other, would require the creation and maintenance of at least a modicum of social order to which all would be subordinate. However the first 'phase' of communism, or socialism, would naturally bear the imprint of bourgeois society. The workers (led by their vanguard party) would of necessity extend discipline 'to the whole of society', to all those wishing to preserve 'bourgeois habits' – including ' the workers who have been thoroughly corrupted by capitalism' – until such time as 'people have become so accustomed to observing the fundamental rules of social intercourse and when their labour has become so productive that they will voluntarily work according to their ability.'[117] Indeed Lenin was quite categorical that 'So long as the state exists there is no freedom. When there is freedom, there will be no state.'[118] The new society would need to pass through a type of Purgatorial process, for such discipline would be 'a necessary *step* for thoroughly cleansing society of all the infamies and abominations of capitalist exploitation, *and for further* progress'.[119]

One final and very significant aspect of *State and Revolution* to consider concerns the nature of democracy envisioned. Engels, writing in 1891, wrote that a democratic republic (to be attained in Germany after the destruction of the semi-absolutist state) would provide the actual form for proletarian dictatorship.[120] By contrast Lenin considered the democratic republic 'the nearest approach to the dictatorship of the proletariat', i.e., not 'the specific form' as Engels had reasoned. Such a republic could not abolish the rule of capital, Lenin thought, it could merely create the conditions necessary for the establishment of proletarian dictatorship, which 'inevitably and solely' would meet the 'fundamental interests of the oppressed masses.'[121] Dictatorship would, by implication, require a class-based republic of soviets or other form of working class organization, it would be for 'the working and exploited people in organizing their social life without the bourgeoisie and against the bourgeoisie.' Lenin appeared to take a more literal interpretation of the dictatorship of the proletariat.

In conclusion, Lenin was convinced of the historical necessity of making a breach in the wall of imperialist capitalism, even if it risked a bloody civil war, and of utilizing the radical rhetoric of civil war, but whether or to what extent this would result in an actual bloody conflict with internal and external enemies would depend on the post-revolutionary situation. Lenin, aware of the distinct possibility of sharp resistance and violent reaction to a Bolshevik-led revolution, was theoretically prepared for the necessity of violently suppressing resistance and waging an international revolutionary war. He seems to have genuinely hoped that the revolution could be relatively 'bloodless', but in any case it was, he believed, absolutely necessary. Certainly he did not enter power with the intention of wielding the blunt instrument of the state to secure the revolution through preventive physical violence, though he did consider a proletarian-revolutionary state an instrument of violence (broadly understood) directed against the bourgeoisie.

Insurrection, Lenin maintained, was an art and, despite the scientific pretensions of Marxism, also involved a considerable leap of faith. The preparations for insurrection went ahead in October, even regardless of the mood of the masses. Lenin was reported to have remarked to his fellow Bolsheviks that 'The Party could not be guided by the temper of the masses because it was changeable and incalculable; the Party must be guided by an objective analysis and an appraisal of the revolution.'[122] Since his return to Russia earlier in the year, the slogan 'All Power to the Soviets' was counter-posed in his mind to the slogan for 'armed insurrection'. Now he conflated the two, convinced that a peaceful development of the revolution had proved unworkable,[123] and he sent his revolutionary troops into power with the assurance that by taking it they 'will save the world revolution [...] and the lives of hundreds of thousands of people at the front.'[124] Power would be seized on behalf of the soviets, not in opposition to them.[125] It was thus that the Bolsheviks seized power in Petrograd between 24 and 26 October 1917.

4 Confronting the 'wolves in the forest'

October 1917–summer 1918

> If the situation were not exceptionally complicated there would be no revolution.
> If you are afraid of wolves don't go into the forest.[1]
>
> (Lenin, October 1917)

Before dawn on 25 October 1917 the Bolsheviks, with Lenin's arrival at Petrograd's Smolny Institute, moved towards overthrowing the Provisional Government. The actions of the Bolshevik-controlled Military Revolutionary Committee (MRC) of the Petrograd Soviet since the beginning of its coup the previous day had been portrayed as defensive in light of Kerenskii's attempts to move against the radical Left before the Second Congress of Soviets, a majority of which was due to favour formation of an exclusively socialist Soviet government.[2] Ironically, in view of its dispersal a few weeks later, the MRC issued an appeal to the citizens of Petrograd justifying its actions in response to Kerenskii's alleged intention to halt convening of the Constituent Assembly.[3] Lenin's rationale 'in insisting on the violent overthrow of the Provisional Government before the opening of the Congress of Soviets' was, as Alexander Rabinowitch explains, 'to eliminate any possibility that the congress would form a socialist coalition in which the moderate socialists might have had a significant voice.'[4] Soviet government could not mean the same petty-bourgeois vacillation that had characterized the last months of the Provisional Government, and the dictatorship of the workers and poorest peasants could now be established. Initially it appeared at the Congress that left-wing Mensheviks and moderate Bolsheviks might succeed in finding agreement to form a multi-party government, but the Menshevik–Defencists and Right SRs were also guilty of considerable intransigence, walking out of the Congress in protest against Bolshevik actions. Bolshevik hardliners then prompted the Menshevik–Internationalists to leave, and with the Left SRs (having broken from the mainstream SRs) initially refusing to join a coalition, the Bolsheviks found themselves in power on their own. Mensheviks and SRs would later retake their vacant seats on the Central Executive Committee (VTsIK), though real power lay with the new executive organ of Bolshevik government.

This new government cabinet was the Council of People's Commissars, Sovnarkom, with Lenin as Chair (in effect Prime Minister). The Bolsheviks were faced with the tasks of consolidating their power throughout the country, restoring the shattered Russian economy, and waging a war against the Central Powers. The tasks facing any new government in Russia in 1917 would have been enormous; the Bolsheviks, however, were attempting to 'transform society.'[5] This desire and the manner in which power was seized were likely to turn not only the upper echelons of Russian society against the Bolsheviks but almost all non-Bolshevik socialists as well, ensuring the distinct possibility of a complicated and protracted civil war without a guarantee of widespread popular support for the Bolshevik cause. The situation Russia then faced was 'chaotic, near-bankrupt and threatened with external attack.'[6] Industrial production had been severely damaged by the war and was concentrated on meeting the state's military requirements, leading to the inflation of prices for scarce manufactured consumer goods. Increasing government attempts to regulate grain trade, culminating in the grain monopoly imposed by the Provisional Government, had led to increasing withdrawal from the market by the peasants.[7] From the beginning the new regime would face the problem of supplying food to the consuming areas, and the crucially important associated problem of ensuring an efficient transport, particularly rail, system as provision of rolling stock had deteriorated and the lines were clogged up with soldiers returning home. These problems were of central importance during Lenin's rule and within months the Bolsheviks would resort to extreme measures of force for their resolution. In addition the Bolshevik state would face economic blockade during its early years – with 14 foreign powers ranged against it during the 'Civil War' – and it was not until the early 1920s that it would succeed in establishing some international trade agreements. The fledgling Bolshevik regime was to receive a baptism by fire in the art of state-building and governance.

Ministries were taken over, re-named People's Commissariats and headed by the new political authorities. In *State and Revolution* Lenin had urged the abolition of the 'bourgeois' distinction between executive and legislature, that the 'Commune' form of government would be a 'working parliament.' A. J. Polan has observed that in his vision of parliamentary representatives as representatives, legislators and executives, there was no place for a parliamentary opposition not willing to implement legislation with which they did not agree.[8] In addition, the investment of executive power in local soviets would undermine their roles as organs of radical, mass democratic activism.[9] The idea of a 'working parliament' would seem to accord primary institutional significance to the Congress of Soviets and its elected VTsIK, and VTsIK was recognized as the highest legislative and administrative body of the state. However Sovnarkom was the real power-centre of government. Formed by and responsible to VTsIK, it was in charge of 'the general direction' of the Russian Socialist Federative Soviet Republic (RSFSR). In accordance with the lack of distinction between executive and legislative functions, it was accorded the right to publish decrees (which it frequently exercised) according to Article 38 of the first Soviet Constitution of July 1918.[10] VTsIK was accorded certain executive functions. Decisions of Sovnarkom were supposed to have the approval of VTsIK, and the latter could rescind decisions of the former, though Article 41 permitted Sovnarkom to bypass VTsIK in 'urgent' cases,[11] and in any case the Bolsheviks dominated VTsIK. In essence, as T. H. Rigby has remarked, 'Bolshevik rule meant [...] Sovnarkom rule.'[12] Sovnarkom was Lenin's institution, through which he directed the activities of state, though from the end of 1918 he also did this through other bodies of party and state. Lenin 'pervaded the whole Sovnarkom system, his activity constantly entering it at all the nodal points, his methods stamped on its very structures and procedure.'[13]

First steps: 'democratic dictatorship'

Even before the 'triumphal march' of Soviet power around most of the former empire, the Bolshevik hold on Petrograd was in immediate danger. General Krasnov, supporting Kerenskii, amassed a force of 700 Cossacks and moved on Petrograd, but was defeated at the Pulkovo Heights outside the city. Supporting the attempted overthrow of the Bolsheviks was the All-Russia Committee for Salvation of the Homeland and the Revolution (ACS), which comprised centrist/right Mensheviks, SRs, Kadets and officers, and whose attempted insurrection was also soon defeated.[14] Regarding these early attempts to reverse the Bolshevik assumption of power, Lenin, through his new cabinet, declared that 'The Soviet Government is making every attempt to avert bloodshed. If bloodshed cannot be avoided and if Kerenskii's units do begin to shoot, the Soviet Government will not hesitate to suppress the new Kerenskii–Kornilov campaign ruthlessly.'[15] In November before an audience of peasants' deputies, and with accusations of 'anarchism' being leveled against the Bolsheviks, he declared that 'A revolutionary army never fires the first shot, and acts in anger only against invaders and tyrants.'[16]

In fact the Soviet government was initially rather mild in its punitive policies towards counter-revolutionaries during these early weeks, after brutal suppression of the counter-revolutionary insurrection. Lenin remarked at the time that 'Krasnov was given soft treatment. He was placed under house arrest.'[17] In Moscow, the MRC reached agreement with the counter-revolutionary 'Committee for Public Safety' after defeating it in an armed power struggle. The agreement guaranteed its members freedom and inviolability of person. Officers were even allowed to retain some weapons for training purposes.[18] Why, then, were the Soviet authorities initially so 'soft'? It appears that, as Il'ia Rat'kovskii argues, this was due to a belief that the resistance of their opponents would be short-lived and futile, for which there would be need neither for the death penalty nor lengthy jail sentences.[19] Nevertheless this was a time of popular lawlessness and lynch rule, against which the new authorities struggled to maintain order.

What, then, was Lenin's attitude towards the death penalty? It was officially abolished by the Second Congress of Soviets, to Lenin's disapproval. He was absent from the Congress during this enactment but was reported to have later protested, 'How can one make a revolution without firing squads?'[20] Yet responding at the Petrograd Soviet to criticisms of Bolshevik 'terrorism' in the form of arrests even of socialists, he explicitly announced his hope of avoiding 'terrorism': 'We have not resorted, and I hope will not resort, to the terrorism of the French revolutionaries who guillotined unarmed men.'[21] 'When we arrested anyone', he explained, 'we told him we would let him go if he gave us a written promise not to engage in sabotage', though this did not apply to the arrested ministers of the Provisional Government, who were to remain incarcerated.[22] More significant was Lenin's reason for the absence of terror: 'I hope we shall not resort to it, because we have strength on our side',[23] believing that the Bolshevik regime was considerably more secure than the Jacobin. This is an interesting statement in light of the explosion of 'red terror' in the second half of 1918 when the regime was coming under extreme threat, not only from the Western, Northern and Eastern Civil War fronts but from peasants and even workers themselves, when the Bolsheviks lacked this 'strength.' In any case he was not rejecting the possible necessity of terror, even against 'unarmed men' – he was merely noting his hope and confidence that it would not be required.

• This discussion coincided with the breakdown of the last real attempt to form a broad socialist government: the negotiations between the socialist parties demanded by the railway workers' union, Vikzhel, which threatened to call a nationwide strike on the railways if a broad socialist coalition were not agreed to. Lenin was opposed to any compromise with parties or organizations not willing to fully support the decisions of the Bolshevik-dominated Congress of Soviets and of exclusively Soviet power, and was not willing to seek agreements. These negotiations merely served to avoid having to deal with a rail strike at the same time that the revolution was threatened by Krasnov and the military cadets.[24] Nonetheless a majority of the Bolshevik Central Committee was committed to the negotiations and the formation of a broad socialist government that would involve a cessation of armed conflict;[25] Kamenev and Zinoviev in particular were key figures seeking agreement. It is clear from Lenin's notes at the Central Committee meeting on 2 November that a majority was not confident of their ability to triumph on their own, and that Kamenev believed that October could only be a 'bourgeois revolution', not a socialist revolution as Lenin insisted.[26]

• During the course of the negotiations Lenin and Trotsky managed to win over the Central Committee to a more hardline, intransigent stance. The negotiations broke down primarily due to this, though initially the moderate socialists were also guilty of deal-breaking intransigence.[27] From Lenin's perspective agreement was impermissible due to the demands of the Mensheviks and SRs to allow non-soviet bodies representation in a new legislative body; the connections of the moderate socialists with counter-revolutionary generals; and moderate socialist refusal to acquiesce to a Bolshevik Soviet majority. Having decided in September that the revolution could not be successful if dependent upon the vacillations of the 'petty-bourgeois' moderate socialists, Lenin's staunch defence of a homogenous Bolshevik government came as no surprise. Rejecting Zinoviev's criticism that 'we are not Soviet power, we are only Bolsheviks', he retorted that the Mensheviks and SRs left the scene 'not by our fault.'[28]

• Lenin's Central Committee resolution of 4 November read that 'to yield to the ultimatums and threats of the minority of the Soviets would be tantamount to complete renunciation not only of Soviet power but of democracy [...] to the majority's fear to make use of its majority',[29] thereby interpreting this majority as legitimation of one-party rule. Such fear he considered intolerable in the only true vanguard party of the proletariat, especially when '*There is not the slightest hesitation among the* mass *of the workers and soldiers.*'[30] There could be no middle course, as Lenin would remark repeatedly over the coming years. He was convinced that the Bolsheviks were not acting in isolation, for 'before us is the whole of Europe.'[31] This, as Alexander Rabinowitch has stressed, was of crucial importance for the intransigence of Lenin and Trotsky during the talks. It would they thought be 'absurd' to artificially 'introduce socialism' in peasant Russia, but the Russian revolution could only be a thorough-going socialist revolution, one that would not shirk from armed violence and civil war, and that would thereby spark revolutions elsewhere in Europe. Having embarked upon this socialist revolution, there could be no agreements – '*bez soglashenii*!' If the Bolshevik compromisers gained a majority in the Central Committee and took power in VTsIK, Lenin threatened to circumvent his own party and 'go to the sailors' – indicating the importance for the revolution of the military – for the people had spoken in favor of exclusively soviet power. Indeed Rabinowitch has demonstrated that Lenin was on strong ground here as regards working class support (at least in Petrograd) for exclusively soviet power.[32] Lenin threatened to continue and indeed heighten 'political terror(ism)', meaning at this time arrests and closures of newspapers, and threatened to arrest the Vikzhel leaders: 'When it is necessary for us to arrest – we will', for 'such is the dictatorship of the proletariat.'[33] The bourgeoisie engaged in sabotage would be arrested but, though criticizing the Bolsheviks for often being 'too good-natured', once again he believed that short-term prison sentences would suffice to break their resistance.[34]

Lenin was not opposed in principle to a coalition with the moderate socialists if they recognized Soviet power and submitted to the policies of the Second Congress of Soviets.[35] In the meantime the Soviet government could only be a Bolshevik one, at least until new soviet elections were held or until the Third All-Russian Congress of Soviets met, but Lenin took the opportunity to publicly call for a coalition once 'the minority' agreed to submit to the Bolshevik programme.[36] In all, there is some truth to the contention of Soviet historians that the establishment of the one-party system was due to the refusal of other parties to comply with the Second Congress.[37] However the reason was more intricate than that. The Bolshevik decision, goaded by Lenin, to present the Congress with an accomplished fact (that the Bolsheviks had taken power) certainly helped to polarize the socialist camp, and continued intransigence militated against any subsequent broad agreement. Bolshevik rule followed from these factors and the general Bolshevik belief that they alone were the vanguard of the working class at such a life-and-death historical juncture. The significance of one-party rule is crucial. The Bolsheviks were effectively unrestricted in ruling Soviet Russia, apart from a brief coalition interlude with the Left SRs, and in addition their socialist opponents would stand to benefit once popular discontent with the new regime manifested itself.

Immediately upon taking power the Soviet government made an historic appeal to all warring nations and their governments to conclude a non-annexationist peace. Lenin did not consider that the ruling classes would comply, for 'The governments and the bourgeoisie will make every effort to unite their forces and drown the workers' and peasants' revolution in blood.'[38] Nonetheless he was confident that the war's experience would soon lead to peace, hinting at the inevitability of international revolutions.[39] He did not embrace the prospect of civil war; regarding the threat posed by the forces of the deposed government, he declared: 'We do not want a civil war [...]. We are against civil war. But if it nevertheless goes on what are we to do?'[40] Though uttered at a meeting of VTsIK with Left SRs, Lenin's 'peaceful' sentiment here was not merely for rhetorical effect. The Bolsheviks, however, were not entirely innocent of the charge of having initiated civil war in Russia. In this regard a distinction should be made between the concept of full-blown armed battles between two opposing sides, the usual definition of civil war,[41] and a broader definition that more completely captures Lenin's and his contemporaries' understanding of it: the defeat of the bourgeoisie; stratification of society along class lines; and use of the class-state to repress and deprive certain sections of society of civic rights, in addition to armed battles. In this sense Lenin openly and unapologetically acknowledged before the Congress of Soviets in January 1918 that 'we have started and are waging civil war against the exploiters.'[42]

The October Revolution itself was the embodiment of Lenin's wartime slogan of converting the imperialist war into civil wars of the exploited against their exploiters.[43] Immediately upon assuming power he insisted that the bourgeoisie 'will have no share whatsoever' in the new government;[44] the RSFSR was to be a class-based regime. One of the first decrees of the new government concerned a temporary closure of the 'bourgeois' press (including some socialist papers), justified by the extraordinary circumstances of the first days of the revolution.[45] It is clear that for Lenin this was not simply a temporary measure. Responding to criticisms in VTsIK on 4 November he declared that 'Earlier on we said that if we took power, we intended to close down the bourgeois newspapers. To tolerate the existence of these papers is to cease being a socialist.'[46] The press, he contended was as dangerous as counter-revolutionary bombs,[47] and the propertied classes were poisoning the minds of the masses and sowing confusion.[48] More fundamentally, the Constitution would disenfranchise all who earned a living through the labour of others, or from sources of income not derived from their own labour, and even those engaged in wage labour to make a profit. These groups formed the so-called *lishentsy*, who would continue to carry the stigma of their alien status whether or not this was the intention. Certain strata of the pre-revolutionary order, such as clerics and members of the former police, were categorically denied the right to vote in Soviet elections.[49]

In fact Lenin's views on punishment were never really 'soft'. During October he drafted regulations such that workers' representatives in factories guilty of dereliction of duty in maintaining order, and office employees guilty of sabotage, would be punished with confiscation of all their property and up to five years' imprisonment.[50] Throughout November he reiterated the message of *State and Revolution* that the proletarian state would be an instrument of 'violence and coercion' directed against the resistance of its enemies, stressing the need for this state to be firm in exercising coercion in the interests of the working classes.[51] In his November *Theses on the Tasks of the Party and the Present Situation* he wrote that October was a socialist revolution and should not be restricted by bourgeois-democratic 'limitations'. The Constituent Assembly that the Bolsheviks were still overtly committed to would be subordinate to the 'conditions of the civil war', and the struggle 'against reformism' would involve a struggle against the 'rejection of terrorism.'[52]

By November/December it was clear to Lenin that the problems faced by the Soviet state were indeed grave. Before October he had wavered between expecting resistance to be short-lived, relatively easy to deal with, and desperate, leading to the most severe class struggles and civil war. There is bread, he declared, but the kulaks (speculators and relatively well-off peasants, such as those who benefited from Stolypin's agrarian reforms) and landowners, together with state officials, railwaymen and bank employees, were prepared to let the workers starve rather than submit to Soviet power. They were to be combated 'mercilessly', with imprisonment in the Kronstadt prison.[53]

By November the formation of the White Volunteer Army was proceeding apace in the southern Don region under Generals Kornilov and Alekseev, and with the support of the Don Cossack ataman Kaledin. Ultra-nationalist and largely conservative, their aim was to launch a 'national crusade' against the Bolsheviks,[54] and to prevent the conclusion of a humiliating peace with Germany. Members of the Kadet Central Committee also proceeded to the Don. Lenin recognized his opportunity to discredit the results of the Constituent Assembly elections in November, which produced a countrywide majority for an undifferentiated SR party, and the Assembly itself. He warned that the Kadets – 'the most malicious enemies of the people' – were in fact attempting to help the White generals to overthrow Soviet power from inside the Assembly.[55] The 'salvation of the country' could only come from a Constituent Assembly formed from the representatives of the working and exploited masses.[56] On 28 November the Kadets were effectively outlawed and their members liable to arrest and trial by revolutionary tribunal,[57] revolutionary courts designed to combat counter-revolution established just a few days previously. This applied to the entire Kadet party, regardless of personal involvement in counter-revolutionary activity.[58]

The Russian Civil War is usually dated from the Czechoslovak Legion revolt in May 1918.[59] Evan Mawdsley has argued that in fact it began in October 1917, though more recently historians have been inclined not to separate neatly the revolution itself from the Civil War. Joshua Sanborn has made the valid point that internecine violence was 'already well underway' in war-ravaged Russia before the October Revolution brought this to full fruition.[60] It can reasonably be concluded that in fact the Civil War properly began in the winter of 1917/18 in the Don, and the Bolsheviks also began to overthrow the Ukrainian government in Kiev at this time;[61] this can be considered the 'early phase' of the Civil War.[62] Certainly this involved fighting between two reasonably structured armies backed by separate civil administrations on Russian soil fighting for control of Russian sovereignty. It is in this context that the merit of Arno Mayer's thesis regarding the importance of the dynamic between revolution and counter-revolution in the rise of revolutionary terror is evident.[63] This contrasts with the idea that the forms of dictatorship that soon arose in Soviet Russia would have arisen effectively regardless of the circumstances,[64] and the arguments of those historians, Russian and Western, who maintain that terror was inscribed in the Soviet system 'from the start' and was close to its 'essence.'[65] Lenin certainly defended vociferously the extraordinary measures and 'political terror' that characterized the regime from its inception, concerned as he was to ensure that the revolutionary power of the people would not be impeded by 'bourgeois' democratic formalities, and he had spoken openly of the possibility of a civil war that would witness 'rivers of blood.' However he by no means desired this in itself or initially viewed it as an essential attribute of revolution. The idea that 'passion for terror' was deeply 'embedded in Lenin's psyche'[66] does not stand up to scrutiny.

In early December the Soviet government sent troops to, as Lenin put it, 'sweep off the face of the earth the criminals and enemies of the people' in the south.[67] This war was fought with great ferocity on both sides, and the Chairman of Sovnarkom urged that the Cossack generals and their Kadet supporters be made to feel 'the iron hand of the revolutionary people.'[68] The Don and Urals (where more counter-revolutionaries were gathering) were declared to be under states of siege, and the local revolutionary garrisons were instructed to act resolutely without waiting for orders from above.[69] In short Lenin was granting local forces unlimited authority to wipe out counter-revolution and anyone supporting it, by whatever means necessary. This was framed within a rhetoric of fear that the rule of landowners and capitalists would be restored.

The concept 'enemies of the people', which was not necessarily class-specific and was a clear indication of the influence of the French Revolution, was encapsulated in Article 23 of the 1918 Constitution. This article removed 'individual rights and the rights of individual groups which use them to harm the interests of the socialist revolution',[70] which was vague enough to ensure that all so-called 'enemies of the people' would be effectively defenceless against the state and, as in the case of the Kadet and Cossack leaders, declared 'outside the law' (*vne zakona*).[71] By contrast, the notion of 'true [*istinnyie*] citizens' – as distinct from hooligans and speculators – was also introduced in Soviet discourse.[72] The notion of the enemy, as Stuart Finkel has noted, was 'a critical component of the Bolshevik *Weltanschauung*', through which a new social identity of the people and of class aliens was to be formed (or 'ascribed' to individuals and social categories by the Party).[73]

By December the growing levels of sabotage, criminality, economic difficulties and the impending convention of the Constituent Assembly prompted an increasingly dictatorial turn in Lenin's utterances. He warned against the dangers of what he understood as 'localism' and anarcho-syndicalism in enterprises – the unanticipated consequences of 'workers' control.' The Bolshevik policy of nationalizing the banks simply involved seizing assets rather than regulating credit, leading to a drying up of the money supply, resort to printing of money, increasing inflation, industrial bankruptcies, increasing unemployment, and in turn increasing peasant withdrawal from the market.[74] In short Bolshevik economic policies 'exacerbated the already chaotic situation in industry.'[75]

- This was still the period of Lenin's virtually unbounded faith in the spontaneous creativity of the masses and the absence of an imposing state-centralist economic model; his emphasis was not upon the capture of state power, but upon its dissolution.[76] Neil Harding has argued that detectable during the first six months of Soviet rule, however, were 'undercurrents' of the duality pervading *State and Revolution*, of both a highly centralized/disciplined, and decentralized structure of power, but that undercurrents of the former did not really surface until the spring.[77] In fact Lenin's response to the accumulation of difficulties was quite 'dictatorial' even from December, though his emphasis was still upon appealing to the masses to realize that this was their revolution, their responsibility, and that 'The last fight is at hand.' His analysis was strikingly class-based and socially-divisive. He did not seek 'to bring together the various sections of society, to achieve an inclusive and universalistic state order'; rather, 'Communism was to be achieved through struggle against class enemies.'[78] 'The whole country and all the nations of our republic', he wished to convince the masses, 'are divided into two great camps', landowners, capitalists, the rich and saboteurs on the one hand; and on the other the workers, rural poor, soldiers and those truly desirous of peace.[79] Either there would be new elections for the Constituent Assembly or 'the bloody extermination of the rich' and their socialist supporters if they chose a bloody and costly civil war, for there could be 'no third path.'[80]

Between 24 and 27 December Lenin wrote two important and insightful articles. In 'How to Organize Competition?', he recognized that the workers and peasants were too 'timid', not yet accustomed to the fact that '*they* are now the *ruling* class.'[81] This was a problem for the Bolsheviks. Their optimism before October was premised upon their belief and hope in the relative ease by which the masses would themselves adapt to taking over the country (as well as the outbreak of revolutions in the West), despite Lenin's reservations regarding the 'petty-bourgeois' mentality of the Russian *narod*. The workers and peasants were not yet 'firm, resolute and ruthless' enough to break the resistance of the capitalists, but 'break it down they will' – his tone was still very optimistic.[82] There was a need for greater proletarian organization, 'accounting and control' of economy and society, and instruction from educated people and specialists, and the Supreme Economic Council (VSNKh) was set up to manage newly nationalized industries. However Lenin's rhetoric also displayed a more dramatically confrontational stance, clearly widening the category of 'enemies of the people' to include not only the 'rich' but 'idlers' as well, i.e. those workers he wrote of in *State and Revolution* as being 'thoroughly corrupted' by capitalism. He wrote furiously:

> No mercy for these enemies of the people, the enemies of socialism, the enemies of the working people! War to the death against the rich and their hangers-on, the bourgeois intellectuals; war on the rogues, the idlers and the rowdies! All of them are of the same brood – the spawn of capitalism, the offspring of aristocratic and bourgeois society.[83]

The 'idlers' were the 'thousands' of working people inevitably engendered by poverty who cared only for themselves and sought escape from social obligations, from 'loathsome labour.' In fact Lenin was encouraging the workers themselves to effectively implement lynch law, to be creative in working out ways of 'exterminating and rendering harmless' these 'parasites', though 'corrigible' elements of these several groups might be given the opportunity 'to reform quickly'.[84] Russia needed to be cleaned of 'all vermin, of all fleas':

> In one place half a score of rich, a dozen rogues, half a dozen workers who shirk their work [...] will be put in prison. In another place they will be put to cleaning latrines. In a third place they will be provided with 'yellow tickets' after they have served their time, so that everyone shall keep an eye on them, as *harmful* persons, until they reform.

There was a clear precedent here for the later practice in Nazi Germany of forcing Jews to wear the Star of David. The next form of punishment proposed was Lenin's first explicit call for executions, for summary justice: 'one out of every ten idlers will be shot on the spot.'[85] In December Lenin introduced a plan for universal labour conscription, as he had advocated before October, for all citizens aged 16 to 55. His proposal was that all citizens would perform work assigned to them by their local soviets or other bodies and envisaged increased workforce discipline, though clearly his emphasis was upon ensuring that the wealthy classes be put to socially-useful labour as a means of abolishing the bourgeoisie as a class.[86] VSNKh initially rejected this and other of Lenin's economic ideas at this time, evidently considering them inappropriate means of quickening the tempo of introducing socialism.[87]

The second article of late December 1917 was 'Fear of the Collapse of the Old and the Fight for the New'. Written in justification of harsh, 'violent' means of transition to socialism, and with armed civil war being waged in the south, it displayed an essentialist attitude towards violence akin to his pre-1917 wartime thought, and was a veritable panegyric on its use. Those 'scared by the class struggle at its highest pitch when it turns into civil war, the only war that is legitimate, just and sacred [...] the sacred war of the oppressed to overthrow the oppressors and liberate the working people from all oppression', could not see the 'historical prospects.'[88] Socialism could not simply be 'introduced'. Lenin reiterated what in essence 'we have always known, said and emphasized', that socialism:

> takes shape in the course of the most intense, the most acute class struggle – which reaches heights of frenzy and desperation – and civil war; we have always said that a long period of 'birth-pangs' lies between capitalism and socialism, that violence *is always* [emphasis added] the midwife of the old society; that a special state (that is, a special system of organized coercion of a definite class) corresponds to the transition period between the bourgeois and the socialist society, namely, the dictatorship of the proletariat. What

dictatorship implies and means is *a state of simmering war*, a state of military measures of struggle against the enemies of the proletarian power.[89]

This was the essence of revolutionary Leninism as it had been since the early years of the century, apart from a brief period before and after October when this discourse was largely absent. It was the idea that revolutionaries could not be so-called if, like the Mensheviks, they were afraid of confronting the necessity of unpleasant but necessary measures. Lenin's reasoning was reminiscent of Robespierre's; the opponents of violence wanted a 'revolution without a revolution', they wanted to avoid its deepening, the combination of radical democracy with dictatorship and terror, and the use of 'divine' popular violence against the people's oppressors.[90] His belief in class-based coercion as a solution to the economic crises was, as Chris Read puts it, 'based on political eschatology rather than economic analysis.'[91] Israel Getzler has argued that what distinguished Lenin from the Mensheviks was not so much his 'intense revolutionism' as 'his simplistic, narrow and brutal understanding of revolution as civil war *tout court*.'[92] Revolution for Lenin was equally, in fact more importantly, about the liberation of the creative abilities of the masses. Yet as we have seen he had since 1905 referred to revolution as war and, confronting the difficulties of making a revolution, it was this conception that he emphasized.

Lenin stressed that the Paris Commune of 1871 – the model of the proletarian state – had failed to act 'with *sufficient* vigour to suppress the resistance of the exploiters.'[93] The dictatorship of the proletariat would characterize 'an entire historical period' and involve the 'systematic application of *coercion* to an entire class (the bourgeoisie) and its accomplices', and he set about making a virtue of necessity, accentuating the positives of revolutionary coercion and violence. He now even welcomed 'extreme resistance' as a means of educating the working class to become the ruling class, for 'The proletariat must do its learning in the struggle, and stubborn, desperate struggle in earnest is the only real teacher.' The greater the exploiters' resistance, 'the more vigorously, firmly, ruthlessly and successfully will they be suppressed by the exploited.'[94]

The very real opposition, counter-revolution and socio-economic difficulties faced by the regime were understood within the framework of Marxist–Leninist class warfare; the awareness of the justness and apocalyptic significance of the revolution the motivation for turning to intensified class civil warfare. The actions of the Bolsheviks since, and indeed by assuming power contributed to the extent of opposition. Sheila Fitzpatrick has argued that 'A civil war, if the Bolsheviks could win it, represented the best hope of consolidating the new regime [through emergency measures], whose position at the beginning of 1918 was extremely precarious.'[95] Lenin seemed to imply something like this, though it should not be thought that he actively sought or desired the full-scale military, bloody civil war that would soon envelop Russia. His thought was moving in a strongly dictatorial and increasingly violent direction.[96] Robert Service has been struck by 'how easily, quickly and frequently he [Lenin] came to conclusions that Sovnarkom had to amplify its repressive zeal. The suspicion must be strong that he had always known that he would deploy greater violence than he was willing to recognize before October 1917.'[97] There is probably some truth in this, but in any case Lenin could fall back on his more violent revolutionary discourse and predictions of previous months and years.

・ On 6 December Sovnarkom entrusted Feliks Dzerzhinskii, an almost ascetical Polish Bolshevik, to form a commission to deal with a threatened general strike of state employees.[98] Dzerzhinskii appeared before Sovnarkom the following evening with a plan for, in effect, a political police that would deal with more than just the threatened strike. The plan was adopted and brought into existence the All-Russia Extraordinary Commission for Combating Counter-revolution, Speculation and Sabotage, or 'Vecheka'. Lenin had not envisaged the creation of a political police,[99] but he agreed with Dzerzhinskii's vision and was to become one of the Vecheka's staunchest supporters. The Vecheka (organized locally as Chekas) was to become the principal repressive instrument of the dictatorship of the proletariat. It was a temporary ('extraordinary') institution, not initially provided with any legal status, and directly subordinate to Sovnarkom. It was clear from the very beginning that the Vecheka would respond to the widespread and manifold problems facing the regime – counter-revolution, speculation, criminality, sabotage and strikes. Lenin had expressed confidence that the revolution would be defended by the self-discipline of the working people but, as noted, he was becoming exasperated with the 'timidity' of the workers and peasants in dealing with some of these problems and was easily convinced of the need for the creation of a political police.[100] Its subordination to Sovnarkom as opposed to VTsIK was to avoid the impression of its being 'part of the regular machinery of state'[101] – for otherwise Bolshevik claims to have 'smashed the state' would appear thin – and to try to ensure exclusive Bolshevik composition and control over it, even though Sovnarkom approved admitting the Left SRs as coalition partners on the very day of the Vecheka's foundation. Martin Latsis, a leading Chekist, later wrote that the Soviet leaders wished to avoid having 'bemoaners' in the Vecheka who would raise questions of moral principles and humanitarian rights and freedoms.[102] The formation of a coalition with the Left SRs broadened the new government's support base, but would also place an important constraint on the Bolsheviks' freedom of maneuver.

Dzerzhinskii set the tone of the Vecheka's future conduct at the Sovnarkom meeting on 7 December: 'Do not think that I seek forms of revolutionary justice; we are not in need of justice. It is war now – face to face, a fight to the finish.'[103] The Vecheka soon acquired its own troop detachments and a year later employed a total of 37,000 people. The Corps of Vecheka Troops was to be recruited 'solely from the proletariat.'[104] Hence, although it exercised a veritable reign of terror from mid-1918 onwards, including the brutal suppression of peasant revolts and workers' strikes, it was in theory a proletarian police, recruited in intent from the best elements of the working classes and the Party itself (though in reality the composition and abuses of conduct of the Chekas would trouble Vecheka leaders through the Civil War).

・ Originally the Vecheka was purely an investigative organ, charged with the task of bringing suspects before the revolutionary tribunals. On 16 December it was granted the power of arrest and soon came into conflict with the Commissariats of Justice (NKIu) and Internal Affairs (NKVD), not so much over its methods as its encroachment on their respective functions.[105] The first major dispute illustrated the special status that Lenin insisted upon for the Vecheka. On 18 December Menshevik and SR members of the 'Union for Defence of the Constituent Assembly' were arrested by the Vecheka but their arrests were countermanded by the Left SR Commissar of Justice, Isaac Steinberg, who was concerned to ensure that a Soviet version of *habeas corpus* be introduced. The Vecheka, by contrast, was largely concerned with pre-emptive, preventive measures. Lenin and Stalin introduced a motion the following day to Sovnarkom condemning Steinberg's infringement of the rights of the Vecheka (and of Sovnarkom), stating clearly that Vecheka arrests could only be overturned by Sovnarkom.[106] Steinberg introduced a resolution, which was substantially adopted, designed to bring all investigative commissions (including the Vecheka) 'into the system.' This would ensure that henceforth the arrests of all 'politically significant' persons would require the written approval of the Commissar of Justice.[107] Two days later these concessions were essentially nullified at Sovnarkom by Lenin's amendments to Steinberg's draft. The work of the Vecheka was to be 'supervised' not only by the (Left SR) NKIu but also by the NKVD, but most significantly these commissariats were merely to be 'notified' of the arrests of politically significant persons – their prior knowledge was not required.[108] Steinberg did gain a victory on 7 January 1918 when Sovnarkom agreed to allow Left SR representation in the Vecheka, and NKIu was authorized to verify the grounds for arrest of political prisoners; those against whom there was not sufficient evidence were to be released.[109]

From the realm of freedom to the realm of necessity

Early in 1918 the Bolsheviks confronted a major political question, the Constituent Assembly. Moderate Bolsheviks had thought that a combination of the Assembly plus soviets would be the form of state, and would unsuccessfully attempt to get the party to agree to this in late November/December.[110] Elections were finally held in November and a nationwide majority was won by the SRs, the Bolsheviks gaining majorities in urban areas. The SR electoral lists did not distinguish between the Left and Right wings of the party, and the involvement of the Kadets with the counter-revolution on the Don further undermined the 'democratic' credentials of the Assembly for most members of the Central Committee. The opposition however, went deeper; Soviet power was to be the medium for proletarian dictatorship, a higher form of democracy.[111] Lenin argued that the assumption by the Assembly of any authority over the soviets would, with the outbreak of civil war, prove to be a fetter on the 'deepening' of the revolution, for it would blunt class struggle. He believed that there should be new elections and that the Assembly should unreservedly accept Soviet power.[112] His opposition to any prerogatives of the Assembly was embodied more starkly in the *Declaration of Rights of the Working and Exploited People*, placed before the Assembly when it convened on 5 January, and which instructed that 'the Constituent Assembly considers that it would be fundamentally wrong, even formally, to put itself in opposition to Soviet power.'[113] Not surprisingly the Assembly did not approve the *Declaration* and was closed, never to reopen. The day before it met, Lenin wrote that 'A bad parliament should be "dismissed" in two weeks. The good of the revolution, the good of the working class, is the highest law.'[114] VTsIK had resolved to use armed force if necessary to ensure that the Assembly did not 'usurp' Soviet power.[115] In the event, there were mass arrests and a number of fatalities among those demonstrating in favour of the Assembly on 5 January.

Following its dispersal, Lenin expounded on the fundamental opposition that he saw between Soviet power and the Assembly, which he described as having 'outlived its purpose.' What were needed were not 'national institutions' but 'only class institutions (such as the Soviets)', which would overcome the resistance of the propertied classes and lay the 'foundations of socialist society.'[116] Would there be a new Assembly, or should there have been a popular referendum before its dissolution? Lenin replied with a categorical 'no', effectively arrogating for the government the right to decide.[117] The Assembly's dissolution gave absolute effect to the Bolshevik policy of excluding the wealthy classes 'and their hangers-on' from the body politic, and of dividing Russian society along class lines. Lenin's reasoning was simple and sharp: the sheep could not live 'side by side with the wolves, the exploited with the exploiters.' He was 'sure' that 'the majority of the workers, peasants and soldiers' shared that sentiment.[118] Civil war he believed inevitable 'in the long process of revolutionary development', and he ridiculed the Menshevik and SR slogan 'Let there be no civil war'. How could the Russian revolution *not* face that issue, he asked, how 'can wolves become lambs?'[119]

Vladimir Brovkin argues that the dissolution of the Assembly marked the 'watershed which set the chain of events in motion leading to the [full-blown] civil war.'[120] Indeed the main phase of Civil War would begin in May with a group of mainly Right SR Assembly representatives establishing a rival government along the Volga. Yet Lenin, justifying the dissolution, spoke once again of only a 'handful of men' in Russia fighting Soviet power. They would disappear in 'a matter of weeks' and Soviet power would triumph as the organizational form of the oppressed class.[121] Such was his absolute confidence in the unity of interests between vanguard (party) and masses that he declared Soviet power to be 'above parties' and a superior form of democracy, that power could be transferred to another party 'without any revolution at all.'[122] This was an incredible statement, as the Bolsheviks set about destroying this very principle in the coming weeks and months according as they lost support in urban soviets. On 14 June, the Mensheviks and SRs would be expelled from VTsIK (though this decision was rescinded in November).[123]

In January, at the Third Congress of Soviets, Lenin confronted non-Bolshevik socialist criticisms of the regime's use of 'terror', civil war and dictatorship. 'Not a single problem of the class struggle has ever been solved in history except by violence', he reiterated, and 'When violence is exercised by the working people, by the mass of exploited against the exploiters – then we are for it!' He dismissed those who 'burst into tears [...] and demand that we perform the impossible, that we socialists achieve complete victory without fighting against the exploiters.' Lenin's reasoning was analogous to that of Robespierre's retort against the Girondin Jean-Baptiste Louvet in the Convention in 1792: 'A sensibility that wails almost exclusively over the enemies of liberty seems suspect to me. Stop shaking the tyrant's bloody robe in my face, or I will believe that you wish to put Rome in chains.'[124] Lenin observed that the regime had not resorted to 'real terror' because the government commanded popular support through the soviets, reiterating that 'it will be sufficient if we nationalize the banks and confiscate their property in order to compel them [the bourgeoisie] to submit.'[125] The transitional period to socialism would be 'the greatest and most difficult transition that has ever occurred in history', but he apparently had little inclination of the forthcoming main phases of civil war. Victory would not be achieved quickly, and the full extent of counter-revolution had not yet come to pass, he thought. Yet the more straightforward the announcement that 'we are waging civil war against the exploiters', he reasoned, the more quickly would 'all the working and exploited people [...] understand that Soviet power is fighting for the real, vital cause of all the working people',[126] and hence the more quickly would the struggle end. Lenin's objective was that of the 'true' pacifist; contrasting the Soviet republic and the imperialist world, he declared 'Over there – conflict, war, bloodshed, the sacrifice of millions of people, capitalist exploitation; here – a genuine policy of peace and a socialist Republic of Soviets.'[127]

Having signed an armistice with Germany in December 1917, Lenin wished to conclude a separate peace and focus on domestic issues, because 'several months at least' would be required for victory, first, over the bourgeoisie at home.[128] Thereafter the initial revolutionary enthusiasm would wane somewhat and the government's emphasis would be upon a centralized, strong state dictatorship. Lenin did not reject the necessity of continuing to prepare for a revolutionary war, but such a war he considered impossible at the present time as the army was 'completely demoralized.'[129] Early in March the Treaty of Brest–Litovsk, an annexationist peace that removed large tracts of territory from Soviet control including grain-rich Ukraine, ended Russian involvement in the European war. This led to bitter debates with the Left wing of the Bolshevik Party and staunch hostility from the Bolsheviks' opponents, and to the departure of the Left SRs from government. The Treaty also ensured that the Allies were now implacably opposed to the Bolsheviks.

The German threat immediately before the Treaty, and the increasingly desperate economic situation (which was exacerbated by the Treaty) led Lenin to formally call for extra-judicial executions. In connection with the extreme food supply crisis he berated the Petrograd workers for being 'monstrously inactive', for they 'must understand that they have no one to look to but themselves.' Urging the creation of worker detachments, on an obligatory basis, to search stations in the capital and even to go to the countryside to ensure the supply of grain, he declared in January that 'We can't get anywhere unless we resort to terrorism': speculators and bandits 'must be shot on the spot.'[130] 'Speculators' were workers and 'middle-men' who carried grain into the cities to sell at inflated prices (the 'bag-men' carried grain for personal consumption or perhaps for speculative, black-market purposes), or peasants who held onto their grain. These speculators, he instructed, needed to be 'fully exposed' first, and he also recommended execution for members of the detachments who were 'dishonest.'[131] On the same day Sovnarkom approved the increase in dispatch of armed detachments to the countryside, though the right to execute 'exposed speculators' on the spot was granted to the local soviets, not to the individual detachments as Lenin had suggested.[132] His advocacy of terror in the countryside, then, preceded the outbreak of the first main phase of the Civil War in May.

For the Bolshevik leaders the rationale for summary justice and the re-instatement of the death penalty for judicial sentences was growing. On 1 January an attempt was made on Lenin's life.[133] The reaction of *Pravda*, the party newspaper, was to propose introducing 'red terror' against the bourgeoisie: 'For every one of 'our heads they will answer with a hundred of their heads.' The proletariat 'does not like to turn the other cheek and "to forgive enemies". It fights for the freedom of all people.'[134] 'They' specifically connoted bankers, bank employees, speculators, factory owners and marauders. The language and logic foreshadowed that used to introduce the official period of Red Terror later in the year. Yet this was not translated into official practice (outside of the zones of civil war). Some regional soviet organizations did however apply the death penalty without sanction over the winter of 1917/18, in response to growing levels of criminality.[135]

These 'bottom-up' pressures, and especially the apparent rejection by Germany of peace terms and the renewed offensive launched on 18 February, resulted in formal sanction of widespread summary justice. Trotsky's decree *The Socialist Fatherland is in Danger!* was issued in the name of Sovnarkom, despite Left SR opposition to the final clause which stated that 'Enemy agents, profiteers, marauders, hooligans, counter-revolutionary agitators and German spies are to be shot on the spot.' To Steinberg's protestation, Lenin is reported to have replied: 'Surely you do not imagine that we shall be victorious without applying the most cruel revolutionary terror?'[136] The decree aimed to mobilize the country for defence and stamp out all threats in the rear.[137] The Vecheka immediately assumed the right of execution. It published a declaration in *Izvestiia*, the newspaper of VTsIK, that 'up to now the Commission has been magnanimous in the struggle with enemies of the people', but henceforth there were no other means of conducting this struggle other than 'merciless destruction at sites of crime.' Once again these declarations did not lead to a 'red terror' as such. There was a limited number of executions, certainly by the Vecheka which executed sixteen people over the coming weeks in Petrograd and Moscow (the Vecheka moved with the government to Moscow in early March),[138] and a Soviet periodical recorded around 100 executions in total in March, not by the Chekas alone. Many of these cases concerned ordinary criminality, not 'political' crimes.[139]

Following the peace treaty, the 'extraordinary' conditions necessitating terror would ostensibly have passed. The Vecheka and its organs, however, continued to execute criminals, and soon political opponents, during the coming months. From

March to June a 'New Course' in Soviet political economy began, what Russian historians refer to as *peredyshka* (breathing spell). Perhaps a more accurate term is that used by Chris Read – 'productionism' – as the priority of the state leaders was to restore and raise economic production.[140] The 'breathing spell' concerned the shift of emphasis from the initial 'assault on capital' to 'state capitalism', to the adoption of the best methods of capitalist production in order to 'build the bricks' of socialism and eventually outmatch capitalism in terms of economic production. It was a time of relatively sober modification of the earlier optimism that suggested that Russia was on the cusp of socialist transformation. This was also a time when Lenin's thought and the practice of the Soviet state displayed signs of a clear and heightened 'totalitarian' impulse, what can be termed Lenin's 'totalitarian consciousness.'[141] This suggests the need to remove any opposition to Bolshevik rule and anything that might be considered a middle or third course between Bolshevik rule and capitalist restoration. The dangers posed by the 'petty proprietors' (peasants) and petty-bourgeois tendencies amongst the populace as a whole Lenin recognized as presenting even graver challenges for the new regime than outright counter-revolution. Chris Read notes that Lenin believed a popular 'cultural' or 'spiritual' revolution would accompany the establishment of a socialist revolution, but this had not yet materialized; his disenchantment with the popular Russian psyche and the desperateness of the situation was leading 'to the search for organizational and institutional substitutes.'[142]

Lenin posited that the peace treaty made a war with Germany all the more inevitable, for the Germans had signed the Treaty to concentrate on the Western Front and then turn their attention eastward.[143] Hence he accepted the need for building up a trained and disciplined regular Red Army of conscripted workers and 'toiling peasants', moving away from the ideal of a voluntary popular militia. This task was entrusted to Trotsky, who began recruiting former military specialists. Brest–Litovsk did not weaken Lenin's theoretical commitment to waging a revolutionary war. In fact he thought that 'We have entered an epoch of *a succession* of wars. We are moving towards a new, *patriotic* war. We will arrive at that war in the midst of a ripening socialist revolution.'[144] His optimism immediately before and after October that successful international revolutions would occur and allow Russia a speedy, relatively uncomplicated advance to socialism had not yet borne fruit, but he had always been theoretically prepared for a lengthy period of struggles, for what he called the 'zigzags of history.' The necessity now was to create the material conditions conducive to the conduct of such a war, a 'holy' war to strengthen and develop socialism,[145] whether it be defensive or offensive in nature (the distinction was not very distinct in Lenin's mind). Lenin's re-adjusted, militarist ideas were introduced at the Extraordinary Seventh Party Congress in early March:

> The Congress therefore declares that it recognizes the primary and fundamental task of our Party, of the entire vanguard of the class-conscious proletariat and of Soviet power, to be the adoption of the most energetic, ruthlessly determined and draconian measures to improve the self-discipline

and discipline of the workers and peasants of Russia, to explain the inevitability of Russia's historic advance towards a socialist, patriotic war of liberation, to create everywhere soundly co-ordinated mass organizations held together by a single iron will [...] and [...] to train systematically and comprehensively in military matters and military operations the entire adult population of both sexes.[146]

His thinking clearly represented a distinct shift from the predominantly libertarian overtones of 1917. He was forced to concede that there would be a 'number of difficult stages of transition' to socialism in view of the 'destruction of culture and means of production' consequent upon the war; how many such stages would depend on the commencement of European revolutions.[147] In the meantime the Russian *narod* must 'learn discipline from the Germans; for, if we do not, we, as a people, are doomed, we shall live in eternal slavery.'[148] That the 'bricks of socialism' had not yet been made in Russia suggested that October could only have been merely a democratic revolution, and that the Bolsheviks had transgressed a fundamental Marxian tenet that a higher socialist revolution could only successfully take place when a society would be economically and culturally ready for it. Lenin would not countenance this, for it would have meant that theoretically the correct political form for Russia would be the Constituent Assembly. The war had convinced him of the ripeness for socialism and necessity of a socialist political revolution in Russia, assured that socialism would soon take hold of Europe. Through 1918 and beyond he was to justify Bolshevik dictatorial rule with the mantra that there could be no 'third way' between the Bolshevik path to socialism, however complicated, and reactionary imperialist restoration with its inherent tendency for war, 'reactionary violence' and destruction.

The road to socialism, Lenin reasoned, would in reality 'never be straight, it will be incredibly involved.' Hence perhaps the need to emphasize the ultimate goal of realizing a communist society; the name of the party now changed to the Russian Communist Party (Bolsheviks) to distinguish it from social-democratic 'opportunism'. Revealingly, Lenin lamented that 'History has not provided us with the peaceful situation that was theoretically assumed for a certain time, and which is desirable for us, and which would enable us to pass through these stages of transition speedily.'[149] He yielded not to a modification of the political nature of the revolution but, as he had been doing since December, to a renewed theoretical awareness of the creative importance of struggle and violence in the Marxist revolutionary conception, almost predicting the course on which Soviet Russia was about to embark:

Marxists have never forgotten that violence must inevitably accompany the collapse of capitalism in its entirety and the birth of socialist society. That violence will constitute a period of world history, a whole era of various kinds of wars, imperialist war, civil wars inside countries, the intermingling of the two, national wars liberating the nationalities oppressed by the imperialists and by various combinations of imperialist powers that will inevitably enter into various alliances [...] This epoch, an epoch of gigantic cataclysms, of mass decisions forcibly imposed by war, of crises, has begun – that we can see clearly – and it is only the beginning.[150]

Lenin's thought at this time evinced a theoretical struggle in his mind between the commune form of radically-democratic dictatorship and a more 'dictatorial' form of dictatorship. In the former the workers would directly participate in political administration; in the latter the state would represent the 'true' interests of the proletariat, and participation would be 'more virtual than real.'[151] One of the insightful themes of Neil Harding's study of Lenin's thought, important to keep in mind as one navigates through the dialectic of theory and practice post-1917, is that its coherency began to break down as a consequence of the failure of theoretical predictions to be materialized.'[152] In early March Lenin still emphasized, as he would always maintain, the utopian elements of *State and Revolution*: 'It is important for us to draw literally all working people into the government of the state [...] socialism cannot be implemented by a minority. It can be implemented only by tens of millions when they have learned to do it themselves.' The state must suppress the exploiters but not through 'police' as such but by the masses themselves acting through state bodies, which must be 'linked' with the masses and 'represent' them.[153] However the state apparatus, he noted, was suffering from ill-discipline and petty-bourgeois habits. Just when would it start to wither away? His answer was that two more party congresses would have convened 'before the time comes to say: see how our state is withering away'.[154] Yet at the same congress he declared that 'the special government apparatus is disappearing, the special apparatus for a certain state coercion is disappearing', for the people themselves were establishing armed forces 'that support the given state system'.[155] The inherent potential danger in Lenin's logic of providing the theoretical basis for a dictatorship over, rather than of, the masses was exposed. The existence of these armed forces – presumably the Red Army, Vecheka and other armed bodies – was, he thought, indicative of the state's disappearing 'as a special coercive force.' This, in addition to his calls for the subordination of the workers to the single will of economic directors appointed by Soviet institutions, was 'tantamount to uniting state and civil society.' The bases of this were contained in the notion of the 'withering away of state and law', the vision of 'nonantagonistic social, economic, and political relations whereby the state [...] will be superfluous.'[156] The state for the Bolsheviks was not an instrument for safeguarding individual liberties but a temporary instrument of strict regulation and class oppression. Lenin indicated that in the future, in so far as the resistance of the 'exploiting classes' would cease, the Constitution would be extended 'to the *whole* population.'[157] Lenin's point was that the state was very far from being superfluous in 1918 but the new 'armed forces' posed no danger to proletarian democracy, and the arming of the entire people remained his aim.

Responding to the dire economic crisis, to the humiliation of Brest–Litovsk, and the consequent criticisms of the government voiced by Mensheviks and SRs, and by the Left Communist opposition within Bolshevik ranks, he turned his thoughts to the bigger historical picture. With the old order collapsing, the new order was being born, albeit 'amid indescribable suffering.' There were those he explained who 'seek salvation from the at times too bitter reality in fine-sounding and alluring phrases', but they were merely proving their ineptitude for the task at hand, the need to 'strain every muscle' and seek 'salvation' along the road of world socialist revolution.[158] The Russian revolution was born of the utter destruction of war, and Lenin ridiculed those who thought that such a revolution could develop 'without torment, without horror.'[159] He was speaking as the representative of the vanguard party, the party that would not give way to despair and seek the easy way out by abandoning this difficult path and making concessions to the agents of capital, to the forces of reaction. He held onto his remarkable dialectical conviction – the war would in fact prove the salvation of the masses for it had shaken them up and was pushing history forward 'with locomotive speed.'[160]

Mensheviks and SRs were attributing the economic crises to Bolshevik policies and reaping electoral successes at the Bolsheviks' expense in the city soviet elections held around the country from early April.[161] Despite some initial acquiescence of local Bolsheviks, some of the newly-elected soviets were forcibly dissolved. On 7 April Lenin berated the Mensheviks for 'trying to overthrow the Soviet government', for being on the side of the bourgeoisie and 'betraying us.' They were allegedly taking advantage of the difficult situation, of 'the hardest months of the revolution', and looking on 'with malicious glee.'[162] The forcible disbandment of popularly-elected soviets or adjustment of electoral rules to facilitate Bolshevik victories in spring 1918 marked the most significant assault on democracy in Russia since the collapse of Tsarism, and was a major step towards the consolidation of one-party dictatorial rule. Regarding Bolshevik repressions Lenin dismissed the 'tears of the Mensheviks and SRs', ridiculed them as 'tender lambs' and accused them of hypocrisy regarding state executions:

> When we apply the death penalty by shooting, they turn into Tolstoyans [...] They have forgotten how, along with Kerensky, they drove the workers into the slaughter [the offensive of June 1917], while the secret treaties were hidden in their pockets. They have forgotten this and turned into meek Christians, fretting about mercy.[163]

Ronald Grigor Suny has noted Lenin's 'complex ambivalence' about the Russian working class: 'at one and the same time the necessary instrument of revolutionary transformation and the inadequately organized and conscious vehicle of that transformation.'[164] In early April Lenin proposed stricter punishments for labour indiscipline, with imprisonment ultimately possible and universal labour conscription embodied in the 1918 Labour Codex.[165] The soviet election results, and the development of independent labour movements with moderate socialist party participation,[166] were worrying trends for the Bolsheviks. Lenin suggested that the state was, in effect, in active combat for the soul of the Russian people, to determine which would prevail – proletarian discipline or petty-bourgeois interests which were opposed to those of the proletariat.[167] The petty-bourgeois psychology in a backward country such as Russia, he lamented, 'is felt at every step', and hence until the higher phase of communism, state and society must organize the 'strictest control.'[168] The protestation of the Left SRs, that such control would lead not to increased labour efficiency but 'serfdom for the working class', Lenin dismissed out of hand. The dictatorship of the proletariat, he reasoned, entailed not simply the overthrow of the exploiters but the establishment of order, discipline, productivity and control.[169] In debate with his Left Communist party colleague Nikolai Bukharin, the message of *State and Revolution* that he now emphasized was that control must be exercised by state and society not only over 'the gentry' but also over the workers 'who have been thoroughly corrupted by capitalism.'[170]

'Control' implies the threat of coercion, but how violent would this coercion be? Lenin repeatedly called for 'the most resolute and draconian measures' to improve discipline.[171] Disciplinary courts were established in the spring and summer of 1918, though their sanctions usually did not exceed that of dismissal from employment. In late 1919, Sovnarkom would authorize these courts to send workers to concentration camps (see chapter 7).[172] In his *Theses on the Current Situation*, written in connection with the introduction of the 'food dictatorship' in late May, Lenin proposed declaring martial law throughout the country and shooting for indiscipline in the army food detachments.[173] He also supported the introduction of appointed 'dictators' to control the railways who would be empowered to shoot for indiscipline.[174]

The principal exposition of Lenin's increasingly statist, dictatorial and violent orientation was provided in his April pamphlet *The Immediate Tasks of the Soviet Government*. Significantly, these ideas were taking shape before the main phase of the Civil War began in late May. Indeed, at a speech in the Moscow Soviet on 23 April Lenin opined that the Civil War, in the sense of actual military battles between opposed armed forces, was at an end.[175] He acknowledged that Tsarism had bequeathed a popular 'hatred and suspicion of everything that is connected with the state'. Plenty of time would be required to overcome this, he thought, but he was convinced that without comprehensive state control of the economy 'a return to the yoke of capitalism is *inevitable*.'[176] His increased reliance on a strong state to cope with difficulties was very much strengthened by ideological conceptions, for it was now 'particularly clear to us how correct is the Marxist thesis that anarchism and anarcho-syndicalism are *bourgeois* trends, how irreconcilably opposed they are to socialism, proletarian dictatorship and communism.' Lenin was espousing the ideological foundations of 'War Communism'.

Expounding upon the petty-bourgeois psychology of the Russian proletariat, Lenin reasoned that 'The Russian is a bad worker compared with people in advanced countries.'[177] What, then, was to be done? The 'last word in capitalism', the 'refined brutality' of the Taylor System was to be introduced, for 'we must not hesitate to use barbarous methods in fighting barbarism.'[178] He saw 'absolutely *no* contradiction in principle between Soviet (that is, socialist) democracy' and the exercise of 'dictatorial powers by individuals.'[179] Indeed, as he had put it at the Seventh Party Congress, such 'draconian measures' would ultimately serve the '*self*-discipline' of the *narod*. He believed that 'strict unity of will' should be enforced by 'thousands subordinating their will to the will of one', and this complemented the fundamentally 'anti-political' essence of his political philosophy. With ideal class consciousness this subordination would be mild leadership; with anything less (clearly the case here) then it would assume 'dictatorial' forms. In any case such subordination he considered an absolute requirement for increasing production. Yet he still believed in the necessity of workers' control from below, reflecting how various strands coexisted in his thought.[180]

Compulsion and state coercion would ensure that proletarian rule could not be accused of meekness and 'desecrated by the practice of a lily-livered proletarian government.' There could, Lenin was convinced, be no third way between the coercive dictatorship of the proletariat and that of the White generals. This coercive state power was necessary, he insisted, because even without an external war a revolution without internal, civil war would be 'inconceivable.' This war would be 'even more devastating' because it concerned 'thousands and millions of cases of wavering and desertion from one side to another.' The dictatorship of the proletariat was the dictatorship of 'the advanced class' and its vanguard, the 'reliable leader' of the masses, and the masses had to be 'won over' from the clutches of petty-bourgeois disintegration. The instability of previous revolutions was due to proletarian weakness, but the proletariat '*alone* is able […] to win over to its side *the majority* of the working and exploited people [i.e. the majority of peasants] and retain power sufficiently long to suppress completely all the exploiters as well as the elements of disintegration.'[181]

Remarking that petty-bourgeois 'anarchy' was even more dangerous than counter-revolution, he stated that: 'We shall be merciless both to our enemies and to all waverers and harmful elements in our midst who dare to bring disorganization into our difficult creative work of building a new life for the working people', i.e. to workers and peasants also who did not prove to be sufficiently disciplined.[182] Dictatorship he described as a 'big word', one that 'should not be thrown about carelessly.' Dictatorship 'is iron rule, government that is revolutionarily bold, swift and ruthless in suppressing both exploiters and hooligans', and he lamented that 'our government is excessively mild, very often it resembles jelly more than iron.'[183] In his speech at the Moscow Soviet in late April he asserted categorically that 'we have always said that we cannot pass from capitalism to the full victory of socialism by the bloodless and easy path of persuasion and conflict, and that we can only reach our goal as the result of a furious struggle.' Yet he wrote that as the civil war was coming to a close, 'the typical manifestation of suppression and compulsion will be, not shooting on the spot, but trial by court.' This was indeed indicative that he considered the law a regular part of proletarian dictatorship,[184] but he also advocated the shooting of 'bribe-takers and rogues.' In May he upbraided the revolutionary tribunal judges for lenient sentences in a case of bribe-taking, demanding the death penalty, but later he insisted that the sentences should be ten years' imprisonment.[185]

The summer of 1918 would witness a transformation in the violent practices of the fledgling Soviet state, in response to the escalation of the state's attempts to resolve the crucial food supply problem, and the onset of the main phases of frontal Civil War. This would lead to an official period of Red Terror in September.

5 The Red Terror

And instead of the many millions of class murders in the war, instead of the slow systematic sucking dry of the blood of the working people by the web of capitalism in the interest of the ruling minority – instead of this we have set about merciless struggle […] And this goes on because we value and love life too much.[1]

(*Vecheka Weekly*, 22 September 1918)

Lenin believed that the summer of 1918 signalled the actual beginning of socialist revolution in agrarian relations. The spring–summer of 1918 represented, as Bertrand Patenaude has put it, the 'second phase' of Bolshevik agrarian policy. This signified a return to class struggle in the countryside, as distinct from the 'first phase' since October characterized by adoption of the SR notion of the peasants as overwhelmingly 'poor' and instinctively socialist.[2] Lenin was a significant force behind the principles of Soviet agrarian policy and its violent conduct. The government adopted a 'food dictatorship' on 9 May that sought largely to politicize the food crisis in terms of class warfare, despite the absence of any 'long-term class dynamics' in accounting for the crisis.[3] The 'defense of the fatherland', Lenin reasoned, could only be achieved through 'a ruthless war to the death begun in one's own country.' To have a strong army and rear there must be a stable food supply, and for that reason he explained that every 'kulak' (covering wealthy peasants and 'profiteers'), 'rich man' and infringer of the state grain monopoly must be punished.[4]

Lars Lih has argued that the political challenge to the Bolsheviks in the soviets provided an important impetus for the Bolshevik discursive emphasis apportioning blame for the food supply crisis on the effects of the war and external and internal foes.[5] This was not merely intended to deflect blame from themselves. Lenin emphasized the need for 'a ruthless and terrorist struggle and war against peasant or other bourgeois elements who retain surplus grain for themselves.'[6] He referred to such peasants as 'enemies of the people' and threatened them with not less than ten years' imprisonment and confiscation of all their property.[7] Responding to Left SR criticisms of the severity of the proposed food dictatorship, he cast them aside as 'anarchist windbags' who denied the necessity of a 'ruthlessly severe' state power. The war for grain he referred to as a 'crusade',[8] warning that the alternative would be a German-installed White dictatorship and White terror, such as was witnessed in Finland and Ukraine.

Lenin's *Theses on the Current Situation* written on 26 May formed the basis for the government's appeal to form armed food detachments (*prodotriady*) of workers and soldiers to conduct this 'crusade'. On the very day that the Civil War broke out in earnest with the revolt of the Czechoslovak Legion along the Trans-Siberian railway, he proposed that the Commissariat of War convert nine-tenths of its work to 'reorganizing the army for the war for grain and on waging this war'. Clearly the war for food was not a response to the Civil War as such.[9] The food dictatorship sought the absolute prohibition of private grain trade and the compulsory delivery of all grain surpluses to the state at fixed prices, and the *Theses* proclaimed martial law throughout the country.[10] In addition to the formation of food armies, including in their composition workers and soldiers from the cities and poor peasants from the famine-stricken areas, the government sought to incite class war and hatred within the villages themselves through the formation on 11 June of the committees of poor peasants (*kombedy*) – the separate formation of the village 'poor' against the village 'rich'. This highly class-political approach to the economic crisis, however, failed to adequately grasp the strength of the basic unity of the Russian countryside and its traditional distrust of the city.

The war for grain

The Bolsheviks' resort to highly dictatorial-statist means of solving the economic crises in spring 1918 was not merely the product of ideological drives and of a more dictatorial, 'vanguard' model of proletarian dictatorship. This was consciously modeled on wartime, especially German, state capitalism. The historians Lars Lih and Peter Holquist, in particular, take a 'Time of Troubles' perspective as regards food supply polices, understanding Bolshevik efforts to ensure an adequate food supply for the troops and general populace within the context of wartime.[11] Lih explains that:

> The Bolsheviks certainly had great faith in the state, but this faith can hardly be ascribed to the civil war. It was the time of troubles that led to a new emphasis on state regulation of society, which predated the Bolsheviks and encompassed almost the entire political spectrum [in Russia].[12]

In Russia's case, as Holquist emphasizes, the lack of a properly constituted civil society and a broad anti-commercial bias were highly significant; all three Russian wartime administrations displayed an anti-market orientation regarding grain procurement. These points, along with pervasive wartime suspicions that 'sabotage' was somehow behind economic crises, prompts Lih to consider that 'Lenin was aggressively unoriginal in his vision of state economic regulation'; the 'food dictatorship' was the Bolsheviks' attempt to re-establish state order.[13] The Bolshevik anti-market orientation in grain supply, however, became theoretically embedded.

The Tsarist administration had been reluctant to resort to force to secure the food supply, and the Provisional Government certainly recognized its necessity in 1917 but lacked sufficient means to pursue as forceful a policy as it intended.[14] The Bolsheviks radically increased the use of armed force for food supply work, and Leninist ideology was a crucial factor behind this. Whereas the Provisional Government sought to unite society to achieve state order, the Bolsheviks 'insisted that world war be transformed into an open-ended class war.'[15]

The concept of 'War Communism' (more correctly translated as 'military' communism[16]) then is somewhat of a misnomer, for this was not simply the result of the Civil War and not confined to its time-frame. Its main features – labour conscription, surplus-grain requisitioning, nationalization of industries and, as at least one scholar considers, state terror[17] – were largely introduced before the Civil War proper, at least in outline. Furthermore, some aspects of War Communism, especially the militarization of labour, were intensified or fully implemented only in 1920 when the worst of the Civil War was over.[18] The Civil War served to intensify these policies but they were responses to the economic collapse, the 'low culture' of the masses, civil war, the terms of Brest–Litovsk that would have granted Germany claim to land and capital assets if these were not nationalized,[19] as well as to the purposeful ideological conceptualizations around these measures. War Communism, as Patenaude puts it, should be understood not just in terms of the 'war' element, but very much also in terms of 'communism'. (Though there were differences within the party regarding the speed at which communism would be achieved.)[20]

Lenin's (private) correspondences in May regarding the food situation were strikingly violent and desperate. He urged the Food Commissar, Aleksandr Tsiurupa, to recognize the necessity of forming an army of 20,000 Petrograd workers 'for a disciplined and ruthless *military* crusade against the rural bourgeoisie', and the Labour Commissar, Aleksandr Shliapnikov, to go to the grain-rich Kuban 'to help pump out grain from there.'[21] Most striking was his telegram of 31 May to workers in Vyiksa, near Nizhni Novgorod, approving their 'excellent plan of a mass movement with machine-guns to obtain grain', with the reservation that the detachment should be formed of 'selected reliable people' to avoid abuses.[22] Such a strikingly militarized approach to a domestic problem, against the civilian peasant population, suggests the Soviet state's practice of total war 'internally, in its efforts to forge a revolutionary society.'[23] This reflected the blurring of distinctions between internal and external foes encapsulated in Lenin's idea of converting the war into a series of civil wars, and indeed his militarized conception of revolution.

Lenin was ambiguous about the extent of support for Soviet power in the countryside. Speaking at a labour gathering he even declared that 'We can count on the politically conscious workers alone; the remaining mass, the bourgeoisie and the petty proprietors, are against us'.[24] In early June to a broader audience he appeared confident that 'the masses' of Russian peasants and workers were in favour of Soviet power.[25] Not surprisingly the frequent heavy-handedness and brutalities of the food detachments and *kombedy* led to peasant hostility toward

Communist rule and the outbreak of revolts and uprisings, as the Bolshevik agrarian expert Vasilii Kuraev would starkly acknowledge at the Party Congress in March 1919.[26]

With the Czechoslovak Legion mutiny along the Trans-Siberian railway and the outbreak of Civil War proper, Lenin reflected on the course of the revolution. The Czechoslovak revolt was, he thought 'obviously being supported by Anglo-French imperialism', and the Civil War was in essence a battlefield of the wider European conflict.[27] In July he explicitly grouped struggle with kulaks, Russian capitalists and foreign imperialists into the same category, that 'the present aggravation of the Soviet Republic's international position is connected with the aggravation of the class struggle at home', and that therefore 'The whole question of the […] Russian socialist revolution has been reduced to a question of war.'[28] The disasters facing Russia were 'international disasters' and could only be solved through world revolution.[29] The revolution in Russia confirmed, he thought, that the nearer the toilers came to their victory the greater the resistance of the exploiters. He acknowledged that the desperate situation inevitably led some sections of the toilers to attack the socialist government, to welcome the Czechoslovak troops 'because of the famine.' Popular consciousness of the necessity for a socialist polity could not be expected at once but would only arrive 'at the end of the struggle.' Lenin was sympathetic to the plight of the peasants, considering it understandable that speculative proclivities should manifest in a country where the peasant was not used to sowing grain on his own land. In this way he pointed to the nefarious, corrupting counter-revolutionary influence of the 'rich peasants, capitalists and imperialists', and justified struggle against these. Nevertheless he considered that a toiling peasant who held onto his grain for a higher price on the black market 'cannot be called a working peasant, he becomes transformed into an exploiter, into someone worse than a robber.'[30]

This confusion persisted in Lenin's rhetoric through the Civil War – speculative peasants were detestable enemies of the people and yet victims of the culture that had spawned them. They appeared at once 'lost' to the revolution and yet eminently salvable through re-education by a class-conscious working class leadership. His analysis was based on his belief that the 'last decisive struggle' was underway, a struggle effectively for the very 'soul' of the Russian people. This convinced him of the necessity of not giving way on grain policy but of waging the war with more class-conscious foot soldiers. He acknowledged that the food detachments were engaged in armed conflicts with the peasants but reasoned that when larger detachments with more class-conscious workers were involved, 'the peasants gave their grain without a single case of violence.' The conclusion that he drew was that if the poor were approached more intelligently, they could be better organized against their real enemies, the rural rich.[31] In fact, despite the extremity of his rhetoric, he thought that in this way grain could be extracted even from the kulaks without armed force.[32]

Demonstrating a 'Time of Troubles' perspective, Lenin once again condemned those moderate socialists who hoped for a revolution that would 'drop from heaven' and not be born with the 'particularly severe' birth-pangs of a revolution arising 'on earth soaked in the blood of four years of imperialist butchery of the peoples.' He justified the 'inevitable severity of the measures' taken to deal with the crises consequent upon the war, presumably even when directed against poor peasants, for 'while individuals [sic] may die in the act of childbirth, the new society to which the old system gives birth cannot die.'[33]

These strands of thought were largely brought together in a speech to a joint session of the Moscow Soviet, the trade unions and VTsIK on 4 June, in which Lenin's narrative stressed the disastrous effects of the imperialist war on Russia and the need for a 'just and sacred war', a 'violent civil war', against imperialism.[34] War, he declared, had accustomed people to settling issues by force, it was 'remoulding people's habits'. Hence to think that the war could be overcome in any way other than civil war, or that socialism could ever come except through civil war, 'is more than strange.'[35] Yes, Lenin accepted, the 'bag-traders' were helping to feed the starving population, but 'along kulak lines [...] to establish, strengthen and perpetuate the power of the kulaks.' Moderate socialists, food supply experts and workers 'led astray' who encouraged the raising of grain prices or even freedom in grain trade were, he thought, in effect trying to help the kulaks to profit from the grain crisis. 'That path we shall never take' he promised; his hostility to any freedom of trade in the essential grain supply appeared absolute.[36] Yes, the food detachments had committed terrible abuses, but 'the working class is not separated by a Chinese wall from the old bourgeois society [...] When the old society perishes [...] the corpse rots and infects us.' The 'New Man' could not be created immediately, but this was no reason to suspend the state's drive towards socialism. He appealed to the workers to 'sanctify and legitimize our food war, our war against the kulaks', to establish 'the distinction between the poor and the rich, which every peasant can understand and which is a profound source of our strength.'[37] Lenin's solution was to fall back on the fundamentals of his class-war mobilization approach to solve the economic and organizational crises facing Russia, to establish strong central state authority and, though prepared to grant 'awards' to poor peasants who fulfilled their duties, he unequivocally stated that against the kulaks 'we shall use force.'[38]

In early August the state began to move (or 'retreat') towards a more restrained system of food supply, the *razverstka* (apportionment), which was formally introduced in January. Lenin acquiesced to the raising of grain prices, though also of the prices of industrial goods. The grain monopoly was supposed to be relaxed under the *razverstka*, as the state now aimed to fulfill a specific required grain target levied by individual districts rather than simply confiscate each peasant's surplus. In practice the levies established from above were excessive and ensured that food stocks and seed that peasants could not afford to relinquish were often forcibly removed. Yet from August the state sought to appease, to 'neutralize' the 'middle' peasants – smallholders between kulaks and the poorest peasants – and to curb the excessive class war terminology of the summer. The kulak remained the enemy, if now more exclusively defined, and force was still to be applied against him, but the overall emphasis was upon restraint in this regard.[39] The difficulty was how to define the 'kulak', for the peasants tried to withhold as much grain as they could. The threat to the regime was particularly acute in August and the grain-rich Volga region was cut off from Red territory. Lenin, still demanding that districts be 'swept clean' of surpluses, instructed Tsiurupa on 10 August to draft a decree designating '25 to 30 hostages from among the rich in each grain-producing volost' answering with their *lives* for the collection and delivery of all surpluses'.[40] He was keen to determine exactly how much grain should be collected from each region; his logic was that estimates should be based on the results of grain-deliveries of exemplary regions and districts.[41]

Food procurement was a most difficult problem for successive Russian governments from 1916 and for much of the twentieth century, for which there does not appear to have been a simple solution. Peasant suspicion of outside forces and unwillingness to make sacrifices for the sake of urban workers would have to be overcome. Revoking fixed prices and simply relying on a free market would not have solved the problem. The Bolshevik approach was certainly not the optimal solution. The detachments did indeed manage to procure grain through force – though transporting it presented considerable problems – but the lack of market incentive and sufficient manufactured goods resulted in a reduction of the sown acreage.[42] Furthermore, the violence of the Bolshevik approach proved politically counter-productive, as it did for their various civil war opponents.

In July and August Lenin was acutely aware of the spread of peasant revolts against Soviet power,[43] largely in response to the abuses and brutalities of armed detachments and Cheka units. In 32 provinces in 1918, there were 258 uprisings.[44] He was also well aware of Cheka abuses from the 'daily' complaints received by the party,[45] and he encouraged shooting those responsible for the abuses of food detachments.[46] The Bolsheviks conveniently conceived these revolts as 'kulak' revolts, meaning at least that the kulaks were the 'ringleaders', a perception undoubtedly fed by Cheka reports from the countryside[47] despite the fact that the revolting communities were largely united in opposition.[48] Conflating external and internal enemies, and pointing to the phenomenon of 'White' terror, Lenin reasoned that 'if the kulaks were to gain the upper hand they would ruthlessly slaughter hundreds of thousands of workers'. That was why 'we call the fight against the kulaks the last, decisive fight.'[49] The significance of such rhetorical conflation of enemies was, as Scott Smith explains, that the Bolsheviks were attempting to monopolize revolutionary discourse and discredit all opposition to their rule by associating such opposition with bourgeois counter-revolution. They were acting both out of genuine ideological conviction regarding the objective correlation of class relations, polarized between the side of the proletariat and the bourgeoisie, but also – certainly towards the socialist opposition – out of dissimulation.[50] In response to the 'kulak revolts', Lenin's 'Manichean' outlook and language of class war and hatred were clear:

> Either the kulaks massacre vast numbers of workers, or the workers ruthlessly suppress the revolt of the predatory kulak minority [...] There can be no middle course. Peace is out of the question [...] Ruthless war on the kulaks! Death to them! Hatred and contempt for the parties which defend them.[51]

His estimation was that of 15 million peasant families in Russia, about two million constituted the 'kulak minority', about three million 'middle' peasants, and about 10 million poor peasant families who survived by selling their labour or without grain surpluses. By 1919 he acknowledged that the majority were in fact 'middle' peasants.

The suppression of the revolts in Penza, a crucially important food supply province for the Bolsheviks in 1918, is the best-known since the publication of an infamous telegram in the 1990s. The Penza revolt broke out on 5 August and spread to a number of districts in the province. Lenin directed local communists to 'carry out a campaign of ruthless mass terror against the kulaks, priests and Whiteguards'. Those suspected of being involved were to be 'shut up in a detention camp outside the city' (concentration camps appeared in July 1918). He demanded to be kept informed immediately of fulfillment.[52] The next day, he instructed that part of the Red Army be sent to put down the rebellions, and that 'all the property of the kulaks and all their grain', not just their surpluses, be confiscated.[53] On 11 August he dispatched two telegrams to Penza. The first pointed out that the uprising must be suppressed in order to clear grain surpluses and that 'all measures' were permitted. Hostages were to be designated in each district from the kulaks and the wealthy, who would 'answer with their lives' for the precise and speedy delivery of the required surpluses determined by the levels 'of previous years.' Reflecting Marx's justification of the execution of hostages by the Communards during the Paris Commune of 1871, Lenin assured his Penza comrades that responsibility for the lives of the hostages lay with the kulaks and the wealthy.[54] The second, 'infamous' telegram was quite brutal and advocated exemplary terror. This brutality was to be justified, once again, because the 'last decisive battle' was taking place. In addition to designating hostages, he now urged that no fewer than 100 'known kulaks, rich men, bloodsuckers' be hanged 'without fail, *so the people see* [...], thrill [*trepetal*], know, shout: they are strangling and will strangle the bloodsucking kulaks.'[55] The mass of peasants was thus to become cognizant of the distinction between the peasant poor and the enemy kulaks, and encouraged by the swift class justice of the regime (and, one can imagine, frightened into abandoning any common cause with the 'kulaks'). To carry this out, Lenin suggested that the Penza comrades find 'some truly hard people.' In fact, the uprising was largely put down on 12 August by means of agitation and limited application of force. Thirteen of the organizers of the revolts were shot.[56] Lenin was evidently disturbed by the lack of concrete information reaching him about actual measures taken, and he was concerned that the local authorities were being too 'soft.'[57]

Red Terror

The publication of Lenin's Penza telegram should not have surprised the reader of his *Collected Works*, though the violence prescribed was expounded more starkly. If the Penza communists were not inclined to implement fully Lenin's advocacy of mass terror, in some other places local commanders often went further than would appear to have been sanctioned from above. The implementation of terror in individual localities typically varied according to particular local circumstances and local leaders.[58] On 20 August, upon learning of the suppression of a 'kulak' revolt in another area, Livny, Lenin urged the local authorities to 'hang the ringleaders.'[59] Following the capture of the town, over 300 people were shot by Red forces.[60] Vecheka reports from the countryside provided a figure of 2,452 executions in the course of the suppression of uprisings in 31 provinces in 1918; but one historian has found an NKVD statistic of 15,000 killed in the course of suppressing uprisings in July and August alone,[61] which appears a more realistic figure. Indeed, a veritable civil war was being waged by the government with the peasantry at precisely the time when the frontal Civil War raged in the Volga and the South.

The expulsion of the Mensheviks and SRs from VTsIK on 14 June was accompanied by closures of their newspapers and the bloody suppression of workers' strikes by Cheka units.[62] Lenin's justification of these suppressions at a trade union conference on 27 June is especially instructive. His reasoning centred on a distinction between the working class as a whole and a 'small strata of the working class', rejecting the charge of moderate socialists that the state was at war with the workers. He observed that the 'overwhelming majority of the working class of Russia' was on the Soviet side, but 'It is quite a different matter that there is an insignificant group of workers still in slavish dependence upon the bourgeoisie.' If those 'insignificant groups which are still in alliance with the bourgeoisie' were hurt in the process of intense class struggle, they would 'have only themselves to blame.'[63] This drew applause from the mainly Bolshevik trade unionists attending. Once again a single proletarian will and a single representative vanguard of that will was assumed, and state violence and coercion even against the working classes was considered justified, for 'chips would fly in cutting down the wood.' By September, with official Red Terror underway, Lenin would openly accept the necessity of waging 'class war' against 'the groups and sections of workers who stubbornly cling to capitalist traditions and continue to regard the Soviet state in the old way: work as little and as badly as they can and grab as much money as possible from the state.' (It was likely that such workers were trying to procure food or had not been paid their wages). Though merely 'a few' of the working class as a whole, he considered that there were 'many such scoundrels' who needed to be 'crushed with an iron hand.'[64]

The main phase of the Civil War had begun on 26 May when Czechoslovak Legion soldiers passing through Russia were disarmed along the Trans-Siberian railway and revolted, capturing Cheliabinsk. By 8 June they had reached Samara and agreed to bolster a rival SR–dominated government, the Committee of Members of the Constituent Assembly (Komuch). In Omsk, Siberia, a liberal–SR coalition government was set up. In September these two anti-Bolshevik administrations would form a Provisional Government, led by a five-person Directorate in Omsk that would be overthrown in November by a rightist coup that installed Admiral Kolchak as Dictator in opposition to the socialist programme of Komuch. By August the 40,000-strong Legion had captured the entire Trans-Siberian railway, and the Czechoslovakian troops allowed Komuch power to spread through much of the grain-rich Volga region, presenting Moscow with serious military and food supply problems. The Allies, Britain in particular, soon realized the benefit of the Czech revolt and of Komuch and supported their efforts, landing troops in Murmansk and Arkhangel'sk in the North and Vladivostok in the East. (British policy, certainly before Brest–Litovsk, had not been essentially anti-Bolshevik. Rather, its priority was to support a Russian government that would renew war with the Central Powers,[65] and secure allied military supplies from German capture). On 8 August Czechoslovak forces captured Kazan, and Nizhni Novgorod along the Volga stood between them and Iaroslavl', north of Moscow.[66]

Lenin's response to the Czech revolt came in a Sovnarkom appeal to the people on 10 June. The 'enemies of the people', he began, were making a last, desperate attempt to return power to the wealthy. The workers and peasants hated their old oppressors, so the Russian bourgeoisie were resorting to support from 'another camp', the Czechoslovaks, controlled by French imperialists. Lenin included the full text of an appeal from the Omsk government to Sovnarkom, laying out its intentions of convoking the Constituent Assembly in Siberia, and offering to supply food to the Bolsheviks on condition that the latter respect the territorial limits of the Siberian government. Lenin dismissed its sincerity, refusing to enter into any negotiations with counter-revolutionaries who were allegedly 'strangling' Siberian workers and peasants and threatening Soviet workers with hunger so as to link up with counter-revolutionaries in the Urals. His practical recommendations were designed to strike pre-emptively at any future counter-revolutionary outbreaks, appealing to all in Sovdepia (central Russia under Soviet control) to exercise close vigilance over the local bourgeoisie, and promising 'severe punishment' for those found to be involved in plots. Regarding the threat of former military officers, the 'honest' ones in Soviet service were to be accorded full personal security, but those involved in nefarious activities were to be 'mercilessly exterminated [*istrebliat'sia*].'[67]

The dictatorial and repressive policies of the Soviet state increased in summer 1918. The Vecheka had practiced relatively limited extra-judicial executions – mainly of criminals – largely because the Left SRs were represented on its Collegium and unanimous decisions were required for death sentences.[68] Once the Left SRs were removed from the Collegium following an attempted Left SR 'uprising' in Moscow in early July, the Vecheka received a freer hand. The death penalty was re-instated for judicial sentences on 16 June by the Bolshevik Commissar for Justice, Piotr Stuchka, and the revolutionary tribunals were empowered to hand down death sentences against political enemies. Lenin's had been one of the voices calling for sharper judicial punishments since early May, and against Left SR opposition to the death penalty, he accused them of hypocrisy regarding their support of extra-judicial Cheka executions: 'when people are sentenced to be shot by Dzerzhinskii's commission [for ordinary criminality] it is all right, but if a court were to declare publicly and openly that a man was a counter-revolutionary and deserved to be shot, that would be wrong.'[69]

Under the impact of the Civil War and peasant uprisings, and motivated by some considerable measure of class hatred,[70] the Vecheka, local Chekas and other bodies were resorting to more extreme forms of safeguarding revolutionary order. This included the executions of 407 people following the suppression of an uprising organized in Iaroslavl' in July by a group led by Boris Savinkov and linked to the Right SRs, which had resulted in a campaign of 'White Terror' against local communists before its suppression. The regime was moving increasingly towards a system of preventive measures such as the widespread registration and accounting (and in places executions) of suspect elements of the population, especially former army officers.[71] The Vecheka also began to apply the death penalty much more frequently for political opposition.[72] One result of this increased move to more widespread terror was the executions of the Tsar's family in Ekaterinburg on 16 July, as the Czechs closed in on the city. There is reason to believe that this decision was taken in Moscow; Trotsky was told that Lenin considered it dangerous to leave the 'Whites' a living monarch to rally around.[73]

- Lenin's rhetoric of intensified terror in summer 1918 resulted from the combination of economic dislocation and these various civil wars, crises that were structured by ideology. The result was a heightened rhetoric of class warfare and the notion of the final and desperate struggle for the freedom of all peoples from the yoke of imperialist oppression. These were millenarian times for Lenin and the Bolsheviks. From late June, Lenin called for mass terror. The assassination of a leading Bolshevik in Petrograd, Volodarskii, led him to upbraid Zinoviev and the Petrograd Bolsheviks for allegedly restraining the workers from responding with mass terror, for preaching it but not implementing it. Lenin insisted that 'We must encourage the energy and mass character of the terror against the counter-revolutionaries, and particularly in Petrograd, the example of which is decisive.'[74] On 5 July the Fifth All-Russian Congress of Soviets, as a result of the reports of Lenin and Iakov Sverdlov, the Chairman of VTsIK, adopted a resolution calling for mass terror against the enemies of Soviet power.[75]

- The day after the Czechoslovak capture of Kazan, Lenin communicated with Nizhni Novgorod to encourage a campaign of mass terror – the shooting of prostitutes and deportation of Mensheviks – due to suspected preparations for a White Guard insurrection there.[76] During August, 101 people were executed in Nizhni by the Cheka, 76 of whom were accused of political crimes.[77] By the end of August, Trotsky's Red Army had managed to stabilize the situation on the Volga and launch a counter-offensive on Kazan, (by early October Samara itself, where Komuch was based, would fall to the Reds).[78] Lenin sent a telegram to Trotsky on 30 August stating that if there were an advantage at Kazan and the soldiers did not prove sufficiently energetic, it would be possible to apply 'the model of the French Revolution', to bring the commanders before court and even shoot them.[79]

- In the last fortnight of August, Lenin reflected on the necessity of terror and of expanding its use. In distinction to the bourgeois and socialist pacifists who opposed the bloodshed of the ongoing war, but 'cannot see its direct connection with the capitalist system', the Bolsheviks and revolutionary socialists alone were able to see that the end to bloodshed required the end of this system globally. In fact he warned that civil war in more 'civilized' countries would be 'far more brutal than in Russia [...] what a terrible fate awaits these civilized countries [...] there is no way out of the imperialist holocaust except by civil war'.[80] This, he explained, was because in Russia the experience of autocracy and of earlier revolutionary upheaval had allowed for a more decisive shift to the Left on the part of several Russian parties.

It was in a letter to American workers, published in *Pravda* on 22 August, that Lenin provided his foremost justification for terror and indeed its further escalation. Those who blamed the Bolsheviks for the collapse of industry and the terror, he alleged, were hypocrites and pedants who revealed 'an inability to understand the basic conditions of the fierce class struggle, raised to the highest degree of intensity that is called revolution.' Reflecting the logic of class warfare and violence in his thought since 1905, and taking aim at socialist opponents, he reasoned that:

> Even when 'accusers' of this type do 'recognize' the class struggle, they limit themselves to verbal recognition; actually, they constantly slip into the philistine utopia of class 'agreement' and 'collaboration'; for in revolutionary epochs the class struggle has always, inevitably, and in every country, assumed the form of *civil war*, and civil war is inconceivable without the severest destruction, terror and the restriction of formal democracy in the interests of this war. [81]

Those 'unctuous parsons – whether Christian or "secular"', could not understand the necessity of brutal civil war, necessary because the revolution engendered by the war 'can not avoid the terrible difficulties and suffering bequeathed it'. They were, therefore, effectively on the side of the bourgeoisie ('hangers-on of the bourgeoisie'), the same bourgeoisie that had reduced Europe to 'barbarism, brutality and starvation' and now insisted that the foundations of a new society could not be built from these ruins and with people who had been brutalized by the war. He attacked their hypocrisy:

> How humane and righteous the bourgeoisie are! [...] The British have forgotten their 1649, the French bourgeoisie have forgotten their 1793. Terror was just and legitimate when the bourgeoisie resorted to it for their own benefit against feudalism. Terror became monstrous and criminal when the workers and the poorest peasants dared to use it against the bourgeoisie!'

The necessity was he believed not to attempt to reduce bloodshed and suffering immediately but, rather, to plunge into battle 'with the utmost ardour and determination at a time when history demands that the greatest problems of humanity be solved by struggle and war.' The truth, he continued, was that 'no revolution can be successful unless *the resistance of the exploiters is crushed* [...] We are proud we have been doing this. We regret we are not doing it with sufficient firmness and determination.'[82]

Terror was for Lenin, then, 'immanent in the dialectics of revolution and counter-revolution.'[83] The world of his times was characterized by violence, and it was obvious to him by autumn 1918 that terror was an essential means of solving deep-rooted political, social and economic problems.[84] He clearly believed in the creative, progressive, regenerative function of 'revolutionary' violence, and once again utilized the powerful trope of a rotting corpse to explain and justify the 'mistakes' committed along the way. Capitalism was disintegrating in a bloody mess and the workers and peasants would need to 'hack a path to victorious socialism' despite the pollutions afflicting them from this corpse. By learning from the experience of their mistakes they would arrive at something life-affirming: socialism.

This was the apogee of Lenin's defence and advocacy of revolutionary state violence and terror. It followed the logic of his thought since 1914, even 1905, fuelled by the ravages of war, revolution and counter-revolution. It sought legitimation in the actions of previous 'bourgeois' revolutionaries, and justification against the evils of the bourgeoisie most forcefully expressed in the brutalities of the imperialist war. The imperialist bourgeoisie 'have slaughtered 10 million men and maimed 20 million' to decide which of the 'vultures' would rule the world, but if 'our war […] results in half a million or a million casualties in all countries, the bourgeoisie will say that the former casualties are justified, while the latter are criminal.'[85] Lenin was determined that the capitalists would reap what they had sown in 1914, and was convinced that 'Bolshevik tactics' alone were 'capable of saving dying culture and dying mankind.'[86]

The assassination of Moisei Uritskii, head of the Petrograd Cheka, and another attempt on Lenin's life on the same day, 30 August, led to the official declaration of Red Terror on 5 September 1918. Members of the SRs had prepared the attack on Lenin, but the party's Central Committee had not approved it. However in a note to Dzerzhinskii written before he was shot after hearing news of Uritskii's assassination, Lenin made clear that the political benefits of the alleged connection of the SRs was to be maximized: 'it is especially important that there is an official certification of a link between the shooters and the party of socialist revolutionaries.'[87] The Red Terror was a period of brutal terror as official state policy against real and perceived enemies of Soviet power, a terror both 'punitive and preventive.'[88] By resorting to such terror the Bolsheviks were both compensating for the lack of adequate popular measures to crush the revolution's enemies, and attempting to mobilize popular support for this cause. The *Vecheka Weekly*, the Vecheka's publication during the Terror, highlighted the need for a powerful organization to counteract and 'compete' with White Guard conspirators who had succeeded in organizing popular revolts against Soviet power in those regions where there were 'strong kulak elements and comparatively weak working peasant ones.' The struggle against counter-revolution, it made clear, could only be successful if the working masses joined with the Chekas in their efforts.[89] The Bolsheviks sought 'to inform workers and peasants of the nature of operational means of their "class and political enemies"', as the *Weekly* expounded in its mission statement. That is, they wished to generate popular support for their vision of revolution as Manichean class warfare, as opposed to the messages from moderate socialists.[90] In the words of one historian who stresses the significance of the accompanying rhetoric, the Terror was an 'ideological performance'.[91]

Terror was certainly the regime's desperate attempt to hold onto power, by whatever means necessary.[92] Power was not an end in itself but necessary according to Marx's injunction that the working class needed to assume state power and retain it, however accurate may have been the charge of their Marxist detractors that they were attempting to introduce socialism in a country not ready for it. In the literature on early Soviet state violence the period of official Red Terror typically appears not as a distinct phenomenon but merely a continuation, extension and legalization of previously existing policy.[93] This is often presented as a de-contextualized reading of the evidence, particularly of Lenin's statements.[94] George Leggett believes that the Terror resulted from Lenin's logic of class struggle, from his 'doctrine of terror, preached and practiced since October as an integral part of his unrelenting pursuit of power.'[95]

There have been remarkably few serious and lengthy studies of the Terror. The Russian historian Il 'ia Rat 'kovskii has recently helped to fill this considerable lacuna, as has Alexander Rabinowitch in his account of the origins and course of the Terror in Petrograd.[96] Rat 'kovskii insists on understanding the Red Terror as a distinct period with a precise time-frame: 5 September to 6 November 1918 (concluding with the declaration of an amnesty by the Congress of Soviets). Terror had intensified over the summer, especially in August, but there was not yet a fully nationwide, systematized terror as policy controlled principally by the Vecheka.[97] Such systematized control by this central institution was designed to give the Terror a more organized form. Importantly, Rat 'kovskii's work has highlighted the impact of White Terror on Bolshevik discourse in 1918. 'White Terror' he defines as 'any action directed against Soviet power' classified as terror. This does not distinguish between the activities of the SRs/Czechoslovaks and the non-socialist 'Whites' who were natural opponents of the SRs as well as the Bolsheviks. Indeed, as we have seen, the Bolsheviks conflated their various opponents into a single category, and such usage of 'White Terror' reflects this Manichean conception. The extent of this terror, however, was considerable in the spring–summer of 1918.[98]

Terror was not the essence of the Soviet system or of Lenin's conception of dictatorship. Soviet repressive policies evolved over the first year of power. Using the historian's beneficial hindsight, however, one can see some element of truth in the contention that terror was inscribed in the logic of October, even if Lenin did not envisage this at the time. Lenin's theory and practice since assuming power were explicitly and, he believed, necessarily socially abrasive and belligerent, and when faced with acute difficulties over the first year of power he exhibited a particular predilection for conflict and violence. Regarding Lenin's personal role, he was the leader of Party and state and a highly theoretical politician. His voice was certainly a significant one in introducing the Terror, though not sufficient alone. He had called for 'mass terror' in June, July and August and yet, as Rat 'kovskii has shown, mass terror was only sporadically conducted by Cheka organs, mainly by the central Vecheka and on the Eastern Front, until late August. (This does not capture the extent of violence in the countryside resulting from armed peasant uprisings and their suppression).

Rabinowitch notes that the directive for the Terror did not simply emanate from Moscow; in Petrograd, the Bolshevik Committee had initiated a policy of mass terror without waiting for Sovnarkom's direction. The Terror was the result of the civil wars being waged, foreign intervention, the perceived threat and very real fear of a full-scale assault on Soviet power from domestic and foreign opponents,[99] allied to a particular millenarian vision, a language of intense class warfare, and a theoretical justification (indeed effective sanctification) of terror in the course of revolution. It was also due to the gradual eclipse of more moderate voices such as, ironically, Uritskii's as head of the Petrograd Cheka. Corresponding to this was a certain radical-socialist consensus that at least increased repressions, some form of terror-revenge, were necessary. The almost-fatal assassination attempt once again on Lenin, and the assassination of Uritskii, provided the sparks that finally caught fire. Even Lev Kamenev, who would soon call for curtailing the terror, advocated increased repressions in early September.[100] On 1 September *Izvestiia* carried a Left SR (internationalist) resolution which lauded revolutionary intransigence and condemned the terrorists as bourgeois counter-revolutionaries. It declared that the working masses must reply with blows against the forces of Russian and foreign capital, that it recognized 'terror as one of the means for struggle of the toilers against the imperialists', and ended with the slogan 'Long live the red terror against all imperialists and hangers-on of the bourgeoisie.' Similarly, the SR Maximalists warned against any 'faint-heartedness' amongst 'revolutionary fighters'.[101]

The Bolshevik reaction to the terrorist attacks of 30 August was instant and extreme. The headline on *Pravda* the following day read: 'The arms of the Right SRs of Russia and the united capitalists wish to remove the head from the workers' revolution. The proletariat will answer by organized mass terror and redoubling of strength at the front. The class murderer, the bourgeoisie, must be crushed.'[102] Sverdlov, expressing no doubt that SRs (and by extension the 'English and French') would be found responsible, cautioned against popular lynch law and appealed to the public for calm to organize 'greater unity of military force' so that the proletariat could answer 'with merciless mass terror against all enemies of the revolution.'[103] The *Pravda* editorial on 31 August specifically warned the Mensheviks and (Right) SRs, officers and saboteurs. This was a struggle that would affect every facet of society, it would be a final and decisive struggle with the class enemy, wherever he or she lurked, 'on the front and in the rear, in the countryside and towns, on the streets *and in homes*' [emphasis added].

Warning the bourgeoisie that 'We have sufficient of your hostages', *Pravda* warned 'In war – as in war.' The response of the proletariat would be disproportionate, for 'To the small, petty, individual terror on us, the worker class will reply with mass, merciless, class terror, of which you cannot yet imagine.' The situation was stark: 'Workers! The time has begun, when either you must destroy the bourgeoisie, or it will destroy you. Be ready for mass, merciless assaults.' The Bolsheviks appeared to be calling for terror against the bourgeoisie as a class, suggesting that the towns needed to be cleansed of 'bourgeois rot'. The editorial clarified however that 'It is necessary to account for *all* bourgeois gentlemen, as you did with the officers, and terminate all, *dangerous* for the affairs of the revolution [my emphases].' The 'hymn' of the working class would 'henceforth be a hymn of hatred and revenge.' Suggesting the de-humanization of the targets of terror, *Pravda* wrote of the 'rabid dog' of counter-revolution that must be killed once and for all.[104] Later on, a leading Chekist, Martin Latsis, outlined the emancipatory, cleansing purpose of terror intended to 'shake off forever the yoke of capital, to destroy class society and with it the bourgeoisie.' Latsis sounded criticism of the state's supposed soft-heartedness heretofore, of the notion that the 'enemy' would be won over 'by our graciousness and humanism.' Hence the necessity for steeled hearts amongst revolutionaries and the working masses, and he justified the Terror as an enforced decision against those enemies who had proven irreconcilable.[105]

In 1996 historian Richard Pipes published an undated note from Lenin that he estimated to have been written on 3 or 4 September, secretly ordering the preparation of the Terror. The editors of a Russian volume of documents subsequently dated this note sometime before 22 February 1921, noting that Lenin did not engage in political activity so soon after being shot.[106] On 5 September Sovnarkom officially adopted mass terror, to be centrally organized by and entrusted primarily to the Vecheka.[107] That the more ruthless and efficient Chekas directed the Terror through their three- and five-person boards, not the revolutionary tribunals as during the French Reign of Terror in 1793 to 1794, suggested, as Matt Rendle puts it, that the regime had for now adopted 'revolutionary terror over revolutionary justice.'[108] Class enemies were to be isolated in concentration camps and all persons concerned in any way with 'whiteguard organisations, conspiracies or uprisings' were to be shot, and notices of such shootings were to be carried in the press. Such notices in the *Vecheka Weekly* attest to the fact that Chekas utilized their powers of execution widely, continuing to execute persons for regular criminality and theft of food, as well as for such activities as 'agitation against Soviet power' and service in the Tsarist regime.[109] In a directive of 2 September the Vecheka ordered the arrests of prominent Mensheviks and SRs, and instructed that bourgeois hostages be taken from amongst the bourgeoisie, clergy and questionable officers; the execution of anyone in Cheka custody who had been in possession of firearms or explosive equipment; and executions of members of the Tsarist gendarmerie.[110] The Chekists were determined to implement terror 'not only in words, as it was before, but in deeds.'[111] In the immediate aftermath of the attempt on Lenin's life, before official announcement of the Terror, 512 arrested hostages were executed in Petrograd and 5,000 more 'bourgeois representatives' were arrested.[112]

Estimates of the total number of executed victims of the Terror vary. Rat'kovskii puts the figure at 8,000 for the period from 30 August until the end of the year, Nicolas Werth at between 10 and 15,000.[113] The majority of the Terror's targets were former Tsarist officers and representatives of the Tsarist regime. In addition the Terror struck against thieves, priests, intellectuals and political activists, and the urban and rural bourgeoisie who were usually held hostage or subjected to various financial punishments. There was also a small portion of worker and peasant victims.[114] The distinction between military and civilian fronts was effectively eradicated with the VTsIK decision of 2 September to convert the country into a 'single military camp'. S. S. Kamenev, Main Commander-in-Chief of the Red Army, noted that through the Civil War Lenin maintained that the country was 'a military machine', with barely any distinction between front and rear.[115]

What, then, was the nature of the Terror? It was intended to excise, to 'cut out' all enemies of the revolution who had proven incorrigible thus far, but in essence it bore a class character, with its victims selected (especially in the days before official declaration of the Terror) not simply 'on the basis of defined criminality, but on the basis of belonging to a defined class', and especially to social position in Tsarist times.[116] It was consequently quite indiscriminate within this broad social categorization. During and after the Civil War, Soviet state violence resulted from security concerns combined with an aesthetic drive to cleanse society of those who would not be transformed. Was one considered 'dangerous' by virtue of one's previous profession or wealth, or by more subjective factors such as one's associations, activities and mental disposition as the decree of 5 September distinguished? This is a particularly interesting aspect of the Terror, and important for comparison with the rhetoric and practices of Stalinist terror. One Chekist in the first edition of the *Vecheka Weekly* called for death to 'thousands' of 'useless', 'irreconcilable' (*neprimirimyi*) enemies of socialist Russia. This article provides a fascinating example of the Bolshevik, in particular Chekist, eschatological and moralistic approach to the Terror. Referring to the slaughter of the Great War, and employing authentic Leninist logic in this regard, he wrote that in this way 'we will save millions of workers, we will save the socialist revolution.' This would be truly humanist terror, because 'we value and love life too much – it is a sacred gift of nature', but the bourgeoisie were slowly draining the 'juices of life' from the proletariat. The 'wheel of history' had turned and in place of the imperialist slaughter there would be 'merciless struggle, not excluding the death penalty, against all irreconcilable enemies of the Russian workers and peasants.' The sword, he concluded, would not be laid down until the sun of socialism would shine.[117] Yet in the same edition another Chekist suggested a different approach. Reacting to an article in *Izvestiia* that dismissed the 'uselessness' of 'individual terror', he agreed with the article that the bourgeoisie needed to be destroyed as a class over a period of time by depriving them of their economic means, but defended the Terror as 'a temporary, exceptional measure.' He also emphasized that its targets were 'inveterate' enemies but his understanding of such appeared narrower, referring not to 'thousands' but the 'individuals and even groups' of the bourgeois 'oligarchy' engaged in active struggle, of not 'voluntarily' submitting to Soviet power.[118]

Later in the year Lenin addressed the question of indiscriminate class terror in connection with a remark on 1 November of a leading Chekist, Martin Latsis. Writing in the organ of the Czechoslovakian Front Cheka, Latsis had opined that Chekists should not search for evidence of a suspect's wrongdoing but, rather, the 'essence of Red Terror' was that a suspect's fate should be determined by their class.[119] Lenin described this as taking the Vecheka's role to 'absurd lengths', that terror was required only for 'the forcible suppression of exploiters who attempted to restore their rule.'[120] This question reflected the tension and confusion surrounding the life-and-death struggle between two irreconcilable camps (bourgeoisie and proletariat) that Lenin had encouraged since the revolution, the necessity of employing ever greater repressive measures not just to punish crime and counter-revolution but to prevent them, and yet the need to use the bourgeoisie to help construct socialism. Such tension was especially true regarding former army officers who were being recruited for the Red Army and yet also targeted by the Terror; notices of their executions in the *Vecheka Weekly* tended to point to specific counter-revolutionary charges against the individuals concerned.

To physically annihilate the bourgeoisie as a class was certainly not something that a Marxist could support. Rather, attaining supreme political power, the proletariat should be able to keep the bourgeoisie in check and ultimately transform this stratum in the process of abolishing class distinctions. The bourgeoisie would be removed as a class by political and socio-economic measures: confiscating their assets, putting them to socially-useful work, and applying punishment, up to the death penalty in cases of aggravated resistance or counter-revolution. Changes in the economic base and socio-political structure would lead to transformations in mentality, in culture. Highlighting the importance of the security considerations of the Terror, one leading Bolshevik, Nikolai Osinskii wrote in *Pravda* that 'From the dictatorship of the proletariat over the bourgeoisie we went to extreme terror – a system of destruction of the bourgeoisie as a class.' However like Lenin he opined that this should not mean 'the physical extermination of all the bourgeoisie'; he thought that execution was necessary only for those involved in active struggle against Soviet power. Registration and categorization he recommended for the bourgeoisie as a whole, reiterating that assault on their economic basis would serve to 'castrate' that 'breed of people.'[121] This would be a lengthy process, but in the heat of Civil War, foreign and domestic encirclement, economic crises and terrorist attacks, could the Bolsheviks afford to carefully sift truly irreconcilable from reconcilable enemies?

These tensions were reflected during the Red Terror, which was a 'temporary' and 'exceptional' two-month period. Ultimately Lenin did not support indiscriminate executions of the bourgeoisie as a class, and the predominant party discourse on the Terror seems to have accepted executions primarily for 'inveterate' enemies, despite the apparently differing interpretations of that adjective. Confinement in concentration camps and hostage-taking, however, were certainly intended to be quite indiscriminate. Hostages were to answer with their lives, and in many cases did, for activities for which they had no responsibility. In any case Lenin's article criticizing Latsis was not published until 1926.[122]

The purpose of the Terror was, through a campaign of mass annihilation but principally intimidation, control and terrorization, to intensify the work of decisively defeating the bourgeoisie as a class and as a serious threat to Soviet power; to enforce loyalty to the new regime and its vision of class struggle;[123] and to reduce potential internal opposition in the event of an invasion of Soviet-held territory (as later in 1937–8). This did not mean a genocidal destruction of the bourgeoisie, even though some Chekists seem effectively to have thought so. Violence, as Stathis Kalyvas notes, can be used both to control and to exterminate a social group.[124] In the Russian Civil War both forms were observed, though the principal and usual form was control (leading to the cessation of the bourgeoisie as a class). Yet it is difficult to disagree with George Leggett that it is not surprising 'that Chekists should take Lenin's doctrine of class conflict to the extreme conclusion of proposing the physical extermination of hostile classes, if the latter resisted the dictatorship of the proletariat.'[125]

By October there was increasing disquiet within the upper echelons of the party regarding the extent of the Terror, and increasing friction in the localities between the Chekas and other Soviet bodies. When an article published in the *Vecheka Weekly* by the Cheka of the town of Nolinsk lauded the use of torture, this attracted Lenin's attention and condemnation. On 25 October the Central Committee resolved to close the *Weekly* because of the article and the editorial sanction of it, which were 'harmful and contradictory to the interests of the struggle for communism', and formed a commission to regulate the Chekas but 'without weakening their struggle with counter-revolutionaries.'[126] By early November the party leadership recognized that the unregulated conduct of the Terror should be halted. By then the Civil War fronts appeared relatively stable. Komuch and the Czech Legion were defeated, the European War was finally being brought to a close, and Kolchak had not yet overthrown the Directory in Omsk and launched an offensive against Soviet power. In addition the critics of Terror within the party and soviet bodies were placing increasing pressures on the leadership to curtail its excesses.

On 2 November Lenin wrote that 'Legality must be raised.' One can imagine that the Bolsheviks as students of the French Revolution were keen to avoid the spiralling irrationality of terror in late 1793–4 after the immediate military threats to the revolution, the ostensible reason for the Terror, had abated. On 6 November, the eve of the first anniversary of the Revolution, the Extraordinary Sixth All-Russian Congress of Soviets declared that the 'worker-peasant power' was 'strengthened and consolidated' and announced an amnesty for political prisoners. Local organs of Soviet power were called upon to continue to apply merciless blows against traitors, conspirators, and White Guards 'and their organizations', but all those against whom charges of immediate involvement in conspiracy and counter-revolution could not be brought were to be amnestied, including all hostages not temporarily necessary for the safety of comrades in enemy hands (in reality, former Tsarist gendarmes and officials were not amnestied).[127]

The period of Red Terror, according to Rat'kovskii, ended at this point due to the increase in legality and the reduced number of victims.[128] This did not mean an end to terror. Lenin was by no means prepared to restrict the work of the Vecheka if and when extreme measures were required, if the corresponding organizations or 'responsible persons' formally declared that the 'extreme conditions of civil war and struggle with counter-revolution demand circumvention from the limits of the laws.'[129] On 20 November, in a *Pravda* article setting out a moderation of approach towards other socialist parties, Lenin noted that 'It would be ridiculous and foolish to refrain from employing terror against and suppressing the landowners and capitalists and their henchmen, who are selling Russia to the foreign imperialist "Allies"', for 'It would be farcical to attempt to "convince" or generally to "psychologically influence" them.'[130] The implication was that these upper strata were certainly irreconcilable to Soviet power. Red Terror continued along the Civil War fronts. On 26 November the Central Committee addressed a circular letter to all party members, commissars, commanders and Red Army men, in which it was stated that 'Red terror is now obligatory, wherever or whenever, on the Southern Front – not only against direct traitors and saboteurs, but against all cowards, self-seekers, connivers and receivers of stolen goods. No crime against discipline and the military revolutionary spirit should remain unpunished.' The Army command was not to stop before any sacrifices (*zhertvyi*) to achieve the lofty task falling now on the Red Army, to win the life and death struggle for the proletariat.[131] Within months the Civil War, and intensified terror, would flare up once again as Bolshevik rule would be confronted with its most serious military threat from the White counter-revolutionary armies of Admiral Kolchak and General Denikin.

With publicly conducted party debates regarding the future and purposes of the Vecheka, Lenin's appearance and address at a Vecheka rally on 7 November served to leave no doubt that the Chair of Sovnarkom supported the Vecheka in its continued work. He acknowledged the Chekas' mistakes but reasoned that these were to be expected and would serve an educative purpose:

> It is not surprising at all to hear Cheka's activities frequently attacked by friends as well as enemies. We have taken on a hard job. When we took over the government of the country, we naturally made mistakes, and it is only natural that the mistakes of the Extraordinary Commissions strike the eye most. The narrow-minded intellectual fastens on these mistakes without trying to get to the root of the matter [...] We, however, say that we learn from our mistakes.

However the learning that Lenin had in mind was 'self-criticism', not condemnation from within or outside the party.[132] The Vecheka's functions he pointed out 'demand determined, swift and, above all, faithful action.' Regarding the attacks on the institution, he remarked that 'this is all narrow-minded and futile talk' that reminded him of 'Kautsky's homily on the dictatorship, which is tantamount to supporting the bourgeoisie.'[133] Lenin was stretching the parameters of Marxist discourse. He argued that the sort of state terror practiced in Soviet Russia was the logical outcome of Marx's ideas, not only justifiable but necessary from a Marxist perspective, for the inevitably desperate resistance of the exploiters would not otherwise be defeated:

> Marx said that the revolutionary dictatorship of the proletariat lies between capitalism and communism. The more the proletariat presses the bourgeoisie, the more furiously they will resist. We know what vengeance was wreaked on

the workers in France in 1848. And when people charge us with harshness we wonder how they can forget the rudiments of Marxism [...] The realization of the need for dictatorship has taken deep root in the people's minds, arduous and difficult though it is [...] The important thing for us is that Cheka is directly exercising the dictatorship of the proletariat, and in that respect its services are invaluable. There is no way of emancipating the people except by forcibly suppressing the exploiters. That is what Cheka is doing, and therein lies its service to the proletariat.[134]

His language and logic were fundamentally the same as in 1905, but the meaning of 'forcibly suppressing the exploiters' now meant in practice something dramatically more violent. However a memoir account of an attendee at Lenin's speech mentions that, in addition to referring to the violent prophylactic functions of the Cheka, Lenin noted that Chekists should not always resort to repression but be engaged in the work of re-education 'in our proletarian spirit.'[135]

Less than a year after Lenin confidently stated that the Bolsheviks would not require the 'guillotine' to suppress their enemies, an official period of terror had been declared in Soviet Russia, accounting for thousands of lives. The actual counter-revolutionary underground had been considerably weakened,[136] but the Terror did not succeed in putting an end to revolts against the regime. The country continued to experience peasant uprisings into October and November of 1918 and beyond,[137] workers continued to strike in 1919, and counter-revolutionary organizations were to continue to appear in the heart of Red territory. The winter of 1918/19 was a time of internal party discussion on the future of the Vecheka and its status within the Soviet system, as it had become the state's instrument of choice for ensuring the security of Soviet power on the home front, but was still an 'extraordinary' commission. Soviet Russia would turn towards a greater sense of 'revolutionary legality' and the gradual institutionalization of the system of extraordinary revolutionary justice and terror.

6 Civil War

The strengthening of dictatorship, 1919

The Soviet Republic must become a single armed camp.[1]

(Lenin, 21 October 1919)

Over the winter of 1918–19 the Bolshevik Party turned its attention to creating a system of greater 'revolutionary legality'. Criticisms of the extent of the Terror and of the powers of the Vecheka were noticeable within the party and soviets from as early as September. 'Left' and 'Right' wing Bolsheviks such as Nikolai Bukharin, Lev Kamenev, Karl Radek, David Riazanov and M. S. Ol'minskii criticized both the fact that the Terror touched workers and poor peasants, and the effectively unregulated, all-powerful Chekas. There was also concern that recourse to executions to defeat the bourgeoisie was all too frequent.[2] In a letter to Lenin in December, a Bolshevik or at least socialist sympathiser from Voronezh criticized the 'degeneration' of democracy in Russia, the state's reliance on force of arms and the Chekas, and the creation of a widespread state of fear consequent upon popular observation of how innocent people could be shot by state forces.[3] Lenin's support for the Vecheka continued, but the proclamation of 'revolutionary legality' on 8 November on the recommendation of the Justice Commissar, Dmitri Kurskii, resulted in a reduction of the repressive powers of the Vecheka and a clarification of its status relative to other bodies.[4]

On 4 February 1919 the Party's Central Committee (which was becoming increasingly directive in affairs of state) formed a three-man commission of Stalin, Kamenev and Dzerzhinskii to work out the relationship between the Vecheka and the revolutionary tribunals.[5] Indicative of the privileged position occupied by the Vecheka as the immediate organ of proletarian dictatorship was the Central Committee's decision on 19 December to request NKIu (Justice Commissariat) to temporarily replace its representative, Kozlovskii, on the Vecheka Collegium on Dzerzhinskii's request. Kozlovskii, the Vecheka complained, had declared that half of those shot by the Vecheka had been innocent, thereby undermining the trust that it required in its work. Furthermore, the Central Committee resolved that there should be no place for 'malicious criticism' of Soviet organizations, such as the Vecheka, in the press organs of party or state.[6] Lenin appears to have been instrumental in the discussions surrounding the Vecheka's future; both Kamenev, who wanted the Vecheka and Chekas abolished, and Jan Peters, Vecheka deputy chairman, wrote directly to him arguing their contrary cases.[7]

The result was that the 'extraordinary commissions' remained in existence; Lenin and hard-line Bolsheviks were not prepared to dispense with their services. In March Dzerzhinskii was appointed Commissar of Internal Affairs, retaining the Chairmanship of the Vecheka, thereby easing some of the institutional conflicts. The right to pass sentences was to be removed from the Chekas and transferred to the revolutionary tribunals. The Chekas were to retain their initial investigatory powers, and would be required to deal with investigations quite quickly. They were however to be permitted to engage in combat during outbreaks of armed struggle, such as against 'banditry' and counter-revolution. Vecheka powers under the Terror were effectively to be retained wherever martial law was declared which, when the Civil War flared up again in the spring, was to be quite widespread. The revolutionary tribunals were to be reorganized into streamlined instruments meting out speedy justice. The Central Committee emphasized that they were not to be neutral courts of law but 'organs of revolutionary reprisal [*rasprava*], as distinct from courts as such.'[8] Sessions would be public and defendants would be present. In circumvention of meaningful legal norms, however, sentences once passed could not be appealed, the calling or not of witnesses and the permissibility or not of the defendant to a defence would 'depend on the tribunal', and tribunals were not to be confined to 'defined measures of punishment' to fit a particular crime.[9] Hence 'revolutionary legality' was a relative term, relative to the effective extra-legality of the Red Terror.[10] These recommendations were adopted by VTsIK on 17 February with the addition that the Vecheka retained the right to confine suspects in concentration camps, evidently a way of circumventing the legal formalities of arrest and trial. Dzerzhinskii was keen to recommend to VTsIK that the labour of concentration camp inmates should be utilized to a greater extent.[11]

On 20 February Dzerzhinskii issued a Vecheka order to all Chekas informing them of their reformed functions, and urging them to deal with all 'old affairs' through the application of 'administrative measures of punishment' – incarceration in camps and possibly also executions – until the reorganized tribunals came into effect.[12] However on 12 March the VTsIK Presidium authorized provincial Chekas to apply the death penalty for bribery and theft without specifying whether or not this would apply only in areas under martial law.[13] On this point, the distinction between 'political'/counter-revolutionary and 'ordinary' crimes was not very distinct in the Bolshevik mind. Most aspects of Soviet life were considered political and most acts of criminality considered crimes against the new social order, especially with the perceived need to consider the state a 'single military camp' under conditions of economic and military hardships.

On 30 November 1918 the Council of Defence had been created. This Council, chaired by Lenin, was charged with the continued task of converting the country into a 'single armed camp', and provided an important institutional means through which Lenin endeavoured to maintain close scrutiny over the running of the country and its defence. On 15 February the Council resolved to authorize the

Chekas and other bodies to arrest members of the soviet executive committees and *kombedy*, and take and shoot peasant hostages, for unsatisfactory snow clearing along the railways.[14] This came before the renewal of serious frontal civil war, in response to the economic and food supply crisis and the central importance in this regard of the railways. Later in the month Lenin drafted a Council decision that reiterated the right of the railway Chekas to use executions as long as martial law on the railways remained in place.[15] In July, when Soviet power was perhaps at its most precarious, Lenin would authorize special Council of Defence representatives entrusted with the right to declare martial law on the railways to impose fines, arrest or confinement in concentration camps for representatives of the state or local inhabitants, or transfer to Military-Revolutionary Tribunals or Vecheka organs if accused of 'severe' misdemeanours.[16] The railways were crucially important for the Soviet state as a whole, but the particularly severe repression of railway workers resulted in their perception that they were being 'senselessly repressed'. The fear instilled by the Chekas on the railways was counterproductive, as Willliam Rosenberg concludes, because it could not solve the problem of a lack of qualified personnel and served to curb individual initiative.[17]

Lenin and the law

It is worth briefly considering at this point Lenin's thinking on the law. The dominant Western scholarly understanding has been that he displayed a greater or lesser degree of legal nihilism when in power.[18] Soviet scholars, on the other hand, tended to exaggerate the importance of legality (albeit 'revolutionary legality') in Lenin's conception of socialist construction.[19] Piers Beirne and Alan Hunt have argued that there was a 'paradoxical relation between law and terror' in Lenin's thought, combining the necessity of unrestricted force to crush opposition, and yet 'the institutionalization of the victorious revolution that required law, rules, and regulations.'[20] Lenin's approach to the law – and its nature in early Soviet Russia more generally – was that 'Socialist legality will be marked by informality, flexibility, and the explicit dominance of political objectives and will therefore directly contrast with the formalism of bourgeois law.'[21]

Lenin oversaw a system of what might be termed, though an oxymoron, legalized arbitrariness. It was necessary to adopt regulations and legal statutes, but considerable 'flexibility' (*gibkost'*), struggle against excessive 'formalism', and when necessary extraordinary measures would be necessary and indeed enshrined in the law itself. Lenin was not a 'legal nihilist' but wanted to ensure that state repression and violence would not be constrained unnecessarily. The law was ultimately considered subordinate to considerations of revolutionary justice, and this was not merely conditioned by the circumstances of civil war but a requisite of the transitional nature of the proletarian state. One of the results or symptoms of the juxtaposition of revolutionary flexibility with commitment to legal procedure was that Lenin regularly received petitions from relatives or acquaintances of persons arrested by the Chekas requesting that he intervene for their release. He would typically request the Vecheka to examine if leniency could be shown, or to provide reasons for arrest. Sometimes his intervention helped secure release, other times it did not.[22] He often demanded mercilessness in his directives, but Lenin was not always opposed to leniency, especially for offenders who committed relatively minor offenses. For example on 6 January 1919 he ordered the Cheka in Kursk to arrest a certain Kagan, a state employee, for 'bureaucratic relations' in dealings with hungry workers. He wanted the press to publish the names of all state officials guilty of such offenses against the starving and inform that severe punishments, up to execution, would be meted out to them, but ten days later Kagan was released on Lenin's own orders.[23]

Lenin had noted in 1918 that courts would serve the dual purposes of education/ cultivation (*vospitanie*) and terror.[24] The Eighth Party Congress in March 1919 professed its commitment to work towards its progressive vision of a judicial system that would involve the participation of the entire population and possess a re-educative rather than punitive character. It noted that progressive punitive reforms had already been instituted, such as sending offenders to educational institutes, or utilizing obligatory labour, instead of incarceration.[25] Such neoclassicist jurisprudential principles, comprising a highly positivist conception of criminality that focused on the socio-economic circumstances leading to crime with a belief in the reformability of the criminal,[26] at least those deemed reformable, would, it was thought, increase the authority and popular legitimacy of the state. This would be recognized by NKIu in the heralding of a 'new course' in punitive policy in 1924.[27]

Contesting Marxism

During the winter of 1918, while he recovered from the assassination attempt, Lenin published a lengthy polemical response to Kautsky's August 1918 work *The Dictatorship of the Proletariat*. Kautsky's book may be summarized briefly as a defence of universal democracy as an indispensable component of proletarian dictatorship, for 'Socialism as a means to the emancipation of the proletariat, without democracy, is unthinkable.'[28] He reasoned, with a more sophisticated understanding of the nature of democratic politics than Lenin's, that classes themselves were not uniform, and that strict proletarian dictatorship along Bolshevik lines would result in some sections of the proletariat finding themselves on the wrong side of a proletarian dictatorship. In any case Kautsky was adamant that democracy should not mean rights for the majority only. Through the 'proletarian-democratic method of conducting the [class] struggle', he reasoned, premature attempts at revolution would be avoided, and less 'sacrifices' would be exacted.[29] Kautsky argued that the dictatorship of the proletariat, according to Marx's comments on the Paris Commune, would be a 'condition' which 'necessarily arose in a real democracy, because of the overwhelming numbers of the proletariat', not a 'form of government' which would mean 'disarming the opposition' by depriving it of the franchise and press freedoms.[30] He was not opposed in principle to revolutionary state violence but the Terror of the French Revolution, he explained, arose out of the circumstances of democratic struggle against absolutism. Socialist revolutions should take considerably less violent forms. Kautsky was an opponent of Bolshevik dictatorship but his principal purpose was not so much to condemn Bolshevism, which he thought 'understandable' in Russian circumstances, as to challenge the pretensions of this 'new theory' to become Marxist orthodoxy.

Lenin began his sharply polemical response that the dictatorship of the proletariat was 'the very essence of proletarian revolution'.[31] His principal thesis was that democracy could not be posed in the abstract but only in terms of the class it would serve. Dictatorship in the 'true' Marxist sense, he reasoned without a very solid basis, meant 'the abolition (or very material restriction, which is also a form of abolition) of democracy for the class over which, or against which, the dictatorship is exercised.'[32] If Kautsky had truly pondered Marx's works, Lenin continued, he would have arrived at the conclusion that 'The revolutionary dictatorship of the proletariat is rule won and maintained by the use of violence by the proletariat against the bourgeoisie, rule that is unrestricted by any laws.'[33] Soviet dictatorship, as we have seen, was not completely unrestricted by law; Lenin's point was that the organs of dictatorship should not be artificially curbed by legal norms. Ridiculing Kautsky's distinction between forms of government and conditions of rule, Lenin accused him of attempting to deprive proletarian rule of revolutionary violence. In fact the true 'condition' of proletarian dictatorship, he sarcastically remarked, was one 'of *revolutionary violence* of one class against another.'[34] 'Revolutionary violence' (broadly understood) had become an integral and essential part of Lenin's definition of the dictatorship of the proletariat – in fact its 'fundamental feature'[35] – in response to Kautsky's tendentious insistence (in a Marxist sense) on protecting democracy, especially in the Europe of that time.

Kautsky had alluded to Marx's *The Civil War in France* to support his argument for universal democracy. Lenin referred to the same source in support of his ideas on violence and dictatorship, making use of the more belligerent and democratically deficient pronouncements of Marx and Engels, thereby highlighting the ambiguities in Marxian thought.[36] Responding to the charge that Marx and Engels considered the possibility of a peaceful transitional period in Britain and America, Lenin countered that the present-day imperialist state was characterized 'by a maximum and universal development of militarism.'[37] He reasoned that every socialist revolution would need to curtail the democratic freedoms of the bourgeoisie,[38] but he accepted that restriction of franchise rights was not necessarily an indispensable characteristic of dictatorship but something called forth by Russian circumstances.[39] There could be no tame 'opposition' at a time of civil war, only 'ruthless enemies' who would be ruthlessly suppressed and deprived of 'all rights'.[40] Later he would explain that the socialist state would naturally take a different form from the 'lies' of so-called democratic freedoms under capitalism, though many 'sincere' socialists could not yet grasp this.[41] Reiterating the ethical distinction between 'revolutionary' and 'reactionary' modes of violence, he reasoned that though socialism 'is opposed to violence against men in general', no one had yet 'drawn the conclusion that socialism is opposed to *revolutionary* violence.' To talk about violence 'in general' without such a distinction, he thought, 'means being a philistine who renounces revolution.'[42] It is true, as Robert Service notes, that Lenin did not specifically mention 'terror' in the work despite the fact that he was writing it during the Red Terror, but it is not true that he 'wanted to practice terror without theoretical justification or political advertisement.'[43]

If Kautsky occupied the 'rightist' Marxist criticism of Bolshevism, Rosa Luxemburg provided a strong 'leftist' criticism. Luxemburg was sufficiently sympathetic to declare that 'the future belongs to "Bolshevism"',[44] and dismissed Kautsky's implication that Russia was too backward for a socialist revolution. She was also concerned by Bolshevik universalistic pretensions, by land redistribution that appeared to strengthen petty-bourgeois peasant instincts, by the corrupting influence of terror, by the restriction of democracy and dissolution of the Constituent Assembly, and she was convinced of the necessity of political pluralism. Lenin and Trotsky, she implied, were excessively fundamentalist in their conception of dictatorship.

Strictly from the perspective of revolutionary Marxist discourse, Lenin's defense of violent revolution, anti-democratic procedures and terror in the context of war and civil war seems more convincing than Kautsky's and Luxemburg's criticisms, though not in regard to suppression of other socialist parties. Yet Lenin had distorted the Marxian conception of dictatorship and a democratic republic, even though this has to be understood against the political climate of 1917–8. He conveniently avoided acknowledgement that the extremist conduct of the revolution had itself contributed significantly to resistance to Bolshevik rule.

Population management

Lenin's attitude towards the wide masses of the population continued to be quite sober and somewhat suspicious in 1919. Regarding the peasantry, in January he noted that:

> ... every peasant is a profiteer by inclination, who has a chance to line his pockets taking advantage of the desperate want and agonising famine [...] among the less educated people, exhausted as they are and worn out by starvation and suffering, there is a tendency, or an undefined feeling of resentment and anger against the comrades engaged in food supplies. They are all people who cannot think, cannot see further than the end of their noses, and it seems to them that food could be procured somehow.[45]

Formally introducing the *razverstka* system, Lenin maintained that the local food bodies must be 'compelled' to meet their targets. Traditional peasant suspicion of the state, which he highlighted rather than the failure of the revolution to deliver on its radical promises, was to be overcome,[46] and he stressed the necessity of proletarian leadership.

Yet his disappointment with the workers also continued. The trade unions would, he thought, eventually fuse with state organizations and take over government functions, but if this were to happen immediately 'they would make a mess of it' because the same petty-bourgeois spirit afflicted the workers. They were 'building a new society without themselves having become new people, cleansed of the filth of the old world.'[47] From an orthodox Marxist perspective, as Kautsky explained, a socialist revolution should only be undertaken when the proletarian mass had become culturally prepared for socialism. The need for greater efficiency and control from the centre led the Bolsheviks to rely more heavily on the party itself to direct the state, and in January a Political Bureau (Politburo) and Organizational Bureau (Orgburo) of the Central Committee were formed. The former soon became the chief repository of power and decision-making in Soviet Russia, and Lenin usually chaired its sessions. Still he constantly encouraged the masses to become involved in administration, and retained his overall optimism regarding the march of the revolution and the creative abilities of the workers.[48]

· The era of 'revolutionary legality' led also to a moderation towards the non-Bolshevik socialist parties, and a reiteration that there would be no application of force 'under any circumstances' against the middle peasants.[49] Lenin acknowledged the more conciliatory attitude of the Mensheviks towards Soviet power as a result of the continuation of foreign support for the Whites. There was no reason to 'repent or renounce' the terror that was previously applied to the Mensheviks and SRs, but now circumstances required a change in approach: 'When we find them [the 'petty-bourgeois democrats'] half turning towards us [...] We must say: "Come along [...] if you think the only way we know how to act is by force, you are mistaken; we might reach agreement."'[50] This moderation towards the socialist opposition did not last long however, and in the spring a renewed assault was initiated.

· Vladimir Brovkin has posed the question whether Lenin 'changed his mind' in the spring in favour of a renewed attack on the 'petty-bourgeoisie and its parties', or whether this was dictated by party hard-liners due to the aggravated circumstances of the time (see below). Defending the moderate line in late November 1918, Lenin made clear that this was a highly tempered 'moderation', for the necessity of 'waging an ideological struggle, a relentless war, against Menshevism' was not abandoned. The task of winning over these socialists was of urgent necessity to bolster the regime 'in the rear', though maybe 'only for a while', but it was imperative never to allow power 'to slip from our hands.' If these socialists were not to make proper use of their freedoms, Lenin warned, 'the whole Extraordinary Commission apparatus is in our hands.'[51] By February Menshevik criticism of the Bolshevik regime in the party's newspaper *Vsegda Vpered* touched on 'red militarism'. The Bolsheviks, they argued, were applying military solutions to political problems, and needed to rely on the Red Army to subdue striking workers and peasants.[52] The Vecheka closed down the paper a few days later. Lenin drafted the (temporary) VTsIK resolution on this, reasoning that the paper's slogan 'Down with the civil war' at a time of civil war and the advance of Kolchak from the East signified that, in fact if not in intent, the Menshevik leaders were in union with the 'landowners and capitalists' in Siberia, Arkhangel'sk, the Volga and Georgia (where the Mensheviks were in power).

The Menshevik leaders, for their part, sought to encourage the Bolsheviks to seek less intransigent ways of organizing the economy and to avoid the spate of strikes and uprisings that were helping Kolckak's advance. Lenin was uncompromising; Soviet power was engaged in 'the last, resolute and most extreme armed struggle against the forces of the landowners and capitalists' and could not endure such people who did not want to 'carry heavy deprivation together with the workers and peasants.' He threatened to exile them to areas under Kolchak's rule.[53] The closure of *Vsegda Vpered* was but the first step in an intensified assault on the Mensheviks, who had been legalized 'so that they could denounce foreign intervention', not undermine the Red Army's stature.[54] The Eighth Bolshevik Party Congress rejected a motion to outlaw the socialist opposition,[55] but in late March several leading Mensheviks were arrested in Moscow and the debate within the Bolshevik Party regarding policy towards the opposition, as with the future of the Chekas, appeared to have been won by the hardliners. The renewal of intensified frontal civil war ensured that the Bolsheviks realized how dependent they were upon the Vecheka and the Red Army.[56]

In late January Lenin replied to a letter from the Menshevik Nikolai Rozhkov urging him to restore some freedom of trade in food, in order to improve the 'desperate' food situation. His response was that the situation was not 'desperate', only 'difficult', and that the only way out was 'forward to socialism through the improvement of the state monopoly' and victory over counter-revolution. The prospects of civil war and revolution in Germany encouraged his sense of optimism.[57] However the application of the *razverstka*, hunger in the factories, and the arrests of socialists throughout the country ensured strikes and uprisings in the spring. Two of the most significant such strikes came at factories in Astrakhan and Tula.[58] Astrakhan was located between Kolchak's troops and Denikin's forces and was of crucial strategic importance.[59] The strike which broke out there in March was brutally suppressed by the Cheka resulting in about 1,500 executed victims, most of whom were workers.[60] The Tula strike in April also affected an area of particular importance for the war effort, for the Tula armaments factories were the main suppliers of munitions for the Red Army. Hundreds of strikers were arrested and 26 'ringleaders' executed.[61] Lenin was informed of the strike on 4 April and told that its causes were hunger and non-payment of wages. His instruction to his secretary was to call Dzerzhinskii and arrange for his (Dzerzhinskii's) departure for Tula.[62] Several days after its suppression, Lenin approved the need for a regular supply of food and wages for Tula factory workers.[63]

The most sinister policy of the central party apparatus at this time, setting a precedent for the nationalities campaigns of later years, was the decision to implement a policy of 'de-Cossackization' in the Don region following its recapture by the Reds. This demonstrated once again ambiguities in official policy concerning prophylactic measures of removing perceived opponents and the use of widespread, indiscriminate violence to this end. In just a few months probably 10,000 to 12,000 Cossacks were killed in the Don, in what Peter Holquist has described as an orchestrated policy of social engineering to render the Don 'healthy' by excising a broad social element perceived inherently harmful.[64] The Russian scholar Vladimir Genis has termed this a genocide.[65] Certainly this policy was genocidal in its consequences, and as Holquist explains it was based on pre-conceived prejudices on the part of the Bolsheviks regarding the Cossacks as inveterate enemies. Lenin had contributed to this in *State and Revolution*, wherein he foresaw the Cossacks as the source of a potential 'Russian Vendée'. On 24 January the Orgburo resolved to 'exterminate one and all' the 'wealthy Cossacks'.[66] The general Cossack population would meet the same fate if they had a 'direct or indirect' part in the struggle with Soviet power. Considering that the Cossack population had been forcibly mobilized by Krasnov to fight the Reds, this directive was in effect the basis for indiscriminate executions. There was also mention of a plan for 'mass resettlement' of poor peasants on Cossack lands, i.e. of introducing forcible migration for the Cossack population, which Sovnarkom converted into policy in April.[67] Forced migrations and executions of Cossack communities in the Don and North Caucasus would be repeated the following year at the end of the Civil War.[68]

Lenin was certainly at least aware of the genocidal consequences of the policy. G. Sokol'nikov, a member of the Southern Front Revolutionary Military Council (RVS; the Revolutionary Military Council of the Republic [RVSR], chaired by Trotsky, was the main army command) directly telegraphed Lenin and Sverdlov on 10 February to complain that the Orgburo directive was in need of 'serious corrections'. Its policy of mass terror, he pointed out, did not take into consideration the mass surrenders of Cossacks to Soviet power.[69] Indiscriminate extermination was soon abandoned and hence, as Holquist observes, this was not an 'open-ended' genocidal policy. Indeed in June Lenin instructed the Southern RVS 'not to irritate the [Cossack] population' by violating 'trivial' features of everyday Cossack life.[70] The popular uprisings in the Don that followed indiscriminate de-Cossackization were, however, met with little mercy. Lenin instructed that Dzerzhinskii provide 'the most energetic people' and enquired if the military had yet been deployed to put down the 'counter-revolutionary' uprising in Veshenskaia in April, and to use 'cunning' if necessary.[71] In August he instructed the use of 'bribery and threats to exterminate the Cossacks to a man' if they burned the oil in the Kazakh city of Gur'ev along the Urals front.[72]

Civil War, phase three: spring–winter 1919

If the first phase of the Civil War began in winter 1917–18, and the second phase began on the Volga with the Czech Legion and Komuch, then the third phase began with Kolchak's offensive launched from Ufa in March 1919. This was soon followed by Denikin's push for Moscow from the South and the threat to Petrograd from General Iudenich. Thus began the main phase of the 'Red versus White' Civil War, pitting the Reds against the forces opposed to socialism: an umbrella of conservatives, monarchists, liberals, landowners, Tsarist army officers and generals etc., supported by Western allied and Japanese forces.

, It is worth analysing in some detail Lenin's rhetoric in spring 1919. Referring to the fact that some Mensheviks, in defiance of their Central Committee, were actively supporting anti-Bolshevik forces, he acknowledged that 'We, of course, persecute Mensheviks, even shoot them, when they wage war against us, fight our Red Army and shoot our Red commanders'.[73] Responding to the spread of peasant revolts, he once again labelled these 'kulak' revolts and justified their suppression, for 'The kulak is our implacable enemy.' The middle peasant, however, 'is a different case, he is not our enemy.' The peasant revolts in fact involved entire villages but in public Lenin was largely incredulous, declaring that: 'An individual village or volost does join the kulaks, but under Soviet power there have been no peasant revolts that involved all the peasants in Russia.'[74] On 14 March the Central Committee agreed to strengthen the Vecheka's forces in direct response to the peasant uprisings, which it described as 'undoubtedly led by the Left and Right SRs', by recalling its most 'reliable workers' who had been transferred to other posts,[75] presumably to better enable the Chekas to win the 'hearts and minds' of poor and middle peasants. There was a distinct contrast in Lenin's thought between the ideal of neutralizing the middle peasant and the perceived practical necessity of resorting to force to suppress risings; as Bertrand Patenaude notes, 'The element of coercion directed against the entire peasantry was to become the hallmark of the *razverstka*.'[76] Lenin did emphasize, though, that the requisition quotas were to be relaxed for the middle peasants.[77]

- One of the principal reasons for the peasant revolts in 1919 was conscription to the Red Army and the consequent rise in desertion and formation of groups of deserter-'bandits'.[78] It is arguable that a more compact but better trained and supplied army rather than the mass conscript army of workers and (mainly) peasants would have resulted in a more effective force, and would have reduced state-peasant conflict. In a speech in May Lenin addressed the dissatisfaction of the *narod* that the Bolsheviks had not kept their promise to deliver peace having presented themselves in 1917 as the only party that could secure it. The Bolsheviks, he explained, had found that 'the whole civilized world' was attacking weak and ruined Russia. He also unapologetically acknowledged in eschatological terms Bolshevik dual responsibility for the Civil War, remarking that the revolution was embarked upon 'to wage a most desperate and violent struggle and war to crush the propertied classes [...] to extricate Russia, and then the whole of mankind, from the imperialist slaughter and to put an end to all war.'[79] Lenin's prediction that the belligerent peoples would come to the rescue of the Russian revolution had not yet materialized, and he reiterated his commitment to the possibility of a revolutionary war 'just as arduous, sanguinary and painful' as any other.[80] His faith that the war would almost instinctively teach the masses the necessity of fighting for their freedom had not yet been justified because of a lack of adequate awareness:

> ... we must not be surprised that extremely ignorant peasants are accusing us of failing to keep our promises [...] In view of their absolute ignorance, we cannot blame them. Indeed, how can you expect a very ignorant peasant to

understand that there are different kinds of wars, that there are just and unjust wars, progressive and reactionary wars [...].[81]

By 1919 his emphasis was once again that socialist consciousness would be brought to the wide masses largely from without. In this regard, he reserved his invective for the socialists who were encouraging the peasants to criticize the state. The socialist was not an ignorant peasant, and was therefore 'a supporter of the bourgeoisie if he in one way or another, *directly or indirectly*, spreads among the people the accusation that the Bolsheviks are dragging out the Civil War [emphasis added]'. There could be no criticism, no 'third way' between the absolute approach of the Bolsheviks and counter-revolutionary triumph.[82] In practice Lenin was not sympathetic to a refusal to serve adequately in the army. On 31 May he drafted a Council of Defence decision on the mobilization of Soviet employees for military service, warning that 'The mobilized men [would have] to answer for each other by collective liability and their families [...]be considered hostages in the event of their deserting to the enemy or failing to carry out assignments etc.'[83]

Directly addressing the industrial strikes of the spring, Lenin acknowledged that some workers were 'not politically conscious' and were 'misled by the appeals of the Socialist Revolutionaries, do not work, go on strike, and come out against Soviet power because of the food shortage.'[84] Clearly he expected the masses to bear these sacrifices because of the historical significance of the revolution. In any case, he reasoned, these 'backward workers' represented the interests of a relatively insignificant minority.[85] On 11 April, addressing the Trade Union Central Council, he justified the arrests of Tula workers and the clampdown on all shades of Menshevism thus: 'Every strike costs the lives of thousands and thousands of Red Army men [...] to deprive us of a number of factories in Tula means depriving thousands of workers of their lives.' The Bolsheviks' very identity as a party of the working classes was at stake; Lenin's identity as a theorist and revolutionary politician rested upon the embodiment of the 'truths' of Marxism in the fundamental unity of workers and their vanguard party.[86] This potential identity crisis was to be solved by laying blame on the socialist opposition for leading the workers from the path of their great mission, and rhetorical reliance on the unity between the party and conscious, vanguard workers. The working masses were naturally weary after five years of war and upheaval, but 'The weary must be encouraged, sustained and led [...] This is exactly what the dictatorship of the proletariat means.' This leadership by the conscious workers was necessary because 'The ignorant masses fall to every bait, and because of their weariness are ready to yield to anything.' They needed to 'hold out' because 'in a few months we shall be victorious all over the world.'[87] Due to the low cultural level of the Russian masses state power, Lenin explained, was being exercised for the working people by the advanced workers, not yet by the working people as a whole.[88]

The stakes could not be higher under circumstances of a life-and-death struggle to retain power, and Lenin made clear that 'He who is not for us is against us.'[89] The party line regarding the Mensheviks and SRs was 'to imprison those who assist Kolchak, *whether deliberately or unwittingly* [emphasis added]'. Were the Mensheviks really fomenting the strikes, Lenin was asked from the floor of the Trade Union Council, and if so what of the distinction between such 'Right' Mensheviks and the party's Central Committee, a 'loyal opposition' in the face of the Kolchak threat? Lenin's reply was starkly honest:

> ... if I were a barrister, a solicitor, or a member of Parliament, I would be obliged to present proof. But I am not the first, the second, or the third, and so I do not intend to and there is no reason why I should. Even supposing the Menshevik Central Committee is better than the Mensheviks in Tula. [...] in fact I have no doubt some of the regular members of the Menshevik Committee are better – in a political struggle, when the whiteguards are trying to get us by the throat, is it possible to draw distinctions?[90]

He added: 'I don't care whether I am accused of committing every mortal sin imaginable and of violating liberties, I plead guilty, but the interests of the workers will be furthered.'[91] Nonetheless later in the month he put his signature on a resolution prepared by the Justice Commissariat, and adopted by Sovnarkom and VTsIK, according to which all workers and peasants involved in strikes/uprisings as a consequence of lack of political consciousness, and who posed no threat to the regime, were to be released.[92]

Responding to confusion within the party regarding the nature of the state's relations with the 'petty-bourgeoisie', in particular the 'petty-bourgeois' socialists, Lenin acknowledged that:

> We shall have to change our line of conduct very often [...] 'Yesterday you were making promises to the petty bourgeoisie, while today Dzerzhinskii announces that the Left Socialist-Revolutionaries and the Mensheviks will be stood against the wall. What a contradiction!' Yes, it is a contradiction. But the conduct of the petty-bourgeois democrats themselves is contradictory.

The Bolsheviks did not want to use force against these 'petty-bourgeois democrats', for they were 'not a serious enemy', but Lenin warned them that 'if you join forces with them [counter-revolutionaries], we shall be obliged to apply the measures of the proletarian dictatorship to you, too.'[93] Would force be applied to the middle peasants also? In practice this was the case and Lenin had no hesitation in supporting the suppression of peasant revolts, but 'in theory' they required 'special treatment'. Later in this speech he acknowledged that 'blows which were intended for the kulaks very frequently fell on the middle peasants. In this respect we have sinned a great deal.'[94]

Discussing agrarian issues at the party Congress in March one contributor noted that since the abolition of the *kombedy* the poor peasant section had effectively dissolved, and the middle peasants were under the influence of the kulaks who were strongly opposed to Soviet power.[95] Socialism, in the opinion of the agrarian expert Vasilii Kuraev, would take about a decade rather than the three or four years initially hoped for its establishment. The individual peasant economy would persist for a long time in Russia he predicted, something that could not be solved simply with international revolutions. Kuraev stated bluntly that the middle peasant felt hatred towards the Bolshevik Party, and openly acknowledged that 'communist politics' were the sources of discontent. To ignore the small peasant economy would lead to uprisings and render impossible the task of meeting the food crisis, and there could be no forced path to collective, communist agriculture. Kuraev broadly approved existing policy under the circumstances; the problem, he believed, was the way Bolshevik agrarian politics were being conducted rather than the politics themselves.[96] The 'Damocles sword' must hang over the kulak, he added, but must not fall on the middle peasant.[97]

On 1 April Lenin warned that 'Kolchak's victories on the Eastern Front are creating an extremely grave danger for the Soviet Republic',[98] threatening loss of the Volga once again. He reiterated the starkness of his conception of the political alternatives facing the country: 'either the absolute power of the working class, or the absolute power of the bourgeoisie – there can be no middle, or third, course.'[99] The problem as Lenin saw it was that the petty bourgeoisie, including the vast mass of Russian peasants and backward workers, could not yet understand this stark distinction. The solution required the experience of 'bourgeois' dictatorship – 'these [petty-bourgeois] masses must be beaten a hundred times to make them understand that the alternative' is either one or the other dictatorial rule – and a Soviet policy of conciliation, as the Congress had emphasized. The confidence of the middle peasants was to be won over through a tactful approach devoid of abuses.

Rather than seeking socialist unity in the face of the White threat, then, Lenin set exclusive, absolutist discursive boundaries. The Mensheviks felt that they could condemn Kolchak and yet remain in opposition to Bolshevik rule, even if a loyal one, dropping the Constituent Assembly slogan. This he believed was impossible. The Mensheviks would be permitted to work for the state but must 'keep out of politics', for 'We shall allow no more opposition.'[101] Freedom, he declared, 'is a very, very important slogan. But our programme says that if freedom runs counter to the emancipation of labour from the yoke of capital, it is a deception.'[102] The particular will of the class-conscious workers and their vanguard party, representing the true general will, would triumph over the uncertain will of the majority.

The world war had formally ended in November 1918, but the Allies continued their intervention on the side of the Whites. In spring 1919 Lenin reiterated his wartime belief that peace without the international triumph of socialism 'means the collapse of all hopes of being able to crawl out of this bloody mire at least partly alive.' The fight must be fought to a conclusion, and there could be no peaceful prospects without the collapse of the capitalist system.[103] The experience of the Bolshevik Revolution convinced him that the resistance of the exploiters would grow both nationally and internationally, and that the distinction between defensive and offensive wars had become 'utterly meaningless.'[104] Drafting parts of the party programme to be adopted at the party Congress, he rejected hopes for safeguarding peace through international disarmament, calling instead for 'the slogan of arming the proletariat and disarming the bourgeoisie […] of completely crushing and ruthlessly suppressing the resistance of the exploiters […] of fighting until victory over the bourgeoisie of the whole world is achieved'.[105] Yet he continued to emphasize the defensive nature of red militarism: 'Everybody knows that this war was forced upon us.' Extrapolating from the Russian experience, he wrote that revolutions 'are subjected to the most serious tests in the fire of battle', and that whoever thought otherwise 'is the worst enemy of the working class.'[106] This was a general observation, for at this time, with the apparently successful revolution in Hungary, he spoke briefly about the possibility of revolution travelling 'by a different, more humane road' in a country where bourgeois resistance would not be so furious.[107]

Lenin noted with some pride that as the armies of bourgeois states were disintegrating, the Red Army was growing. The Red Army Commander (until July) I. I. Vatsetis had warned Lenin in February of the need to increase the armed forces, especially reservists, in light of the gathering military threat from the South and West (from Iudenich in Estonia).[108] The Red Army, despite the problem of desertion, grew to a force of three million men in 1919.[109] The 'military question' received particular prominence at the Eighth Party Congress, especially due to the existence within the party of a 'Military Opposition' that was troubled by Trotsky's policy of empowering former Tsarist officers, and by a general sense that the old army and militarist ethos were returning. The organization of a regular army, Lenin acknowledged, 'was an entirely new question' for Marxists, but 'Those who accused us of being militarists are hopelessly muddled.' It was, he explained, 'inconceivable for the Soviet Republic to exist alongside of the imperialist states for any length of time. One or the other must triumph in the end.' In the meantime there would be some 'frightful collisions' between the Soviet and bourgeois states. In order to hold onto power the proletariat would need to 'prove its ability to do so by its military organization.' What this meant was the necessity for the workers and peasants 'to master modern technology and modern methods of warfare' and build an effective, disciplined army. The dual task facing the state was to utilize the means of warfare ultimately to negate it, and to combine 'the new revolutionary creative spirit of the oppressed' with 'the store of the bourgeois science and technology of warfare in their worst forms.'[110]

Generally speaking, the Bolsheviks did not appear to be sensitive to the potential dangers posed to the flourishing of a healthy society by its organization along largely militarist lines, including the use of terror in the rear. The result, as John Erickson noted, was 'a peculiarly non-socialist warping of the state' that would persist after the cessation of the Civil War.[111] The Bolsheviks had, before October, disparaged the phenomenon of militarism and regular standing armies, and yet had advocated the dialectical notion of overcoming war with war. The Congress acknowledged that the army was a source of hardship on an already exhausted country, as it reduced the agricultural workforce and put great strain on food supply and transport. This 'transitional' army would however gain victory over its enemies and give way to the ideal of a people's militia formed on a class basis. The Congress envisioned soldiers' barracks as schools for military and political education, and recommended that universal military education be implemented so that the militia that would replace the 'transitional' regular army would be trained in the latest military technology and science.[112] In May 1919 Lenin oversaw the formation of the Troops for the Internal Defence of the Republic (VOKhR), centralizing all the auxiliary troop formations belonging to individual organizations and departments, subordinate to Dzerzhinskii's NKVD through the Command of Vecheka Troops.[113] The special importance attached to ensuring that the armed forces assigned for food supply work would not be weakened by such centralization was reflected on 1 August when Lenin signed a Council of Defence resolution that a separate department be set up within the Vecheka Command exclusively for food affairs.[114]

The Central Committee, as Lenin described it, was 'the militant organ of a militant party in time of civil war'.[115] Yet he was concerned not to glorify violence in itself, not to yield to the spirit of viewing force as a panacea for all ills – despite his own propensity to resort to force and violence – and not to use it under the wrong circumstances, with no chance of success. That he did not consider revolutionary violence a constant feature of the Soviet system he was keen to stress in the spring of 1919. 'Under certain circumstances violence is both necessary and useful', he explained, but there were circumstances 'under which violence cannot produce results.' Revolutionary violence and dictatorship he characterized as 'excellent things' when applied 'in the right way and against the right people', but 'they cannot be applied in the field of organization.'[116] It would be foolish to imagine that economic organization could be achieved 'by violence alone'; after the defeat of the bourgeoisie, prolonged education and re-education would be required, 'proletarian influence over the rest of the population.' Yet the bourgeois specialists, and the Mensheviks and SRs, were 'bourgeois through and through' and surveillance would be required over their activities.[117] Lenin realized that violence alone was not constitutive of order. Hannah Arendt reasoned that violence 'can destroy power [but] is utterly incapable of creating it.'[118] Lenin, as a theorist professing that the new power would triumph, indeed could only triumph in forceful struggle with the old, would not have agreed with this dictum, but he would have seen some merit in it.

Sending greetings to Hungarian workers in May, Lenin seemed to encourage them to shoot petty-bourgeois vacillators.[119] By the end of that month, the Red counter-offensive on the Eastern Front had resulted in the Whites being driven from the Volga, but Lenin feared that the revolution would be lost if the Reds did not manage to gain the security of controlling the Urals.[120] The influence of the hardships of civil war and economic crises on his thought was particularly apparent in a speech he delivered on 19 May to an adult education congress. Denikin was breaking out from the south, and Lenin reflected that the time was past when it was conceivably possible to 'convince the majority' to adopt socialism by persuasion. There could be no 'peaceful evolution towards socialism.' He reasoned that this was not simply because of the World War; even without the war, and even if the revolution had initially proceeded peacefully, he thought that the counter-revolutionary bourgeoisie would have instigated 'furious wars'. The exploiters, he explained, 'will surrender only after a desperate and relentless struggle', and the majority of the *narod* would only be won over through such a struggle. Dictatorship Lenin now defined as 'a cruel, stern, bloody and painful' word, not one to be played with.[121] The peasants formed this majority and, the Bolsheviks believed, constituted a 'special class'; they were both workers and property-owners who could be persuaded by Kolchak's promise to restore free trade.[122]

Under dictatorship, Kautsky critically noted, a decision is 'taken by military means. Hence, if you do not win by force of arms you will be vanquished and annihilated, because in civil war no prisoners are taken, it is a war of extermination.' Lenin replied: 'Quite right. What you say is true.' He clarified once again that this was not a naked struggle for the physical annihilation of the bourgeoisie, but of 'the economic conditions of this class's existence.' In short: 'Dictatorship does not mean only violence [*nasilie*], although it is impossible without violence, but also a form of the organization of labour superior to the preceding form.'[123] Writing about the Communist *subbotniks* he stressed this even more: the dictatorship of the proletariat was 'not only the use of force against the exploiters, and not even mainly the use of force' but, rather, the leadership of the masses by the industrial workers.[124] Forceful grain requisitioning was justifiable, Lenin maintained, for if the proletariat organized distribution correctly along equitable socialist lines, the task of convincing the peasants of the sense of socialist economics would be facilitated.[125] Force, he reasoned, was doomed to failure when applied without 'economic roots', but not when backed by the advanced class and relying on this 'loftier' system of socialist organization; in desperation he declared: 'We must sacrifice everything to save the lives of the workers.'[126]

In June the atrocities committed by the newly-formed Ukrainian Cheka were brought to Lenin's attention. He ordered a purge of the Ukrainian Cheka and that henceforth only communists were to be permitted to enter its ranks.[127] Having just driven the Whites east to the Urals, and with reinforcements unavailable for the Eastern Front due to the importance of the Southern Front, Lenin was concerned that Kolchak might advance once again. He ordered that the local population in Simbirsk (Lenin's home town) be mobilized and, fearful of popular revolts in the rear of the Red Army, ordered that persons concealing weapons be shot. In June one such revolt broke out near Simbirsk and Lenin enquired of the Eastern RVS 'whether the insurgents can be crushed by means of aeroplanes? Immediate and complete suppression is essential.'[128] The means of total war in Europe were to be applied on the home front against the peasants. In a communication with Aleksandr Beloborodov in the South, as the advancing Whites moved to link up with the Veshenskaia rebels, Lenin stated that it was necessary not to 'wear down' but 'destroy' the enemy, and he requested precise information on exactly 'how many taken' (presumably hostages) and how many [Cossack] stanitsas had been 'cleansed'.[129]

The mobilization of former officers presented another problem, with increasing cases of betrayal. Early in June Lenin recommended increasing hostage-taking from the bourgeoisie and the families of officers on the Southern Front. It would be a 'disgrace' he noted 'to hesitate to shoot [hostages] for non-appearance' of officers for Red Army service.[130] It is doubtful though that such hostages were actually executed, certainly on a very large scale.[131] On 20 June VTsIK adopted the Central Committee's plan for widening the scope for Cheka executions in areas declared under martial law, including for membership of 'counter-revolutionary organizations', treachery, concealment of traitors, robbery and illegal trade in cocaine.[132]

On 3 July, Denikin issued his plan to seize Moscow, following his capture of Tsaritsyn.[133] Lenin immediately wrote a letter in the name of the Central Committee to local Party bodies describing the situation as probably the most critical of the revolution.[134] British support for Denikin, as for Kolchak, was considerable in terms of equipment and morale, though particularly after this initial summer campaign.[135] It was necessary, Lenin maintained, that the Soviet Republic become '*a single military camp*, not in word but in deed', and that all institutions be 'placed on a military footing.'[136] In effect, what Lenin meant by a 'single military camp' was that, considering the Soviet Republic to be 'a fortress besieged by world capital', one's right to inhabit the country depended upon one's participation in its defence, and hence the state's right to mobilize the entire population to this end.[137]

This appeal demonstrated in sharp relief the absolutist, 'totalitarian' nature of Lenin's thought during 1919, under the impact of prolonged and aggravated civil war and foreign intervention. The extreme dangers posed to the regime in summer 1919 combined with ideological precepts explain Lenin's directives. The 'nutritive medium' for counter-revolutionary activities in the rear, he explained, was the bourgeoisie, kulaks, '"non-Party" public', and the 'spineless', wavering socialists neither clearly for the Bolsheviks nor for Denikin. The party's vigilance was to be multiplied tenfold, as counter-revolutionary attempts from the bourgeoisie, kulaks, the intelligentsia, Mensheviks and SRs were 'absolutely inevitable.' Once again Lenin warned against being deceived by 'the words and ideology' of the opposition socialist leaders attempting to find a 'third way' between either dictatorship. He explicitly justified the imprisonment and shooting of these socialists (amongst others) who came out against Soviet power – 'in other words, in favour of Denikin' – whether through force of arms or of agitation against mobilization. It was either red terror, or Kolchak and Denikin would be 'able to slaughter, shoot and flog to death tens of thousands of workers and peasants'.[138] To speak of 'Bolshevik atrocities' under such circumstances, he remarked, required 'all the hypocrisy of bourgeois writers.'[139]

Lenin wrote that unless these practices, including the taking of hostages, were 'extended and multiplied', the war could not be waged and the victory of the proletariat could not be achieved. His absolutism extended to the individual moral conscience: those 'capable of whining over the "iniquity" of such a decision [of introducing terror], must be given up as hopeless and held up to public ridicule and shame.'[140] On 8 July he instructed that special troop detachments should patrol the frontline areas, taking hostages from amongst the 'kulaks' and suppressing peasant rebels and deserters ('greens').[141] The 'green' movement acquired particular importance in 1919 and was discussed by the Council of Defence on 11 July, with the result that Vecheka forces were to be increased to deal with peasant rebellions.[142] On the same day Lenin brought the Council's attention to the problem of 'counter-revolutionary elements in the army', supposedly bourgeois and petty-bourgeois elements who were allegedly conducting counter-revolutionary agitation and inciting other soldiers to desert. Circulated at the meeting was Lenin's draft resolution that recommended the institution of surveillance over all those in the armed forces identified as bourgeois and petty-bourgeois elements by their past or present possessions, practices or personal relationships, including relations with 'petty-bourgeois' political parties. The draft suggested that a mere indication that these elements were engaged in counter-revolutionary activities would suffice for arrest. The execution of such soldiers, and the arrest of their families or deprivation of family food rations were the most severe forms of punishments that he recommended, especially regarding those deemed particularly hostile to Soviet power.[143]

Lenin also supported the harsh measures in the army that Trotsky insisted upon to ensure discipline. In response to the persistent charges circulating against the latter that he was 'shooting communists' (including political commissars), and in response to his threat to resign, Lenin addressed a letter to 'worker leaders' in July expressing his 'absolute confidence' that Trotsky's 'severe orders' were 'correct, expedient and necessary.' Trotsky later recalled his 'bewilderment' upon receipt of this letter, with the upper portion blank for him to write whatever order he wished so that it would have Lenin's support and approval.[144]

This was an extreme civil war, and terror to safeguard front and rear is part of the logic of such conflicts. However, with the continuation of this brutal civil war into a second year and the failure of international revolutions to mature, these measures reflected an extreme hardening and escalation of certain aspects of the logic of this ideology-in-power – most notably literal class warfare, political absolutism and belief in the historical significance of revolutionary violence. White terror in areas under the control of the White armies was also extremely brutal but it was largely unorganized, not established as government policy, and 'not based on principles of class differences.'[145] Furthermore taking Menshevik Georgia as a comparison of Russian Marxist polities, despite the more favourable circumstances confronting that government, Ron Suny has highlighted that 'Collaboration rather than class or ethnic warfare marked the Menshevik approach'.[146]

It is questionable to what extent a policy of collaboration with other socialist parties during the dangerous months of 1919 would have allowed the Bolsheviks to enforce the harsh measures that they felt were necessary to repulse the advancing armies. It seems reasonable to conclude, though that the Soviet rear would have been strengthened through active enlistment of cross-party support for struggle with the Whites (perhaps with a moratorium on partisan conflict) rather than the Bolshevik approach of heightened suspicion and pursuit of suppression. On this point Alexander Rabinowitch has suggested that had the Bolshevik-Left SR alliance not broken down the previous year, 'it seems likely that the Russian civil war would have been significantly less torturous' considering the latter's links with the peasants.[147] Modification of agrarian policy whilst retaining a strong state food supply apparatus, as was attempted from 1921, would surely have served the same purpose. These options however appeared ideologically foreclosed to the Bolsheviks in 1919, though Lenin reiterated the official policy of accommodating individual socialists who moved toward support for the Bolsheviks.

Theory and practice interacted upon each other, as explained at the outset of this book. Brovkin perceptively notes that the Bolsheviks 'made rational choices among other options [...] which had an impact on the ideology itself.'[148] Samuel Farber, has observed that:

> ... responses will likely reveal particular sets of political values and assumptions on the part of the revolutionary leaders. Consequently, we are dealing here with political belief systems that shape what are considered to be the appropriate actions against real or supposed dangers, and the manner in which those actions are justified.[149]

Lenin's refrain since spring 1919 was that the regime needed to 'hold out' for a few more months, for victory over the counter-revolutionaries in Russia and revolutions in Europe were inevitable.[150] Dictatorship he justified because 'our war is a just, legitimate and unavoidable war of defence.' Brovkin has even argued that the militant Marxism of 1917 had turned into 'totalitarian Stalinism' by 1919.[151] Lenin and the Central Committee were attempting to control and/or change the very thinking of the Russian population as a whole. Similar to the Tsarist regime (which was, however, not quite 'totalitarian'), the Bolshevik state worked to establish surveillance over opposition parties that would necessitate information on the names, addresses, professions etc. of 'agitators', and details on their 'plans, intentions, and influence on the masses.' Supervision would be exercised over all known current or former members of these parties and their acquaintances, contacts, relations etc.[152] Nonetheless the notion that Stalinism had somehow come into existence by 1919 is certainly an exaggeration, as well as an anachronism. The Bolsheviks after all were fighting a life-and-death struggle against regular armies for their very survival.

Despite his strained relationship with the Russian people throughout 1919, Lenin continued to profess apparently unbounded 'faith' in the proletariat, or at least its advanced section, in its moral influence on the masses. The Soviet Republic was to become a single armed camp but, he wished, would also allow the masses to readily participate in public life themselves.[153] However the enemy was 'still far from being defeated', and the capitalists and landowners were still strong, he explained, not only because of the ties of international capital but because of the force of bourgeois habits and the 'darkness' of the wide masses.[154] In the heat of battle Lenin urged the mobilization of tens of thousands of workers to fight and make sacrifices for the revolution, such as his call for the 'total mobilization of all Tsaritsyn workers' in June before the fall of that city. His most extreme proposal came in a letter to Trotsky on 22 October. To 'bring real pressure on Iudenich', he enquired about the possibility of mobilizing 20,000 Petrograd workers plus 10,000 bourgeoisie, putting machine guns behind them and shooting 'a few hundred.'[155] He reasoned that, apart from responding to necessity, the sacrifices made by the advanced workers and finest party members (they 'will die in desperate battles') would increase support for Soviet power amongst the less-advanced workers and peasants and encourage the war-weary troops at the front to achieve 'miracles'.[156]

Responding to criticism by the British socialist Ramsay MacDonald of the recently created Third Communist International (Comintern) in Moscow, Lenin remarked that 'when history places the dictatorship of the proletariat on the order of the day it is not voting, but civil war that decides *all* serious political problems'.[157] The 'sympathy and support' of the majority of the population were necessary for a successful revolution, but he emphasized to foreign communists what he had learned in the course of the Russian revolution: that such support could not be determined by elections. Rather it would be '*won* in the course of long, arduous and stern class struggle' waged by the proletariat *for* this support.[158]

On 11 July Lenin delivered a lecture on the state, the 'most burning' of political questions. There was a clear difference in emphasis here from the idea of smashing the state which pervaded *State and Revolution*, attesting to the impact on Lenin's thought of two years of revolution and state-building. The bourgeois state would still need to be 'smashed' initially, but he appeared closer now to Marx's earlier idea of the proletariat simply wielding the state in its own (although supra-class) interests.[159] The more statist and repressive connotations of *State and Revolution* were emphasized: 'We shall use this machine, or bludgeon, to destroy all exploitation [...] when there is no longer a situation in which some gorge while other starve, only when the possibility of this no longer exists shall we consign this machine to the scrap-heap.'[160]

During the summer and winter of 1919 Lenin began to pronounce more regularly on the justification for terror and the culpability of the Allies, thereby excusing the state for its violence. It was only after the capitalists had developed their resistance, he explained, 'that we began to crush that resistance systematically, applying even terror.'[161] That was 'the source of terror', and therefore 'those who preach renunciation of terror in Russia are nothing but conscious, or unwitting, tools and agents of the imperialist terrorists.'[162] In September/October he jotted down some notes for a never-written pamphlet on the dictatorship of the proletariat, revealing the prominence of violent forms in his conception of proletarian dictatorship in 1919, and how this conception had developed since and remained faithful to *State and Revolution*. Dictatorship had not been understood by socialist critics of the Soviet regime, he reiterated, because of their failures to understand that dictatorship represented the logical culmination of class struggle in its most severe forms. The forms of proletarian class struggle, under its dictatorship, 'cannot be what they were before', and he outlined the five forms of class struggle under proletarian dictatorship: suppression of the resistance of exploiters; civil war; 'neutralization' of the petty-bourgeoisie; 'utilization of the bourgeois specialists'; and inculcation of a new discipline. He associated civil war with terror, and significant also was that 'neutralization' of the peasantry involved both violent suppression in the event of 'deviations' [*ukloneniie*], and persuasion.[163]

⋅ During the autumn Lenin oversaw the introduction of shooting on the spot for those guilty of causing material damage to railways, and the creation of a special revolutionary tribunal under the Vecheka to combat theft, speculation and other abuses amongst state employees.[164] This tribunal was to mete out punishment, not conduct a trial as such; it was to be guided 'exclusively by the interests of the revolution and not connect with any form of legal proceedings.' Dzerzhinskii explained that open, public sessions would ensure that the bourgeoisie would know 'that we will be merciless with them', and would teach the public not only of the 'external' enemy but also of the 'internal' enemy lurking within the Soviet state apparatus. 'We are not trying to destroy those who were capitalists', Dzerzhinskii explained, but those wishing to restore the past 'we will destroy mercilessly, as class enemies.'[165] Following an Anarchist attack on the Moscow party headquarters in late September there was an intensified wave of violence against prisoners and hostages, and the Central Committee reinforced its injunction that whoever did not 'actively' support the defence of Soviet power was a traitor.[166]

By November 1919, the dangers from Kolchak, Denikin and Iudenich, in addition to the support for them from the Allies, had diminished or effectively been defeated. Lenin encouraged the complete rout of the retreating enemies; to the Petrograd workers and soldiers, he appealed that 'At this moment we can and must strike harder than ever in order to finish off the enemy.'[167] Yet the Bolsheviks believed that the Civil War had been won and could now adapt to rebuilding and strengthening the Soviet state. How they would set about this task would illustrate the effects of the Civil War upon the ideology and institutional practices of Bolshevism, although the transition from war to peace would not be a smooth one as the Soviet economy was in dire straits by 1920. In addition, a war with Poland would break out in the spring of that year, another front of the Red–White Civil War would ignite briefly later in the year, and civil war between the state and peasantry would return with intensity.

7 War and peace

From Civil War to NEP, 1919–1921

> [...] at this moment of transition from civil war to the new tasks we must transfer everything to the labour front and there concentrate all our forces, with the utmost effort and with ruthless, military determination.[1]
>
> (Lenin, 27 January 1920)

The winter of 1919–20 was a time for dealing with another struggle, the 'bloodless front' of economic recovery. Lenin declared in December that the 'main difficulties are behind us', but soon he would recognize that this 'bloodless front' would be perhaps the most challenging. This was also a time of reflection and justification. Speaking in early December, he justified his pre-Civil War belief that through civil warfare the *narod* would be strengthened in political awareness, for it had come to understand, through its 'class instinct', that 'our government is a sound one, it is a government that demands rather a lot, it is a government that is able to ensure the fulfilment of those demands at all costs.'[2] Indeed, as Erik Landis notes, the popular experience of White occupation during the Civil War served to embolden local soviet officials (as well as the Moscow leadership) in their policies, for it 'effectively legitimized the conduct and policies of the Soviet government's revolution.'[3]

Lenin was also putting forward a further source of the legitimation of violence, as deriving from and constituting what Christopher Finlay describes as 'revolutionary subjectivity', or more simply class awareness. 'War', Lenin told the Congress of Soviets, 'is not only the continuation of politics, it is the epitome of politics'; it was 'political education.'[4] Yet terror had been an enforced policy, he repeated, for confronted with the 'terrorism' of the Entente 'we have the right to resort to terror ourselves.'[5] In March 1920, responding to socialist charges that the Bolsheviks had 'drenched the country in blood', he declared that 'capitalists are capitalists, and the only thing to do with them is to vanquish them [repression broadly conceived]. Because it is impossible to come to terms with the capitalists and secure their obedience peacefully, especially after four years of war.' In this way he insisted that the bloodshed of the Civil War was not due to Russia's 'backwardness' but was a consequence of the nature of imperialism and the necessity of struggle against it.[6] Every victory achieved was leading towards that time when the country would operate without terror as a 'method of persuasion and influence.'[7] Lenin was a little more cryptic on this point: 'we shall be the first to take steps to confine it [terror] to the lowest possible minimum', he remarked, 'as soon as we put an end to the chief source of terrorism – the invasion of world imperialism, the war plots and the military pressure of world imperialism on our country.'[8] With victory in the Civil War and the expulsion of foreign powers minimal levels of terror might still be required, but in fact this chief source of terrorism would only cease with the triumph of international socialism.

Transition from war to peace

Lenin warned that Denikin had not yet been completely defeated, but with the Civil War effectively over the Bolsheviks could now devote themselves to addressing the catastrophic economic crises afflicting the regime. Dictatorial methods would likely have been resorted to by any government under such conditions, but the Bolshevik approach was characterized by a continuation of the mentality and means of wartime into peacetime. The Bolshevik leaders, having defeated the Allied-sponsored White armies, sought to harness the spirit of militarization to mobilize society for economic recovery. Lenin retained a wartime outlook and rhetoric, reasoning that the enemy 'is always watching every step we take and will make many more attempts to overthrow us by all the means in their power, force, fraud, bribery, conspiracies'.[9] He also re-iterated the ideological basis of War Communism. The requisitioning of surplus grain would remain the basis of food supply policy, with the peasant as yet required to sell grain for fixed prices without an equivalent goods exchange. Requisitioning 'must be carried out in full', he insisted, and when the food supply system becomes properly regularized, then 'we [shall] have a socialist foundation.' He was convinced that there could be no return to freedom of trade without bringing the country back to capitalism[10] and, as Bertrand Patenaude has demonstrated, food supply officials began to speak of the *razverstka* system as a means of effecting a 'revolution in peasant consciousness.'[11]

Lenin dismissed the notion that the Bolsheviks were 'a party that coerces the peasantry'; forceful requisitioning was being carried out only against the 'profiteer'.[12] The question remained how to distinguish the profiteering from the working peasant? Lenin acknowledged the difficulty involved, for 'however contradictory they may be', they 'are fused into one whole.'[13] He considered demarcation possible but his understanding posited that the categories were fluid and that the 'petty-bourgeois masses' would waver between the two. So long as the old self-interested outlook persisted, and peasants would not volunteer grain to the state as a loan, there was 'no alternative but to requisition grain surpluses as a loan to the hungry workers.' In order to change this peasant *mentality*, he underlined, 'nothing' could be accomplished by force.[14] He implied acknowledgement that wartime requisitioning had been excessive and politically damaging. In November with regard to Ukraine he instructed that requisitioning must be 'to the strictly limited extent necessary',[15] and he was also aware of the 'outrageous excesses' being committed, such as by army food agents in the recaptured Don.[16]

In accordance with the notion of the 'front' of economic reconstruction, 'labour armies' were formed from Red Army soldiers. Such labour units served as means of utilizing this disciplined apparatus for combating the principal economic difficulties, and of addressing the potential dangers of demobilizing soldiers amidst economic dislocation. The principle of conscripted labour was to be applied to the workforce more generally, with Lenin declaring that 'we must strain all the live forces of the workers and peasants to the utmost and demand that they give us help in this matter.'[17] Such labour mobilization signified the adaptation of army organization for civilian purposes; with 'soldiers as workers and workers as soldiers', as Brovkin puts it.[18] Further indicative of the application of military-style administrative methods in economic organization was the renaming of the Council of Defence as the Council of Labour and Defence (STO) in early 1920, and this 'streamlined inner cabinet' gradually eclipsed Sovnarkom in importance.[19]

Trotsky was the principal instigator of militarized labour, viewing it as a long-term strategy for the transition to socialism. Some scholars, such as Robert Service, reason that for Lenin such a militarized approach 'was a regrettable necessity and not a policy to glory in.'[20] Jonathan Aves perceptively notes that Lenin did not wish to identify too closely with enthusiasm for military methods,[21] but he certainly openly proclaimed the importance of such an organizational model, declaring that 'we must transfer everything to the labour front and there concentrate all our forces, with the utmost effort and with ruthless, military determination.'

The militarization of labour had truly begun in 1919, initially for industries vital for the war effort. In January 1920 militarized labour conscription was introduced for all workers. In addition to food supply and transport, there were serious problems in securing and transporting fuel. In November 1919 Lenin had called for 'labour conscription for the whole population' to solve the fuel crisis and instructed local Party organizations thus:

> Punish with ruthless severity those who despite repeated insistence […] are found to have shirked the work. Any lenience or weakness will be a crime against the revolution […] All fuel work in general must be organized in military fashion, with the energy, speed and strict discipline that is demanded in war.[22]

On 12 November he had instructed the RVS to establish military-revolutionary tribunals when necessary along the railways to deal with the fuel crisis.[23] On 1 February he instructed his Defence Council colleagues to introduce martial law in areas either side of railway lines to mobilize labour for clearing the lines of snow. Bread rations were to be reduced for those not working on the vitally important railways and increased for railway workers, with the rationale 'Let thousands more perish but the country will be saved.'[24]

The Soviet historian Gimpel'son argued that War Communism was not abandoned in early 1920 due to the dire economic situation and the dangers of a renewal of war.[25] However Lenin was not unduly troubled about a renewal of war in early 1920.[26] Aves argues that 'ideological considerations' were also very important. Bolsheviks were convinced that the general line of War Communism was correct; they probably believed their own rhetoric regarding workers' acceptance of Bolshevik economic policies; and, despite acknowledgement of the limits of force to realize proletarian organization, coercion and its threat rather than material incentives was chosen as 'the main instrument for raising labour productivity.'[27]

Bolshevik labour policies in 1920 have been described by one Russian historian as the 'enserfment' of the workers.[28] The Central Committee, defending its policy of militarized labour at the Ninth Party Congress, noted that the transition to 'organized social labour' was unthinkable without state compulsion of parasitical and backward elements of society and of the working class, and that the 'instrument of state compulsion' was 'military force'. Such compulsion would decline in proportion to improvements in economic development and increase in socialist upbringing of 'the rising generation'. Defending against what it called 'philistine-intellectual and trade-union prejudices' against militarized labour, the Central Committee sought to explain the 'inevitable and progressive' significance of applying 'military compulsion' to the task of raising economic production.[29] The Congress declared with confidence that the 'greatest achievement' to date had been a large turn towards awareness of the necessity of sacrifice on the economic front on the part of the mass of workers and part of the peasantry. Despite this, the Congress resolved to employ imprisonment in concentration camps as a possible punishment for labour 'desertion' due to the 'significant section' of the workers moving from factory to factory and shirking work to look for food.[30] (Forced labour camps had already been established by VTsIK in 1919.)

There was therefore a duality in Bolshevik rhetoric: the idea of mobilizing the masses through propaganda and continued confidence in their increased awareness, and yet belief in the importance of state compulsion for restoring the economy, and the ever-present threat of coercion against workers for indiscipline. The Bolsheviks appeared convinced that the justness of the purpose justified labour conscription, but there was also realization of the limits of force and the importance of education and propaganda to ensure popular acceptance of such measures.[31]

Lenin at times displayed a distinct hostility towards the peasants in 1920. Certainly with the apparent end of the major Civil War threat there was less of a pragmatic necessity to 'neutralize' the peasants.[32] In addition the extent of peasant uprisings in the major grain-producing regions was very considerable from the spring onwards.[33] The Bolsheviks were faced with a logical conundrum, as Lenin recognized: 'We must remember that we are grappling with the task of making a socialist revolution in a country where peasants form the greater part of the population.'[34] It was essential to ensure an adequate food supply to restore industry, but the majority of Bolshevik leaders had no intention in early 1920 of tolerating any notion of free trade. Lenin continued to distinguish the category of 'working' peasants, but his expressed attitude towards the 'millions' of 'petty-bourgeois property-owners' who possessed grain while the dwindling numbers of workers in collapsed industries were starving was 'one of war'.[35]

Consistently Lenin referred to the 'well-fed' peasant in contrast to the starving worker, particularly regarding the grain-producing regions recently re-conquered for Soviet power: Ukraine, Siberia, the Kuban' and the Don. In February he telegrammed Stalin in Khar'kov approving reduction in requisition quotas,[36] but in general he thought that 'In those regions there are rich peasants; there are no proletarians, and what proletariat there is, has been corrupted by petty-bourgeois habits.'[37] Regarding the Don and Volga regions Moscow continued to insist through 1920 that the high requisition quotas be met, dispatching military force to ensure this despite the evident fact that these quotas could not be met.[38] The 'peasant profiteer', Lenin maintained, was aiming to overthrow Soviet power by means of 'peaceful disintegration', through restoration of freedom to trade and speculate. This he believed was being exploited by the Entente and signified that 'The war has changed its front and its forms.'

Lenin was convinced that the proletariat had a right 'to exercise coercion in order to hold its own at all costs'.[39] Yet he was even clearer that 'Our methods of violence towards the peasantry will help us little', that 'violence alone cannot ensure victory', even declaring that 'organization and moral authority are all that is needed.'[40] Having declared 'war' on the petty-proprietors, he then explained that such a battle would be fought on the 'bloodless front' and would take a long time. Dictatorship, Lenin explained, 'means a persistent struggle – bloody and bloodless, violent and peaceful, military and economic, educational and administrative – against the forces and traditions of the old society.'[41] In early April he suggested that the employment of the coercive state apparatus for suppressing resistance was 'not even largely' dictatorship's purpose; rather, dictatorship signified organization and the unity of the working masses.[42] With a shift to the 'peaceful front', violence appeared a less central component of Lenin's conception of proletarian dictatorship. In April he was emphasizing once again the task of 'winning over' the peasant masses, including in the newly-acquired territories. Socialism could only be victorious in Russia, he insisted, if the distinction between peasant and worker were eventually abolished, confident that the peasantry itself was 'splitting up more and more' along class lines. Yet he noted menacingly that 'This is how unity of will was expressed during the war – anybody who placed his own interests [...] above the common interests, was branded as a self-seeker and was shot.' He explained: 'we realized that we could not emerge from the old society without resorting to compulsion as far as the backward section of the proletariat was concerned.' The peasant's 'two souls' of property-owner and worker needed to be separated. They would only be won over with a 'firm policy', there could be no capitulation to the peasant's proprietary tendencies, and 'as for the peasant proprietors, we have to fight them.'[43]

Lenin made it quite clear that the dictatorship of the proletariat, in theory as in practice, was foremostly the dictatorship of the proletarian party, for the party was essential to counteract petty-bourgeois 'relapses' amongst the proletariat.[44] Lenin was located on the dominant élitist rather than popular democratic strand of

Bolshevik thought, the latter voiced in particular by the 'Workers' Opposition' that was critical of what it considered the party leadership's 'distrust' of worker initiative.[45] In the course of the trade union controversy within the party later in the year, Lenin would declare that the proletarian dictatorship could not be exercised by the whole of the class but only by its vanguard which had been 'absorbed by the Party'.[46] There could be no tolerance of indiscipline within or outside the Party, for Lenin's absolutist scenario remained intact: 'Whoever brings about even the slightest weakening of the iron discipline of the party of the proletariat (especially during its dictatorship), is actually aiding the bourgeoisie against the proletariat.'[47] Yet he was, as always, a champion of 'a truly mass and truly revolutionary movement', and he ridiculed the distinction made by German communist critics between dictatorship either of a class or of a party.

Lenin's was not the most militant Bolshevik voice in favour of applying force to solve economic problems, and of theorizing the central transformative power of the workers' state rather than the workers *per se*. Trotsky's 1920 book *Terrorism and Communism*, written in response to Kautsky's work of the same title, was the boldest defence of revolutionary terror though it was certainly consonant with Leninist logic. Kautsky had directly challenged the contradictory duality of humanism and terror in Leninism, contending that the aim of socialism and the Bolshevik commitment to the sanctity of life did not justify its taking in the manner practiced by the Bolshevik state.[48] Trotsky ridiculed Kautsky's democratic humanitarianism. He agreed that terror was not a necessary concomitant of revolution but reasoned that the enemy must be made harmless, and 'in wartime this means that he must be destroyed.'[49] Trotsky explained that proletarian state power was 'an exceptional regime' required for 'a transitional period,'[50] and he neatly summarized the above-mentioned duality in Bolshevik thought: 'To make the individual sacred we must destroy the social order which crushed him. And this problem can only be solved by blood and iron.'[51] Expounding on militarized labour, Trotsky reasoned that the population must be treated 'as the reservoir of the necessary labour power.'[52] He did not believe that compulsory labour represented 'violence done to the working class', for it was not opposed by the majority of workers. Nonetheless the state would be required to punish for labour indiscipline, as 'Repression for the attainment of economic ends is a necessary weapon of the Socialist dictatorship.'[53]

It fell to the party theorist Nikolai Bukharin to provide the most in-depth theoretical justification for the application of force in economic transformation, in his 1920 book *Economics of the Transformation Period*.[54] He explained that the state, directed by the party, reflected the 'collective reason of the working class' and hence was charged with safeguarding it, and was entitled to use force to achieve it. Force is itself an economic power Bukharin wrote, quoting Marx, and 'revolutionary state power is the mightiest lever of economic revolution.'[55] Force served two functions: it was an 'absolute necessity' against the inevitable active resistance of the bourgeoisie; but state force, effecting a revolution of popular mentalities, would also 'turn inward' as 'the *self-organization and the compulsory self-discipline of the working people*.' In this case force would constitute 'the power of cohesion'.[56] 'In the transition period', Bukharin explained, force 'is transferred – in altered forms – to the working people themselves, even to the ruling class.' When reading the book, Lenin underlined 'even to the ruling class' and wrote 'True!' in the margin.[57] This was logical, reasoned Bukharin, for in capitalist society there was no 'self-activity for the working masses', in communist society there would be no 'external regulation of relationships between people' at all, but in the transition period there would be a combination of compulsion and liberation such that the workers would go through their school of socialism. Compulsion would of course also be required for the masses of middle, and sometimes even poor peasants.

Bukharin, like Lenin, justified such 'compulsion' because it was 'for the first time really the tool of the majority in the interest of this majority.'[58] Reflecting the Bolshevik eschatological belief in the historical purpose of the workers' revolution, which required the forging of a 'New Man', and the ethical duality surrounding the use of violence, Bukharin expounded further:

> From a broader point of view, i.e. from the point of view of a historical scale of greater scope, proletarian compulsion in all its forms, from executions to compulsory labour, constitutes, as paradoxical as this may sound, a method of the formation of a new communist humanity from the human material of the capitalist epoch […] as concentrated application of force, the dictatorship finally abolishes all force.[59]

Lenin's reaction to this was to write 'Precisely!' Thus, the approach to socialist transformation of the country had by 1920 developed quite significantly from that envisaged in 1917, but state policies were not merely responses to the circumstances of war and revolution. They were also reflective of highly theorized ideological adjustments to the problems presented and experiences acquired during that time. On 17 January 1920, following a proposal from Dzerzhinskii, VTsIK and Sovnarkom resolved to abolish the death penalty for both judicial and administrative sentencing (i.e. for both the tribunals and the Vecheka and other bodies), over the signatures of Lenin and Dzerzhinskii.[60] Lenin explained the reasons for this on 2 February at VTsIK, focussing on the political capital to be gained abroad:

> When bourgeois democracy in Europe does all in its power to spread the lie that Soviet Russia is predominantly terrorist, when this lie is spread about us by bourgeois democracy and by the socialists of the Second International […] In order to refute this lie we have decided on the step taken by Comrade Dzerzhinskii.[61]

Reiterating that terror was an enforced response to the terror of the Entente, he reasoned that 'the use of violence arises from the need to crush the exploiters, the landowners and capitalists. When this is accomplished we shall renounce all extraordinary measures. We have proved this in practice.' However Lenin had maintained since November that the exploiters had not yet been entirely crushed. The abolition of the death penalty at this point seemed at variance with his views on 'revolutionary legality'. In any case the threat of its re-imposition remained, for 'any attempt by the Entente to resume methods of war will force us to reintroduce the former terror'. Such attempts would embolden, and heighten the risk from, domestic opponents of the regime. This was still 'a time of the law of the jungle', Lenin reminded his audience, 'when kind words are of no avail.'[62]

Speaking to a Cheka audience on 6 February 1920, he clarified the issue:

> we do not close our eyes to the possibility of restoring capital punishment. With us it is a matter of expediency. It goes without saying that the Soviet government will not keep the death penalty longer than is absolutely necessary, and by doing away with it, has taken a step that no democratic government or any bourgeois republic has ever taken.[63]

Dzerzhinskii instructed the Cheka Special Departments at the front that the abolition did not apply to them.[64] To one such front, the north Caucasus, Lenin sent a telegram on 28 February reading: 'We badly need oil, consider a proclamation to the population, that we will slaughter (*myi pererezhem*) all if they burn the oil.'[65] Most notably, attesting to the idea that the abolition served a largely publicity value, on 19 February Sovnarkom resolved to extend the rights of the Vecheka and the central Revolutionary Tribunal to establish military-revolutionary tribunals in areas outside the frontal zones, as a consequence of the rise in 'banditry'.[66] 'Banditry' was defined as 'armed robbery', but this term was used by the Bolsheviks to include hostile peasant movements. Military tribunals, as Dzerzhinskii made clear, retained the right to pass sentences of shooting.[67]

Defence and offense: war with Poland

The abolition of the death penalty was reversed with the onset of the Polish–Soviet War in April, when Polish forces invaded Soviet Ukraine. Norman Davies notes that the war in fact began in 1919 with the instalment of a Lithuanian–Belorussian Socialist Republic after some skirmishes with Polish troops.[68] Soviet and Polish expansionist aims, and Soviet rhetoric of 'revolutionary war', led the Poles under Jozef Piłsudski to launch a pre-emptive strike in April 1920.[69] Davies has argued that 'Lenin was in favour of the war, but chose for several very good reasons not to reveal his views too openly.'[70] For historian Adam Zamoyski, Lenin was 'not interested in peace', and he claims that as early as 14 February Lenin 'took the final decision to attack Poland.'[71] It is worth exploring the accuracy of these claims.

On 23 February the Western Front RVS had reported to Lenin a large concentration of Polish forces and the need for the Red Army to similarly increase its concentration of divisions.[72] Four days later Lenin sent a telegram to Trotsky in which he wrote 'All the symptoms are that Poland will present us with absolutely unreasonable terms', referring to peace negotiations then underway. Urging the 'rapid transportation of everything possible to the Western Front', Lenin feared that 'we have been in a little too much of a hurry with the labour armies' and opined that 'We have to give out the watchword of preparing for war with Poland.'[73] The next day he warned that the Polish threat was all the greater, and enquired if Denikin could be crushed quickly to enable the release of reinforcements.[74] What these correspondences signify is that Lenin was, by March, convinced of the inevitability of war and the need to prepare for it; they do not necessarily imply a pre-emptive aggressive intention. Indeed Polish historian Piotr Wandycz pointed out that there were 'good strategic, economic, and political reasons' for Lenin to desire peace with Poland in 1920, reasons downplayed or overlooked by Davies and Zamoyski.[75]

In early February, announcing peace with Estonia, Lenin spoke proudly of 'proving our ability to renounce, in all sincerity, the use of force at the appropriate moment, in order to change to a peace policy'. This proved that 'we do not have to resort to force to win the sympathy and support of the bourgeoisie.'[76] However his private correspondences were less pacifistic than his public pronouncements. On 14 February he requested the formation of a 'Galician striking force' and instructed Stalin that Soviet diplomacy ought to 'keep silent' about this.[77] Evidently this is what Zamoyski has in mind when stating that Lenin decided on war that day. It is more likely that, realizing that war would be inevitable, Lenin was preparing to convert it into a revolutionary war and work out a strike plan. In September, at a session of the party Conference, he would acknowledge that his reasoning at this time was 'In order to avoid war, we are prepared for an offensive.'[78] It was not until 17 March that Lenin provided a clear-cut indication that he was prepared to launch an offensive war, in connection with a supposed seizure of part of Berlin by the Spartacists (Communists): 'it is necessary to speed to the maximum the capture of the Crimea so that we have a completely free hand, for the civil war in Germany could compel us to move to the West to help the communists.'[79]

Davies is undoubtedly correct that Soviet strengthening of the Western Front 'produced a classic situation of mistrust in which each side interpreted the other's defensive precautions as proof of aggressive intentions.'[80] Yet to claim that Piłsudski 'won the race' to the offensive overlooks the fact that Lenin wished at that time to concentrate on domestic problems. War would have come sooner or later if the Polish socialist revolution did not itself take place, but the point is that in early 1920 Lenin would have preferred later, his commitment to supporting revolution in Germany notwithstanding.

Once war did come, and the Polish incursion was repulsed, the Red Army's offensive on Warsaw was certainly informed by ideology. The differences between offensive and defensive, and foreign and civil wars were not very distinct for the Bolsheviks. When the British Foreign Secretary, Curzon, proposed a Polish–Soviet boundary, Lenin's response was to ask Stalin to 'furiously intensify the offensive.'[81] In mid-July the Politburo decided to cross the 'Curzon Line', despite the scepticism of Stalin and Trotsky concerning the organization of the army and the threat remaining from the Whites in Crimea.[82] This decision signified, as Lenin put it at the party Conference in September, that the 'defensive period of the war with worldwide imperialism was over, and we could, and had the obligation to, exploit the military situation to launch an offensive war.'[83] Lenin maintained in his speech at the Conference, first published in the 1990s, that he had wished to concentrate on peaceful economic construction to which the army had been assigned, and that the peace offer whereby Poland would have (temporarily) retained its 'good chunk of the Ukraine' was sincere.

In March Lenin had reiterated that 'the present policy of all bourgeois states is the *preparation* of *fresh* imperialist wars – wars are not only being prepared but are objectively inevitable as a result of all their politics.' Hence to bemoan civil wars in such states that 'may cost tens of thousands of lives' would be to allow 'another imperialist bloodbath that yesterday cost millions of lives and tomorrow will cost millions more.'[84] Lenin certainly intended to inspire civil wars in the 'border states' and Poland, and to 'sovietize' these lands. In Ukraine he proposed that troops march through the entire country, organize food supply according to the *razverstka* model, and take a list of 'rich peasants' to answer for fulfilment.[85] For western Ukraine he wanted the army to ruthlessly crush the Polish landowners and 'kulaks', transfer their land to the peasants, and thereby win support for Soviet power amongst 'the farm hands, and the mass of the peasants.'[86] Yet the Polish war was not intended to be one of conquest as such; Lenin's intention was that the Red Army would arm the Polish workers and leave Poland as soon as possible.

The Red offensive would soon be repulsed and the Reds driven back beyond the Curzon Line, until peace negotiations culminated in the Treaty of Riga in March 1921. During these negotiations recruitment for the Whites was taking place in Latvia and Estonia. Considering a 'diplomatic protest' insufficient, Lenin wanted to 'punish' Latvia and Estonia by military means. In late October/early November he instructed Efraim Sklianskii, Trotsky's deputy in the RVSR, that the army should cross the borders by a distance of about a kilometer and 'hang there 100 to –1,000 of their officials and rich men.'[87] In one of his most cynical correspondences, he then wrote to Sklianskii instructing him to work out his 'beautiful plan' with Dzerzhinskii that 'under the guise of "greens" (we will then pin it on them) advance for "10 to 20 versts" and hang kulaks, priests, landowners. Prize: 100,000 roubles for each hanging.'[88] (George Leggett dated this document to August, not October/November as have the editors of a recent Russian collection of Lenin documents, and thought it was in connection with the Polish offensive. It is probable that it was directly connected with the other correspondence with Sklianskii mentioned above.)

During the Polish campaign Lenin attended the Second Congress of the Comintern. He declared that the fundamental mistake of the German Independents (Kautsky's new party), which ultimately did not accept Lenin's conditions for joining Comintern, was that they recognized the conquest of power but not dictatorship. One of their members opined that terror and coercion were 'two different things'. Lenin's retort was quite interesting:

> ...such a distinction is possible in a manual of sociology, but it cannot be made in political practice [...] Of course, there is no need to proclaim in

advance that we shall positively resort to terror but if the German officers [...] remain the same as they now are [...] the employment of terror will be inevitable [...] A party that makes shift with such ideas cannot participate in the dictatorship.[89]

The practice of terror Lenin wanted enshrined as a principle of international revolutionary Marxist orthodoxy, though with the proviso that this would depend on the nature of counter-revolutionary opposition. Each party, during this period of 'acute civil war', should be organized on the basis of 'iron discipline bordering on military discipline.'[90] Important to note also is that Lenin repeated that agricultural collectivization must proceed cautiously in the aftermath of revolutions in the principal capitalist countries, without 'any coercion' of the middle peasants. The middle peasants he defined quite clearly as those who produced a small surplus crop and hired labour, but he also noted that though it would be necessary to struggle against the 'big peasants' (kulaks), this latter group was capable of loyalty to the proletarian state once the ruthless resolve of this state had been demonstrated.[91]

Once the Polish war broke out, Lenin reasoned that 'However much we may desire to go over to peaceful construction as soon as possible [...] the fact that war has been forced upon us makes it imperative that we subordinate everything to the demands of that war so as to achieve the most successful and rapid results.'[92] On 11 May the STO and VTsIK adopted a resolution signed by Lenin that placed much of European Russia under martial law, with the justification that the Polish 'bourgeois-landowner government' was attempting to revive counter-revolution within the country.[93] Depicting a picture of the German government's support for Piłsudski, Entente support for General Wrangel – who had revived the Civil War in Crimea – and Wrangel's intention to link up with Polish forces, Lenin and Trotsky introduced a Politburo resolution on 4 June urging an increase in measures of reprisal against all 'elements undermining the military capacity of the Soviet Republic in its struggle against the new whiteguard alliance'.[94] This was broad enough to include just about any opposition to Soviet power.

The second half of 1920 saw a renewed determination to combat the Mensheviks and SRs, in connection with the persistence and increase in popular, mainly rural, unrest.[95] Lenin was fully aware of the extent of this unrest from regular Cheka *svodki* (reports) dispatched to Moscow, copies of which were sent personally to him. In one such *svodka* for June, the majority of provinces mentioned was reported as dangerous or unsatisfactory regarding the general popular attitude towards Soviet power. The continuation of war with Poland was an important source of this dissatisfaction, especially in Moscow and Vladimir provinces.[96] Lenin, as the instigator of the Red Army's Polish offensive, was fully aware of domestic discontent with the continuation of the burdens of war. The Bolsheviks were, first, the party of the advanced, vanguard workers. In Saratov province it was reported that the 'conscious part' of the urban population was supportive of the Polish offensive. However several factories there were not disposed to 'friendly relations' with the government 'thanks to the counter-revolutionary activities of the SRs and Mensheviks.'[97] The discursive orthodoxy was reinforced that, though food deficiency was a key factor, the presence of 'counter-revolutionary agitators' was another crucial factor in generating popular unrest and its nature.

 Lenin had approved a reduction in requisitions in Khar'kov in February, yet the mood of the peasants in a particular region of that province was worsening owing to the 'resolute measures of pumping-out grain from the kulaks.'[98] In Cheliabinsk province, unrest was largely due to the 'incorrect activities of the food detachments.' The section on uprisings must have made the most troubling reading for Lenin. In the Kuban'-Black Sea region, the insurgents were calculated to number up to 7,000. In Voronezh province, widespread 'counter-revolutionary agitation' under the slogan 'without communists and no removal of grain' resulted in up to 2,000 armed insurgents. In Omsk province, an uprising mobilized 'all the peasantry'.[99] On 11 July Lenin was informed that 'Half of the Altai and Tomsk gubernias [in southern Siberia] are in the grip of a kulak movement which we are suppressing by force of arms. The cause of the insurrection is lack of commodities.'[100] Two days later Lenin advised provincial authorities that food supplies were extremely limited, and that if they were to provide rations for all elements of society they would have to fulfil completely their requisition quotas.[101] Confronted with violent popular opposition to the 'workers' and poor peasants' revolution', facing economic collapse, waging a revolutionary war and civil war, and as yet unwilling to re-conceptualize the *razverstka*, the state resorted to brutal suppressions.

 Placing a significant part of the blame on 'counter-revolutionary agitators', who were certainly involved in giving organization to outbreaks of revolt, made it easier for the Bolsheviks to rationalize this popular indignation and intensify suppression of the socialist parties. The poor and middle peasants were supposedly being misled and hence unable to understand the significance of Soviet power. Correspondingly, Chekists drew attention in these reports to the lack of adequate party work in areas afflicted by popular disaffection, and to the 'dark unconscious masses' in such places.[102] In November Lenin would speak of 'the variety of shades and forms of counter-revolution in various parts of Russia' as represented, in effect, by all parties aside from the Bolsheviks, and he was convinced that 'we [the party] have every reason to consider ourselves far more steeled in the struggle [against the 'world bourgeoisie'] than anybody else is.'[103] Even the 'minority' offshoot of the SRs who disagreed with their Central Committee and favoured co-operation with the Bolsheviks – although they wanted free elections to the soviets – were met with hostility. The Vecheka was instructed to issue a circular letter warning that these 'minority' SRs were merely trying to revive the SR Party and 'harm the normal course of socialist revolution.'[104]

 The *svodki* also kept the Moscow leadership informed about the continuing problem of desertion. In Tver province in June it was estimated that there were nearly 8,500 Red Army deserters; in the Northern Dvina, around a thousand, especially comprising middle and 'even poor' peasants. The local population was reported providing support to the deserters. Lenin could take consolation from such provinces as Briansk where, despite the 'harsh circumstances' for the army, soldiers were reported to be supportive of Soviet power and desertion comparatively low.[105] The struggle with desertion, waged openly in the press, took the forms of agitation and propaganda to shame deserters and encourage men to voluntarily appear for service; the incentive of material provisions for soldiers' families; and threats to confiscate half or all the property of deserters' families or of those sheltering them.[106] The Central Committee tried to restrict the shooting of deserters to cases where there were direct links with 'banditry' and attempts to encourage desertion amongst others, or depending on the gravity of the situation at the front.[107]

Before NEP: state versus peasantry

By October the war with Poland was reaching a ceasefire but civil war against Wrangel's forces persisted. The *svodki* continued to paint a picture of a country very far from the socialist ideal. The presentation of differences in attitude towards the regime of various social elements was quite clear. In one such report received in late October, workers in Tula were reported to be satisfied. In Riazan both workers and peasants were 'indignant' at the lack of food and the *razverstka*. In Vladimir, however, the workers were reported to be 'fully sympathetic' towards the regime, with the peasants – middle and poor – unhappy, even 'openly hostile'. In Iaroslavl' the workers were described as 'conscious', the peasants 'undefined' and the petty-bourgeoisie (a term that usually included the peasantry) 'openly hostile'.[108] The peasants, as Lenin declared in December, were not socialists.[109]

The situation in Ukraine was particularly troubling. 'Banditry' was described as on the increase in connection with the 'new *razverstka*' in Khar'kov; kulaks were allegedly spreading rumours to dissuade the peasants from complying with the quotas. The entire population, apart from the poor peasants, was described as 'waiting for Wrangel.' In Kiev the population was 'literally starving'.[110] Lenin was informed that in other parts of the country armed uprisings, due to the *razverstka*, were put down by the army and the Chekas, sometimes with the use of machine guns.[111]

The Civil War effectively concluded in November. Having failed to crush the Whites before the Polish war, Lenin was determined that there would be 'rapid and complete liquidation' of all enemy forces in the 'Caucasus and the Kuban', urging the use of heavy artillery against the remnants of Wrangel's troops there.[112] Following the evacuation of Wrangel's forces from Crimea, the Soviet authorities executed about 50,000 of the local population. Historian Nicolas Werth has apparently implicated Lenin in this, based on the latter's declaration to Moscow Communists on 6 December that there were 300,000 bourgeoisie in Crimea who constituted a source of future enemies. However Werth does not mention the remainder of Lenin's statement, that 'we are not afraid of them' and will 'subordinate and assimilate [or bear – *perevarit'*] them.'[113]

In early October, following the suppression of uprisings in connection with Wrangel's forces landing in the Kuban', Lenin had approved increased grain requisitioning in the area above the estimated quota.[114] In the middle of the month he laid out the principles of future grain-requisitioning. Responding to criticisms of government policies from provincial Moscow soviets, he recognized that 'Most of the peasants are feeling all too severely the effects of famine, cold and excessive taxation.' The quotas imposed upon Central Russia were 'often extremely rigorous', but Sovnarkom had decided to reduce them. To meet the balance, there would henceforth be even greater reliance upon the principal grain-producing regions.[115] There was no talk as yet of discontinuing the *razverstka*, due to the acute food shortage, and thus these reports from the country did not yet induce Lenin to adopt a new economic course.

From November the tasks of peaceful construction took precedence once again, and Lenin now recognized that 'we have become almost totally accustomed to tackling political and military tasks', leading to a revival of bureaucratic methods. He felt it necessary to remind his colleagues of the requirement ultimately to smash the old state apparatus and transfer power to the soviets.[116] On 30 November he first mentioned a possible changeover from the surplus-appropriation system to a tax-in-kind,[117] but the adoption of a new course came only after a wave of industrial strikes and major peasant uprisings in late 1920/early 1921. These uprisings led to what Oliver Radkey labelled a 'second civil war' between state and peasantry. The primary cause of the uprisings was the *razverstka* and how it was taken; as Lenin would acknowledge and criticize in May 1921, the levies had in cases been taken 'two or three times' in one period.[118]

ᐧ The largest peasant uprising occured in Tambov province, constituting a huge movement that cut through an important grain-producing region and the transportation route from the south-eastern grain-producing regions.[119] Initially, in September 1920, Lenin enquired whether the quota for Tambov province should be reduced.[120] By October he gave a 'definite order to *achieve rapid and complete liquidation*' of the uprising. Four days later, informed of an increase in the revolt, he instructed that 'Speediest (and exemplary) liquidation is absolutely essential',[121] and in a *svodka* received the same month he was informed that 600 insurgents had been killed in Tambov.[122] In early 1921 Lenin was still demanding that the Red Army '*rout* and *catch* Antonov [leader of the Tambov insurrection] and Makhno [Ukrainian 'bandit' leader].'[123]

The problems in Tambov were explained clearly in a March 1921 report sent to Lenin by Vladimir Antonov-Ovseenko, chair of a VTsIK commission that was sent there. Regarding the *razverstka*, Antonov-Ovseenko criticized the centre for completely failing to take into account the weak organizational apparatus, the bad harvest, the bandit movement, and the protestations of district authorities that quotas could not be fulfilled. On 8 February Moscow actually decided to suspend grain requisitioning in 12 provinces, including Tambov.[124] Regarding the Cheka, Antonov-Ovseenko complained that it was 'saturated with corrupt and suspicious persons and completely paralyzed.' Regarding the uprising itself, Antonov-Ovseenko highlighted the solid organization provided it by the local SRs, whose programme had 'success amongst the peasants.'[125] His assessment was that the Bolsheviks Party had effectively 'lost all contact with the country' and was relying only on the urban workers. Yet it should not be thought that this was simply a traditional conflict between state/city and country; it was also a political conflict between the state and those peasants and their leaders who had been politically mobilized by the revolution, and Bolshevik failures to deliver on the promises of 1917.[126]

Antonov-Ovseenko stressed the need to win over the peasants from the 'SR-bandits' through political education (open court sessions), destruction of the SR organization, and also control of the work of the state apparatus, especially the food organs. He indicated that he did not believe radical policy changes were required.[127] That same month, however, the party decided to address the 'exhaustion' of the masses and abolish the *razverstka* system. It was the adoption of NEP that finally broke popular support for the uprising,[128] allowing the peasants to return to some semblance of normalcy.

The suppression of the uprising however was brutal. Moscow was finally persuaded by Antonov-Ovseenko to send a major military force to Tambov. On 26 April Sklianskii wrote to Lenin considering it 'desirable to send [Red Army General Mikhail] Tukhachevskii' to Tambov, though Sklianskii was concerned about the possible 'political effect', especially abroad, of sending the Red Army's leading commander to fight the insurgent peasants.[129] Lenin agreed that Tukhachevskii be sent, without publicity. Not only would this be a striking example of the state using its troops against its own people, but there were fears that such indication of the insecurity of Soviet power would encourage foreign aggression.[130] Tukhachevskii conceived his task to be not merely or even principally the routing of the insurgent 'Partisan Army' but the 'sovietization' of the affected countryside; as Holquist observes, the Bolshevik Civil War campaigns were not intended simply to pacify the countryside but to cleanse it of the 'tumour' of 'banditry'.[131] Thus, Orders Nos. 130 and 171 provided for a massive campaign of hostage-taking and summary executions in villages noted for commitment to the rebels. Over 5,000 hostages had been put in concentration camps by July, including women and children. These brutal measures also reflected a brutal security logic. One of the key components of Order No. 171 was the necessity of removing all weapons from the villages, as Soviet officials were convinced that rebels might seek surrender and rehabilitation only to strike again following the departure of the Red Army.[132] In total, 11,000 insurgents lost their lives during the uprising, and the executions of 'bandit hostages' were reported to Lenin.[133] Camp inmates, in Tambov as elsewhere, were considered according to their sociological past and perceived reconcilability to the regime – whether they were fervent, irredeemable foes of Soviet power, or victims of their own ignorance and circumstances and capable of re-education. Perhaps as many as 25,000 people or more ascribed to the former category were executed by the state in the eighteen months following the Civil War.[134]

In December 1920 Lenin appeared before the Eighth All-Russian Congress of Soviets. The Bolsheviks had accepted the need to reach agreement with the imperialist powers, offering economic concessions to the USA and Japan, and working toward a trade agreement with Britain. The rationale was to acquire, in return, the best machinery to restore the shattered Soviet economy, but Lenin retained his commitment to socialist revolutions as the only means 'out of eternal warfare'. The task of Soviet Russia was to attempt to convince the workers of the world of this fact.[135] Despite demobilization, he believed that 'we must keep our Red Army in a state of combat readiness at all costs, and increase its fighting efficiency', for 'history teaches us that no big question has ever been settled, and no revolution accomplished, without a series of wars.'[136] He would not rule out the possibility that the Red Army would 'resort to certain actions' which could be regarded as aggressive,[137] i.e. offensive revolutionary wars. There was then as yet no real idea of 'peaceful co-existence' with the capitalist world; Lenin declared that 'We are lagging behind the capitalist powers and shall continue to lag behind them; we shall be defeated if we do not succeed in restoring our economy.'[138]

To meet these tasks Lenin reiterated the continued need for dictatorship, and the tensions within his dual concept of dictatorship – 'compulsion with persuasion' – were evident. The present tasks, as he put it, demanded 'enthusiasm and self-sacrifice from the vast majority of workers and peasants [...] They must be organized, *not to resist* the government but to support and develop the measures of *their* workers' government and to carry them out to the full.'[139] Were they convinced of the necessity of sacrificing everything for the sake of victory of the labour front?', Lenin asked, replying in the negative. Yet he was confident that the *narod* would be won over to the task of creating the new order. Lenin's 'heroic scenario' (as Lars Lih terms it) of the vanguard of the *narod* leading it to salvation remained a constant guiding star for his political thought.

During its dictatorship the proletariat, Lenin repeated, 'is entitled to use compulsion [against the 'landowners and capitalists'], because it is doing so in the interests of the working and exploited people'.[140] Only through the firm will of the proletariat would the peasants and workers unite into a single force capable of creating the new society. In a speech to young Communists in October he accepted the existence of a 'communist morality' and explained that 'our morality is entirely subordinated to the interests of the proletariat's class struggle.' There was, he explained, no 'eternal morality' outside of the interests of class struggle; rather, morality 'serves the purpose of helping human society to rise to a higher level.'[141] Hence the more severe forms of state coercion could be considered justifiable and indeed moral in the interests of the Marxist teleology. Such coercion would apply also to the 'backward' lower classes, as clearly justified in Bukharin's book, though Lenin was confident at the Congress that proletarian dictatorship held 'no terrors' for the mass of peasants and workers. Nonetheless the 'truth is on our side', he was convinced, and he warned that 'Whoever reveals the least weakness, the least slackness in this matter, is an out-and-out criminal towards the workers' and peasants' government', because the capitalist powers were waiting to jump on any weaknesses displayed by Soviet Russia.[142]

Incentives were now to be granted to 'industrious' peasants but a more ambitious plan was generated within the food supply apparatus to assert state control over agricultural production.[143] Lenin made perfectly clear that he had no intention of making significant concessions to the small-scale peasant economy; in a small-peasant country, he warned, the economic basis of capitalism was stronger than that of socialism.[144] Hence the enthusiasm with which he explained the necessity of bringing electrification throughout the country, of bringing 'light' and 'enlightenment' to the 'darkness' of rural life. There were clear tensions in his thought between, on the one hand, the importance of restoring agricultural production and the self-criticism now voiced of 'being carried away by our struggle against the kulaks', and on the other the prevention of any strengthening of the position of the 'kulaks' – who, he acknowledged, operated 'the best-run farms'. He remarked at the Congress that 'No machines should be given, not even to the most hardworking farmer, not even if he has achieved success without the least resort to kulak practices.' Machines by their very nature required hired labour and thereby the industrious peasant would turn into a kulak.[145] He was convinced that the 'most decisive class struggle' was still raging in the countryside.[146] However in response to questions from representatives of regional soviets as to how to differentiate kulaks from non-kulaks, he was vague and dismissive: 'the local people know this perfectly well.' On this point, Donald Raleigh has explained that allegiance to Soviet power, rather than sociological belonging, increasingly came to define social identity in early Soviet Russia. One representative at the Congress wanted to know if he should continue forcibly confiscating 'kulak' property because the grain quotas had not been fulfilled, even if this led to the ruin of farms. Lenin's reply was that he should follow the government policy and his own 'communist conscience'.[147]

In December Dzerzhinskii sent a secret report to the Central Committee in which he proposed the abolition of the right of Chekas to implement the death penalty without Vecheka approval, except in cases of open armed actions against Soviet power. The Vecheka would once again largely transfer its functions to the judicial apparatus, the tribunals. Dzerzhinskii recommended that the arrests of socialists be considered means of 'temporary' isolation from society in the interests of the revolution, and that their incarceration should not have a 'punitive character'.[148] On 8 January 1921 he issued a Vecheka order that the 'old methods' of the Civil War – 'mass arrests and repressions' – would no longer be appropriate means of dealing with the SRs. Mass repression would merely provide fuel for counter-revolution and intensify popular discontent with the regime, and he recommended instead 'more subtle' methods of controlling these parties and combating their popular influence, such as infiltration.[149] This relatively moderate approach to socialist political opposition would contrast with the more severe approach soon adopted by the Bolshevik leadership according to its understanding of the nature of the new course in Soviet politics from March 1921, the NEP.

Yet Dzerzhinskii's correspondences with Chekists and the party leadership in the winter of 1920–21 would reflect the party's philosophy of repression during the early years of NEP, and provide an insightful illustration of its philosophy of repression generally. He explained that during the Civil War the least economic malfeasance and petty speculation could have hindered the Red Army and was considered impermissible. Political police discourse for much of the 1920s would emphasize the distinction between 'inveterate', recidivist opponents and criminals (the true focus of Cheka attention), and workers and peasants who infringed the law due to harsh material conditions and/or ignorance. Dzerzhinskii lamented that Soviet prisons at the end of 1920 were 'overflowing' with workers and peasants, not class enemies, and he wanted to see this situation reversed. 'Comradely leadership' rather than prison should henceforth be employed for working elements suffering from 'poor consciousness', but repression of the bourgeoisie he wanted intensified through their isolation from society and the creation of concentration camps solely for bourgeois inmates.[150] State violence against the bourgeoisie and all 'inveterate enemies' was then certainly not simply induced by wartime necessity but was, more accurately, immanent in Bolshevik ideology and political practice, and cultivated by the experience of extreme circumstances. Bourgeois resistance, opposition and hostility to Soviet power remained inside and outside the country, Dzerzhinskii warned, and the complexity of the domestic and international situation ensured that 'flexibility' rather than rigid adherence to legality was still necessary. He stressed that the Vecheka was not a police force of old, expressing his desire that its activities would be perceived by the proletariat as those 'of its own dictatorship.'[151]

The Vecheka's existence as the organ of state violence seemed secure and its armed forces were accorded 'special status' to remain under its own control.[152] With the introduction of NEP, the party would have to reconsider the Vecheka's position within the state structure. Nonetheless 'flexibility' in coercive/repressive practices would certainly continue.

8 'We will cleanse Russia for a long time'

The contradictions of NEP

[…] it would be necessary to deport several hundred such gentlemen pitilessly. We will cleanse Russia for a long time.[1]

(Lenin to Stalin, 16 July 1922)

In March 1921 the Bolshevik Party realized the need to change its course towards socialism in response to the widespread peasant and worker unrest. Lenin demonstrated his ability to take and secure decisive and pragmatic, though deeply unpalatable, political and economic decisions. The result was the substitution of a reduced tax-in-kind in grain for the state monopoly. Peasants would be permitted to trade their resultant surplus stocks and the restoration of a private market was soon permitted. Lenin introduced this as 'state capitalism', which he understood as capitalist relations under the control of a socialist, proletarian state. What the Bolsheviks had considered not just execrable but intolerable just a few months previously – the encouragement of the capitalist tendencies of the petty-bourgeois peasantry – was now considered necessary. Initially Lenin envisaged that this would be based on simple commodity exchange, but within several months a further retreat to a monetary economy was announced. In industry, small and middle enterprises were largely de-nationalized, though essential and large-scale industries remained under state ownership. Thus after three years of civil war and War Communism, a limited mixed economy was introduced in Soviet Russia, known as the New Economic Policy (NEP), and was only to be replaced with the inauguration of forced industrialization and forced collectivization at the end of the decade.

NEP represented an attempt to reintegrate state with society and witnessed a blunting of the weapon of class warfare, a significant reduction in state violence as a whole, and a greater culture of legality. Yet in many respects in its early years it also represented a period of intensified dictatorship of the ruling party. This was to ensure that changes in economic practices would not result in significant similar changes in the politico-ideological sphere. State coercion and terror persisted, despite the cessation of major armed confrontations on Russian soil and the relative international security of the Soviet Republic. With the defeat of the White armies, the state received a freer hand to attempt to decisively confront sources of (potential) political opposition. NEP was in fact conceived as perhaps the high-point of the Leninist concept of *'kto-kogo?'* (who-whom?), that is, a particularly crucial period in the struggle between the proletariat and the bourgeoisie/petty-bourgeoisie for victory over the other, precisely because concessions to capitalism had been granted.[2]

. The study of NEP has traditionally been of particular interest for scholars examining the continuities and disparities between Leninism and Stalinism. Was NEP a temporary retreat from the principles of the preceding years, in which case Stalin's 'revolution from above' appears as a largely rational continuation of an original Leninist project ('totalitarian' school)? Or was it the beginning of a new course, supposedly more akin to the original and true essence of the Leninist conception of socialist transformation as opposed to the temporary policies of War Communism, in which case Stalinism represented a radical and distorted new departure ('revisionist' school)?[3] Stephen Cohen provides a particularly charged version of the latter argument, asserting that NEP represented 'a historical model of Soviet Communist rule radically unlike Stalinism.'[4] For Vladimir Brovkin, who rejects the idea that NEP was an alternative to Stalinism, NEP was merely a 'temporary obstacle to overcome' and was 'never conceived of as a path to socialism.'[5] Roger Pethybridge questions whether the gap between the respective aims of state and society could ultimately have been bridged without 'wide-ranging political coercion.'[6] Certainly the greater freedoms in the private sphere accompanying NEP, including the possibility of enjoying 'bourgeois' tastes, troubled party members who remained focused on the creation of a new society. Efim Gimpel'son argues that it was primarily the state's unwillingness to accompany relative economic liberalization with similar political liberalization that ultimately spelled failure for NEP.[7]

The question of whether NEP was merely a retreat or a different course to socialism (and hence perhaps whether the market economy could develop into socialism 'without a revolution against the [new] bourgeoisie'[8]) has been the crucial debating point. Immediately before and during the Gorbachëv era, some Soviet historians emphasized that NEP was not simply a retreat but a long road to socialism.[9] Lars Lih argues that Lenin's belief in the heroism of civil war policies persisted, and that Lenin and Stalin's later opponent Bukharin always conceived NEP as a retreat certainly but one that would lead to an advance to a planned economy and the supersession of capitalism.[10] For Lenin, as we will see, NEP was both a retreat and a reconceptualization of the route to socialism, and there was no question but that NEP was designed ultimately to completely eradicate capitalism and petty-bourgeois production, to overcome itself as Lih notes. It was primarily a reconceptualization in the sense that Lenin recognized the mistake of attempting to move towards communism too soon, but he certainly believed that there were inherent dangers in the new course and that class struggle could not be dispensed with. NEP was a serious attempt on the part of Lenin and the Bolshevik leadership to accommodate the structural problems facing the revolution, not just peasant hostility and the virtual collapse of the industrial proletarian base but also the cultural backwardness of the country. This, however, was seriously constrained by the limits of permissible Bolshevik discourse and hostility to a private economic and public sphere. This discourse stressed the principle of '*kto-kogo?*', of the Bolshevik Party as the true embodiment of proletarian will, and of the need to relinquish as little as possible of the perceived gains of the previous three years.

The 'retreat' of NEP then, at least in terms of ideological discourse, should not be exaggerated. Tolerance of capitalist relations was required, not simply to relieve social tensions but to create the bases of socialism, but the Bolsheviks were constantly fearful of the removal of their socialist polity. Igal Halfin has made the important observation that the eschatological premise of Bolshevism, prescribing forward movement toward communism, ensures that 'radical tension between present and future describes the [Bolshevik] mind-set of the 1920s.'[11] It is hardly surprising, then, that many in the party were supportive of Stalin's abandonment of NEP by 1930. The most useful analyses are those that point to the contradictions of NEP and yet take seriously what it was about, ultimately arguing that Stalin would replace it with something quite different to what was conceived earlier in the decade.

Lenin, argues Robert Service, 'still breathed fire' in his advocacy of terror during NEP and had no change of heart before he died.[12] Joan Witte argues similarly that he extracted from the failures of War Communism 'no generalized lesson of the limitations of force as a policy instrument'. She finds it surprising then that 'in his retirement he pleaded for peaceful, harmonious development.'[13] Whereas Witte implies a more essentialist approach to violence in Lenin's thought and therefore finds it strange that Lenin would 'change', Moshe Lewin, with equal exaggeration, finds this not at all unusual. Unlike 'some of his successors', Lewin remarks, Lenin 'hated repression; for him, it should be used only in the defense of the regime against serious threat and as a punishment for those who contravened legality.'[14] The record of Lenin's pronouncements and practice during NEP conflicts with Lewin's understanding. Lenin never (as far as we can tell) relinquished his fervent belief, derived from his interpretation of Marxism and reinforced by the experience of revolution in practice, that dictatorship 'is a state of intense war', that '*À la guerre, comme à la guerre*', and that 'Until the final issue is decided, this awful state of war will continue'.[15] Yet Lenin had always recognized that force and violence were not sufficient solutions to the problems facing the revolution and not always appropriate. His last writings testify to his realization that Soviet Russia could not be forced into communism but would require a more peaceful and evolutionary path because of the 'petty-bourgeois' nature of the masses.

Lenin and NEP

In early February 1921 Lenin delivered a speech in which he declared that 'The peasants are another class', but that 'We must do our best to establish proper relations' between them and the workers. He warned that 'We never promised a liberal regime; the one we have has helped us to escape the bondage of the landowners and capitalists.'[16] Four days later he drafted a plan to introduce the tax-in-kind, set below *razverstka* levels,[17] that was approved at the Tenth Party Congress in March. Lenin now acknowledged that miscalculated Bolshevik policy, aggravated by crop failure, had contributed to the particularly extreme food crisis already in evidence.[18] Yet he was wistful that grain-rich Ukrainian peasants could not understand that confiscations were intended to ease the plight of workers and peasants. The peasant 'cannot help being ignorant' and it would, 'take us years to re-educate him.'[19]

The Congress met amidst the Kronstadt sailors' mutiny, as well as continuing peasant revolts. Relations between 'workers and peasants', Lenin stated, were 'not what we had believed them to be.' The petty-bourgeois peasantry raised the serious prospect of the Russian Revolution going the way of the French (Thermidor then Bonapartism), for 'The petty-bourgeois counter-revolution is undoubtedly more dangerous than Denikin, Iudenich and Kolchak put together, because ours is a country where the proletariat is in a minority.'[20] NEP then was political in nature: 'Politics are relations between classes, and that will decide the fate of our Republic.'[21] There was for Lenin no question but that the proletariat still had a right to exercise its dictatorship despite being in a minority, indeed despite being 'largely declassed', for 'in a peasant country only the will of the mass of proletarians will enable the proletariat to accomplish the great tasks of its leadership and dictatorship.'[22] Marxism, he believed, taught that only the Communist Party could train the working people to embody the single proletarian will and withstand not just petty-bourgeois vacillation but narrow 'craft unionism' within the proletariat itself, and he characterized the Party's Workers' Opposition as a 'radical departure from communism and a deviation towards syndicalism and anarchism.'[23] The petty-bourgeois peasantry – which he referred to clearly as an independent class – was certainly to be won over eventually to the proletarian camp; however his justification for the persistence of proletarian dictatorship on the basis of a proletarian majority, or its position as a significant minority amongst 'middle' elements[24] appeared to be wearing very thin.

NEP was designed to reckon with the fact that the peasantry as a class had 'levelled' out, had become an almost unitary body of 'middle peasants', and with the fact that revolutions had not matured abroad.[25] Lenin's prediction that the rule of the bourgeoisie would not survive the imperialist war had proved as yet unfounded. His other prediction, that without such an outcome a socialist revolution in Russia could not survive, had also not come to pass. Neither proletariat nor bourgeoisie was yet strong enough to obliterate the other, therefore 'only agreement with the peasantry can save the socialist revolution in Russia',[26] a *smyichka* between worker and peasant. The proletariat required tact in understanding the precariousness of its power-base, the need to sow dissension in the enemy camp, and to ensure that the petty-bourgeois peasantry would be won over. The peasants were to be the primary recipients of concessions, but these were only permissible within the limits required to sustain the power of the proletariat, which was advancing 'towards communism.'[27] Would not freedom of trade for the small farmer undermine proletarian power, Lenin wondered, addressing the deep concerns of many Congress delegates? Ostensibly yes, he acknowledged, but this was necessary to stimulate the economy and restore large-scale industry, the basis of proletarian power.[28] Lenin spoke of NEP both as a means of saving proletarian power and as an alternative to international revolutions to secure the triumph of socialist revolution in Russia,[29] but certainly he believed that the complete triumph and security of socialism would require an international victory for socialism (as basically Stalin would also later maintain).

What, then, of the role of state coercion and violence? This was, Lenin noted, one of the last and most crucial of the proletariat's battles, against petty-bourgeois anarchy at home.[30] The landowners and capitalists of old had effectively been expelled, and he thought that there were only two classes in Russia, the proletariat and the peasantry.[31] He later clarified that though crushed politically, the capitalists still existed in Soviet organizations and especially in émigré groupings abroad, hoping and striving for a return to power in Russia.[32] In a sentence that seemed to prefigure Stalinist sentiment a decade later, Lenin told the Eleventh Party Congress that 'the fight against capitalist society has become a hundred times more fierce and perilous, because we are not always able to tell enemies from friends.'[33] Hence the Bolshevik reasoning that counter-revolution would result from any softening of political dictatorship. Coercion and indeed violence, then, could not be dispensed with. Referring to the Kronstadt mutiny, Lenin declared that when 'faced with that sort of thing, we must [...] counter it with rifles, no matter how innocent it may appear to be.'[34]

Expanding on the theme of '*kto-kogo?*', Lenin remarked that in fact 'government must be much stricter and much firmer than it was before'. The essential question in this new 'war' was:

> who will win, who will first take advantage of the situation: the capitalist, whom we are allowing to come in by the door, and even by several doors [...] or proletarian state power? [...] Either the capitalists succeed in organizing first – in which case they will drive out the Communists and that will be the end of it. Or the proletarian state power, with the support of the peasantry, will prove capable of keeping a proper rein on those gentlemen, the capitalists, so as to direct capitalism along state channels and to create a capitalism that will be subordinate to the state and serve the state.[35]

He explained that behind the slogans of freedom and democracy advanced by the Mensheviks and SRs, and by the petty-bourgeois masses, lay the rule of the White Guards lying in wait, and hence the impossibility of any middle course. Proletarian dictatorship he continued to understand as 'war, much more cruel, much more prolonged and much more stubborn than any other war has ever been',[36] and the restoration of capitalist relations brought into sharp relief the general rule of war that 'danger threatens us at every step.' What this demanded was that Soviet society must be governed 'with a firmer hand than the capitalist governed before you', despite the fact that the state now permitted the peasants to control their own economy. There could be no room for 'sentiment' in wartime, he continued, and 'Whoever now departs from order and discipline is permitting the enemy to penetrate our midst.'[37] There was thus a fundamental continuity in Lenin's political thought between the eras of civil war and NEP.

The introduction of NEP would not necessarily remove the use of force to extract the grain tax. The reductions in sown areas and crop yields would undoubtedly diminish whatever surplus the peasant would initially have, but the imperative for the state was still to feed the towns and factories. Lenin did not expect the peasant, who 'lack[ed] faith', to understand this, so 'we shall not be able to do without coercion, on which [subject] the impoverished peasants are very touchy.'[38] The point was, though, that 'Persuasion must come before coercion'.[39] The task was to ease the peasants' situation as far as possible. For many peasants NEP would result in relative enrichment, to their becoming kulaks, and Lenin was clear that that this would not be prohibited as such but combated by other means. He was confident that overall state control, and improvements in technology and eventual conversion to large-scale agricultural production, would eventually wipe out the kulaks. In May at the Party Conference he asserted that NEP was both a retreat and a new course to be undertaken 'seriously and for a long time', as Nikolai Osinskii had put it. Rather prophetically, he thought that the policy would probably be changed again in about five to ten years.[40] However long NEP might last, it appears that the Bolsheviks continued to assume that they would not likely survive for more than a decade or two in the absence of international revolutions.[41]

· Violent measures continued to be 'inalienable elements of social relations' in NEP Russia.[42] The official number of victims shot by the Vecheka and Chekas in 1921 was 9,701, for such crimes as belonging to counter-revolutionary organizations, espionage, preparing and participating in uprisings, 'banditry' and theft. Those executed also included Red Army soldiers who refused to go to Kronstadt to put down the mutiny.[43]

NEP was not initially extended to the peasants of the rich grain-producing areas of Ukraine and the Caucasus.[44] For the peasants as a whole the methods of collecting the tax differed little from those used for the *razverstka*. Taxes were often set at unrealistically high levels, and state personnel were frequently guilty of abuses of position and drunkenness. Peasant opposition manifested itself in sometimes passive, sometime active resistance, and rebellion continued through the early- and mid-1920s.[45] In addition the state's pricing controls (and the activities of the 'NEPmen' traders) during the initial years of NEP continued to dis-incentivize peasants to part with their produce for as yet sparse, expensive consumer products. From 1922 the state attempted to resolve some of the difficulties associated with the operation of NEP, and from the second half of that year a general improvement in peasant attitudes towards the state was evident.[46]

One of the principal factors complicating the new agrarian course was the crop failure and famine that arose principally along the grain-producing Volga by July. The famine and its devastating consequences, resulting in the deaths through starvation and disease of some five million people, were not simply the results of drought and years of war and revolution. They were to a considerable extent the results of state requisitioning, including confiscations of peasants' seed grain for the sowing season, and the failure of the government to take preventive measures.[47]

On 2 July Lenin as Chair of the STO (Council of Labour and Defence) proposed to suspend free grain exchange in Siberia only and restore forced exchange with the Siberian food authorities.[48] On 30 July he and Viacheslav Molotov, Central Committee secretary, sent a telegram to all provinces and regions noting that, owing to crop failures in certain provinces and the inadequacies of free trade, the significance of trade relative to taxation should not be exaggerated in ensuring an adequate food supply (i.e. provincial officials should not assume that opening the market would solve the food supply problems). Taxation was to be fully collected through a combination of agitation and administrative or judicial punishments of tax evaders – the 'total power of the state apparatus of coercion.'[49]

Indicative also of how Lenin had not suddenly revised his belief in the efficacy of severe coercion and violence in the face of an economic crisis was a note he wrote in August instructing 'instant, exemplary and highly severe punishment of 10 of the *richest* peasants per volost *for any delay*, however slight, over the tax-in-kind or for *slack* delivery'.[50] During the same month the STO resolved that 'the most resolute measures of a forceful character' would be applied by revolutionary tribunals with the first signs of opposition to the tax or delays in its fulfilment.[51] In times of crisis the Bolsheviks had greater instinctual trust in requisitioning backed with the full armed might of the state (than in market incentives to acquire more grain), ironically the (former) approach that had helped bring about the famine to begin with.

Lenin, though, was very honest about the mistake of attempting to organize the economic production and distribution of a small-peasant country on communist lines.[52] In a major policy pamphlet, *The Tax in Kind*, he acknowledged Bolshevik 'defeat' on the economic front. Yet he was defiant that War Communism had been necessary under the circumstances of the Civil War, even when it involved confiscating a peasant's personal requirements for the army and the workers. He even suggested that 'We deserve credit for it.'[53] In addition he reiterated that 'in countries beset by an unprecedented crisis', meaning 'all the countries of the world' in the aftermath of the Great War – 'terrorism' could not be dispensed with. It was 'Either the Whiteguard, bourgeois terrorism of the American, British (Ireland), Italian (the fascists), German, Hungarian and other types, or Red, proletarian terrorism.'

Four years after the revolution and given the failure of Bolshevik policies yet to lead to a better life for the Russian toilers, Lenin turned once again to the 'great accelerator' of history, the imperialist war, for moral justification for Bolshevik actions over the previous years. The picture that Lenin painted was stark, but once again prophetic, if capitalism were not defeated internationally:

> It is a question of life and death for millions upon millions of people. It is a question of whether 20 million people (as compared with the 10 million who were killed in the war of 1914–18 [...]) are to be slaughtered in the next imperialist war, which the bourgeoisie are preparing [...].[54]

However much the bourgeois press might condemn the 'horrors' of Russian Bolshevism the point, Lenin insisted, was 'to distinguish firmly, clearly and dispassionately what constitutes the historic service rendered by the Russian revolution from what we do very badly'.[55] The anti-war Basle Manifesto of 1912 had become outdated: it was necessary for socialists not merely to make anti-war speeches and oppose moves towards war in their own countries, but to copy the example of the Russian Bolsheviks in 1917.[56] Were the Mensheviks correct in arguing that the failure of revolutionary methods proved that a more cautious reformist approach should have been adopted from the outset of the revolution? No, he replied, the adoption of NEP merely proved that there were times for revolutionary methods and times for a more reformist approach.[57]

The Red Army was supposed to be reduced by 1.5 million troops by September but in July, the month that he had acknowledged the extent of the famine catastrophe, Lenin declared that 'we must continue to think first of all of our Red Army' in matters of food supply.[58] Long-term peaceful coexistence with the West was not envisioned, yet NEP called for a cautious foreign policy due to the need to 'normalize' relations somewhat with the capitalist powers in the interests of economic reconstruction.[59] Revealing of Lenin's cautious tactic were his instructions to the Soviet delegation at the Genoa Conference in 1922 (the first international economic conference attended by a Soviet delegation). He wanted no mention of 'inevitable forcible revolution and the use of sanguinary struggle' in any declarations. It would be sufficient to note that Communists were not pacifists, but it would be 'our duty to give our fullest support to any attempts at a peaceful settlement of outstanding problems' in order to achieve the necessary economic agreements.[60] He explained to the Foreign Commissar, Chicherin, that there was no question of pacifism as a point of party principle, but only 'to soften up the enemy, the bourgeoisie.'[61]

NEP was accompanied by a general diminution of terror, and a period of greater revolutionary legality was proclaimed. This resulted in the reorganization of the Vecheka, diminution of its functions and powers, and rise in the importance of NKIu. The basis of 'revolutionary legality' remained the class principle;[62] Lenin emphasized that 'Our courts are class courts directed against the bourgeoisie', and more particularly his concern was that the courts would exercise state regulation of capitalist relations. Those found abusing NEP, he insisted, should be chastised ruthlessly through the courts 'with every means, including the firing squad'.[63] Lenin wanted to employ model trials (*obraztsovyikh protsessov* – 'model' in terms of forceful repression and publicity of the significance of the trials) for such economic crimes, without which NKIu would be 'good for nothing', because he considered that it would be a 'great mistake to think that NEP puts an end to terror.'[64] Indicating the contradictory tensions in his conceptualization of NEP, Lenin insisted that the state was to extend its rights to the 'private legal relations' made possible by a more liberalized economy, exercising 'our revolutionary concept of law' in this field, for 'We do not recognize anything "private"'.[65]

Due to the need for greater legality it was essential to reform the Vecheka, define its powers and limit it to political problems. The Politburo also recognized the need to remove stereotyped images of Cheka terror abroad.[66] In June 1921 the Vecheka's right to administer extra-judicial repression was once again confined to areas under martial law and only for direct participation in espionage, 'banditry' and armed uprisings.[67] Within a year of NEP the Vecheka would be abolished. Heightened legality would provide greater domestic stability and serve to increase the legitimacy of the state in the popular imagination. In 1922 greater importance was attached to the system of people's courts and the revolutionary tribunals were abolished in October, though military courts for special cases remained.[68]

How meaningful, though, would Vecheka reform be? Vecheka reform was introduced and explained by Lenin at the Ninth All-Russian Congress of Soviets in December. The Vecheka, he noted, was one of those institutions where 'faults are sometimes the continuation of our merits'. Lenin promised always to defend the Vecheka when confronted with talk of 'Russian barbarism'. He made clear that there was no question of the complete dissolution of this institution for it was considered an integral part of proletarian dictatorship:

> As long as there are exploiters in the world, who have no desire to hand over their landowner and capitalist rights to the workers on a platter, the power of the working people cannot survive without such an institution [...] The Soviet government grants admission to foreign representatives, who come here under the pretext of giving aid, but these same representatives turn round and help overthrow Soviet rule [...] Our government will not find itself in this position, because we shall value and make use of an institution like the Cheka.[69]

In November Sovnarkom had appointed a commission of Dzerzhinskii, Kamenev and Kurskii (the Commissar of Justice) to work out regulations for the Vecheka.[70] There were clear differences between the commission's members, but Lenin was determined that Vecheka functions be severely curtailed, at least in outward form. On 29 November he wrote to Kamenev to encourage this, declaring himself to be 'closer' to Kamenev's position than to Dzerzhinskii's.[71]

VTsIK decreed the reorganization on 6 February 1922. The Vecheka was to be renamed the State Political Administration (GPU), subordinate to the NKVD (still headed by Dzerzhinskii) though with 'special status', with regional organs attached to local soviet executive committees. Cases of counter-revolution, speculation and abuses of office were to be transferred to the revolutionary tribunals or people's courts. The GPU was charged with border control, protection of railways and waterways, counter-espionage and suppression of overt counter-revolutionary activity, including 'banditry'.[72] It was also granted the right, through a clause inserted in the decree, to fulfil any 'special task' assigned it by VTsIK or Sovnarkom. Particularly noteworthy in this regard was the responsibility devolved upon the GPU to gather information on the domestic mood of the populace and the influence of the 'petty-bourgeois element';[73] the GPU, as the Vecheka, was to be the 'eyes and ears' of the party. The full military apparatus of the Vecheka was to be retained such that in the event of an 'aggravation' of civil war, it would be prepared to act resolutely.

Lenin made clear that these restrictions in function would largely serve to maintain a mere veneer of legality. Even before the VTsIK decree, in January he had written to Iosif Unshlikht, deputy leader of the Vecheka, to assuage his concerns about Vecheka competency. Tribunal sessions should not be publicized as a rule, he noted, and their panels were to be 'augmented by "your" men and their ties (of all sorts) with the Vecheka strengthened.' The 'force and speed' of reprisals were to be intensified.[74] In other words, Lenin envisaged that a significant role for the political police would remain during NEP, even as conducted through legal channels. This reflected internal state discussions at the end of the Civil War concerning the transition from war to peace and the necessity of strengthening legality yet retaining sufficient 'flexibility' in the operation of the state's repressive apparatus, though by September Dzerzhinskii was voicing concerns that the Chekas were not exercising sufficient influence in court sessions.[75]

Lenin wrote to Unshlikht that the 'slightest increase in banditry' would be sufficient for martial law to be declared and 'shootings on the spot' to commence, and he assured him that Sovnarkom (i.e. very largely Lenin himself) would see to this if requested (even informally over the telephone).[76] None of this was mentioned officially, and indeed the Politburo did not authorize the GPU formally to practice summary justice in cases of 'banditry' until 27 April (though not officially decreed by VTsIK until October), when it also granted it power to exile criminal elements.[77] The right of employing administrative exile within the RSFSR for three years for counter-revolution was granted to the NKVD (and hence the GPU) on 10 August.[78] Leading Chekists such as Dzerzhinskii had opposed separation of political and large-scale 'economic' crimes in view of the 'unprecedented' nature of the 'bacchanalia' in the field of such crime, and the GPU regained powers to combat serious economic crimes in January 1923.[79]

· Revolutionary legality presupposed greater weight for the courts. Lenin's conception from the beginning was that the courts were to be empowered with the right to effectively administer arbitrary justice on serious matters, becoming the new instruments of terror against enemies of the regime, and that the party would direct court sentencing.[80] That the courts were to serve when necessary as organs of terror, and that this was an important function of what Lenin understood as 'revolutionary legality', he expounded upon in greater detail in a letter to Kurskii on 20 February. Previously 'the militant organs of the Soviet power' had been the army and the Chekas, but 'An *especially* militant role now falls to the People's Commissariat for Justice'. It was especially important, he continued, that reprisals should be intensified against the Mensheviks and SRs, 'the political enemies of the Soviet power and the agents of the bourgeoisie'. Show (or 'model') trials were to be employed both against these parties and those persons guilty of exceeding the limits of state capitalism.[81] If these courts did not punish 'public manifestations of Menshevism' with the death penalty, Lenin stated at the party Congress, 'they are not our courts.'[82]

· The first Soviet Criminal Code came into force in June 1922. Writing again to Kurskii, Lenin recommended the extension of the death penalty for a wide variety of crimes, especially for 'all forms of activity by the Mensheviks, *SRs and so on*', to be formulated in such a way as to tie these parties with the bourgeoisie abroad. In a draft preamble to the Code he wrote that, pending 'the establishment of conditions guaranteeing Soviet power against counter-revolutionary encroachments upon it', tribunals would be empowered to apply capital punishment, but death sentences could be commuted to deportation, on pain of death for illicit return.[83] Such was the extent of Bolshevik belief in the continued necessity of violent struggle with counter-revolution that some members of VTsIK considered it as yet untimely to provide such legal codification. Lenin addressed this with another letter to Kurskii on 17 May, revealing of his approach to jurisprudence. He wanted to:

> … put forward publicly a thesis that is correct in principle and politically (not only strictly juridical[ly]), which explains the *substance* of terror, its necessity and limits, and provides *justification* for it. The courts must not ban terror […] but […] legalize it as a principle […] It must be formulated in the broadest possible manner, for only revolutionary law and revolutionary conscience can more or less widely determine the limits within which it should be applied.

The courts, as Lenin envisaged, were to be instruments of a politicized struggle against criminality. Lenin then offered Kurskii two variants regarding the basis and justification for execution for counter-revolution. The first would comprise active and intentional assistance or membership of an organization that assisted that section of the international bourgeoisie actively attempting to overthrow Soviet power by blockade, intervention, espionage or financing of the anti-Soviet press; the second, agitation that 'serves or is likely to serve' the above, i.e. not necessarily with intent.[84] VTsIK adopted a resolution closer to the first variant as Article 57 of the Criminal Code, which defined counter-revolution as any action intended to overthrow Soviet power.[85] This was still a vague understanding and could easily be used, as indeed it was, to implicate membership of any group or organization perceived to be opposed to Soviet power.

NEP was, though, a period of greater legality than before. The GPU was regulated more strictly relative to the Vecheka, especially with the establishment of a Procuracy in August 1922 and the Workers' and Peasants' Inspectorate.[86] Lenin was at the forefront of insistence that respect for the rule of law be observed – however 'flexible' he felt should be its application – reasoning that this was a 'necessary concomitant' of the task of improving cultural standards.[87] Legal and punitive discourse through the mid-1920s continued to speak of the necessity for firm dictatorship against the enemies of Soviet power, including recidivist criminals, but there was also continued recognition of the need to establish a class-based system of justice that would allow for an approach based on 'moral leadership' rather than prison for workers and peasants who were not recidivist criminals.[88] The principle of *habeas corpus* was enhanced for the population as a whole, but the perceived necessity for the continuation of terror and judicial 'flexibility' had become enshrined in law at a time of relative peace and security, and precisely because Soviet power was in retreat.

Indeed the Civil War powers of the Vecheka largely continued through the GPU, which oversaw the state's assault on intellectuals and the Church in 1921–2.

This attests to the fact that, as Stuart Finkel puts it, 'wartime methods of dealing with the population remained appropriate.'[89] Yet as time wore on Dzerzhinskii recognized the harm that institutionalized terror was doing to the success of NEP. Excessive persecution of socialists, he argued, was creating martyrs and removing valuable intellectuals. In August 1923 he wrote with concern that the extent of the death penalty, both judicial and administrative (GPU), was contradicting the purpose of NEP. He thought that execution should be considered an exceptional measure not a permanent institution, and should be reserved exclusively for 'banditry' and suppression of uprisings. Dzerzhinskii suggested that the time had come when dictatorship could be exercised, in effect, without the death penalty – except in exceptional cases – and that this would have considerable value abroad in attracting support for communism. It would also help secure international recognition of the Soviet Union (the USSR had been established in December 1922). Dzerzhinskii was sure that if Lenin were still in charge of government – his illness had forced his retirement by then – the latter would support this restriction even more insistently.[90]

Kronstadt 1921

The Kronstadt mutiny accompanied the party's adoption of NEP and characterized Lenin's approach to politics and security thereafter. It epitomized, as the Bolsheviks saw it, the dangers posed to socialist construction by 'petty-bourgeois' anarchy. They feared that the naval base of Kronstadt, situated 20 miles from Petrograd in the Gulf of Finland, would be used as a base from which to launch an assault on the mainland if taken by counter-revolutionaries supported by Western powers, and that this 'would have meant nothing less than a resumption of the Civil War'.[91]

The Bolsheviks were deeply troubled by the extent of the strike movement in Petrograd during February. Workers, exasperated by militarized labour, were demanding an end to trade restrictions but also, reflecting Menshevik and SR influence, advancing demands for freely-elected soviets.[92] There were even calls to overthrow the government.[93] On 28 February unrest spread to the sailors of Kronstadt, the 'pride and glory' of 1917, when the crews of the battleships *Petropavlovsk* and *Sevastopol* issued an ultimatum to the government. In political terms, the sailors were not seeking the removal of the Bolsheviks from power but the removal of single-party dictatorship.[94] The Mensheviks and SRs, as Paul Avrich notes, 'did not exert a dominant influence'; the ideology of the mutineers was 'a kind of anarcho-populism'.[95] Nevertheless the head of the Petrograd Party, Zinoviev, telegrammed Lenin late on 28 February to inform him that the sailors had adopted 'SR-Black Hundred resolutions', and that the SRs were probably forcing these events.[96]

Lenin's response, without waiting for any detailed information, was that the mutiny 'very quickly revealed to us the familiar figures of Whiteguard generals'. He was convinced that there was something quite sinister behind it, referring to Parisian newspaper reportage a fortnight earlier of a mutiny at Kronstadt as evidence that it was ultimately 'the work of Socialist-Revolutionaries and whiteguard émigrés', with the knowledge of the French. He accepted that the sailors' demands ostensibly represented 'a small shift, which leaves the same slogans of "Soviet power" with ever so slight a change or correction.'[97] We have seen, though, that a defining characteristic of Leninism-in-power was that ultimately there could not be the slightest weakening of proletarian political dictatorship as exercised by the Bolsheviks without placing Soviet power in grave peril. One week later, he famously acknowledged that the sailors did not want 'either the Whiteguards or our government', but reasoned that there was no other alternative.[98]

Lenin's understanding was that the mutiny was the product both of popular misguidance and anarchy, and more sinister elements encouraging and preparing to take advantage of it, even if in the case of the socialist parties he seemed prepared to accept that they may not have consciously aimed at restoring capitalist rule. Avrich has demonstrated that there was good reason for the Bolsheviks to be fearful of the consequences of a popular revolt in Kronstadt. The National Centre, a coalition of Kadets, monarchists and other groupings that had been uncovered by the Vecheka during the Civil War, had headquarters in Paris and had certainly made preparations to utilize an uprising in Kronstadt to launch an assault on the mainland.[99]

Shortly after the Red Army had been sent across the ice to suppress the mutiny on 18 March, Lenin received a report from the Vecheka Special Department that traced its origins to the Anglo-Soviet trade agreement negotiations. The French government was opposed to such an agreement, therefore French agents working with SR groups in Riga allegedly decided to begin an uprising in Petrograd and Kronstadt to 'play for time', during which pressure would be applied on the British government to break negotiations. This was what led to 'an acceleration of the Kronstadt events.'[100] Lenin read the report 'attentively' and wrote a letter to Dzerzhinskii in which he opined that 'this is very important and, probably, fundamentally true.'[101] One month later he received information from the Vecheka that Victor Chernov, SR. leader, had sent greetings to the sailors and offered to arrive personally at Kronstadt to provide his support. The Kronstadt Revolutionary Committee thanked Chernov but 'temporarily refrained' from accepting his offer of help.[102] This, then, clearly suggested that the mutiny was not organized by the SRs, but that they were anxious to support it.

In the aftermath of the suppression there was a suggestion in Bolshevik quarters to legalize individual Mensheviks, SRs and Anarchists not implicated in the strikes and mutiny in advance of elections to the Moscow Soviet. This would have (belatedly) contributed to meeting the sailors' political demands, but Lenin and the Politburo rejected this on account of the part they believed Menshevik leaders had played in the mutiny.[103] If the Bolshevik aim was to put an end to the disquiet and prevent a slide to counter-revolutionary restoration, this could surely have been achieved, and more effectively, through negotiation and compromise when needed.

Recently published documents attest to the unnecessary brutality in the aftermath of the mutiny. During the fighting, thousands of people were taken prisoner. On 20 April the Petrograd Cheka met to discuss sentencing prisoners. The members of the Revolutionary Committee were sentenced to be shot. The majority were described as 'non-party', one a Menshevik, and others members or former members of the Bolshevik Party.[104] Other sailors involved in the mutiny were also sentenced; in all, there were 41 sentences of execution passed at this one meeting. To take one example, Vasilii Nevskii, described as sympathetic to Soviet power though non-party, had investigated the rebel resolution and, although he initially rejected it, later voted with the majority and travelled to the *Petropavlovsk*. He was sentenced to be shot.[105] During the coming weeks and months, 2,103 persons would be sentenced to death and many others to lesser forms of punishment, though 1,464 would be released from custody.[106] There were mass evacuations from the island of mutineers, their families and private citizens,[107] often to the newly-established Solovetskii Camp of Special Purpose on the remote northern Solevtskii islands. The reality of the suppression of the uprising, then, was at considerable variance with the notion espoused by some Soviet historians that the state dealt violently only with 'several active leaders of the mutiny', and demonstrated mercy towards the majority of the mutineers guilty of errors arising from material difficulties and lack of political consciousness.[108]

'Cleansing' Russia: socialists and intellectuals

On 4 June 1921 the Politburo directed the Vecheka to intensify struggle with the Mensheviks in view of their increased 'counter-revolutionary activities.'[109] In accordance with Lenin's instructions, the Vecheka worked out a plan of action of 'mass operations' against the Mensheviks and SRs to remove their influence on the masses by closing their legal newspapers and exiling 'the most active [and perceived incorrigible] Mensheviks' to remote areas of the country.[110] The Vecheka had reported the participation of SRs in 'kulak and bandit movements' and, though acknowledging that the Mensheviks condemned 'kulak uprisings' and other violent means of struggle with Soviet power, noted that they supported 'any movement directed against the proletarian dictatorship.'[111]

In March 1922 Lenin announced that the economic retreat was over and that it was time to 'deploy and regroup our forces properly': the limits of concessions to capitalism had been defined.[112] Zinoviev added that the political offensive was continuing. The aim was to 'completely liquidate' anti-Soviet groups, including the Mensheviks and SRs, taking from them their 'valuable human material' capable of supporting Soviet power, and 'breaking the rest.'[113] There was a certain *cultural* tolerance and pluralism during NEP, but the Bolsheviks aimed to destroy all non-Soviet organizations with ideas alien, or potentially alien to Soviet power, and excise dangerous population elements – foretasting some of the extremities of this process in the later 1920s and 1930s. This was especially apparent in 1922. It involved the destruction of the Menshevik and SR organizations; deportations of intellectuals perceived to be irreconcilable to Soviet power; an assault on organized religion and a state-sponsored schism in the Orthodox Church; systematized censorship and control of academia; and a clamp-down on independent professional organizations.[114] The juridical process, through political show trials of clergy and SRs in 1922, was utilized as a means of ascribing legitimacy to Soviet power and the use of state terror, and as an instrument of popular political education. Lenin suffered a major stroke in May 1922 and essentially left the Kremlin for the estate of Gorki outside Moscow. Yet as scholars of this 'ideological front' note, he was still very much involved in these events.[115] One of his biographers observes that some of his remarks of this time were 'particularly irritable and aggressive'.[116] The personal frustrations associated with his illness and inability to sustain work may have played a part in this.

Lenin elucidated the Bolshevik problem early in 1921. The Mensheviks and SRs, he contended, were helping the 'amorphous, indefinite and unconscious' petty-bourgeoisie 'to recoil from the Bolsheviks, to cause a "shift of power" in favour of the capitalists and landowners.' Whatever helped to achieve this was evidence of Menshevism, whether 'avowed or in non-party guise', and its advocates should be in prison or abroad.[117] Reflecting the pervasive Bolshevik proclivity to politicize all social phenomena, the GPU explained that struggle for professional autonomy (such as for medical professionals) was necessarily political, intended to diminish the influence of the Communist Party and the class principle.[118] In its report of 1 June 1922 on anti-Soviet groups amongst the intelligentsia (requested by Lenin), the GPU warned the Politburo of the danger that elements of these several groups – socialist parties, independent publishers, professionals, students, clergy – would 'in the near future' unite into a 'dangerous force opposed to Soviet power',[119] due to a perceived weakening of the state's repressive instruments. The GPU urged resolute prophylactic measures. Trotsky gave an interview to an American journalist in which he in fact justified the deportations of intellectuals on humanitarian grounds, for in the event of another war these 'irreconcilables' would prove to be agents of counter-revolution and would have to be shot.[120] Even the relatively moderate Commissar of Enlightenment Anatolii Lunacharskii[121] wrote in October 1922 that, though NEP required some 'tolerance' of 'capitalist ideology', the expulsions were justified and action should be taken to deal not just with open counter-revolutionaries but also those engaged in academic work that would conflict with maturation of the 'proletarian worldview.'[122]

Stuart Finkel notes that during NEP 'control did not mean the full abolition of heterodoxy as much as circumscribing its manifestations', though the Bolsheviks certainly desired that the public sphere in a socialist society 'should be unitary and univocal'.[123] Chris Read has argued that the Bolshevik tendency to perceive two irreconcilable ideological camps – simply for or against Soviet power – was also a consequence of a particularly absolutist Tsarist Russian political culture that induced revolutionaries born in its environment to create such a sharp distinction between those for and against the regime.[124] The revolutionary process had encountered numerous setbacks and in 1921–2, fearful as they were of losing control of it when making concessions to capitalism, the Bolsheviks felt the need to hasten the removal of all ideological influences that might undermine the socialist 'cultivation' (*vospitanie*) of the *narod*. Proletarian class-consciousness depended on large-scale industry, Lenin explained, and in the absence of industry, the greater was the danger from Mensheviks and SRs. The workers, he thought, were being provoked into political instability and 'scepticism'.[125]

. In a circular letter of 27 June 1922 the GPU noted the 'dual tactics' of the Mensheviks: ostensibly they sought merely to democratize Soviet power, but they were also engaged in counter-revolution even if they were not connected with 'out-and-out counter-revolutionaries'.[126] The Mensheviks, according to the letter, were a bourgeois party for they believed NEP as a return to capitalism should be accompanied by the right of 'the propertied classes' to peacefully agitate for influence over the masses, but a workers' party could advocate no such thing. The Mensheviks, it concluded, were a 'workers' party' in name only in order to penetrate the workers, especially backward elements, and lead them astray.[127] On 22 August Unshlikht issued an instruction to regional GPU offices to immediately arrest 'active Mensheviks', who would be either exiled or, in cases whereby weighty evidence could be brought to bear, put on trial.[128]

In August at the Party Conference, Zinoviev explained Bolshevik repressive policies towards these groups. We cannot reject repression, he began, indeed repression was a 'sacred' thing, but he emphasized its instrumental nature. The Mensheviks and SRs had repressed the Bolsheviks when in government in 1917 but to little avail, for then 'life was with us'. Bolshevik repression by contrast would succeed because the Mensheviks and SRs were historically redundant, and force against them would be historically progressive. However repression could not be the same as it was during the Civil War, he thought, for now 'we can resort to more complex, more mechanical measures'. In this regard he referred to the Bolshevik tactic of supporting the *Smena Vekh* movement of émigré intellectuals who, convinced as were the Mensheviks that the regime would evolve into a democracy, decided to abandon hostility to the Bolsheviks. They remained 'ideological enemies of Communists', Zinoviev explained, but they represented a new departure amongst the 'bourgeoisie' and would be useful in splitting enemy ranks.[129] Referring to Lenin's philosophy on repression, he concluded that it was necessary to know 'when, who, where, and under what circumstances to shoot. That is all.'[130]

, This did not reflect the vitriol in Lenin's remarks concerning punishment of Mensheviks and SRs in his contributions to the Criminal Code, or indeed his general propensity to advocate execution. His recommendation of capital punishment to deal with opposition socialists (though regarding the Mensheviks he countenanced exile and deportations as alternatives) was embodied in the trial of the SRs begun in early June 1922. Twelve death sentences were handed down by the Supreme Tribunal but, on the basis of an agreement reached with international socialists, these were suspended. The decision to bring the SRs to a show trial designed to publicly discredit them was due to the Bolshevik fear of a peasant party in a peasant country. The SRs were described as 'most dangerous' because they were considered most desirous of returning to power themselves.[131] Persecution of the SRs is more easily understood than that of the Mensheviks. SR gatherings during NEP continued to speak about overthrowing the Bolsheviks, though the party's Central Committee tried to persuade party activists that armed struggle was futile.[132]

↓ Some Bolsheviks were opposed to the passing of death sentences due to the adverse international reaction such sanctions would invoke.[133] When, at a Moscow province party conference, the moderate David Riazanov questioned the 'morality' of Bolshevik willingness to execute individual SRs as opposed to destroying the party as a party, he was rounded upon by his party colleagues and subsequently removed from 'responsible work' by the Politburo.[134] VTsIK justified the death sentences in the context of 'the great historical struggle' between on one side the rule of capital and all forms of violence against the masses, and on the other the working masses of Russia and the world, with the SRs 'wholly' on the side of the former.[135] Marc Jansen notes that Lenin was actually pleased with the suspended death sentences, his secretary, Lidia Fotieva, later attributing the idea of suspended sentences to Lenin.[136]

▸There were cases of conspiracy that surely encouraged Bolshevik fears. In late August 1921 61 people, including intellectuals and professors, were executed in what is known as the 'Tagantsev Affair' when the Petrograd Battle Organization led by V. N. Tagantsev was discovered by the Cheka. This conspiratorial group, with links to émigrés, sought the overthrow of the regime.[137] Bolshevik fears of intellectual conspiracy were at their height during the famine in 1921, when non-Bolshevik socialists and intellectuals were temporarily permitted to provide a public duty in famine relief in the form of the Famine Relief Committee (as distinct from the state relief committee, Pomgol). In émigré circles the famine signalled the inevitable doom of Bolshevism, and there were even rumours that the Committee could be a government in embryo.[138] The Bolsheviks were highly suspicious of it, and the Politburo ordered the arrest of all its non-Communist members on 27 August 1921 on counter-revolutionary charges.[139]

↘ Lenin played an active role in the deportations of intellectuals and socialists. On 19 May 1922 he wrote to Dzerzhinskii that the list of members appearing on the cover of an edition of the journal *Ekonomist*, which was openly criticizing the regime's policies, included 'almost all the most legitimate candidates for deportation.'[140] Yet the Politburo was by no means willing to comply reverently with his requests and demands regarding the deportation process.[141] Lenin wrote to Stalin on 16 July expressing his frustration that the process was not yet completed, listing several persons who, along with 'several hundred such gentlemen', should be deported 'pitilessly' (*bezzhalostno*). He was not concerned about providing reasons: 'Arrest several hundred and *without declaration* of motives – leave, gentlemen!' His notes on particular individuals read as follows: 'will be insidious, as far as I can judge by reading his article'; 'Rozanov (doctor, cunning)', N. A. Rozhkov (necessary to deport him, incorrigible).'[142] In one case, L. N. Radchenko and his 'young daughter' were recommended for deportation because 'by hearsay [they are] malicious enemies of Bolshevism.'[143] Thus, 'hearsay' and his impression of someone's mindset on the basis of his reading of one article were for Lenin sufficient reasons for deporting someone and their family from their homeland. In early September he issued a directive to steadily continue the deportations, principally of Mensheviks. By then Dzerzhinskii, evidently acting on Lenin's direction, raised concerns that the process was being undertaken too hastily and urged greater accuracy, for the task was to sort the irreconcilables from those capable of supporting Soviet power.[144]

These expulsions were the method of excision employed by the Soviet regime in the early 1920s against intellectuals; expulsion rather than execution suggests that the Bolsheviks wished to appear relatively moderate to the outside world.[145] These measures resulted from an absolutist and uncompromising ideology confronted with an unforeseen and threatening reality. This unanticipated reality – a revival of capitalism in Soviet Russia, the persistence of threatening alien ideas that could capture the masses, and indeed the capitalist world outside of Russia – was however indicative of the weaknesses in the ideological predictions that had driven the Bolsheviks to total revolution in the Russia of 1917–8. The irony was that they were resorting to the repressive measures of Tsarist times, removing harmful persons to sparsely populated regions of the country (or abroad) where their influence on the *narod* would be minimal. This was a clear demonstration of institutionalized policing methods of controlling sections of the population deemed dangerous to the regime (as opposed to the ideal of a state 'withering away'), which would be most clearly illustrated by the actions of the police in the 1930s. The Bolsheviks believed that such repressions were justified because 'life' was on their side, that they constituted not so much repression as means of liberation, and could not be compared with the 'reactionary violence' of Tsarism. In the process Soviet Russia was brought closer to the creation of a near 'totalitarian' order.

'Cleansing' Russia: the Orthodox Church

One particularly interesting and complex example of the state's effort to realize an ideologically uniform society free of independent organizational influences over the people was the attempt in 1922 to break the Russian Orthodox Church. This involved the support of a Church 'reformation' in the form of the Renovationist movement, show trials and executions of clergy, and a campaign of intensified anti-religious as well as anti-clerical propaganda. Organized religion as a whole was targeted, not just Orthodoxy. Indeed the Bolshevik state was the first to openly proclaim its intention to eradicate religion in the name of modernizing rationality. The reason for this intensified anti-clerical/religious struggle was Church opposition to forcible confiscation of church valuables, especially consecrated items, for famine relief. Existing scholarship has demonstrated that the state's campaign of confiscating church valuables in gold, silver and precious metals was not intended for famine relief directly but, using the famine as pretext, to bolster Soviet economic recovery and launch an assault on the Church. The Bolsheviks were concerned to restore the value of the Soviet rouble following the restoration of a monetary economy in 1922.[146]

This is also an interesting and complex case study of the role of ideology in early Soviet state violence and repression; after all, the Bolsheviks regarded the

Orthodox Church as an integral part of the oppressive Tsarist apparatus and the 'last bastion of organized resistance to the new regime'.[147] This does not mean that Lenin believed in launching an all-out assault on religion; rather, religion would supposedly wither away like the state with the creation of the material requisites for true socialism. During the first years of Soviet power the party officially separated Church from state but in a way aimed at directly attacking the Church's material means of existence, and removing its legal rights as an entity.[148] Churches and religious objects were granted to the Church for use but were now the property of the state. The Orthodox Patriarch, Tikhon, had initially proclaimed anathema on the Bolsheviks, though the Church leadership wanted the Church to refrain from politics during the Civil War.[149] Nonetheless sections of the clergy often rendered full and active support of the White cause. This, and the position of the Church in Tsarist society, ensured that at times Lenin mentioned clergy as direct targets when advocating terror. The clergy received special surveillance treatment from the Vecheka, indicating the threat the Bolsheviks considered they posed.[150]

The Bolshevik state did not need another reason for popular unrest, and during the first year of NEP Lenin's attitude towards religion was especially moderate. In April 1921 he instructed Molotov 'absolutely to avoid any insult to religion' because of the Easter holidays, not to publicly 'expose the lies of religion' at that time because it would be 'without tact'.[151] Organized religion was however incompatible with the party's political dictates during NEP, and the Vecheka plan approved by Lenin in June sought, though with caution, to prohibit any religious congresses or publications.[152] Why, then, did the Politburo launch an assault on the Church in 1922, attempt to 'divide and conquer' it, intensify anti-religious propaganda, and publicly try and execute clergy and believers accused of counter-revolution? Jonathan Daly answers this question very clearly: this was the Party's opportunistic response to exploiting the circumstance of famine for political considerations.[153] However this should also be understood through the meaning and significance of NEP.

By February 1922 the party decided that voluntary donations of church valuables for famine relief had not been sufficient. On 23 February VTsIK decreed, in view of the urgent need to mobilize all the country's resources for famine relief, to remove all valuables of all religions so long as this did not 'affect the interests of these cults', and by agreement with believers.[154] Collections would henceforth be obligatory, ultimately leading to a clash between Church and state over ownership of the valuables. The Patriarch responded defiantly on 28 February, condemning the VTsIK decree as 'an act of sacrilege [sviatotatstva]'. He expressed his wish that believers continue to donate church valuables voluntarily but warned that consecrated valuables could not be confiscated or voluntarily donated on pain of excommunication.[155] In fact Tikhon issued a 'secret instruction' to priests encouraging them to 'struggle against' confiscations at meetings with their congregations, noting that, even as regards consecrated items, 'What is important is not what to give, but whom to give it.'[156] This was crucially important – Tikhon's opposition to the decree on grounds of canon law was enforced because of his hostility to an overtly anti-religious state.

The crux of the matter was the interpretation by clergy and believers of Tikhon's appeal, with many considering that the valuables were not intended for famine relief but for the Bolsheviks' own purposes. In April, under GPU questioning, Tikhon would explain that he had not at all intended 'to call believers to resist [Soviet] power; if it was understood as such somewhere, that was incorrect.'[157] The reactions of clergy and believers throughout the country was mixed. Lenin was informed by GPU reports that in some provinces the masses were 'hostile' to the confiscations, in others the popular mood was described as 'alarming' (in its opposition to the campaign), and elsewhere there was support from clergy and believers for confiscations.[158]

The effect of popular and clerical reaction to the VTsIK decree was, initially, to inspire caution on the part of the GPU, which recommended on 8 March a suspension of operations until there were clearer results from a more intensified political agitation campaign.[159] Yet by April there were, according to official state figures, 1,414 bloody incidents in front of churches leading to the deaths of 28 bishops and 1,200 priests by April 1922. The most significant such incident occurred on 15 March at Shuia, in Ivanovo-Voznesenk province, when a crowd of believers opened fire on Red Army soldiers accompanying the confiscation commission after disarming some of them. The soldiers tried to disperse the crowd and ended by shooting into it, killing five and wounding 15.[160] One member of the local soviet executive committee subsequently resigned due to his sharp condemnation of the local soviet's conduct of the campaign.[161] The Central Committee responded to Shuia by ordering a temporary suspension of the campaign in order to undertake more intensive propaganda work.[162]

It was at this point that Lenin contributed his by now infamous letter of 19 March, sent to Molotov for the Politburo.[163] First published in Paris in 1970, it has typically generated scandal amongst historians since its authenticity has been confirmed. It is therefore important that it is read within the full context of the 1922 campaign, as a reaction both to violent resistance to the state's confiscation decree, and to any hint of retreat or moderation on the part of his Party colleagues. The Shuia events, he began, demonstrated conclusively that the 'Black Hundred clergy' led by Tikhon were attempting to deliberately 'give battle' to Soviet power. This was precisely the moment, the 'only moment when we have a 99 out of 100 chance for full success to rout the enemy and guarantee for us the necessary position for many decades.' Hence the confiscation campaign must be conducted 'with the most furious and merciless energy and not shirking from suppressing any resistance.' Why was the timing so opportune? It was because at this moment thousands of corpses littered famine-stricken areas. The vast majority of the peasant masses would ultimately prove to be either *for* Soviet power or at least would not support the 'handful' of reactionary clergy and urban petty-bourgeoisie. Would the valuables be used to reduce the number of starved corpses on the Volga? Lenin did not suggest this. 'We can secure for ourselves one hundred million gold roubles' (a much-inflated estimate as it turned out), he explained, remembering the 'gigantic wealth' of the monasteries, and without this 'no general state work, no economic construction in particular and no settling of our position in Genoa [the first international economic conference attended by a Soviet delegation] especially will be possible.'

This unique moment, he thought, required a Machiavellian approach:

> One clever writer on questions of state justly stated that if it is necessary in order to realize a certain political aim to use cruelties, then it is necessary to fulfil them in the most energetic manner and in the shortest time, for lengthy use of cruelties the masses will not endure.

Following Genoa and the hoped-for international agreements, clerical repression would be politically harmful. Destruction of the reactionary clergy would also, he thought, lessen the threat posed by hostile Russian émigrés. Lenin was convinced that 'we must give the most resolute and merciless battle to the Black Hundred clergy and suppress its resistance with such cruelty that they will not forget it for several decades.' In Shuia, 'no less than some tens of representatives' of the local clergy and petty-bourgeoisie' should be arrested 'on suspicion of direct or indirect participation in violent resistance to the VTsIK decree' and brought to trial. This should end no other way than the 'shooting of the largest number of the most influential and dangerous Black Hundreds in Shuia', and not just in Shuia. In fact he suggested that 'The more members of the reactionary clergy and reactionary bourgeoisie we succeed in this regard to shoot, the better.'

Lenin's letter would influence a hardening of the party's approach to the campaign, and reveal divergences amongst the Bolshevik political élite. His fury contrasted with the decision of the Central Committee the same day, and with Trotsky's Commission in charge of the confiscations. On 20 March, with Trotsky present and perhaps having not yet read Lenin's letter, the Commission decided to temporarily suspend operations in those areas where there existed a risk of 'excesses'.[164] The tenor of Lenin's letter was approved by the Politburo. Trotsky, who was in charge of both the collection of valuables and the state's anti-religious policy, succeeded in having approved by the Politburo a recommendation to execute the 'ringleaders' at Shuia, to instruct the press to adopt a 'furious tone' towards these ringleaders, to arrest the Church Synod, and to set about the confiscation campaign across the country. Molotov, however, suggested that Lenin's colleagues were not prepared to be so cavalier in their approach when he recommended in response that the campaign be extended not to all provinces and towns but only to those where there were substantial valuables to be confiscated.[165]

It appears that Trotsky was influenced by Lenin's letter to adopt a more focussed and belligerent approach to the campaign directed against the Church.[166] In a policy directive of 30 March, Trotsky suggested that the campaign that had begun as a means of bolstering the state's gold reserve had become, in addition, an attempt finally to reckon with the Orthodox Church, agreeing with Lenin that 'The campaign regarding the famine is extremely advantageous for this.'[167] It was thus an opportunistic response to an unresolved ideological problem. It should not be thought however that famine relief had been forgotten; Trotsky ordered that one million gold roubles be released for this purpose, and that trains of food purchased with this money be sent to the Volga. He did make it clear though that this would be very much a public relations exercise.[168]

On 24 March *Izvestiia* published a front-page warning to the hierarchy and those vocally opposed to the confiscation decree. The article established first that resistance to the decree indicated counter-revolution, and second that this was due to the inflammatory attempts of a consciously counter-revolutionary stratum. In some places priests had indeed expressed their intention to see the collapse of Soviet power.[169] The article warned that when a choice had to be made between the lives of millions of starving peasants and a 'wretched small group of unrepentant Black Hundreds', the decision would be simple.[170] Therefore duplicitous use was made of the famine to accord clearly-implied repression with a type of moral sanctity.

Repression of the clergy culminated in show trials in the spring and summer of 1922, the two largest in Moscow and Petrograd; in total, there were 44 executions arising from 55 tribunals throughout the country.[171] On 2 May the case of two priests sentenced to death for their roles in the Shuia events came before the Politburo. Mikhail Kalinin, the Chairman of VTsIK, proposed the repeal of the death sentences but the majority (Lenin, Stalin, Trotsky and Molotov) voted in support of the Shuia tribunal's sentences.[172] Two days later the Politburo resolved to direct the Moscow Tribunal to hand down death sentences for the accused priests (without mentioning the lay accused), and instructed Moscow newspaper editors to engage in a campaign to expose the counter-revolutionary activities of the Church hierarchy.[173]

The front page of *Izvestiia* on 6 May publicly expounded the state's case against the clergy, describing the hierarchy headed by Tikhon as the 'general staff of the counter-revolution' within Russia.[174] The priests within Russia and the White émigrés abroad were considered parts of the one counter-revolutionary organization, even if acting separately, for their aims were the same: to overthrow Soviet power, suppress the workers and peasants, and restore the powers of the landowners, capitalists and Tsar.[175] There were only 'two camps', those for, and those against the revolution, and the counter-revolutionary clergy were firmly placed at the head of the latter. 'Revolutionary law' should demonstrate no hesitation in delivering the final excisional blow to this counter-revolutionary leadership in Soviet Russia, for this would be 'in the interests of the salvation of millions of starving, in the interests of the salvation of the revolution's achievements, i.e. in the interests of millions of workers and peasants.'[176] The trials and accompanying publicity thereby attempted to accord legitimacy to Soviet power and its repressive measures.

Eleven death sentences were handed down by the Moscow Tribunal for seven priests and four lay believers. Those sentenced to death were accused of the 'counter-revolutionary activities' of having 'consciously and intentionally' planned to incite opposition to the VTsIK decree, declaring the confiscations 'robbery'; distributing the Patriarch's appeal and having resolutions approved at believers' meetings to resist the decree 'with all means and forces'; and not taking action to pacify the 'dark mass' of believers they had incited.[177] *Pravda* wrote of the impermissibility of clerical resistance when the Soviet state was in a weakened condition surrounded by enemies who could attack at any moment, and of the clergy's links with counter-revolutionary forces abroad.[178] Once again the possibility of clemency came before the Politburo when Kamenev sought to reduce the number of death sentences to two. Lenin was in a majority in casting his vote against reducing the number of death sentences (against a minority of Kamenev, Tomskii and Rykov).

In the end, six of the death sentences were commuted. Of the five who were not pardoned, the Tribunal reasoned that mercy could not be shown them largely because of their personal characters. The Tribunal ruled that a contributing factor to the sentences was that the defendants did not repent but attempted to devolve personal responsibility on the hierarchical system of discipline, and continued to refer in court to the correctness of God's law regarding donation of church valuables.[179] They were considered particularly 'irreconcilable' enemies who had clearly and consciously used religion for counter-revolutionary purposes. Hence, the defendants were not simply judged according to their social background and affiliations but how these had apparently shaped the extent of their (conscious) personal dispositions to Soviet power.[180]

Those sentenced to death at the Petrograd trial were, similarly, considered individuals particularly 'harmful and dangerous' to Soviet power.[181] The final sentencing, as at the Moscow trial, was the result of reconciling the perceived counter-revolutionary dangers of the defendants with 'political considerations'. Petr Krasikov, the prosecutor at the Petrograd trial, successfully secured the commutation of six of the death sentences in order to meet the Renovationist clergy's request for mercy.[182] However Archbishop Veniamin of Petrograd was executed, having been described by Krasikov as a 'fully conscious conductor of counter-revolutionary politics under the flag of the Church'. Yet Veniamin had been more flexible than Tikhon on the question of permitting donation of consecrated valuables, and the leading Renovationist priest had written to assure the government that Veniamin was not guilty of counter-revolution.[183] Veniamin's 'crime' was clearly not counter-revolution, but he fell victim to the Bolshevik conviction that the Church in which he occupied a leading position and to which he was obedient was engaged in counter-revolution.

Once again VTsIK requested clemency for those who would be executed in Petrograd but, even though it was constitutionally the highest state authority, the party's Central Committee refused.[184] In what appears to be an unsigned internal Justice Commissariat memo outlining the reasons for rejecting the legal arguments of the defence lawyers, it was argued that tribunals possessed the right to apply whatever sentences they considered appropriate according to 'socialist legal consciousness'. Most revealing of Soviet legal philosophy in such cases, it argued that tribunals should merely be satisfied that there was enough evidence to indicate guilt rather than be concerned about objectively examining the evidence to support the prosecution.[185] This is not to suggest that due process or leniency were entirely dispensed with; many were released from custody, including those against whom there was insufficient evidence, and those who had mitigated their 'crimes' by attempting to pacify the rest of the protesting crowds.[186]

State repression of the Church in 1922 ultimately resulted from ideological intolerance towards organized religion. Repression did not follow simplistically and inexorably from this premise; ideology and circumstances were inextricably linked. The campaign to collect church valuables was not originally conceived with the express purpose of allowing the Bolsheviks to deal decisively with the Church. Subsequent events were interpreted through ideology and fed ideological conceptions and inclinations. Lenin, as we have seen, actively sought confrontation with anyone who offered resistance, Church-inclusive, though Trotsky hoped that adequate propaganda work and avoidance of unnecessary offence to religion would minimize popular violence.[187]

Undoubtedly Church leaders had been strongly hostile to the Bolshevik order since its inception, and political police reports into the early 1920s attested to continued hostility amongst lower clergy. The messages emanating from the émigré Church gathering, the Karlovatskii Sobor, were overtly counter-revolutionary and though condemned by Tikhon, this must surely have further convinced the Bolsheviks that the Church was an inveterate foe. Clerical opposition to the decree served to politically discredit the Bolsheviks as sacrilegious robbers, but it appears that the Church and most of those who resisted the decree were primarily reacting against what they understood as the state's invasion of their religious sphere. Undoubtedly, for many peasants the confiscations were seen as another outrageous act of the state following the abuses and hardships associated with years of forcible grain requisitioning.

The Bolsheviks tended to exaggerate the political nature of social phenomena and equate political opposition with counter-revolution, and the predominant Bolshevik conception was that the Tikhonite Church was inherently counter-revolutionary. The conceived impossibility of any middle ground between absolute Bolshevik power and restoration of the old order, encouraged by the Civil War experience and theoretically enshrined in the meaning of NEP, encouraged interpretation of resistance as counter-revolution or at least ultimately serving it. This, and the opportunism of utilizing the valuables campaign to propagate the alleged counter-revolutionary nature of the Church and defeat it, ensured a more violent and confrontational approach than might otherwise have been.

Overall, NEP demonstrated a struggle in Lenin's mind between the need to accommodate the shortcomings of the revolution and reintegrate state with society, and yet to hold onto the essentials of Bolshevism and preserve as much as possible of what had been achieved. These tensions persisted in his last writings in 1923. There could be no question in his mind whether the Bolsheviks were correct 'to implant socialism in an insufficiently cultured country', as their socialist critics contended. It was simply the case that the process in Russia had 'started from the opposite end to that prescribed by theory'. The political revolution had preceded the cultural revolution, but he reasoned that there was nothing incorrect from a Marxist viewpoint about departing somewhat from the 'textbook' orthodoxy of a Kautsky.[188] Having started his Marxist career in opposition to revolutionaries who placed primacy on violent revolution and not the laws of historical progression and preparatory work amongst the masses, Lenin found himself justifying such 'Jacobinism'.

In these last writings, Lenin pointed out that 'a radical modification in our whole outlook on socialism' was necessary. There needed to be a shift of emphasis from political struggle to 'peaceful, organizational, "cultural" work'. His hope was that through the organization of peasant co-operatives, the development of industry, the education of the masses, and the promotion to governmental responsibility of selected exemplary workers and specialists, the result would be a remoulding of the Russian masses, the construction of a properly socialist governmental apparatus, and ultimately the realization of socialism and communism. Through a successful, if rather lengthy 'cultural revolution' of the 'entire people', NEP would give way to socialism. The great 'advance' of NEP, Lenin thought, was that it 'does not demand anything higher' of the ordinary peasant than that which the peasant could be expected to contribute at that time. He expected that the mass of Soviet peasants and workers would undergo this cultural transformation through education and with the creation of a certain level of material production. They would be transformed into citizens of a socialist state who would naturally adopt socialist principles of organization, production and distribution, and this would take only a few decades.[189] Indeed the plan for co-operativization, as Erik van Ree argues, indicated that Lenin already wanted to begin a systematic move from peasant control to state control of the land, however lengthy and 'peaceful' a process he might have intended this to be.[190]

Stalinism was not the inevitable result of Lenin's apparently simplistic and, with hindsight, unrealistic reasoning. Yet it was one, though extremely brutal, logical way for the Bolsheviks to actively re-engage the realization of their millenarian mission when it was apparent to the Stalinist Party that NEP was not fulfilling it, that the Bolsheviks had not succeeded in establishing firm control and support in the countryside,[191] and that dangers from outside the country (and correspondingly within) were increasing. In any case the strengthening of absolutist political dictatorship during NEP, despite its relative moderation after 1922, ensured that nothing approaching a 'liberal' alternative to Stalinism was at all likely. Ultimately Lenin would bequeath a state system wherein terror was sanctioned and indeed institutionalized, even if he would have been scandalized if he knew how the Stalinist regime would come to forcibly collectivize agriculture within a decade, and turn the instrument of terror on the party itself.

Conclusion
Lenin's terror

> ⚘ Our generation will have carried out a task of tremendous historical importance. The cruelty of our lives, imposed by circumstances, will be understood and pardoned. Everything will be understood, everything! [1]
>
> (Lenin, as recounted by Maksim Gor´kii)

For Lenin, 'revolutionary' violence was an instrument with which to realize his vision of a socialist, ultimately communist world, a world without violence. He considered it an essential means to topple the Russian autocracy, and after 1917 considered it an essential component of proletarian dictatorship, but in general he did not consider it something desirable for itself – despite official encouragement of popular 'hatred and revenge'. Overall it was not an intrinsically necessary component of his thought, and he did not always choose or advocate the violent option, though many of his pronouncements at various times suggested an 'essentialist' approach to violence. He accepted that coercion and violence would be required to transform the country, but his conception of proletarian dictatorship, even during the Civil War, emphasized that violence alone could not solve the country's problems, and that violence could not accomplish the more essential function of dictatorship: proletarian organization, unity of workers and peasants, and the mental/cultural transformation required for socialism. Indeed, as Joshua Sanborn notes, though 'there was a strong current of revolutionary glorification of violence […] there was a simultaneous desire to contain violence in rather traditional ways', by asserting the state's control over its use and the highly difficult differentiation between its 'acceptable and unacceptable' expressions.[2]

By the end of the Civil War the Bolshevik state had become accustomed to dictatorial practices and its leaders spoke repeatedly of applying the experience of wartime measures and military discipline to the 'economic front'. The Bolshevik leadership was predisposed to resort to coercion, even against its core constituency, and to reject other means of confronting crises. Indeed difficulties and crises, whether political, economic or military, were considered as warfare and Bolshevik leaders provided elaborate theoretical justifications for the existence of a violently coercive state.

Marxist morality placed the good of the revolution above all else and in philosophical terms rejected the idea of an ahistorical and immutable 'good' and 'bad',[3] and indeed of what the Bolsheviks sarcastically referred to as the sacredness of human life in a 'bourgeois' sense, meaning a principled opposition to violence. The concept of life does indeed appear 'sacred', and a conception of good and evil present, in Marxist–Leninist thought, but those served to justify the revolutionary process and 'revolutionary violence' rather than restrict it. Individual lives were quite easily considered dispensable in light of the greater, transcendental historical destiny that the revolution embodied for the collective existence of humanity as a whole – past (as a means of giving meaning to the sacrifices and sufferings of previous generations), present and future. The Bolsheviks were certainly not unique in moralizing about violent acts in the interest of a higher cause, whether in a Russian or global historical context,[4] but they did tend to be very explicit in so doing. Without glorifying violence for itself, a virtue was made of perceived necessity. Undoubtedly this helps explain how life could often appear so 'cheap' to Lenin and many of his comrades (as to political and military leaders and theorists generally before and during the Great War).

It is imperative to note, as Soviet historians did, that Lenin clearly distinguished two different typologies of violence – revolutionary violence and reactionary, counter-revolutionary violence – which he believed could not be compared as like.[5] Indeed the works of Soviet historians, written within the parameters of Leninist discourse, offer insights into the Leninist conceptualization of violence in the interests of revolution (which is not the same as an objective analysis of this conceptualization). They emphasized the reactive nature of such violence (reacting to counter-revolution), and that the revolution served a fundamentally 'humanistic' mission because the most important questions of class struggle were solved by force. However terror was not to be raised to a point of essential principle.[6] In addition, they pointed to the dialectical Marxist–Leninist approach to mastering the 'bourgeois' means of warfare in order to overcome oppression and indeed warfare itself.[7]

One could ask why the Bolsheviks were so desperate to take power and felt the need to resort to violence and terror at all, if the triumph of communism was inevitable in any case? That would be to accept an overly positivist, deterministic understanding of the Marxist philosophy of historical materialism. The triumph of communism was considered historically necessary but this did not remove historical contingency. Merleau-Ponty stresses this dialectic of necessity and historical contingency, reasoning that 'history is terror because there is a contingency.'[8] Using the metaphor of childbirth, the new society which had been already effectively brought into being by advanced capitalism and the World War, as Lenin believed, could yet be still-born. This was what Lenin and indeed Martov feared during the war, especially with the growth of imperialist Leviathan states possessing unprecedented weapons of coercion. Following the revolution, Lenin and the Bolsheviks were constantly fearful that various factors – cultural backwardness, criminality, 'bourgeois habits', counter-revolution and imperialist intervention – could result in the death of the 'infant' in Russia, thereby seriously hampering the international spread of socialism. The triumph of communist revolution, however confident Lenin was about it and though referred to as inevitable in the *Communist Manifesto*, could not actually be guaranteed – it had to be struggled for, with violence when necessary.

Ideology and violence in early soviet Russia

This book, a study of Lenin's thinking on violence throughout his political life and his practice of violence as leader of the Soviet state, has argued that ideology provides the primary explanatory framework for the phenomenon of early Soviet state violence as directed from the centre of power. However, ideology cannot be said to have caused state violence in early Soviet Russia; the 'action' of the Bolshevik assumption of power and practice of politics guided by Marxist–Leninist ideology did not lead simply to the 'effect' of state violence. The reasons for according primacy to ideology in explanation of Lenin's relationship with violence, and early Soviet state violence as approved 'from above', stem from what that particular ideology was and its nature, and how ideologies in general function. Ideologies structure how political actors perceive the world, how they interpret events, incorporate them into an existing meta-narrative and belief system, and contribute to how actions are prescribed. Political ideologies are not just sets of beliefs, however doctrinaire, and are not static but exist in the real world, informed by events and particular personalities.

Martin Malia set out an ostensibly neo-totalitarian perspective in the mid-1990s in his broad history of the Soviet Union, the 'agenda' of his book being to 'reassert the primacy of ideology and politics over social and economic forces in understanding the Soviet phenomenon.'[9] Malia's fundamental argument was that a distinct 'logic' pervaded Soviet history, rendering it meaningful, and that this logic conspired to create the Soviet system even if the historical actors were unaware of where this would lead. This Malia termed the 'if-then' approach, such that once a certain course of action was taken the path of subsequent historical development was thereby constrained within a certain direction. So, the difficulties faced by the Bolsheviks when in power and the choices made, far from diverting them from 'genuine socialism', revealed to them 'who they in fact were'. Lenin remained faithful to Marxism's 'deeper structure', Malia argued, though he 'recast' it to accommodate Russian conditions.[10] The notion of a definite logic running through Soviet history is certainly an important observation. Malia's argument, though, strongly suggested ideological determinism despite the fact that he explicitly rejected this.

The world certainly possesses a determinacy in its own right 'irrespective of the discursive constructions that are put upon it.'[11] The most influential case for the primacy of events and circumstances in explaining early Soviet terror is Arno J. Mayer's comparative study of terror in the French and Russian revolutions. Mayer reasons that violence was fuelled by 'the dialectic of revolution and counter-revolution', considering that ideology cannot primarily account for Bolshevik violence because the Bolshevik leaders were not prepared for what happened after seizing power.[12] His conception of ideology is a somewhat confusing mixture of ideologies as systems of inflexible beliefs and yet 'flexible and adaptable', setting limits on possible policy choices rather than fixing 'iron parameters' of action.[13] His understanding suggests that for ideology to be accorded explanatory primacy it must exercise a general causal function, something that ideologies, he believes, do not.

Mayer's assessment of ideology as an explanatory factor suffers from this concern to discard the causal determinism traditionally associated with the proponents of the ideology thesis: 'The concept of ideology is at once too vague, charged, and mechanical to provide an explanatory frame'. Instead ideology largely serves, in Mayer's estimation, merely to legitimize actions. However the ideology itself helped to create the particular circumstances that the Bolsheviks faced, and provided an interpretive frame and motivation for repressive actions that can be considered 'excessive' by any balanced estimation. Malia provided an important insight into the relationship between ideology and circumstances: 'a dialectic where events prompted drastic action and then ideology radicalized these actions still further.'[14] This book and other recent historiography helps to circumvent both excessive emphasis upon ideological determinacy, and the contrary idea that ideology was used merely as rationalization and legitimation for actions already implemented.

Ideologies take root and develop within particular political cultures. Marxism, with its eschatological vision, secular religious-like characteristics, and Manichean inclinations, found in Russia an intellectual culture conducive to the development of a particularly absolutist world view. Some scholars have pointed to a characteristic dualistic/'bipolar' system of values in Russian culture derived from Orthodox Christianity, a 'totalizing value system based on absolute right and wrong', and have explicitly linked this to political violence and its justification in Russian history.[15] Russian/Soviet history has, however, provided merely 'one dramatic example' of a broader phenomenon that helps explain the mentalities of justification behind much of modern political violence: that is, value systems based on absolutist conceptions of right and wrong that prescribe the realization of utopian conceptions on earth.[16] Political violence is not somehow intrinsic to Russian culture, and Russian history is not a long story of exceptional violence; indeed the 'bipolar' model also ensured a particularly strong Russian intellectual tradition of non-violence. The Manichean Bolshevik worldview was not just the product of an absolutist Marxism and an inherited Russian cultural trait. It received its clearest expression after 1917 in struggle with domestic and foreign enemies and catastrophic economic crisis. Yet the paradoxical notion of the rejection of violence through means of violence runs deeply in Russian culture and history. The tragic irony of this, considering Lenin's particularly noticeable advocacy of violence against violence itself, is that 'the application of violence in order to fight violence ironically turns those who would banish bloodshed into people little different from those they seek to overthrow.'[17]

Current scholarship on twentieth-century European violence highlights the importance of looking beyond national histories in isolation, to understand modern forms of political violence within general European processes begun in the late nineteenth century.[18] Locating Russia's experience of revolution within the context of the First World War, as we have seen, is crucial to understanding the Bolshevik revolution itself and its attendant violence; and, as Peter Holquist notes, this makes it 'a European, rather than a solely Russian, story'.[19] Holquist, rejecting an explanatory 'binary model' of either ideology or circumstances,[20] situates the practices of the Soviet state within the framework of wartime European, especially Russian, state practices: population surveillance, mass mobilizations, deportations of suspect population categories, and heightened state powers more generally. The Bolsheviks adapted the means of waging 'total war' to a waging of 'total revolution' at home. He also emphasizes a Russian political-intellectual culture that placed primacy on the state's importance in social transformation and the Tsarist legacy of a deeply divided society, with disparities between the social ideals of educated society and the mass of the people themselves.[21] Indeed the 'roots' of the violence in Russia and Europe more generally after the war, as Ian Kershaw reminds us, lay 'deeper than the war itself'.[22] Ideological fury, the class warfare mentality and the millenarian Bolshevik vision attached to the general European culture and 'ethos' of violence and state intervention at the time that the Russian Revolution occurred. Hence the crucially important point that the Bolsheviks inherited the means of state coercion and 'the tools of wartime mobilization', but added the particularities of their ideology to the practice of state violence.[23] Ideology also provided a powerful explanation along class lines for the ruin and destruction of the experience since 1914, such that 'those employing [revolutionary] violence invested it with a redemptive and purifying significance.'[24] Part of what made the Russian/Soviet experience of inter-war European violence unusual, Holquist observes, was that the Bolsheviks continued to wield the instruments of wartime – popular mobilization and state violence – on a considerable, albeit reduced scale into peacetime (after 1921) for revolutionary purposes, as other European powers managed to return to a more regularized order.[25]

The Soviet project reflected broader intellectual and institutional patterns of nineteenth- and twentieth-century European 'modernity' through state social interventionism, including the Enlightenment ideal of acting upon and reshaping societies according to rational scientific and aesthetic principles.[26] The realization of this was envisaged through education and the inculcation of new values, but sometimes by more coercive means. In extreme and even distorted fashion, in Nazi-controlled territory and Soviet Russia/Soviet Union such 'social engineering' was implemented through extremely coercive and violent forms – the excision of social impurities whether through concentration camp incarceration, reform through penal labour, or execution. Soviet state violence, as Holquist importantly observes, was not merely 'repressive', designed to eliminate political threats. It served an envisioned project of social 'cleansing', of creating an aesthetically pure unitary social order based on a mythologized conception of a 'new' modernity that would replace the alienation and anomy of capitalist modernity.[27] This would likely entail considerable coercion and at least some violence, especially within the matrix of extreme violence that was wartime Europe. Such an ethos characterized the state's functioning from its beginning; Stalinism appears more a considerable extension of this project rather than a radical break with it. Yet the uniqueness and particularities of the Bolshevik modernizing project and repressive practices should not be overlooked, and Bolshevik repression should not be understood simply in terms of modernity.[28] Daniel Beer notes that Russian liberal-biomedical norms of social 'renovation' were by definition coercive but that Russian liberals largely stepped back from widespread state-sponsored violence. The Bolsheviks, however, 'showed far less inhibition.'[29] Violent language and emphasis upon struggle were characteristics of the iconoclastic intellectual currency of Marx, Engels, Friedrich Nietzsche, and later the Bolsheviks, along with their rejections of 'bourgeois' and Christian morality.[30] What Roger Griffin has written about fascists applies equally to Marxist–Leninists, that 'their ambitions, failures, and crimes against humanity' are unintelligible without understanding their sense of 'standing on the edge of history and proactively changing its course, freed from the constraints of "normal" time and "conventional" morality.'[31]

There has appeared recently in the scholarly literature a re-conceptualization of the validity of the notion of the Soviet regime as 'totalitarian', inspired by the late Claude Lefort.[32] This is not concerned with describing an existing system but, rather, the 'almost limitless ambition' of the regime to remake society in an aestheticized image according to its ideological postulates. This book is situated within this trend. It is certainly not enough to understand the intellectual origins of Marxism–Leninism simply within the Enlightenment rationalist tradition. In a seminal study published in the 1950s Jacob Talmon identified the origins of 'totalitarian democracy', that particular form of the liberal idea in Western political thought that emerged from the same premises as liberal democracy in the eighteenth century, combining Enlightenment rationalism with a secular Messianism,[33] and which is particularly valuable for understanding the origins of Marxism and Marxism–Leninism.[34] It differed from liberal democracy in that it posited 'a sole and exclusive truth in politics', a belief that human freedom and the creation of a society of unitary purpose were necessarily compatible, and the politicization of all aspects of human society. It postulated a 'preordained, harmonious and perfect scheme of things;' for totalitarian democrats, coercion could be justified in the interests of this ideal 'without any real violation of the democratic principle being involved'.[35]

Contextualization of Bolshevik ideology and practices complements incisive analysis of the particularities of the ideology in question. Igal Halfin has highlighted the comparison that can be drawn between Bolshevik ideology and elements of the Christian tradition, explaining the former as a 'secularized eschatology'. Bolshevism was fundamentally motivated by its vision of historical teleology – the transformation of the working people from the 'darkness' of capitalism to 'salvation' in a classless society through the agency of the proletariat as equivalent 'divine messenger.'[36] Halfin convincingly demonstrates that Marxism–Leninism was not just another political ideology, or a version of political realism motivated by calculations of maximizing political power and influence. The 'Russian revolutionary eschatology sought to change society radically […] to abolish politics, and to open a new, conflict-free, transparent page in the story of human existence.'[37] Bolshevism cannot be considered a 'degenerated' intellectual trend due to its genesis in 'backward' Russia; rather, as Halfin demonstrates, the radical 'transcendence of the existing society' that the Bolsheviks attempted to implement was 'the very mainspring of Marxism's ethical drive'.[38]

•   Marxism then, despite its 'scientific' pretensions, was driven by an ethical notion of the salvation and redemption of humanity. Lenin, as we have seen, and like Robespierre before him, was motivated to revolutionary state terror by lofty moral impulses, by belief that through such exercise of state power true liberty would be achieved and advancement towards an idealized human society facilitated. Robespierre famously declared that terror as a means of striking against the revolution's enemies was an emanation of virtue, and that without deployment in the name of virtue terror would prove merely destructive and harmful. Lenin and his followers proclaimed a similar line of reasoning; during the height of terror in 1918 a Chekist could write that violence against the bourgeoisie was justifiable because 'we value and love life too much'. The centrality in Romantic thought of the notion of history's 'apocalyptic design' – that 'the evil of the world had to reach its climax' before being swept away, whether by God or by the proletariat and its vanguard party – was one shared by Marx.[39]

Halfin explains that 'Although events generated various interpretations' for the Bolsheviks, the 'shared eschatological premise eliminated any historical options that were incongruent with the Marxist eschatological narrative.'[40] The eschatological fervour associated with the messianic role to be played by the Party as vanguard of the working class generated an ideological intransigence and unwitting élitism, though Marxism–Leninism was certainly also characterized by 'faith' in the socialistic instinctiveness of the working people. For the Bolsheviks, ideological orthodoxy and popular spontaneity were two sides of the same conceptual coin. Indeed, as Joshua Sanborn explains, ideology is really about the 'covenant' between rulers and ruled regarding the way that a polity is organized and events are understood. However, this covenant does not always function smoothly, and as a result 'sovereign and subject frequently collide.'[41] Possessed of the 'objective truth' and acting on that basis, the Bolsheviks were not going to retreat easily from implementing their revolutionary design in the face of widespread social opposition to their rule,[42] despite the resultant problems of identity for Bolshevik leaders as the supposed vanguard of the working people.

This book has explained how Lenin dealt with this and constructed a justification for state violence through an absolutist conception of a scenario of either advance towards the 'light' of socialism for the peoples of the world, or return to the 'darkness' of the supremacy of imperialist forces, with counter-revolutionary agents exploiting the 'darkness' of sections of the masses for their nefarious ends. Thus we can understand the functioning of the Soviet system, and the way it was structured, in Weberian terms – that is, the relationship between forms of authority and the way such authority is legitimized.[43]

How, then, can we appraise Lenin in the 'court of history'? 'It was left to Lenin', as A. James Gregor observes, to first put together in the twentieth century 'the tentative outlines of the totalitarian state.'[44] Due to the fact that executions, deportations and political (and to a lesser extent religious) persecution were widespread and systematic, targeting not just combatants but civilians also, and tolerated by the regime when committed by its organs (indeed often as state policy), some of the violent practices of the Leninist regime constitute crimes against humanity according to the Rome Statute of the International Criminal Court.[45] Part of Lenin's legacy was the creation of a system of institutionalized state violence, coercion and repression that arose during an era of unprecedented violence, with the capacity for even greater violence in the future. Nonetheless one should not assume that responsibility for the actions of some of the most unimaginably brutal political regimes in history that have ostensibly adhered to Marxist–Leninist ideas can be placed on Lenin. The case for Stalinism as a possible offshoot of Leninism appears a strong one but to accord, for example, any considerable responsibility to Lenin's ideas for the genocidal reign of the Khmer Rouge in Cambodia would be quite incredible. (Interestingly, in one of his last publications Lenin opined that revolutions in Asia 'will undoubtedly display even greater distinctions [than the 'classical', Western-oriented Marxist conception of socialist revolution] than the Russian Revolution').[46] The left-wing historian Paul Le Blanc makes a quite valid point that the personal qualities that led Lenin to brutal policies were not necessarily any stronger than in some of the major Western leaders of the twentieth century.[47] Lenin's politics were far more explicitly violent, justified in his mind by the ends to which such violence would serve. Yet Churchill, Roosevelt and Truman led their countries through the bloodiest war in history, justifying the use of enormous levels of violence against civilian populations to defeat the Axis alliance. History, as Geoffrey Roberts notes, cannot be reduced to a simplistic morality tale,[48] pitting a 'good' side against a 'bad' one.

Jacob Talmon posed the question whether when 'the deeds of men [sic] in power believe their words, are they to be called hypocrites and cynics or are they victims of an intellectual delusion?' The answer provided here regarding the Bolsheviks is more complex than this question would suggest but agrees primarily with the latter notion. The Bolshevik project had immense pretensions: to establish a new system cleansed of the evils of the old, and the creation of a society reflecting belief in the ultimate perfectibility of humanity. The Bolsheviks proved radical in the extreme in their approach to achieving this, with a willingness to resort to an enormous scale of violence and terror. The project was utopian, and with hindsight clearly unattainable as conceived. However the violence and terror of early Soviet Russia cannot be explained away simplistically as the actions of violent fanatics, or the products of a violent Russian political culture. Bolshevik violence (and the communist vision) was a reaction to violent, unjust and flawed Russian and European political systems, and to the struggle for survival. Does the Russian Revolution teach us of the futility and inherent humanitarian dangers of thorough-going political revolutions? This is ultimately for the reader to decide, but the extent of the violence and dictatorial rule associated with the Bolshevik attempt to remake the world can primarily be explained by the particularities of Bolshevism and its responses to very violent times, not simply by the nature of revolution itself.

The more significant lessons to be learned from the experience of the Russian Revolution, as relevant today as in the last century, concern fundamental issues of how we as human beings relate to each other. Writing of the lessons of the Terror of the French Revolution, historian David Andress makes a profound observation, the continued relevance of which has been demonstrated by the events of the first years of this century, and which is especially appropriate to conclude this study of Lenin and violence. The maxim that 'the price of liberty is eternal vigilence' needs to be applied not so much externally, to perceived enemies, but internally, 'against ourselves'. We should

> not assume that we are righteous, and our enemies evil; that we can see clearly, and others are blinded by malice or folly; that we can abrogate the fragile rights of others in the name of our own certainty and all will be well regardless. If we do not honour the message of human rights [...] we too are on the road to Terror.[49]

The purpose of this book has been to contribute to explaining Bolshevik violence, through the theory and practice of the first Bolshevik leader, but certainly not to justify or excuse it.

Notes

Introduction: ideology and violence

1 Alexander Solzhenitsyn, *The Gulag Archipelago 1918–1956: An Experiment in Literary Investigation I–II*, trans. by Thomas P. Whitney, London: Collins and Harvill Press, 1974, pp. 173–4.

2 Christopher Read, *Lenin: a Revolutionary Life*, London and New York: Routledge, 2005, p. 250.

3 Joshua A. Sanborn, *Drafting the Russian Nation. Military Conscription, Total War, and Mass Politics, 1905–1925*, DeKalb, IL: Northern Illinois University Press, 2003, p. 174.

4 Paul R. Gregory, *Terror by Quota. State Security from Lenin to Stalin: an Archival Study*, New Haven: Yale University Press, 2009, p. 29.

5 See for example the preface, introduction and conclusion in Stephane Courtois (ed.), *The Black Book of Communism: Crimes, Terror, Repression*, trans. Mark Kramer and Jonathan Murphy, Massachusetts: Harvard University Press, 1999.

6 See Richard Pipes (ed.), *The Unknown Lenin: Revelations from the Secret Archive*, Annals of Communism Series, New Haven: Yale University Press, 1998, pp. 1–11.

7 Robert Gellately, *Lenin, Stalin and Hitler: The Age of Social Catastrophe*, London: Jonathan Cape, 2007, p. 9.

8 See for example Sebastian Budgen, Stathis Kouvelakis and Slavoj Žižek (eds.), *Lenin Reloaded: Towards a Politics of Truth*, Durham: Duke University Press, 2007.

9 The phrase is Lars Lih's. See discussion in Christopher Read, 'Retrieving the Historical Lenin', in Ian D. Thatcher (ed.), *Reinterpreting Revolutionary Russia*, Hampshire: Palgrave Macmillan, 2006, p. 131.

10 Read, *Lenin*, p. 246.

11 There is however a work by a Soviet historian, Iu. N. Shumakov, *V. I. Lenin o revolutsionnom nasilii v istoricheskom razvitii*, Moscow: 1973 but the author has been unable to locate a copy.

12 Robert Service, *Lenin: A Political Life*, vol. 3, Bloomington: Indiana University Press, 1995, p. xix.

13 Ken Jowitt, *New World Disorder: The Leninist Extinction*, Berkeley and Los Angeles: University of California Press, 1993, p. vii.

14 Though agreeing with the spirit of Michael David-Fox's essay on ideology in Soviet studies, I take a different view from his on this point. See Michael David-Fox, 'On the Primacy of Ideology. Soviet Revisionists and Holocaust Deniers (In Response to Martin Malia)', *Kritika*, 2004, vol. 5, No. 1, 81–105.

15 See Igal Halfin, *From Darkness to Light: Class, Consciousness, and Salvation in Revolutionary Russia*, Pittsburgh: University of Pittsburgh Press, 2000. For the social, intellectual and institutional requisites for 'high-modernist' state schemes of social

engineering, see James C. Scott, *Seeing Like a State. How Certain Schemes to Improve the Human Condition Have Failed*, New Haven: Yale University Press, 1998.

16 See Martin Conway and Roberth Gerwarth, 'Revolution and counter-revolution', in Donald Bloxham and Robert Gerwarth (eds.), *Political Violence in Twentieth-Century Europe*, Cambridge: Cambridge University Press, 2011, pp. 140–75.

17 Peter Holquist, *Making War, Forging Revolution: Russia's Continuum of Crisis, 1914–1921*, Massachusetts: Harvard University Press, 2002, p. 45.

18 See Barry Cooper, *Merleau-Ponty and Marxism: From Terror to Reform*, Toronto: University of Toronto Press, 1979, p. 47.

19 Ronald Grigor Suny has demonstrated this in his study of Menshevik rule in Georgia before 1921, the Mensheviks being the Bolsheviks' former Party colleagues. The Georgian Mensheviks, however, had a more secure power base than the Russian Bolsheviks, were faced with less extreme circumstances, and in addition they did not consider the country to be ripe for a truly socialist revolution as did the Bolsheviks in Soviet Russia. See Ronald Grigor Suny, 'Social Democrats in Power: Menshevik Georgia and the Russian Civil War', in Diane P. Koenker, William G. Rosenberg and Ronald Grigor Suny (eds.), *Party, State, and Society in the Russian Civil War: Explorations in Social History*, Bloomington: Indiana University Press, 1989, pp. 324–45.

20 See Peter Holquist, 'State Violence as Technique: The Logic of Violence in Soviet Totalitarianism', in Amir Weiner (ed.), *Landscaping the Human Garden: Twentieth-Century Population Management in a Comparative Framework*, Stanford: Stanford University Press, 2003, p. 26.

21 Neil Harding, *Leninism*, London: Macmillan, 1996, pp. 156–7.

22 Joseph Schull, 'What is Ideology? Theoretical Problems and Lessons from Soviet-Type Societies', *Political Studies*, 1992, vol. XL, No. 4, 729.

23 Steve Smith, 'Two Cheers for the "Return of Ideology"', *Revolutionary Russia*, 2004, vol. 17, No. 2, 133.

24 See Gopal Singh, 'Politics and Violence', *Social Scientist*, 1976, vol. 4, No. 11, p. 63.

25 See Slavoj Žižek, *Violence*, London: Verso, 2008.

26 Though typically translated as 'violence', the word has also been translated as 'force' in the English-language edition of Lenin's *Collected Works*. I have, in places, changed this translation to 'violence' where I consider this more accurate.

27 Ruslan Vladimirovich Tikhomirov, 'Problema revolutsionnogo nasiliia v rossiiskoi sotsial-demokraticheskoi pechati (bol'shevikov i men'shevikov), fevral' 1917 – mart 1918gg.', Ph.D. (Candidate's) dissertation, St. Petersburg, 2000, pp. 52–8.

28 Virginia Held, *How Terrorism is Wrong: Morality and Political Violence*, New York: Oxford University Press, 2008, p. 128.

29 One of the interesting things about the development of Soviet jurisprudence is the legalization of the arbitrary use of force.

30 Stathis N. Kalyvas, *The Logic of Violence in Civil War*, New York: Cambridge University Press, 2006, p. 20. The understanding of state violence adopted here does not include regular military battlefield operations between Red and White forces after October 1917, at least in areas not under the nominal rule of the Bolsheviks.

31 Hannah Arendt, *On Violence*, Orlando: Harcourt, 1970, p. 51.

32 A. James Gregor, *Marxism, Fascism, and Totalitarianism. Chapters in the Intellectual History of Radicalism*, Stanford: Stanford University Press, 2009, p. 22.

33 Andrew Heywood, *Political Ideologies: An Introduction*, Fourth Edition, Hampshire: Palgrave Macmillan, 2007, p. 11.

34 Ibid., pp. 11–12.

35 Michael Freeden, *Ideologies and Political Theory: A Conceptual Approach*, Oxford: Clarendon Press, 1996, p. 3. Such complex understanding of how ideologies function owes much to the anthropological work of Clifford Geertz. See 'Ideology as a Cultural System' in Clifford Geertz, *The Interpretation of Cultures: Selected Essays* [1973], New York: Basic Books, 2000.

36 Charles Reynolds, *Modes of Imperialism*, Oxford: Martin Robertson, 1981, p. 126.
37 Graeme Gill, 'Ideology and System-Building: The Experience under Lenin and Stalin', in Stephen White and Alex Pravda (eds.), *Ideology and Soviet Politics*, London: Macmillan/SSEES, 1988, p. 75.
38 Trevor Purvis and Alan Hunt, 'Discourse, Ideology, Discourse, Ideology, Discourse, Ideology…', *The British Journal of Sociology*, 1993, vol. 44, No. 3, p. 485.
39 David Priestland, *Stalinism and the Politics of Mobilization: Ideas, Power, and Terror in Inter-war Russia*, Oxford: Oxford University Press, 2007, pp. 16–18.
40 Freeden, *Ideologies and Political Theory*, pp. 69–70. For the relationship between 'conscious' ideological thoughts and broader, 'more anonymous' cultural idioms, see also Theda Skocpol, 'Cultural Idioms and Political Ideologies in the Revolutionary Reconstruction of State Power: A Rejoinder to Sewell', *The Journal of Modern History*, 1985, vol. 57, No. 1, p. 86–96.
41 Freeden, *Ideologies and Political Theory*, p. 79.
42 Priestland, *Stalinism and the Politics of Mobilization*, p. 17.
43 Freeden, *Ideologies and Political Theory*, p. 3.
44 Giovanni Sartori, 'Politics, Ideology, and Belief Systems', *The American Political Science Review*, 1969, vol. 63, No. 2, pp. 403, 410. Lars Lih, in the most recent biography of Lenin, particularly emphasizes the importance of the emotive component of Lenin's political convictions (Lars T. Lih, *Lenin*, London: Reaktion Books, 2011).
45 Alain Besançon, *The Intellectual Origins of Leninism*, trans. Sarah Matthews, Oxford: Blackwell, 1981, p. 200.
46 See also Andrew Vincent, *Modern Political Ideologies*, Third Edition, West Sussex: Wiley-Blackwell, 2010, p. 20.
47 See for particular Mark Sandle, *A Short History of Soviet Socialism*, London: UCL Press, 1999 and Halfin, *From Darkness to Light.* See discussion in Smith, 'Two Cheers for the "Return of Ideology" ', pp. 119–35.
48 Priestland, *Stalinism and the Politics of Mobilization*, p. 11.
49 For an example of a clear recent account in this vein see Stephane Courtois, 'Conclusion', in Courtois (ed.), *The Black Book of Communism*, esp. p. 735–7. For the historiographical trends in writing about Soviet history, including repression, see Priestland, *Stalinism and the Politics of Mobilization*, pp. 2ff.; see also David Priestland, 'Marx and the Kremlin: writing on Marxism–Leninism and Soviet politics after the fall of communism', *Journal of Political Ideologies*, 2000, vol. 5, No. 3, 377–8. Regarding Lenin's recent biographers, Dmitri Volkogonov provided the foremost account in the totalitarian vein, see Dmitri Volkogonov, *Lenin: A New Biography*, New York: The Free Press, 1994, esp. pp. 83; xxxviii. Robert Service and Christopher Read both advance more complex understandings of Lenin's ideas and political practice. Service sees no simple connection leading from Leninism to the worst horrors of Stalinism, while Read implies that it was circumstances that primarily explain Leninist state terror, though not coercion more generally. See Robert Service, *Lenin: A Political Life*, vol. 3, Bloomington, IN: Indiana University Press, 1995, pp. xv–xix; Read, *Lenin*, p. 247.
50 See Courtois, 'Conclusion', in *The Black Book of Communism*, p. 735.
51 Anna Geifman, *Thou Shalt Kill: Revolutionary Terrorism in Russia, 1894–1917*, New Jersey: Princeton University Press, 1993, p. 254. For the notion that some of Lenin's violent injunctions reflected a 'pathological character', a mental imbalance, see A. G. Latyshev, *Rassekrechennyi Lenin. Liudi i vlast'*, Moscow: Mart, 1996, pp. 33–4.
52 See for example Boris Levytsky, *The Uses of Terror: The Soviet Secret Police, 1917–1970*, trans. H. A. Piehler, New York: Coward, McCann and Geoghegan, 1972, p. 13; Marcel Liebman, *Leninism Under Lenin*, trans. Brian Pearce, London: Jonathan Cape, 1975, p. 311; Nicolas Werth, 'A State against Its People: Violence, Repression, and Terror in the Soviet Union', in Courtois (ed.), *The Black Book of Communism*, and Suny, *The Soviet Experiment*, pp. 64–5.

53 Alexander Rabinowitch, *The Bolsheviks in Power: The First Year of Soviet Power in Petrograd*, Bloomington, IN: Indiana University Press, 2007.
54 Suny, 'Social Democrats in Power', in Koenker, William G. Rosenberg and Ronald Grigor Suny (eds.), *Party, State, and Society in the Russian Civil War*, pp. 324–5.
55 Smith, 'Two Cheers', 122.
56 Joan Witte, 'Violence in Lenin's Thought and Practice: The Spark and the Conflagration', *Terrorism and Political Violence*, 1993, vol. 5, No. 3, 188–9; 137–8. Rustam Singh has also written a lengthy article on violence in Lenin's concept of revolution, 'Violence in the Leninist Revolution', *Economic and Political Weekly*, 1990, vol. 25, No. 52, p. 2843ff.
57 Witte, 'Violence in Lenin's Thought and Practice', p. 189.
58 Eckard Bolsinger, *The Autonomy of the Political: Carl Schmitt's and Lenin's Political Realism*, Connecticut: Greenwood Press, 2001, pp. 6; 11.
59 John Gray, *Black Mass: Apocalyptic Religion and the Death of Utopia*, London: Allen Lane, 2007, p. 18.
60 Peter Waldron, *Governing Tsarist Russia*, Hampshire: Palgrave Macmillan, 2007, p. 181. See also Richard Pipes, *Russia Under the Old Regime*, London: Weidenfeld and Nicolson, 1974, esp. Chapter 11.
61 Jonathan Daly, *The Watchful State: Security Police and Opposition in Russia, 1906–1917*, DeKalb, IL: Northern Illinois University Press, 2004, p. 226.
62 Significantly, the Tsar and conservatives explicitly maintained that Russia had remained an autocracy after 1905; even a reforming minister such as Petr Stolypin, whose vision if implemented would have led to a properly constitutional (though not parliamentary) order, apparently still thought of the new constitutional order in 1906 as a uniquely Russian combination of autocracy and the rule of law. See Abraham Ascher, *P. A. Stolypin: The Search for Stability in Late Imperial Russia*, Stanford: Stanford University Press, 2001, pp. 109; 126–8.
63 Daly, *The Watchful State*, pp. 223ff.
64 Ibid., p. 225.
65 Ibid., p. 225.
66 Ibid., p. 226.
67 See David McLellan, *Marxism after Marx*, Fourth Edition, Hampshire: Palgrave Macmillan, 2007, p. 2.
68 See Karl Kautsky, 'The Social Revolution', 1902, vol. 1, Part 3. Online. Available http://www.marxists.org/archive/kautsky/1904/ (accessed 27 March 2007). Future references to Kautsky's works are from this source, unless otherwise stated.
69 See Ibid., Part 2.
70 Kautsky, 'The Social Revolution', Part 3, p. 12.
71 Karl Kautsky, 'The Road to Power', 1909, v, p. 2.
72 See Vladimir Il'ich Lenin, *Teoriia Nasiliia*, Moscow: Algoritm, 2007, p. 8.
73 Quoted in David McLellan (ed.), *Karl Marx: Selected Writings*, Oxford: Oxford University Press, 1977, p. 272.
74 See Robert Service, *Lenin: A Political Life*, vol. 1, London: Macmillan, 1985, pp. 33ff.
75 See Engels to Nikolai Danielson, 17 October 1893, in Karl Marx and Friedrich Engels, *Collected Works*, vol. 50, London: Lawrence and Wishart, 2004, pp. 214–5.
76 See Robert V. Daniels, *The Rise and Fall of Communism in Russia*, New Haven: Yale University Press, 2007, p. 44 and Lesley Chamberlain, *The Philosophy Steamer: Lenin and the Exile of the Intelligentsia*, London: Atlantic Books, 2006, pp. 24–5. Marxism traditionally stresses the primacy of economic factors in socio-historical development, not politics.
77 Lars T. Lih, *Lenin Rediscovered: What is to be Done? in Context*, Brill: Leiden, 2006. The contours of this argument are not new, see Harding, *Lenin's Political Thought*, vol. 1, 1984, and Moira Donald, *Marxism and Revolution: Karl Kautsky and the Russian Marxists, 1900–1924*, New Haven: Yale University Press, 1993.

78 Donald, *Marxism and Revolution*, p. 126.
79 Karl Marx, 'The German Ideology', in McLellan (ed.), *Karl Marx: Selected Writings*, p. 179.
80 Robert Mayer, 'The Dictatorship of the Proletariat from Plekhanov to Lenin', *Studies in East European Thought*, 1993, vol. 45, No. 4, p. 266.
81 See also Hal Draper, *Karl Marx's Theory of Revolution*, vol. III, New York: Monthly Review Press, 1986.
82 Gregor, *Marxism, Fascism, and Totalitarianism*, p. 232.
83 See for example Neil Harding, *Leninism*, London: Macmillan, 1996, pp. 262–3.
84 Lih, *Lenin*, p. 203.
85 V. I. Lenin, 'Speech Delivered at the Third All-Russian Trade Union Congress',vol. 30, pp. 7–8. Marxists Internet Archive. Online. Available http://www.marxists.org/archive/lenin/works/1905/rd/index.htm (accessed 10 April 2007). The 'Marxists Internet Archive' is the principal source of Lenin's *Collected Works* to be used throughout this book and all references to Lenin's works are from this source unless otherwise stated. Considering the numerous editions of the *Works* that exist, each work is referred to by title in footnotes so as to make easier the task of consultation. Page numbers follow the printed version of each work on standard A4-size paper, whereby each work, and each major chapter thereof, begins on page 1. The reader is advised that page numbers indicated are accurate within one page, due to minute differences in printer types (e.g. material indicated on p. 4 might be partially located on p. 5). For accuracy of translation, the author has consulted the third and the last, fifth, Russian edition of Lenin's *Works*. See V. I. Lenin, *Sochinenii*, Third Edition, 30 volumes, Moscow: Partizdat, 1930–1937, and V. I. Lenin, *Polnoe Sobranie Sochinenii*, Fifth Edition, 55 volumes, Moscow: Institute of Marxism–Leninism, 1958–1965.
86 See Norman M. Naimark, 'Ethnic Cleansing Between War and Peace', in Weiner (ed.), *Landscaping the Human Garden*, pp. 218–35.
87 The most recent argument for considering Stalinist violence in general as a series of genocides is Norman M. Naimark, *Stalin's Genocides*, New Jersey and Oxford: Princeton University Press, 2010.
88 See Mark von Hagen, *Soldiers in the Proletarian Dictatorship: The Red Army and the Soviet Socialist State, 1917–1930*, Ithaca: Cornell University Press, 1990.
89 Rana Mitter, *A Bitter Revolution: China's Struggle with the Modern World*, Oxford: Oxford University Press, 2006, p. 209.
90 See Nikolai Osinskii in *Pravda*, 11 September 1918.
91 The most informative work for a scholarly readership is Michael Geyer and Sheila Fitzpatrick (eds.), *Beyond Totalitarianism: Stalinism and Nazism Compared*, New York: Cambridge University Press, 2009. See also Ian Kershaw and Moshe Lewin (eds.), *Stalinism and Nazism: Dictatorships in Comparison*, Cambridge: Cambridge University Press, 1997 and Richard Overy, *The Dictators: Hitler's Germany and Stalin's Russia*, London: Allen Lane, 2004.
92 Stephane Courtois, 'Introduction', in Courtois (ed.), *The Black Book of Communism*, p. 16.
93 For an illuminating study of how the body politic was defined and categorized in the Soviet Union, see Golfo Alexopoulos, *Stalin's Outcasts: Aliens, Citizens, and the Soviet State, 1926–1936*, Ithaca and London: Cornell University Press, 2003.
94 See Amir Weiner, 'Introduction', in Weiner (ed.), *Landscaping the Human Garden*, p. 15.
95 Holquist, 'State Violence as Technique', pp. 38ff. Nonetheless, biological understandings of criminality in Soviet repression were nonetheless significant, especially in the 1930s. See Daniel Beer, *Renovating Russia: The Human Sciences and the Fate of Liberal Modernity, 1880–1930*, Ithaca and London: Cornell University Press, 2008, p. 200.

96 For an excellent account of the shift in Soviet policing and terror practices in the 1930s, see Paul Hagenloh, *Stalin's Police: Public Order and Mass Repression in the USSR, 1926–1941*, Washington, DC: Wilson Center/John S Hopkins University Press, 2009.

97 Jörg Baberowski and Anselm Doering-Manteuffel, 'The Quest for Order and the Pursuit of Terror', in Geyer and Fitzpatrick (eds.), *Beyond Totalitarianism*, p. 213.

98 See in particular Martin Malia's forward to the English-language edition of that volume, where he seems to imply that Communism was the greater evil.

99 See Peter Fritzsche and Jochen Hellbeck, 'The New Man in Stalinist Russia and Nazi Germany', in Geyer and Fitzpatrick (eds.), *Beyond Totalitarianism*, pp. 302–41.

100 Igal Halfin (ed.), *Language and Revolution: Making Modern Political Identities*, London and Portland, OR: Frank Cass, 2002, p. 5.

101 Holquist, 'State Violence as Technique', p. 38.

102 Quoted in Fritzsche and Hellbeck, 'The New Man', p. 336.

103 For a similar argument, see Robert O. Paxton, *The Anatomy of Fascism*, London and New York: Penguin, 2005, p. 213.

104 See also Christian Gerlach and Nicolas Werth, 'State Violence – Violent Societies', in Geyer and Fitzpatrick (eds.), *Beyond Totalitarianism*, pp. 176–8.

1 'Revolution is war': the genesis of a militant Marxism 1894–1907

1 Much of this chapter has appeared as James Ryan, '"Revolution is War"': The Development of the Thought of V. I. Lenin on Violence, 1899–1907', *Slavonic and East European Review*, 2011, vol. 89, No. 2, pp. 248–73.

2 V. I. Lenin, 'Revolutionary Days', Part III, vol. 8, p. 1.

3 Waldron, *Governing Tsarist Russia*, p. 123.

4 Abraham Ascher points out that the upheaval of these years in fact began in 1904 with liberal disenchantment with the autocracy, and that the 'revolution' did not come to an end until 3 June 1907 when electoral changes designed to curb opposition were introduced by the Prime Minister, Petr Stolypin. See Abraham Ascher, *The Revolution of 1905: A Short History*, Stanford: Stanford University Press, 2004, p. xiii.

5 See Franziska Schedewie, 'Peasant Protest and Peasant Violence in 1905: Voronezh Province, Ostrogozhskii Uezd', in Jonathan D. Smele and Anthony Heywood (eds.), *The Russian Revolution of 1905: Centenary Perspectives*, London: Routledge, 2005, pp. 137–48.

6 John Keep, 'Terror in 1905', in Ian D. Thatcher (ed.), *Reinterpreting Revolutionary Russia: Essays in Honour of James D. White*, Hampshire: Palgrave Macmillan, 2006, p. 21.

7 Geifman, *Thou Shalt Kill*, p. 112.

8 For a broader understanding of Soviet 'militarized socialism', see von Hagen, *Soldiers in the Proletarian Dictatorship*, pp. 6–7.

9 See Bruce Hofmann in David J. Whittaker (ed.), *The Terrorism Reader*, 2nd Edition, London and New York: Routledge, 2003, p. 5.

10 Boaz Ganor, 'Defining Terrorism: Is One Man's Terrorist Another Man's Freedom Fighter?', *Police Practice and Research*, 2002, vol. 3, No. 4, 287.

11 V. I. Lenin, *What the 'Friends of the People' are and how they fight the Social-Democrats*, Moscow: Progress Publishers, 1966, Part III, p. 88.

12 See V. I. Lenin, 'The Tasks of the Russian Social-Democrats', vol. 2, p. 6.

13 V. I. Lenin, 'Frederick Engels', vol. 2, p. 1.

14 V. I. Lenin, 'Draft and Explanation of a Programme for the Social-Democratic Party', vol. 2, p. 16.

15 See for example Lenin, 'The Tasks of the Russian Social-Democrats', pp. 6ff.

16 On revolutionary terrorism in Russia before 1917, and the Russian Marxist response to terrorism, see Geifman, *Thou Shalt Kill*; Norman M. Naimark, *Terrorists and Social Democrats: The Russian Revolutionary Movement under Alexander III*, Massachusetts: Harvard University Press, 1983; O. V. Budnitskii, *Terrorizm v Rossiiskom Osvoboditel'nom Dvizhenii: ideologiia, etika, psikhologiia (vtoraia polovina XIX–nachalo XX v.)*, Moscow: Rosspen, 2000; and David Allen Newell, 'The Russian Marxist Response to Terrorism', Doctoral Dissertation, Stanford University, 1981.

17 Newell, 'The Russian Marxist Response to Terrorism', p. 197.

18 Biographers of Lenin have usually spent some time pondering the effects of the execution of his brother Aleksandr for his part in an attempt on the life of the Tsar in 1881. Soviet opinion was that this act had convinced Lenin immediately of the necessity of rejecting individual terrorism, as his sister had claimed, though the consensus now is that Lenin's ideas were not sufficiently developed at that time to support such a claim. Undoubtedly the execution of his brother added an extra emotional element to Lenin's visceral hatred of the autocracy, strengthening his deeply emotional commitment to a strategy that would realize their common revolutionary dream (see Lih, *Lenin*, p. 194).

19 V. I. Lenin, 'A Draft of Our Party Programme', vol. 4, p. 8.

20 V. I. Lenin, 'Where to Begin?', vol. 5, p. 3.

21 Ibid., pp. 6–7.

22 See V. I. Lenin, 'The Tasks of the Russian Social-Democrats', vol. 2, p. 14.

23 Lenin, 'Where to Begin?', p. 3.

24 Ibid., p. 4.

25 V. I. Lenin, 'Second Congress of the RSDLP 5. Draft of Minor Resolutions: Terrorism', vol. 6, p. 2.

26 See V. I. Lenin, 'Left-Wing Communism: An Infantile Disorder', vol. 31, p. 2.

27 Lenin, 'Where to Begin?', p. 3.

28 V. I. Lenin, 'The Urgent Tasks of Our Movement', vol. 4, p. 3.

29 V. I. Lenin, 'Revolutionary Adventurism', vol. 6, p. 3.

30 Newell, *The Russian Marxist Response*, p. 231.

31 Lenin, 'Revolutionary Adventurism', pp. 8–9.

32 V. I. Lenin, 'What is to be Done? Burning Questions of Our Movement', vol. 5, Chapter V, p. 17.

33 Ibid., Chapters I, p. 3 and IV, pp. 29–30.

34 V. I. Lenin, 'Material for the Preparation of the Programme of the RSDLP Notes on Plekhanov's Second Draft Programme', vol. 6, p. 13.

35 See Karl Marx, 'Conspectus on Bakunin's Book *Statism and Anarchy*', 1874. Online. Available   http://www.marxists.org/archive/marx/works/1874/04/bakunin-notes.htm (accessed 19 September 2009).

36 V. I. Lenin, 'Revolution in Russia', vol. 8, p. 1.

37 Just two weeks before, observing liberal discontent with the regime due to the war with Japan and the Tsar's refusal to compromise the principle of autocracy, Lenin had wondered whether the workers would soon decide if 'the moment for the decisive struggle for freedom has come.' See V. I. Lenin, 'The Autocracy and the Proletariat', vol. 8, p. 1.

38 V. I. Lenin, 'The Revolutionary Army and the Revolutionary Government', vol. 8, p. 5.

39 See Iu. O. Martov, 'Deviatoie ianvaria' and 'Revoliutsionnyie Perspektivyi', in O. V. Volobuiev and V. V. Shelokhaev (eds.), *Men'sheviki: Dokymentyi i materialyi, 1903– fevral' 1917 gg,* Moscow: Rosspen, 1996, pp. 90–94; p. 103.

40 This was the opinion of Elena Stasova, an associate of Lenin's. Quoted in Geifman, *Thou Shalt Kill*, p. 91.

41 See V. I. Lenin, 'Tasks of Revolutionary Army Contingents', vol. 9.

42 Quoted in Geifman, *Thou Shalt Kill*, p. 91; Budnitskii, *Terrorizm v Rossiiskom Osvoboditel'nom Dvizhenii*, p. 324. In addition Lenin urged 'the shooting on the spot' for anyone in the Party who refused to organize wide Bolshevik circles in Russia, especially amongst the youth. How serious he was is questionable but it certainly demonstrates his ruthlessness towards questions of Party organization and discipline. See Ascher, 'Introduction', in Smele and Heywood (eds.), *The Russian Revolution of 1905*, p. 9.
43 V. I. Lenin, 'A Militant Agreement for the Uprising', vol. 8, p. 2.
44 See for example Lenin, 'Working-Class and Bourgeois Democracy', p. 6.
45 See for example V. I. Lenin, 'The Struggle of the Proletariat and the Servility of the Bourgeoisie', vol. 8, p. 2.
46 V. I. Lenin, 'A New Revolutionary Workers' Association', vol. 8, pp. 3–4.
47 V. I. Lenin, 'No Falsehood! Our Strength Lies in Stating the Truth!', vol. 9, p. 2.
48 V. I. Lenin, 'Between Two Battles', vol. 9, pp. 6–7.
49 V. I. Lenin, 'Two Tactics of Social-Democracy in the Democratic Revolution', vol. 9, Afterword, III, p. 2.
50 Ibid.
51 V. I. Lenin, 'The Black Hundreds and the Organisation of an Uprising', vol. 9, pp. 1–2; p. 5.
52 Keep, 'Terror in 1905', in Thatcher (ed.), *Reinterpreting Revolutionary Russia*, p. 30.
53 See Abraham Ascher, *The Revolution of 1905: Russia in Disarray*, vol. 1, Stanford: Stanford University Press, 1988, p. 335.
54 See *Chetvertyi (Ob'edinitel'nyi) s''ezd RSDRP. Aprel'-mai 1906 goda. Protokolyi*, Moscow: Gospolitizdat, 1959, p. 483.
55 See Ascher, *The Revolution of 1905*, pp. 5–6.
56 Lenin, 'Two Tactics', section 6.
57 See Volobuiev and V. V. Shelokhaev (eds.), *Men'sheviki*, p. 123.
58 Lenin, 'Two Tactics', vol. 12, p. 2.
59 V. I. Lenin, 'The Revolutionary-Democratic Dictatorship of the Proletariat and the Peasantry', vol. 8, p. 7.
60 Volobuiev and V. V. Shelokhaev (eds.), *Men'sheviki*, p. 124.
61 Lenin, 'Two Tactics', Conclusion: Dare we Win?, p. 9. Hence Lenin did not understand the 'dictatorship of the proletariat' as simply the condition of proletarian rule as Hal Draper has understood Marx's original meaning. For Lenin, dictatorship signified an active political form of rule.
62 Ibid., section 6.
63 Gregory Varhall notes that Lenin first used the expression 'dictatorship of the proletariat' in *What is to be Done?*, 1902. See Gregory Varhall, 'The Development of Lenin's Conception of the Dictatorship of the Proletariat', Ph.D. Dissertation, University of Notre Dame, 1982, p. 9.
64 See Donald, *Marxism and Revolution*, Chapter 3.
65 Karl Kautsky, 'Revolutions, Past and Present', 1906, pp. 2–4.
66 Lenin, 'Two Tactics'. See section entitled 'The Vulgar Bourgeois Representation of Dictatorship and Marx's View of It', p. 3.
67 Ibid., vol. 4, p. 2.
68 V. I. Lenin, 'Sketch of a Provisional Revolutionary Government', vol. 8, p. 1.
69 This was the resolution of the alternative (Menshevik) Party Conference in Geneva. See Volobuiev and V. V. Shelokhaev (eds.), *Men'sheviki*, p. 123.
70 Lenin, 'Two Tactics', vol. 4, p. 2.
71 See Ibid., section 6. Engels referred to the Terror of 1793 as 'useless cruelties'. Marxists were confident that, through concern for social as well as political revolution, in addition to distinguishing democratic and socialist revolutions, twentieth-century revolutions would not witness the 'cruelties' born of an insecure regime lacking popular strength.

72 Ibid., vol. 4, p. 2.
73 Ibid., Conclusion, p. 9.
74 Lenin, 'Social-Democracy and the Provisional Revolutionary Government', Part II, p. 4.
75 See V. I. Lenin, 'A Contribution to the History of The Question of Dictatorship. A Note', vol. 31, pp. 2ff.
76 Ibid., p. 6.
77 Varhall, 'The Development', p. 86.
78 Lenin, 'A Contribution to the History', pp. 10–2.
79 Lenin, 'A Contribution to the History', pp. 3, 9. See also Leopold Haimson, 'Lenin's Revolutionary Career Revisited: Some Observations on Recent Discussions', *Kritika*, 2004, vol. 5, No. 1, 65.
80 For discussion around this see also Varhall, 'The Development', pp. 87ff.
81 Geifman, *Thou Shalt Kill*, p. 11.
82 Plekhanov, 'Vroz' idti, vmeste bit'', in Volobuiev and V. V. Shelokhaev (eds.), *Men'sheviki*, p. 98.
83 V. I. Lenin, 'Third Congress of the RSDLP Speech on an Agreement with the Socialist-Revolutionaries', vol. 8, p. 6. No formal agreement was actually concluded, but on the ground agreements were implemented. See Budnitskii, *Terrorizm v Rossiiskom Osvoboditel'nom Dvizhenii*, p. 321.
84 Lenin, 'Third Congress of the RSDLP. Draft Resolution of the Armed Uprising', p. 1. See also Erik van Ree, 'Reluctant Terrorists? Transcaucasian Social-Democracy, 1901–1909', *Europe–Asia Studies*, 2008, vol. 60, No. 1, p. 129.
85 V. I. Lenin, 'From the Defensive to the Offensive', vol. 9, p. 1.
86 Geifman, *Thou Shalt Kill*, p. 91.
87 Lenin, 'From the Defensive to the Offensive', p. 2.
88 V. I. Lenin, 'A Militant Agreement for the Uprising', vol. 8, pp. 3–4.
89 Ibid., p. 3.
90 Lenin, 'From the Defensive to the Offensive', p. 2.
91 V. I. Lenin, 'The Present Situation in Russia and the Tactics of the Workers' Party', vol. 10, p. 5.
92 Geifman, *Thou Shalt Kill*, p. 92.
93 V. I. Lenin, 'Lessons of the Moscow Uprising', vol. 11, p. 6.
94 Ascher, *The Revolution of 1905*, vol. 1, pp. 289–90.
95 Though the Russian for 'guerrilla' is *partizan*, 'partisan' connotes underground resistance during occupation by an invading force.
96 *Chetvertyi (Ob'edinitel'nyi) s''ezd RSDRP*, pp. 567–8; pp. 526–7.
97 Ibid., pp. 480–1.
98 Lenin, 'Lessons of the Moscow Uprising', pp. 3–4.
99 *Chetvertyi (Ob'edinitel'nyi) s''ezd RSDRP*, p. 528
100 Ibid., p. 482.
101 V. I. Lenin, 'The Events of the Day', vol. 11, p. 2.
102 Samuel Baron, *Plekhanov: The Father of Russian Marxism,* Stanford, 1963, p. 267.
103 Lenin, 'Lessons of the Moscow Uprising', p. 1.
104 Ibid., p. 3.
105 V. I. Lenin, 'Guerrilla Warfare', vol. 11, No. III, p. 2.
106 Lenin, 'Guerrilla Warfare', II, p. 2.
107 Lenin, 'Lessons of the Moscow Uprising', pp. 5–6.
108 See V. I. Lenin, 'Tactical Platform for the Unity Congress of the RSDLP', Fighting Guerrilla Operations, vol. 10, pp. 1–2.
109 Newell, 'The Russian Marxist Response to Terrorism', p. 430.
110 Ibid., p. 400.
111 Lenin, 'Lessons of the Moscow Uprising', p. 2.
112 Lenin, 'Guerrilla Warfare', III, p. 3.

113 V. I. Lenin, 'Against Boycott. Notes of a Social-Democratic Publicist', vol. 13, No. III, p. 3.
114 Newell, 'The Russian Marxist Response to Terrorism', pp. 441–2.
115 Ascher, *The Revolution of 1905*, pp. xiii, 145.
116 V. I. Lenin, 'The Boycott', vol. 11, pp. 4–5.
117 Lenin, 'Guerrilla Warfare', vol. III, p. 3.
118 *Piatyi (londonskii) s''ezd RSDRP. Aprel'-mai 1907goda. Protokolyi*, Moscow, 1963, pp. 615–6; see also pp. 638, 650–1.
119 See R. C. Williams, *The Other Bolsheviks: Lenin and his Critics, 1904–1914*, Bloomington: Indiana University Press, 1986, Chapter five.
120 Iu. N. Amiantov, Yu. A. Akhapkin and V. T. Loginov (eds.), *V. I. Lenin. Neizvestnyie dokumenty, 1891–1922*, Moscow: Rosspen, 1999, Document No. 9, p. 27.
121 Lenin, 'Against Boycott', IV, p. 2.
122 Lenin, 'The Black Hundreds and the Organisation of an Uprising', p. 5.
123 Lenin, 'Guerrilla Warfare', III, p. 3.
124 Bolsinger, *The Autonomy of the Political*, p. 5.
125 Quoted in Tikhomirov, '*Problema revolutsionnogo nasiliia*', p. 59.
126 Lenin, 'Revolutionary Days', Part III, p. 1.
127 Lenin, 'The Revolutionary Army and the Revolutionary Government', p. 5.
128 Jacob W. Kipp, 'Lenin and Clausewitz: The Militarization of Marxism, 1914–1921', *Military Affairs*, 1985, No. 49, vol. 4, p. 189.
129 Israel Getzler, 'Lenin's Conception of Revolution as Civil War', *Slavonic and East European Review*, 1996, vol. 74, No. 3, p. 466.
130 Mayer, 'The Dictatorship of the Proletariat', p. 273.
131 V. I. Lenin, 'Social-Democracy's Attitude Towards the Peasant Movement', vol. 9, p. 9.
132 V. I. Lenin, 'Petty-Bourgeois Tactics', vol. 12, p. 3.
133 Abraham Ascher, 'Introduction', in Smele and Heywood (eds.), *The Revolution of 1905*, pp. 3–4.
134 V. I. Lenin, 'The Three Sources and Three Component Parts of Marxism', vol. 19, p. 1.
135 V. I. Lenin, 'Should We Organize the Revolution?', vol. 8, p. 6.
136 Anna Krylova, 'Beyond the Spontaneity-Consciousness Paradigm: "Class Instinct" as a Promising Category of Historical Analysis', *Slavic Review*, 2003, 62, pp. 1–23.
137 Indeed, Lenin dated the origins of Bolshevism as a distinct tendency to 1905 (See V. I. Lenin, 'The Historical Meaning of the Inner-Party Struggle in Russia', II, vol. 16, p. 1.) Neil Harding has argued that Leninism became 'a cohesive and militant ideology' during the First World War (See Harding, *Leninism*, p. 52.). However, Lenin's ideas expressed as a reasonably coherent system owed much to 1905, though certainly more to 1914. Chris Read has also made the case for the importance of 1905 for the birth of Leninism (see Read, 'Lenin and the 1905 Revolution', in Smele and Heywood (eds.), *The Russian Revolution of 1905*, p. 238).

2 'Violence to end all violence': ideological purity and the Great War, 1907–1917

1 V. I. Lenin, 'The Revolution in Russia and the Tasks of the Workers of All Countries', vol. 23, p. 1.
2 Irving H. Smith, 'Lenin's Views on the First World War, 1914–1917', *Europa*, 1979–80, vol. 3, No. 1, p. 69.
3 See Robert Service, *Lenin: a Political Life*, vol. 2, London: Macmillan, 1995, pp. 222; 289.
4 See V. I. Lenin, 'The Second Duma and the Second Revolutionary Wave', vol. 12.

5 See Lenin's 12 August 1906 article in *Proletarii*, 'The Boycott', vol. 11, p. 1. See Service, *Lenin*, 2000, pp. 178ff.

6 Lenin, 'The Second Duma and the Second Revolutionary Wave', p. 2.

7 Ibid., p. 4.

8 Ibid., p. 5.

9 V. I. Lenin, 'The Imminent Dissolution of the Duma and Questions of Tactics', vol. 12, p. 2.

10 V. I. Lenin, 'The Second Duma and the Tasks of the Proletariat', vol. 12, pp. 2–3.

11 V. I. Lenin, 'Against Boycott: Notes of a Social-Democratic Publicist', vol. 13, No. III, p. 4.

12 Ibid., IV, p. 1.

13 V. I. Lenin, 'The Third Duma', vol. 13, pp. 4–6. Chris Read, then, is not entirely correct that 'The ebbing of the revolutionary tide meant that, instead of promoting armed uprising about which he was now silent, Lenin was prepared to settle for using the Duma delegation as a political mouthpiece for the movement.' See Read, *Lenin*, p. 85.

14 V. I. Lenin, 'Materialism and Empirio-Criticism: Critical Comments on a Reactionary Philosophy', vol. 14, Chapter 6.2, p. 4.

15 Ibid., Chapter 2.6, p. 5. In fact, Chris Read argues that 'Lenin rejected the fundamental premise of philosophy – the search for truth.' See Christopher Read, *Religion, Revolution and the Russian Intelligentsia, 1900–1912: The 'Vekhi' Debate and its Intellectual Background*, London: Barnes and Noble, 1979, p. 55.

16 V. I. Lenin, 'L. N. Tolstoy and the Modern Labour Movement', vol. 16, p. 3.

17 See in particular V. I. Lenin, 'Tolstoy and the Proletarian Struggle', vol. 16, p. 2.

18 Nikolai Rozhkov, a Bolshevik who would later part with Lenin and be exiled from Soviet Russia, believed that Russia would need to develop a 'civilized' higher form of capitalism that would create the possibility of a peaceful revolution. See John Gonzalez, 'N. A. Rozhkov and V. I. Lenin: The Forgotten Polemics of the Inter-Revolutionary Years, 1908–1917', *Revolutionary Russia*, 2005, vol. 18, No. 2, p. 172ff. See Lenin's response in 'A Liberal Labour Party Manifesto', vol. 17, No. III, p. 1.

19 V. I. Lenin, 'Lessons of the Commune', vol. 13, p. 3.

20 See V. I. Lenin, 'The Assessment of the Russian Revolution', vol. 15.

21 V. I. Lenin, 'Economic and Political Strikes', vol. 18, p. 1.

22 V. I. Lenin, 'The Revolutionary Upswing', vol. 18, p. 5.

23 Ibid., p. 6. Lenin even claimed in this article that the liberal newspapers were exaggerating the extent of unrest amongst the sailors so that the proletariat would be provoked into a premature assault.

24 V. I. Lenin, 'Concerning the Event of November 15: An Undelivered Speech.', vol. 18, p. 3. The popular demonstration in question took place in connection with the opening of the Fourth State Duma in November 1912.

25 V. I. Lenin, 'A Game of Chance', vol. 18, p. 2.

26 V. I. Lenin, 'Who Stands to Gain?', vol. 19, p. 1.

27 It was Kautsky's decision to vote war credits that did really occasion shock for Lenin. In 1915 he had already opined that the SPD might defend Germany in an international war. See Lenin, 'Bellicose Tactics', p. 3.

28 R. Craig Nation, *War on War: Lenin, the Zimmerwald Left, and the Origins of Communist Internationalism*, Durham: Duke University Press, 1989, p. ix.

29 See discussion in Harding, *Leninism*, Chapter 9.

30 Nation, *War on War*, p. 38.

31 Lenin, 'The European War and International Socialism', vol. 21, p. 1. The expression in italics reads 'a holy war of all the oppressed, for the conquest of their own fatherland!'

32 V. I. Lenin, 'The War and Russian Social-Democracy', vol. 21, p. 1.

33 Such as Prussian intervention in the Italian war of 1859, and the wars for German unification.
34 V. I. Lenin, 'Under a False Flag', vol. 21, p. 7.
35 V. I. Lenin, 'The Tasks of Revolutionary Social-Democracy in the European War', vol. 21, p. 3.
36 Lenin, 'The European War and International Socialism', p. 3.
37 Lenin, 'The War and Russian Social-Democracy', p. 2.
38 Volobuiev and V. V. Shelokhaev (eds.), *Men'sheviki*, p. 353.
39 Lenin, 'The Tasks of Revolutionary Social-Democracy', p. 2.
40 This declaration is in Volobuiev and V. V. Shelokhaev (eds.), *Men'sheviki*, pp. 350–1.
41 Ibid., pp. 354–7. See also Ibid., pp. 368–72.
42 See Volobuiev and V. V. Shelokhaev (eds.), *Men'sheviki*, p. 371.
43 See Ibid., pp. 359–364.
44 See also White, *Lenin*, p. 110.
45 See Nation, *War on War*, p. 34.
46 Lenin, 'The War and Russian Social-Democracy', p. 2.
47 See Harding, *Lenin's Political Thought*, vol. 1, p. 305.
48 Lenin, 'The War and Russian Social-Democracy', vol. 21, p. 6.
49 V. I. Lenin, 'The Position and Tasks of the Socialist International', vol. 21, p. 5.
50 Marx had written: 'The contradictions of capitalist development were leading inevitably toward revolutionary transformations […] to the creation of a true world order, purged of war and enmity between peoples.' See Nation, *War on War*, p. ix.
51 For Kautsky on 'ultra-imperialism', see Donald, *Marxism and Revolution*, pp. 204–6.
52 The expression 'war on war' had been voiced by one of the leaders of the Second International at the Basle Congress in 1912, without prescribing what exactly that would mean in practice. See James Joll, *The Second International, 1889–1914*, London: Weidenfeld and Nicolson, 1974, p. 156.
53 Lenin, 'The Position and Tasks', p. 5.
54 Ibid.
55 Ibid.
56 V. I. Lenin, 'The Conference of the RSDLP Groups Abroad', vol. 21, p. 3.
57 V. I. Lenin, 'Dead Chauvinism and Living Socialism: How the International Can be Restored', vol. 21, p. 4.
58 Lenin, 'The Position and Tasks', p. 5.
59 Daniels, *The Rise and Fall*, p. 130.
60 See Service, *Lenin*, vol. 2, 1995, pp. 86–90 for a discussion of internal Bolshevik debates.
61 Lenin, 'Conference of the RSDLP Groups Abroad', p. 3.
62 Ibid.
63 Ia. G. Temkin, 'Razvitie leninskoi programmyi mira na puti k Velikomu Oktiabriu', *Voprosi istorii KPSS*, 1977, vol. 6, pp. 8–9.
64 Lenin, 'The Conference of the RSDLP Groups Abroad', pp. 3–4. This may be contrasted with the four points put forward by the oppositional Menshevik worker group to the Central War-Industry Committee in 1915, whereby the War's end was urged by means of struggle for democratic freedoms, convocation of a Constituent Assembly, and support for the bourgeoisie in its struggles with the regime. See Volobuiev and V. V. Shelokhaev (eds.), *Men'sheviki*, pp. 408–9.
65 Lenin, 'The Position and Tasks', p. 5.
66 See Daly, *The Watchful State*, pp. 163–4.
67 Lenin, 'The Conference of the RSDLP Groups Abroad', p. 5.
68 See also Smith, 'Lenin's views', pp. 66–7.
69 V. I. Lenin, *Neizvestnyie dokymentyi*, Document No. 100, pp. 201–2. Even Kautsky, despite his reserved support for the German war effort, was according to Moira Donald 'so wholeheartedly [opposed to war] that he could no longer view the prospect of war

in any positive light whatsoever, not even as a necessary stage in the breakdown of capitalism.' See Donald, *Marxism and Revolution*, pp. 204–5.

70 See 'Vyipiski i zamechaniia na knigu klauzevitsa "o voine i vedenii voin"', *Leninskii sbornik*, vol. 12, Moscow-Leningrad, 1930, pp. 388–452. For a discussion of Lenin's reading of Clausewitz, see Kipp, 'Lenin and Clausewitz'.
71 'Vyipiski i zamechaniia', *Leninskii sbornik*, p. 425. Lenin wrote 'Important' beside this, noting in brackets an inaccuracy: 'all the people' should denote the bourgeoisie (presumably in keeping with his view that the war begun in 1914 was driven by the bourgeoisie, who were duping the working classes). See also A. A. Strokov, *V. I. Lenin o voine i voennom isskustve*, Moscow: Nauka, 1971, pp. 18–9.
72 Etienne Balibar, 'The Philosophical Moment in Politics Determined by War: Lenin 1914–16', in Sebastian Budgen, Stathis Kouvelakis and Slavoj Žižek (eds.), *Lenin Reloaded*, pp. 215–6.
73 Rosenthal, *New Myth, New World*, p. 130.
74 V. I. Lenin, 'A Caricature of Marxism and Imperialist Economism', vol. 23, No. 6, pp. 2–3.
75 See Service, *Lenin*, vol. 2, p. 86.
76 V. I. Lenin, 'The Question of Peace', vol. 21, p. 3.
77 V. I. Lenin, 'The Defeat of One's Own Government', vol. 21, p. 5.
78 Lenin, 'Appeal on the War', vol. 21, p. 2. In December 1914 Lenin had applied the idea of 'salvation' in another sense reminiscent of Christian discourse – that of the idea of 'confused', 'vacillating' socialists who could still 'be saved and restored to socialism, but only through a policy of a most decisive break and split' with the true renegades. See Lenin, 'Dead Chauvinism and Living Socialism', p. 6.
79 Lenin, 'The Defeat of One's Own Government', p. 5.
80 V. I. Lenin, 'The Collapse of the Second International', vol. 21, No. v, p. 5.
81 V. I. Lenin, 'The "Disarmament" Slogan', vol. 23, p. 3.
82 Ibid., p. 2.
83 Ibid.
84 Ibid.
85 V. I. Lenin, 'Proposals Submitted by the Central Committee of the RSDLP to the Second Socialist Conference', vol. 22, p. 4.
86 See also V. I. Lenin, 'Imperialism and the Split in Socialism', vol. 23, pp. 1ff. There were however apparent ambiguities/inconsistencies in Lenin's thinking on the 'moribund' nature of imperialism. See Gregor, *Marxism, Fascism, and Totalitarianism*, pp. 227–33.
87 V. I. Lenin, 'Imperialism, the Highest Stage of Capitalism: A Popular Outline', vol. 22, VII, pp. 4–5.
88 See V. I. Lenin, 'On the Slogan for a United States of Europe', vol. 21, p. 3.
89 Lih, *Lenin*, p. 129.
90 V. I. Lenin, 'Socialism and War: The Attitude of the Russian Social-Democratic Labour Party Towards the War', vol. 21, Chapter I, p. 1.
91 Lenin, 'On the Slogan for a United States of Europe', pp. 1–2.
92 V. I. Lenin, 'On the Two Lines in the Revolution', vol. 21, p. 5.
93 Lenin, 'The Defeat of Russia and the Revolutionary Crisis', vol. 21 p. 2.
94 Ibid.
95 V. I. Lenin, 'The Socialist Revolution and the Right of Nations to Self-Determination. Theses', vol. 22, p. 1.
96 Lenin, 'The Conference of the RSDLP Groups Abroad', p. 3.
97 Lenin, 'The Socialist Revolution and the Right of Nations to Self-Determination', p. 2.
98 Lenin, 'Reply to P. Kievsky (Y. Pyatakov), vol. 23, p. 4.
99 Ibid., p. 5.
100 Ibid.

101 Lenin, 'Imperialism and the Split in Socialism', pp. 12–13.
102 Balibar, 'The Philosophical Moment', in Sebastian Budgen, Stathis Kouvelakis and Slavoj Žižek (eds.), *Lenin Reloaded*, p. 215.
103 V. I. Lenin, 'A Caricature of Marxism and Imperialist Economism', vol. 23, No. 6, p. 5.
104 Ibid., p. 5.
105 Lenin, 'The Military Programme of the Proletarian Revolution', vol. 23, No. I, p. 3.
106 Ibid., p. 2.
107 See V. I. Lenin, 'On the Slogan for a United States of Europe', vol. 21, p. 4.
108 Lenin, 'The Military Programme', I, pp. 2–3.
109 Ibid., p. 3. See also Plimak, *Politika perekhodnoi epokhi*, pp. 124–5.

3 'History will not forgive us if we do not seize power now': the revolutionary imperative, 1917

1 V. I. Lenin, 'The Tasks of the Proletariat in the Present Revolution (aka *April Theses*)', vol. 24, p. 2.
2 Robert Service, for example, has argued that Lenin 'eulogised force' and displayed 'an abiding fascination with terror as a technique of rule' in the February to October period. See Service, *Lenin*, vol. 2, p. 222.
3 See I. Kh. Urilov, *Istoriia rossiiskoi sotsial-demokratii (men'shevizma). Chast' chetvertaia: stanovlenie partii*, Moscow: Sobranie, 2008, pp. 361–2.
4 See V. I. Lenin, 'Farewell Letter to the Swiss Workers', vol. 23, p. 5.
5 Ibid., p. 4.
6 V. I. Lenin, 'Telegram to the Bolsheviks Leaving for Russia', vol. 23, p. 1.
7 I draw here on Chapter 17 of the first volume of Ron Suny's biography of Stalin, as yet unpublished, with thanks to Professor Suny for letting me see the manuscript.
8 V. I. Lenin, 'Letters from Afar', vol. 23, First Letter, pp. 1–2.
9 Ibid., p. 5. The April Crisis concerned the revelation that Pavel Miliukov, the Foreign Minister, had agreed to honour the treaties that Nikolai II had signed with the Entente.
10 V. I. Lenin, 'The Tasks of the Proletariat in Our Revolution (Draft Platform for the Proletarian Party)', vol. 24, p. 1.
11 Lenin, 'Letters from Afar', Second Letter, p. 7.
12 Ibid., Third Letter, p. 3.
13 V. I. Lenin, 'Letters on Tactics', vol. 24, p. 3.
14 Lenin, 'Letters from Afar', Third Letter, p. 8. See also Service, *Lenin*, vol. 2, 1995, p. 148.
15 Lenin, *April Theses*, p. 2.
16 Lenin, 'The Tasks of the Proletariat in Our Revolution', pp. 2–3.
17 V. I. Lenin, 'I. G. Tsereteli and the Class Struggle', vol. 24, p. 4.
18 Lenin, 'Letters on Tactics', p. 6.
19 See Marx, 'Conspectus on Bakunin's *Statism and Anarchy*'.
20 V. I. Lenin, 'Resolution on Measures to Cope with Economic Disorganisation', vol. 24, p. 3.
21 V. I. Lenin, 'The Seventh (April) All-Russia Conference of the RSDLP (B) April 24–29, 1917', 'Resolution on the Current Situation', vol. 24, p. 3.
22 V. I. Lenin, 'The Revolution in Russia and the Tasks of the Workers of All Countries', vol. 23, p. 1.
23 Lenin, 'Farewell to the Swiss Workers', p. 4.
24 Lenin, *April Theses*, p. 3.
25 Ibid.
26 V. I. Lenin, 'The Petrograd City Conference of the RSDLP (Bolsheviks)', vol. 24, No. 1, pp. 4–5; Lenin, 'The Tasks of the Proletariat in Our Revolution. What Should be the

Name of Our Party?'. Yet, Lenin was not completely convinced that the workers would be sufficiently conscious and heroic to perform 'miracles of proletarian organization', noting that practice alone would tell. See Lenin, 'Letters from Afar', Third Letter, p. 8.

27 See Lenin, 'The Petrograd City Conference', vol. 1, p. 5.
28 See Service, *Lenin: a Political Life*, vol. 2, p. 166–80.
29 V. I. Lenin, 'Resolution of the Central Committee of the RSDLP (Bolsheviks) Adopted April 21, 1917', vol. 24, p. 1.
30 V. I. Lenin, 'The Third Congress of the Communist International', vol. 42, pp. 11–12.
31 V. I. Lenin, 'The Dual Power', vol. 24, p. 3.
32 Lenin, 'The Seventh (April) All-Russia Conference', p. 7.
33 Ibid.
34 There was an anomaly here in that during the Civil War the Red Army would resort to conscripting non-class-conscious peasants. I am grateful to Gayle Lonergan for pointing this out to me.
35 V. I. Lenin, 'First All-Russian Congress of Peasants' Deputies', vol. 24, p. 2.
36 Lenin, 'First All-Russian Congress of Soviets of Workers' and Soldiers' Deputies', vol. 25, p. 6.
37 Lenin, 'The Petrograd City Conference', p. 4, and 8 'Draft Resolution on the War', p. 4.
38 Rabinowitch, *The Bolsheviks in Power*, p. 4.
39 See Leonid Obukhov, 'Ideia Odnorodnogo Sotsialisticheskogo Pravitel'stva i Politicheskie Partii na Urale', paper presented at the Study Group on the Russian Revolution Annual Conference, Aberdeen, January 2008. Cited with the kind permission of Professor Obukhov.
40 Lenin, 'The Tasks of the Proletariat in Our Revolution. A New Type of State Emerging from Our Revolution', p. 3.
41 Ibid., 'What Should be the Name of our Party?', p. 2.
42 Ibid. Aleksandr Guchkov was a key member of and minister in the Provisional Government.
43 See Lenin's report on the current situation at the April Bolshevik Party Conference, Lenin, 'Seventh (April) All-Russia Conference of the RSDLP(B)'.
44 V. I. Lenin, 'Counter-Revolution Takes the Offensive: Jacobins Without the People', vol. 24, pp. 1–2.
45 V. I. Lenin, 'First All-Russian Congress of Soviets of Workers' and Soldiers' Deputies', vol. 25, pp. 3–6.
46 V. I. Lenin, 'The Enemies of the People', vol. 25, pp. 1–2.
47 Service, *Lenin*, vol. 2, pp. 226–7.
48 V. I. Lenin, 'An Epidemic of Credulity', vol. 25, p. 1.
49 V. I. Lenin, 'The Political Situation', vol. 25, p. 1.
50 On the July Uprising, see Alexander Rabinowitch, *Prelude to Revolution: The Petrograd Bolsheviks and the July 1917 Uprising*, Bloomington and London: Indiana University Press, 1968.
51 Lenin, 'The Political Situation', p. 1.
52 Ibid., p. 2.
53 See Alexander Rabinowitch, *The Bolsheviks Come to Power: The Revolution of 1917 in Petrograd*, New York: W. W. Norton, 1976, p. 152.
54 Read, *Lenin*, p. 162.
55 See *Men'sheviki v 1917 gody. Ot iiul'skikh sobyitii do kornilovskogo miatezha*, vol. 2, Moscow: Progress-Akademia, 1995, p. 94. See also 'Vyistuplenie I. G. Tsereteli' and 'Vtoroe vyisuplenie F. I. Dana', in Ibid., pp. 92–3.
56 'Vyistuplenie Iu. O. Martova', in Ibid., p. 99.
57 V. I. Lenin, 'They Do Not see the Wood for the Trees', vol. 25, p. 2.
58 See Service, *Lenin*, 2000, p. 288.

59 V. I. Lenin, 'On Slogans', vol. 25, p. 2.
60 Ibid.
61 Ibid., p. 6.
62 V. I. Lenin, 'Rumours of a Conspiracy', vol. 25, p. 5.
63 *Shestoi s''ezd RSDRP (bol'shevikov). Avgust 1917 goda: Protokolyi*, Moscow: Politizdat, 1958, p. 256.
64 Ibid., pp. 256–7.
65 Ibid., p. 257.
66 Ibid., pp. 269–70.
67 See the last footnote to V. I. Lenin, 'On Compromises', vol. 25.
68 Rabinowitch, *The Bolsheviks Come to Power*, pp. 154–61.
69 V. I. Lenin, 'On Compromises', p. 2. In fact, Lenin's sudden change for conciliation and support of a multi-party soviet government once again met with some opposition from within the Bolshevik Party, see Rabinowitch, *The Bolsheviks Come to Power*, p. 173. Several historians have found it difficult to take Lenin's 'compromise' offer very seriously (see for example Leonard Schapiro, *The Origin of the Communist Autocracy: Political Opposition in the Soviet State: First Phase, 1917–1922*, Massachusetts: Harvard University Press, 1966, p. 56), though it does appear to have been intended genuinely.
70 Lenin, 'They Do Not See the Wood for the Trees', p. 2.
71 Rabinowitch, *The Bolsheviks Come to Power*, pp. 162–4.
72 See Leopold Haimson (ed.), *The Mensheviks: From the Revolution of 1917 to the Second World War*, Chicago and London: Chicago University Press, 1974, p. 24. That is, the Provisional Government would be replaced but the soviets would not exclude from power representatives of all democratic institutions, such as urban dumas, not represented in the soviets.
73 See Haimson, *The Mensheviks*, in particular pp. 26–31.
74 In this regard, Rex Wade notes that Bolshevik rhetoric of this time was, though oversimplified and 'even erroneous', especially effective in presenting the chaos and collapse of Russia as the result of the actions of the ruling elements, implying that if the Bolsheviks assumed political leadership they would solve these complex problems. See Rex A. Wade, *The Bolshevik Revolution and Russian Civil War*, Connecticut: Greenwood Press, 2001, p. 47.
75 V. I. Lenin, 'The Russian Revolution and Civil War: They Are Trying to Frighten Us with Civil War', vol. 26, pp. 10–11.
76 Ibid., p. 5. Interestingly, in this article Lenin identified the Cossacks as the source of a potential 'Russian Vendee' (p. 6).
77 This debate has been excellently conducted in the articles of Ronald Grigor Suny, Reginald E. Zelnik and Sheila Fitzpatrick in Diane Koenker, William G. Rosenberg and Ronald Grigor Suny (eds.), *Party, State, and Society in the Russian Civil War: Explorations in Social History*, Bloomington: Indiana University Press, 1989.
78 Sheila Fitzpatrick, 'The Legacy of the Civil War', in Ibid., p. 388.
79 Service, *Lenin*, vol. 2, p. 212.
80 Lenin, 'The Russian Revolution and Civil War', pp. 8–9.
81 V. I. Lenin, 'The Bolsheviks Must Assume Power: A Letter to the Central Committee and the Petrograd and Moscow Committees of the RSDLP(B)', vol. 26, p. 2.
82 Lenin, 'Imperialism and the Split in Socialism', p. 12.
83 Lenin, 'The Bolsheviks Must Assume Power', pp. 1–3.
84 Ibid., pp. 2–3.
85 Esther Kingston-Mann has explained that Lenin considered that a Constituent Assembly convened before an 'anti-bourgeois' revolution would simply reflect the interests of the bourgeoisie. See Esther Kingston-Mann, *Lenin and the Problem of Marxist Peasant Revolution*, New York: Oxford University Press, 1985, p. 167.

86 Lenin, 'The Bolsheviks Must Assume Power', pp. 1–3. There was, however, scepticism amongst workers toward an impending pre-emptive uprising.
87 V. I. Lenin, 'Marxism and Insurrection: A Letter to the Central Committee of the RSDLP(B)', vol. 26, p. 2,
88 Lenin, 'Marxism and Insurrection', p. 4. In an appeal of the Military Revolutionary Committee (MRC) of the Petrograd Soviet to all citizens on 7 November 1917, it was declared that 'The wealthy classes and their attendants [*prisluzhniki*] will be denied the right to receive food' if they persisted in hindering the food supply and in industrial sabotage. See G. A. Belov, A. N. Kurenkov, A. E. Loginov, Ya. A. Pletnev, V. S. Tikunov (eds.), *Iz Istorii VChK, 1917–1921gg. Sbornik dokumentov*, Moscow: Gospolitizdat, 1958, Document 37, p. 37. Hereafter *Iz Istorii VChK*. The MRC was set up to oversee the military operations of the October Revolution and remained as the forerunner of the Vecheka, the Soviet political police, until the creation of the latter on 7 December 1917.
89 V. I. Lenin, 'The Impending Catastrophe and How to Combat It. Can We Go Forward if we Fear to Advance Towards Socialism?', vol. 25, pp. 2–3.
90 See Larisa Vladimirovna Borisova, *Voennyi kommunizm: nasilie kak element khozaistvennogo mekhanizma*, Moscow, 2001, p. 17.
91 See Lars T. Lih, *Bread and Authority in Russia, 1914–1921*, Berkeley: University of California Press, 1990, pp. 97–194.
92 V. I. Lenin, 'Can the Bolsheviks Retain State Power?', vol. 26, p. 25.
93 Lenin, 'Letters from Afar', Fourth Letter, p. 4
94 I. S. Rat'kovskii, *Krasnyi terror i deiatel'nost VChK v 1918 gody*, St Petersburg: St Petersburg University Press, 2006, p. 9.
95 Lenin, 'The Russian Revolution and Civil War', p. 9 I am grateful to Tony Heywood for raising this question with me.
96 Ibid., p. 11.
97 Service, *Lenin*, vol. 2, pp. 243.
98 Erik van Ree, 'Lenin's Conception of Socialism in One Country, 1915–17', *Revolutionary Russia*, 2010, vol. 23, No. 2, 171.
99 Service, *Lenin*, vol. 2, p. 244.
100 V. I. Lenin, 'The Tasks of the Revolution', vol. 26, pp. 8–9. This article was published on September 26 and 27, 1917, in *Rabochy Put'*, though evidently written in early September.
101 V. I. Lenin, 'Letter to the Central Committee, The Moscow and Petrograd Committees and the Bolshevik Members of the Petrograd and Moscow Soviets. October 1, 1917, vol. 26, p. 3.
102 Lenin, 'Can the Bolsheviks Retain State Power?', p. 27.
103 Fitzpatrick, 'The Legacy of the Civil War', p. 388.
104 For a more detailed analysis of this text, see James Ryan, 'Lenin's Terror. Violence in the Thought of V. I. Lenin and an Assessment of the Significance of Ideology in Early Soviet State Violence', Ph.D. Dissertation, University College Cork, 2009, Chapter 3.
105 The classic example of this is found in Daniels, *The Rise and Fall*, pp. 59–67.
106 See A. J. Polan, *Lenin and the End of Politics*, London: Methuen, 1984 and also El'khon Rozin, *Leninskaia mifologiia gosudarstva*, Moscow: Iurist', 1996.
107 Polan, *Lenin and the End of Politics*, p. 139.
108 Ibid., p. 52.
109 V. I. Lenin, 'The State and Revolution', *Selected Works*, vol. 2, Moscow: Progress Publishers, 1963, pp. 252–3.
110 Quoted in Ibid., p. 257.
111 Ibid., pp. 248–9.
112 Ibid., p. 254.
113 Ibid., p. 262.
114 Ibid., pp. 303–4

115 Ibid., pp. 303–4.
116 Ibid., p. 273.
117 Ibid., p. 308.
118 Ibid.
119 Ibid., p. 312. The idea of the transition from capitalism to communism as a type of Purgatory has also been noted by Halfin, *From Darkness to Light*, p. 25.
120 See Friedrich Engels, 'A Critique of the Draft Social-Democratic Programme of 1891', in Marx and Engels, *Collected Works*, vol. 27, pp. 225–30.
121 Lenin, 'The State and Revolution', *Selected Works*, vol. 2, p. 289.
122 Ibid., p. 255. For a criticism of Lenin's view see Iurii S. Novopashin, 'Mif o diktature proletariata', *Voprosi istorii*, 2005, vol. 1, 43.
123 V. I. Lenin, 'Meeting of the Central Committee of the RSDLP(B) October 16, 1917', vol. 26, pp. 1–2.
124 V. I. Lenin, 'Letter to the Bolshevik Comrades Attending the Congress of Soviets of the Northern Region', vol. 26, p. 4.
125 V. I. Lenin, 'Letter to the Central Committee, The Moscow and Petrograd Committees', p. 2.
126 V. I. Lenin, 'Letter to Central Committee Members', vol. 26, p. 2.

4 Confronting the 'wolves in the forest': October 1917–summer 1918

1 Lenin, 'Can the Bolsheviks Retain State Power?', *Selected Works*, vol. 2, p. 376.
2 See Rabinowitch, *The Bolsheviks in Power*, p. 9.
3 *Iz Istorii VChK*, Document No. 3, p. 5.
4 Rabinowitch, *The Bolsheviks in Power*, pp. 9–10.
5 Evan Mawdsley, *The Russian Civil War*, Boston: Allen and Unwin, 1987, p. 76.
6 Read, *Lenin*, p. 185.
7 See Peter Gatrell, *Russia's First World War: A Social and Economic History*, Harlow: Pearson, 2005, esp. pp. 206ff; Orlando Figes, *Peasant Russia, Civil War: The Volga Countryside in Revolution, 1917–1921*, Oxford: Clarendon Press, 1989, p. 247; and Holquist, *Making War*, pp. 30–3.
8 Polan, *Lenin and the End of Politics*, p. 82.
9 See Piers Beirne and Alan Hunt, 'Law and the Constitution of Soviet Society: The Case of Comrade Lenin', in Piers Beirne (ed.), *Revolution in Law: Contributions to the Development of Soviet Legal Theory, 1917–1938*, New York and London: M. E. Sharpe, 1990, p. 89.
10 O. I. Chistiakov, *Konstitutsiia RSFSR 1918 goda*, 2nd Edition, Moscow: Zertsalo, 2003, p. 205.
11 Ibid.
12 T. H. Rigby, *Lenin's Government: Sovnarkom 1917–1922*, Cambridge: Cambridge University Press, 1979, p. 53.
13 Ibid., p. 108.
14 See Rabinowitch, *The Bolsheviks in Power*, pp. 23ff.
15 V. I. Lenin, 'Wireless Message of the Council of People's Commissars. October 30 1917', vol. 26, pp. 1–2.
16 V. I. Lenin, 'The Extraordinary All-Russian Congress of Soviets of Peasants' Deputies', vol. 26, p. 5.
17 V. I. Lenin, 'Meeting of the All-Russian Central Executive Committee. November 4 1917', vol. 26, p. 2.
18 *Iz Istorii VChK*, Document No. 26, p. 28; Document No. 27, pp. 29–30.
19 Rat'kovskii, *Krasnyi terror*, p. 11.

Notes 211

20 Quoted in George Leggett, *The Cheka: Lenin's Political Police: The All-Russia Extraordinary Commission for Combating Counterrevolution and Sobotage, December 1917–February 1922*, Oxford: Clarendon Press, 1981, p. 62.

21 V. I. Lenin, 'Speech at a Joint Meeting of the Petrograd Soviet of Workers' and Soldiers' Deputies and Delegates from the Fronts', vol. 26, p. 2.

22 See *Iz istorii VChK*, Document No. 21, pp. 23–4; see also Lenin, 'Meeting of the All-Russian Central Executive Committee', p. 2.

23 Lenin, 'Speech at a Joint Meeting of the Petrograd Soviet', p. 2.

24 See V. I. Lenin, 'Meeting of the Central Committee of the RSDLP(B) 1 November 1917', vol. 26, p. 1.

25 Rabinowitch, *The Bolsheviks in Power*, pp. 27ff.

26 V. I. Lenin, *Neizvestnyie dokumentyi*, Document No. 111, p. 220.

27 See Vladimir N. Brovkin, *The Mensheviks after October: Socialist Opposition and the Rise of the Bolshevik Dictatorship*, Ithaca: Cornell University Press, 1987, pp. 27ff; Rabinowitch, *The Bolsheviks in Power*, pp. 26ff.

28 V. I. Lenin, *Neizvestnyie dokumentyi*, Document No. 109, p. 216.

29 V. I. Lenin, 'Resolution of CC of the RSDLP(B) on the Opposition within the CC 2 November 1917', vol. 26, p. 2.

30 V. I. Lenin, 'From the Central Commmittee of the Russian Social-Democratic Labour Party (Bolsheviks)', vol. 26, p. 3.

31 *V. I. Lenin. Neizvestnyie dokumentyi,* Document No. 109, pp. 216–7.

32 Rabinowitch, *The Bolsheviks in Power*, pp. 31–3.

33 *V. I. Lenin. Neizvestnyie dokumentyi*, Document No. 109, p. 217.

34 Ibid., p. 216.

35 Lenin, 'Resolution of CC November 2 1917', p. 2.

36 V. I. Lenin, 'From the Central Commmittee of the Russian Social-Democratic Labour Party (Bolsheviks)', vol. 26, p. 3, pp. 4–5. See the second dispatch from the Central Committee that day.

37 See M. P. Iroshnikov, *Vo glave Sovnarkoma. Gosudarstvennaia deiatel'nost' V. I. Lenina v 1917–1922 gg.*, Leningrad: Nauka, 1976, p. 63.

38 V. I. Lenin, 'Second All-Russian Congress of Workers', Peasants' and Soldiers' Deputies. Report on Peace', vol. 26, p. 4.

39 Ibid., Report on Peace', pp. 3–4.

40 Lenin, 'Meeting of the All-Russian Central Executive Committee. November 4 1917', p. 2.

41 Stathis N. Kalyvas, *The Logic of Violence in Civil War*, New York: Cambridge University Press, 2006, p. 17.

42 V. I. Lenin, 'Third All-Russian Congress of Soviets of Workers', Soldiers' and Peasants' Deputies', vol. 26, p. 6.

43 V. I. Lenin, 'Extraordinary Seventh Congress of the RCP(B) March 6–8, 1918', vol. 27, No. 1, p. 2. Soviet historians of the Civil War acknowledged this but argued that the unleashing of actual bloody civil war was due to the armed actions of international and domestic counter-revolutionaries. See I. B. Berkhin, *Voprosi istorii perioda grazhdanskoi voinyi (1918–1920gg.) v sochineniiakh V. I. Lenina*, Moscow: Nauka, 1981, pp. 4–5.

44 V. I. Lenin, 'Meeting of the Petrograd Soviet of Workers' and Soldiers' Deputies', vol. 26, p. 2.

45 *Iz istorii VChK*, Document No. 16, pp. 20–1.

46 Lenin, 'Meeting of the All-Russia Central Executive Committee', p. 2.

47 Cited in Peter Kenez, 'Lenin and the Freedom of the Press', in Abbott Gleason, Peter Kenez and Richard Stites (eds.), *Bolshevik Culture: Experiment and Order in the Russian Revolution*, Bloomington: Indiana University Press, 1985, p. 139.

48 *Iz istorii VChK*, Document No. 16, p. 20. Early in 1918, a Revolutionary Tribunal for the Press was established. See Brovkin, *The Mensheviks after October*, p. 108.

49 See Article 65 in Chistiakov, *Konstitutsiia*, pp. 211–2.
50 See V. I. Lenin, 'Draft Regulations on Workers' Control', vol. 26, p. 2; V. I. Lenin, 'Draft Rules for Office Employees', vol. 26, p. 1.
51 See V. I. Lenin, 'The Extraordinary All-Russian Congress of Soviets of Peasants' Deputies', vol. 26, p. 6; V. I. Lenin, 'Speech at the First All-Russia Congress of the Navy', vol. 26, p. 2.
52 V. I. Lenin, 'Theses on the Tasks of the Party and the Present Situation. November 1917', vol. 42, pp. 1–2.
53 *Iz istorii VChK*, Document No. 44, pp. 56–7.
54 Holquist, *Making War*, p. 115.
55 See G. Adibekova and V. P. Pirozhkov (eds.), *V. I. Lenin i VChK: sbornik dokumentov (1917–1922)*, 2nd Edition, Moscow: Politizdat, 1987, Document No. 10, p. 13.
56 *V. I. Lenin i VChK*, Document No. 12, p. 16.
57 V. I. Lenin, 'Decree on the Arrest of the Leaders of the Civil War against the Revolution', vol. 26, p. 1.
58 For Lenin's justification of this, see V. I. Lenin, 'Speech Delivered at the Second All-Russian Congress of Soviets of Peasants' Deputies', vol. 26, p. 3.
59 See for example Geoffrey Swain, *The Origins of the Russian Civil War*, London: Longman, 1996, p. 2.
60 Joshua A. Sanborn, 'Unsettling the Empire: Violent Migrations and Social Disaster in Russia during World War I', *The Journal of Modern History*, 2005, vol. 77, No. 2, 322.
61 See Mawdsley, *The Russian Civil War*, pp. 24–6. See also *Protokolyi zasedanii soveta narodnyikh komissarov RSFSR. Noiabr' 1917–mart 1918gg.*, Moscow: Rosspen, 2006, Protocols 3 and 4, pp. 72; 84.
62 William Henry Chamberlin, *The Russian Revolution 1917–1921*, vol. 1, New Jersey: Princeton University Press, 1987, pp. 374–5.
63 Arno J. Mayer, *The Furies: Violence and Terror in the French and Russian Revolutions*, New Jersey: Princeton University Press, 2000. Peter Holquist challenges the idea that Red and White violence simply exerted causal influence upon each other; rather, they were 'inextricably intertwined' but emerged more from the 1914–1921 'maelstrom of war, revolution, and civil wars.' See Holquist, *Making War*, p. 203.
64 For this argument see David W. Lovell, *From Marx to Lenin: An Evaluation of Marx's Responsibility for Soviet Authoritarianism*, Cambridge: Cambridge University Press, 1984, p. 9.
65 See for example Hellmut Andics, *Rule of Terror: Russia under Lenin and Stalin*, New York: Holt, 1969, pp. 15–16; A. L. Litvin, 'Krasnyi i belyi terror v rossii, 1917–1922', *Otechestvennaia istoriia*, 1993, vol. 6, 49.
66 Richard Pipes, *The Russian Revolution, 1899–1919*, London: Collins Harvill, 1990, p. 791.
67 See Holquist, *Making War*, p. 120; see *Iz istorii VChK*, Document No. 56, p. 65.
68 *Iz istorii VChK*, Document No. 56, p. 65.
69 Ibid.
70 Chistiakov, *Konstitutsiia*, p. 203.
71 *Iz istorii VChK*, Document No. 56, p. 65.
72 See Ibid., Document No. 42, p. 54.
73 Stuart Finkel, *On the Ideological Front: The Russian Intelligentsia and the Making of the Soviet Public Sphere*, New Haven: Yale University Press, 2007, pp. 10–11; see also Sheila Fitzpatrick, 'Ascribing Class: The Construction of Social Identity in Soviet Russia', *Journal of Modern History*, 1993, 65, pp. 745–70.
74 Brovkin, *The Mensheviks after October*, p. 53.
75 Brovkin, *The Mensheviks after October*, p. xvi.
76 Harding, *Lenin's Political Thought*, vol. 2, pp. 172–8.
77 Ibid., p. 187.

78 Holquist, *Making War*, pp. 166–7.
79 V. I. Lenin, 'Draft of a Manifesto to the Peasantry from the Second All-Russian Congress of Soviets of Peasants' Deputies,' vol. 26, p. 2. 6 December 1917.
80 Ibid., p. 5.
81 V. I. Lenin, 'How to Organize Competition?',vol. 26, p. 4.
82 Ibid., p. 3.
83 Ibid., p. 5.
84 Ibid., p. 7.
85 Ibid., p. 8.
86 See V. I. Lenin, 'Draft decree on the nationalisation of the banks and on measures necessary for its implementation', vol. 26, p. 2.
87 See Borisova, *Voennyi kommunizm*, pp. 20–1.
88 V. I. Lenin, 'Fear of the Collapse of the Old and the Fight for the New', vol. 26, p. 1.
89 Ibid., p. 2.
90 See Maximilien Robespierre, *Virtue and Terror: Introduction by Slavoj Žižek*, London: Verso, 2007, p. xi.
91 Christopher Read, 'Values, Substitutes, and Institutions: The Cultural Dimension of the Bolshevik Dictatorship', in Vladimir N. Brovkin (ed.), *The Bolsheviks in Russian Society: The Revolution and Civil Wars*, New Haven: Yale University Press, 1997, p. 301.
92 Getzler, 'Lenin's Conception of Revolution as Civil War', p. 464.
93 Lenin, 'Fear of the Collapse of the Old', p. 2.
94 Ibid., pp. 2–3.
95 Sheila Fitzpatrick, 'The Civil War as a Formative Experience', in Abbott Gleason, Peter Kenez and Richard Stites (eds.), *Bolshevik Culture*, p. 74. See also Holquist, 'Violent Russia, Deadly Marxism', p. 8.
96 See also A. S. Velidov, 'Na puti k terroru', *Voprosi Istorii*, 2002, 101.
97 Service, *Lenin*, vol. 2, p. 291. Trotsky famously claimed in December that 'in one month at most this terror will assume more frightful forms, on the model of the great revolutionaries of France.' Quoted in Anna Geifman, 'The Origins of Soviet State Terrorism, 1917–21', in Marcus C. Levitt and Tatyana Novikov (eds.), *Times of Trouble: Violence in Russian Literature and Culture*, Wisconsin: The University of Wisconsin Press, 2007, p. 153.
98 See *Protokolyi zasedanii SNK*, Protocol No. 7, p. 89.
99 See Leggett, *The Cheka*, p. 19; Rat'kovskii, *Krasnyi terror*, p. 19.
100 This point has been made by S. V. Leonov, *Rozhdenie Sovetskoi Imperii: gosudarstvo i ideologiia 1917–1920gg*, Moscow: Dialog MGU, 1997, p. 213 and by Lennard D. Gerson, *The Secret Police in Lenin's Russia*, Philadelphia: Temple University Press, 1976, p. 7.
101 Leggett, *The Cheka*, p. 21.
102 Rat'kovskii, *Krasnyi terror*, p. 16.
103 Quoted in Leggett, *The Cheka*, p. 17.
104 Ibid., p. 100.
105 Ibid., p. 121.
106 *V. I. Lenin i VChK*, Document No. 20, p. 26.
107 Ibid., Document No. 21, p. 27.
108 Ibid., Document No. 73, pp. 84–6.
109 *Protokolyi zasedanii SNK*, Protocol No. 5, pp. 192–3; see also *V. I. Lenin i VChK*, Document No. 28, p. 34.
110 I draw here on Chapter 18 of Ron Suny's as yet unpublished biography of Stalin, and Rabinowitch, *The Bolsheviks in Power*, pp. 88–91.
111 See Thesis 2 in V. I. Lenin, 'Theses on the Constituent Assembly', vol. 26, p. 1. These theses were written on 11 or 12 December.
112 Ibid., p. 4.

113 V. I. Lenin, 'Declaration of Rights of the Working and Exploited People', vol. 26, p. 2.
114 V. I. Lenin, 'Plekhanov on Terror', vol. 42, pp. 2–3.
115 V. I. Lenin, 'Resolution of the All-Russia Central Executive Committee, 4 January 1918', vol. 26, p. 1.
116 V. I. Lenin, 'Draft Decree on the Dissolution of the Constituent Assembly', vol. 26, p. 2.
117 V. I. Lenin, 'Extraordinary All-Russian Railwaymen's Congress', vol. 26, pp. 10–11.
118 Lenin, 'Extraordinary All-Russian Railwaymen's Congress', pp. 10–11.
119 V. I. Lenin, 'People from Another World', vol. 26, p. 2.
120 Vladimir N. Brovkin, *Behind the Front Lines of the Civil War: Political Parties and Social Movements in Russia, 1918–1922*, New Jersey: Princeton University Press, 1994, p. 11.
121 Lenin, 'Extraordinary All-Russian Railwaymen's Congress', p. 11.
122 Ibid.
123 These expulsions were ostensibly due to the alleged involvement of the Mensheviks and SRs in fomenting strikes and uprisings, but it appears that the Bolsheviks felt threatened by the rise in support for these parties, the growing demands of the workers' representatives' movement, and fears that both parties would unite against the Bolsheviks at the forthcoming Congress of Soviets in July. See Leonard Schapiro, *The Origin of the Communist Autocracy: Political Opposition in the Soviet State: First Phase: 1917–1922*, Massachusetts: Harvard University Press, 1966, p. 152; and Brovkin, *The Mensheviks after October*, p. 221.
124 Quoted in Robespierre, *Virtue and Terror: Introduction by Slavoj Žižek*, London: Verso, 2007 , p. 47.
125 Lenin, 'Third All-Russian Congress', p. 6.
126 Ibid.
127 Ibid., p. 14.
128 V. I. Lenin, 'On the History of the Question of the Unfortunate Peace', vol. 26, p. 2.
129 Ibid., p. 6.
130 V. I. Lenin, 'Meeting of Presidium of the Petrograd Soviet with Delegates From Food Supply Organisations, 14 January 1918', vol. 26, p. 2.
131 Ibid.
132 *Protokolyi zasedanii SNK*, Protocol No. 2, p. 205.
133 It is not clear who was responsible for this, see Rat'kovskii, *Krasnyi terror*, p. 53 for a discussion.
134 *Pravda*, 3 January 1918.
135 Rat'kovskii, *Krasnyi terror*, pp. 52–3.
136 Quoted in Leggett, *The Cheka*, p. 57.
137 V. I. Lenin, 'The Socialist Fatherland is in Danger!', vol. 27, pp. 1–2.
138 Rat'kovskii, *Krasnyi terror*, p. 55.
139 Ibid., pp. 56–7.
140 Read, *Lenin*, p. 216.
141 This term, 'totalitarnogo soznaniia', is borrowed from Novopashin, 'Mif o diktature proletariata', 47.
142 Read, 'Values, Substitutes, and Institutions', p. 301.
143 See V. I. Lenin, 'Draft of an Order for all Soviets', vol. 27, p. 1, written on 2 March.
144 V. I. Lenin, 'A Serious Lesson and a Serious Responsibility', vol. 27, p. 5.
145 V. I. Lenin, '"Left-Wing" Childishness', vol. 27, p. 6.
146 V. I. Lenin, 'Extraordinary Seventh Congress', p. 1.
147 Lenin, 'Extraordinary Seventh Congress', vol. 9, pp. 3–4.
148 Ibid., vol. 1, p. 14.
149 For Soviet historians, this statement represented convincing evidence that Lenin's recognition of the need for 'turning to class struggle' arose from the experience of

violent counter-revolutionary struggle after October. See V. D. Polikarpov, 'Nekotoryie voprosyi leninskoi kontseptsii istorii grazhdanskoi voinyi v rossii', in I .I. Mints and Yu. I. Korablev (eds.), *Zashchita velikogo oktiabria*, Moscow: Nauka, 1982, pp. 90–1.

150 Lenin, 'Extraordinary Seventh Congress', vol. 9, p. 4.
151 See Ronald Grigor Suny, 'Class and State in the Early Soviet Period: A Reply to Sheila Fitzpatrick', *Slavic Review*, 1988, vol. 47, No. 4, p. 618.
152 Harding, *Lenin's Political Thought*, vol. 2, p. 328.
153 Lenin, 'Extraordinary Seventh Congress', 9, p. 7.
154 Ibid., 15, p. 2.
155 Ibid., 9, p. 1.
156 See Piers Beirne and Alan Hunt, 'Law and the Constitution of Soviet Society: The Case of Comrade Lenin', in Piers Beirne (ed.), *Revolution in Law: Contributions to the Development of Soviet Legal Theory, 1917–1938*, New York and London: M. E. Sharpe, 1990, p. 88.
157 Lenin, 'Extraordinary Seventh Congress', 18, p. 3.
158 V. I. Lenin, 'The Chief Tasks of Our Day', vol. 27, p. 2.
159 See V. I. Lenin, 'Speech in the Moscow Soviet of Workers', Peasants' and Red Army Deputies', vol. 27, p. 4.
160 Lenin, 'The Chief Tasks', p. 4.
161 See Chapter 5 in Brovkin, *The Mensheviks after October*.
162 V. I. Lenin, 'Speech at a Meeting in the Alexeyevsky Riding School', vol. 27, pp. 1–2.
163 Ibid.
164 Suny, 'Class and State', p. 616.
165 V. I. Lenin, 'Speech at a Meeting of the Presidium of the Supreme Economic Council', vol. 42, pp. 1–2; Borisova, *Voennyi kommunizm*, pp. 21–2.
166 See for example Rabinowitch, *The Bolsheviks in Power*, pp. 223ff.
167 V. I. Lenin, 'Session of the All-Russian CEC, April 29, 1918', vol. 27, p. 5.
168 Lenin, 'Session of the All-Russian CEC', p. 13.
169 Ibid., pp. 16ff.
170 Lenin, '"Left-Wing" Childishness', p. 23.
171 Borisova, *Voennyi kommunizm*, p. 28.
172 Ibid., p. 29.
173 V. I. Lenin, 'Theses on the Current Situation', vol. 27, p. 1. See also Borisova, *Voennyi kommunizm*, p. 28.
174 See V. I. Lenin, 'Six Theses on the Immediate Tasks of the Soviet Government', vol. 27, p. 3.
175 The apparent reason for Lenin's declaration was the unsuccessful White ambush on Ekaterinodar, capital of the Kuban' Soviet Republic, and the death in battle of General Lavr Kornilov. See Mawdsley, *The Russian Civil War*, pp. 21–2.
176 V. I. Lenin, 'The Immediate Tasks of the Soviet Government', vol. 27, pp. 13–4.
177 Ibid., p. 18.
178 Lenin, '"Left-Wing" Childishness', p. 13.
179 Lenin, 'The Immediate Tasks', p. 25. Freedom, Lenin had remarked in 1914 in his notes on Hegel, contained necessity transcended within it.
180 Ibid., pp. 30ff.
181 Ibid., p. 22.
182 Lenin, 'Speech in the Moscow Soviet', pp. 4–5.
183 Lenin, 'The Immediate Tasks', p. 23.
184 P. Beirne and A. Hunt, 'Law and the Constitution', in P. Beirne (ed.), *Revolution in Law*, p. 71.
185 V. I. Lenin, 'To the CC, RCP', vol. 27, p. 1. See also *V. I. Lenin i VChK*, Document No. 46, p. 51.

5 The Red Terror

1 *Ezhenedel'nik VChK,* 22 September 1918, in V. K. Vinogradov (ed.), *VChK upolnomochena soobshchit'...1918g,* Moscow: Kuchkovo pole, 2004, p. 56.

2 Bertrand M. Patenaude, 'Peasants into Russians: The Utopian Essence of War Communism', *Russian Review,* 1995, vol. 54, No. 4, p. 554.

3 Lih, *Bread and Authority,* p. 141.

4 V. I. Lenin, 'Report on Foreign Policy Delivered at a Joint Meeting of the All-Russian Central Executive Committee and the Moscow Soviet. May 14, 1918', vol. 27, p. 12.

5 Lih, *Bread and Authority,* p. 153.

6 V. I. Lenin, 'Main Propositions of the Decree on Food Dictatorship', vol. 27, pp. 1–2.

7 V. I. Lenin, 'Addendum to the Decree on the Food Dictatorship', vol. 42, p. 1.

8 See V. I. Lenin, 'On the Famine. A Letter to the Workers of Petrograd, 22 May 1918', vol. 27, pp. 2–6.

9 V. I. Lenin, 'Theses on the Current Situation', vol. 27, p. 1; Lih, *Bread and Authority,* p. 133.

10 Lenin, 'On the Famine', p. 2.

11 See in particular Lih, *Bread and Authority,* pp. 264ff.

12 Ibid., p. 267.

13 Ibid., pp. 98, 128.

14 Holquist, *Making War,* p. 107.

15 Ibid., pp. 109; 166–7.

16 See the introduction to G. Paul Holman, '"War Communism", or the Besieger Besieged: A Study of Lenin's Social and Political Objectives From 1918 to 1921: Part I', Ph.D. Dissertation, Georgetown University, Washington, DC, 1973, pp. 3–18; Alfred G. Meyer , *Leninism,* Massachusetts: Harvard University Press, 1957, p. 193.

17 See L. A. Kogan, 'Voennyi kommunizm: Utopia i real'nost', *Voprosi istorii,* 1998, vol. 2, p. 126.

18 Jonathan Aves, *Workers Against Lenin: Labour Protest and the Bolshevik Dictatorship,* International Library of Historical Studies, New York: Tauris, 1996, p. 17.

19 See Gatrell, *Russia's First World War,* 226.

20 See Bukharin's more optimistic assertions (*Vos'moi s''ezd RKP(b). Mart 1919goda. Protokolyi,* Moscow: Politizdat, 1959, p. 40), and Lenin's response that 'heterogeneous phenomena' had not ceased to exist, that 'The capitalism described in 1903 remains in existence in 1919 in the Soviet proletarian republic.' (Lenin, 'Eighth Congress of the RCP(b). March 18–23, 1919', vol. 29, No. 3, p. 2.)

21 See V. I. Lenin, 'To A. D. Tsiurupa, 10 May, 1918', vol. 44, p. 1; 'To A. G. Shliapnikov, 28 May, 1918', vol. 44, p. 1.

22 V. I. Lenin, 'Telegram to the Vyksa Workers, 31 May 1918', vol. 44, p. 1.

23 Holquist, *Making War,* p. 167.

24 V. I. Lenin, 'Speech at the Second All-Russian Congress of Commissars for Labour', vol. 27, p. 4.

25 V. I. Lenin, 'Joint Session of the All-Russian Central Executive Committee, the Moscow Soviet of Workers, Peasants and Red Army Deputies and the Trade Unions', vol. 27, pp. 7–9.

26 See *Vos'moi s''ezd,* p. 235.

27 V. I. Lenin, 'Fourth Conference of Trade Unions and Factory Committees of Moscow', vol. 27, pp. 4–5.

28 V. I. Lenin, 'Speech at a Joint Session of the All-Russia Central Executive Committee, the Moscow Soviet, Factory Committees and Trade Unions of Moscow. July 29, 1918', vol. 28, pp. 8–11.

29 Lenin, 'Fourth Conference', p. 5.

30 Ibid., pp. 7–10.

31 Ibid., p. 12.

32 V. I. Lenin, 'Organisation of Food Detachments', vol. 27, p. 2.

33 V. I. Lenin, 'Prophetic Words', vol. 27, p. 5.

34 Lenin, 'Joint Session', pp. 6–9.

35 Ibid., pp. 17–8.

36 Ibid., pp. 10–11. (See footnote 25). This did not yet apply to other foodstuffs, though from 1919 only the least important foodstuffs were permitted for commodity-exchange marketization by the peasants.

37 Lenin's injunction here to identify the enemy and the 'true' citizen should be read in light of Bolshevik attempts to construct social identities in a country with a weak class structure, especially after years of war and revolutionary upheaval (Fitzpatrick, 'Ascribing Class').

38 Lenin, 'Joint Session', pp. 12–16.

39 Lih, *Bread and Authority*, pp. 188ff.

40 V. I. Lenin, 'To: A. D. Tsiurupa, 10 August, 1918', vol. 44, pp. 1–2. Lenin also directly instructed local Agriculture Commissars to designate hostages, see V. I. Lenin, 'Telegram to V. N. Kharlov, 29 August, 1918', vol. 44, p. 1.

41 See V. I. Lenin, 'Telegram to V. N. Kharlov, 21 August, 1918',vol. 44, p. 1.

42 Patenaude, 'Peasants into Russians', p. 557.

43 See Lenin, 'Fifth All-Russian Congress of Soviets', p. 10.

44 Leonov, *Rozhdenie sovetskoi imperii*, p. 218.

45 *V. I. Lenin i VChK*, Document No. 71, p. 73.

46 See V. I. Lenin, 'Theses on the Food Question, 2 August, 1918', vol. 28, p. 2.

47 See A. Berelovich and V. P. Danilov (eds.), *Sovetskaia derevnia glazami VChK-OGPU-NKVD. 1918–1939, Dokumentyi i materialyi*, vol. 1: 1918–1922, Moscow: Rosspen, 1998, pp. 24–5.

48 Figes, *Peasant Russia, Civil War*, p. 156.

49 V. I. Lenin, 'Comrade Workers, Forward to the Last, Decisive Fight!', vol. 28, p. 2.

50 Scott B. Smith, *Captives of Revolution: The Socialist Revolutionaries and the Bolshevik Dictatorship, 1918–1923*, Pittsburgh: University of Pittsburgh Press, 2011, p. 84.

51 Lenin, 'Comrade Workers, Forward to the Last, Decisive Fight!', pp. 2–4. These parties were principally the Right and Left SRs, the latter having resigned from government following the Treaty of Brest-Litovsk. Interestingly, Manichean philosophy did not actually predict an end to the conflict between light and darkness, whereas Marxism did. See Gray, *Black Mass*, p. 34.

52 Lenin, 'Telegram to Yevgenia Bosch', p. 1.

53 V. I. Lenin, 'Telegram to V. V. Kuraev, 10 August, 1918', vol. 35, p. 1.

54 *Leninskii sbornik*, vol. 18, p. 203. See Karl Marx, 'The Civil War in France', vol. 4, in Marx and Engels, *Collected Works*, vol. 22, pp. 343–56.

55 Pipes, *The Unknown Lenin*, Document No. 24, p. 50.

56 See *V. I. Lenin. Neizvestnyie Dokumentyi*, Document No. 137. See Note 3, pp. 246–7.

57 See V. I. Lenin, 'Telegram to A. Y. Minkin, 14 August, 1918', vol. 35, p. 1.

58 Alistair Wright, 'The Cheka and the Red Terror in Karelia during the Russian Civil War, 1918–1919', p. 24. Paper delivered at the Study Group on the Russian Revolution Annual Conference, Glasgow, January 2011.

59 V. I. Lenin, 'Telegram to the Livny Executive Committee', vol. 35, p. 1.

60 Rat'kovskii, *Krasnyi terror*, p. 132.

61 See Leonov, *Rozhdenie sovetskoi imperii*, p. 218.

62 See Nicholas Werth, 'A State against Its People: Violence, Repression, and Terror in the Soviet Union', in Courtois (ed.), *The Black Book of Communism*, p. 68.

63 Lenin, 'Fourth Conference of Trade Unions', pp. 19–21.

64 V. I. Lenin, 'The Character of our Newspapers', vol. 28, p. 2.

65 See especially Swain, *The Origins*, pp. 156ff.

66 Brovkin, *Behind the Front Lines*, p. 20.

67 *V. I. Lenin i VChK*, Document No. 51, pp. 54–7.
68 Rat'kovskii, *Krasnyi terror*, p. 85. Leonov notes that the Bolshevik Central Committee had decided as early as 19 May to introduce the death penalty for defined crimes (*Rozhdenie sovetskoi imperii*, p. 221).
69 Lenin, 'Fifth All-Russian Congress of Soviets', p. 10.
70 Rat'kovskii, *Krasnyi terror*, p. 134.
71 Ibid., pp. 127ff.
72 Ibid., p. 133.
73 See Leonov, *Rozhdenie sovetskoi imperii*, p. 224. The executions were approved by VTsIK and published in *Izvestiia* on 19 July.
74 V. I. Lenin, 'To: G. Y. Zinoviev, 26 June, 1918', vol. 35, p. 1.
75 Velidov, '*Na puti k terroru*', p. 116.
76 V. I. Lenin, 'To: G. Y. Fyodorov', vol. 35, p. 1.
77 Rat'kovskii, *Krasnyi terror*, p. 142.
78 See Mawdsley, *The Russian Civil War*, pp. 67ff.
79 *V. I. Lenin. Neizvestnyie dokumentyi*, Document No. 142, p. 250.
80 V. I. Lenin, 'Speech in Polytechnical Museum, August 23, 1918', vol. 28, pp. 3–4.
81 V. I. Lenin, 'Letter to American Workers', vol. 28, p. 7.
82 Ibid., pp. 7–9.
83 Mayer, *The Furies*, p. 255.
84 See this argument in Leonov, *Rozhdenie sovetskoi imperii*, p. 226.
85 Lenin, 'Letter to American Workers', pp. 8–9.
86 Ibid., p. 12.
87 *V. I. Lenin i VChK*, Document No. 83, p. 84.
88 Vera Broido, *Lenin and the Mensheviks: The Persecution of Socialists under Bolshevism*, Aldershot: Gower/Temple Smith, 1987, p. 32.
89 See *Ezhenedel'nik VChK*, 22 September 1918, in *VChK upolnomochena soobshchit'*, p. 54.
90 This has been stressed by Scott, *Captives of Revolution*, pp. 86ff.
91 Smith, *Captives of Revolution*, p. 81. Smith's account of the Terror is particularly illuminating.
92 See Pipes, *The Russian Revolution*, pp. 793–4; Donald J. Raleigh, *Experiencing Russia's Civil War: Politics, Society, and Revolutionary Culture in Saratov, 1917–1922*, Princeton, NJ: Princeton University Press, 2002, p. 414.
93 S. P. Melgounov, *The Red Terror in Russia*, Connecticut, Hyperion Press, 1975, pp. 22ff; Mawdsley, *The Russian Civil War*, p. 81; A. L. Litvin, 'Krasnyi i belyi terror v rossii, 1917–1922', *Otechechestvennaia istoriia*, vol. 6, 1993, p. 49; W. Bruce Lincoln, *Red Victory: A History of the Russian Civil War*, New York: Simon and Schuster, 1989, pp. 135ff; R. J. Rummel, *Lethal Politics: Soviet Genocide and Mass Murder since 1917*, New Brunswick: Transaction Publishers, 1990, p. 35.
94 See for example Anna Geifman, 'The Origins of Soviet State Terrorism, 1917–21', in Marcus C. Levitt and Tatyana Novikov (eds.), *Times of Trouble*, pp. 153ff.
95 Leggett, *The Cheka*, p. 102.
96 See Rabinowitch, *The Bolsheviks in Power*, pp. 313–56.
97 Rat'kovskii, *Krasnyi terror*, p. 145.
98 See Ibid., pp. 95ff.
99 See Rabinowitch, *The Bolsheviks in Power*, p. 330ff.
100 Rat'kovskii, *Krasnyi terror*, p. 160.
101 *Izvestiia VTsIK*, 1 September 1918, p. 3.
102 *Pravda*, 31 August 1918.
103 Ibid.
104 Ibid.
105 Martin Latsis, 'Krasnyi Terror', in *Krasnyi Terror*, 1 November 1918, in *VChK upolnomochena soobshchit'*, p. 275.

106 See Pipes, *The Unknown Lenin*, Document No. 28, p. 56 and V. I. Lenin. *Neizvestnyie dokumentyi*, Document No. 272, p. 417. See Pipes, *The Unknown Lenin*, Document No. 28, p. 56.

107 For text, see *Iz istorii VChK*, Document No. 155, pp. 182–3.

108 Matthew Rendle, 'Revolutionary tribunals and the origins of terror in early Soviet Russia', *Historical Research*. Online. Available http://onlinelibrary.wiley.com/ doi/10.1111 (accessed 12 February 2011).

109 See for example *VChK upolnomochena soobshchit'*, pp. 79–80.

110 See A. I. Kokurin and N. V. Petrov (eds.), *Gulag 1917–1960*, Rossiia XX vek, Moscow: Materik, 2000, Document No. 2, pp. 14–5.

111 *Ezhenedel'nik VChK*, 22 September 1918, in *VChK upolnomochena soobshchit'*, p. 58.

112 Rat'kovskii, *Krasnyi terror*, p. 153.

113 Ibid., p. 199; Werth, 'A State against its People', p. 78.

114 See Rat'kovskii, *Krasnyi terror*, pp. 170ff.

115 *Vospominania o Vladimire Il'iche Lenine*, vol. 2, Moscow: Gospolitizdat, 1957, p. 252.

116 Rat'kovskii, *Krasnyi terror*, pp. 162–3.

117 *Ezhenedel'nik VChK*, 22 September 1918, in *VChK upolnomochena soobshchit'*, pp. 55–6.

118 Ibid., p. 58.

119 See *Krasnyi terror*, 1 November 1918, in Ibid., p. 276.

120 V. I. Lenin, 'A Little Picture in Illustration of Big Problems', vol. 28, p. 3.

121 *Pravda*, 11 September 1918.

122 See Litvin, '*Krasnyi i belyi terror*', p. 59, n.48.

123 Scott Smith's argument that the real significance of the Terror was this propaganda effort amongst the masses, not so much to terrorize the bourgeoisie, appears not to distinguish sufficiently its rhetorical, theatrical significance from its security imperatives.

124 Kalyvas, *The Logic of Violence in Civil War*, p. 26.

125 Leggett, *The Cheka*, p. 114. One of the reasons Leggett cites for making this assessment is Lenin's response to Steinberg's exasperated statement in January 1918 regarding the Vecheka: 'Let's call it frankly the Commissariat for Social Extermination and be done with it!', to which Lenin replied 'Well put […] that's exactly what it should be […] but we can't say that.'

126 *V. I. Lenin i VChK*, Document No. 86, p. 87.

127 Ibid., Document No. 91, p. 91. For the Vecheka's interpretation of the amnesty, see V. Vinogradov, A. Litvin and V. Khristoforov (eds.), *Arkhiv VChK: sbornik dokumentov*, Moscow: Kuchkovo pole, 2007, p. 295.

128 Rat'kovskii, *Krasnyi terror*, p. 207.

129 *V. I. Lenin i VChK*, Document No. 89, p. 89.

130 V. I. Lenin, 'The Valuable Admissions of Pitirim Sorokin', vol. 28, p. 6. This may have meant execution, arrest or confinement in concentration camps.

131 *V. I. Lenin i VChK*, Document No. 99, p. 97. Mawdsley notes 2,000 death sentences in the Eighth Army alone, with 150 being carried out.

132 V. I. Lenin, 'Speech at a Rally and Concert for the All-Russian Extraordinary Commission Staff, November 7 1918', vol. 28, p. 1.

133 Ibid., p. 2.

134 Ibid.

135 V. Vinogradov and N. Peremyishlennikova (eds.), *Arkhiv VChK*, p. 92.

136 Rat'kovskii, *Krasnyi terror*, p. 239.

137 See A. Berelovich and V. P. Danilov (eds.), *Sovetskaia derevnia glazami VChK-OGPU*, p. 26.

6 Civil War: the strengthening of dictatorship, 1919

1 V. I. Lenin, 'Results of Party Week in Moscow and Our Tasks', vol. 30, p. 4.
2 See Rat'kovskii, *Krasnyi terror*, pp. 219ff.
3 See '"Diktatura partii pogubit delo". Iz pisem V. I. Leninu', *Novyi mir*, 1992, vol. 6, p. 219.
4 See note to *V. I. Lenin i VChK*, Document No. 89, p. 90. The problem of the excessive powers and punitive practices of the Chekas was highlighted by Stalin and Dzerzhinskii in their report to Lenin on the reasons for the fall of Perm to Kolchak's troops in December. See J.V. Stalin and F.E. Dzerzhinskii, 'Report to Comrade Lenin on the Commission of the Party Central Committee and the Council of Defence on the Reasons for the Fall of Perm in December 1918', in J. V. Stalin, *Works*, vol. 4. Online. Available http://www.marxists.org/reference/archive/stalin/works/ (accessed 11 May 2009).
5 *V. I. Lenin i VChK*, Document No. 131, p. 118.
6 Russian State Archive for Social-Political History (RGASPI), f.17, op. 2, d.7, l.5; *V. I. Lenin i VChK*, Document No. 113, p. 107.
7 *V. I. Lenin i VChK*, Document No. 131, p. 119.
8 Ibid., p. 118.
9 Ibid., Document No. 143, p. 126–7. In general, Soviet courts were to be guided by correct 'socialist consciousness'.
10 Indeed, 'repressive regimes are consistent with the rule of law precisely because their policies follow legal forms. Law, then, does not solve the problems of state violence'. (John T. Parry (ed.), *Evil, Law and the State: Perspectives on State Power and Violence*, Amsterdam and New York: Rodopi, 2006, p. ix.)
11 *F. E. Dzerzhinskii. Predsedatel' VChK-OGPU 1917–1926. Dokumentyi*, Rossiia XX Vek, Moscow: Materik, 2007, Document No. 158, p. 104.
12 Ibid., Document No. 159, p. 105.
13 See Ibid., Document No. 167, p. 110.
14 *V. I. Lenin i VChK*, Document No. 139, p. 123.
15 V. I. Lenin, 'Draft Decision for the Council of Defence on regulating relations between the Vecheka, the Railway Cheka and the Commissariat for Railways', vol. 42, p. 2.
16 RGASPI, f.19, op. 3, d.53, l.56.
17 William G. Rosenberg, 'The Social Background to Tsektran', in Diane P. Koenker, William G. Rosenberg and Ronald Gigor Suny (eds.), *Party, State, and Society*, pp. 368–9.
18 See, for example, Service, *Lenin*, vol. 2, p. 282.
19 See for example R. A. Rudenko, 'V. I. Lenin o sotsialisticheskoi zakonnosti', in *V. I. Lenin o zakonnosti i pravosudii*, p. 4.
20 Piers Beirne and Alan Hunt, 'Lenin, Crime, and Penal Politics, 1917–1924', in P. Beirne (ed.), *Revolution in Law*, p. 100; see also Jane Burbank, 'Lenin and the Law in Revolutionary Russia', *Slavic Review*, 1995, vol. 54, No. 1, 24–31.
21 Beirne and Hunt, 'Law and the Constitution of Soviet Society', p. 63.
22 See RGASPI, f.5, op. 1, Section IY '*Gosudarstvennaia bezopasnost*' (State Security), 3.
23 *V. I. Lenin i VChK*, Documents No. 122, 127, pp. 113, 116.
24 See Burbank, 'Lenin and the Law', p. 40.
25 *Vos'moi s''ezd*, p. 400.
26 Beirne and Hunt, 'Lenin, Crime', p. 107.
27 For debate on this 'new course' in 1924 see RGASPI, f.76, op. 3, d.149, ll.63–71.
28 Karl Kautsky, *The Dictatorship of the Proletariat*. Ann Arbor: University of Michigan Press, 1971, p. 5.
29 Ibid., pp. 36–7.
30 Ibid., p. 46.

31 V. I. Lenin, 'The Proletarian Revolution and the Renegade Kautsky. How Kautsky Turned Marx into a Common Liberal', vol. 28, pp. 1–2.

32 Ibid., p. 4.

33 Ibid., p. 5.

34 Ibid.

35 Ibid., p. 7.

36 Marx had remarked that 'The Commune does not [do] away with the class struggles [...] but it affords the rational medium in which that class struggle can run through its different phases in the most rational and humane way.' See Karl Marx, 'Draft Notes to *The Civil War in France*', in McLellan (ed.), *Karl Marx Selected Works*, pp. 556–7. Yet Engels, in his introduction to this work in 1891, noted how savagely the Commune was suppressed, 'what insane cruelties of revenge it [the bourgeoisie] will be goaded the moment the proletariat dares to take its stand against them as a separate class, with its own interests and demands,' which would seem to suggest support for Lenin's position at least on the need for revolutionary violence and even restricting democratic rights. See Friedrich Engels, '1891 Introduction to *The Civil War in France*', in Marx and Engels, *Collected Works*, vol. 27, pp. 179ff.

37 Lenin, 'The Proletarian Revolution. How Kautsky Turned Marx' pp. 6–7.

38 See Ibid., 'Can There be Equality between Exploited and the Exploiter?', pp. 5–6.

39 Ibid., 'The Soviet Constitution', p. 1.

40 Ibid., p. 7.

41 V. I. Lenin, 'The State: A Lecture Delivered at the Sverdlov University', vol. 29, p. 14.

42 Lenin, 'The Proletarian Revolution. What is Internationalism?', p. 4.

43 Service, *Lenin*, vol. 3, p. 37.

44 Quoted in Plimak, *Politika perekhodnoi epokhi*, p. 197. For a discussion of Luxemburg's response to the Russian Revolution, see Marcel van der Linden, *Western Marxism and the Soviet Union: A Survey of Critical Theories and Debates Since 1917*, trans. Jurriaan Bendien, Chicago: Haymarket, 2009, pp. 26–36.

45 V. I. Lenin, 'Speech at a Joint Session of the All-Russian Central Executive Committee, The Moscow Soviet and All-Russian Trade Union Congress, January 17, 1919', vol. 28, p. 4. Hence, for the Bolsheviks kulakism was, as Lars Lih notes, the most evident expression of 'a disease to which the whole peasantry was susceptible.' (Lih, *Bread and Authority*, p. 145.)

46 Lenin, 'Speech at a Joint Session', p. 8.

47 V. I. Lenin, 'Report at the Second All-Russian Trade Union Congress, January 20, 1919', vol. 28, p. 11.

48 Ibid., p. 12.

49 V. I. Lenin, 'Speech at Moscow Party Workers' Meeting', vol. 28, p. 3.

50 Ibid., p. 9. The Bolshevik motivation in this regard was not also to gain 'a moral victory' in terms of the regime's international reputation. See Ibid., pp. 19–20; Brovkin, *Behind the Front Lines*, pp. 26–7.

51 Lenin, 'Speech at Moscow Party Workers' Meeting', pp. 19–20.

52 Brovkin, *Behind the Front Lines*, p. 38.

53 *V. I. Lenin i VChK*, Document No. 148, p. 130.

54 Brovkin, *Behind the Front Lines*, p. 40.

55 See *Vos'moi s''ezd*, pp. 31–2.

56 Brovkin, *Behind the Front Lines*, pp. 55–6.

57 V. I. Lenin. *Neizvestnyie dokumentyi*, Document No. 161, pp. 267–8.

58 See Borisova, *Voennyi kommunizm*, pp. 56ff.

59 Werth, 'A State against its People', p. 87.

60 Borisova, *Voennyi kommunizm*, p. 64.

61 Werth, 'A State against its People', p. 87.

62 *V. I. Lenin i VChK*, Document No. 172, p. 145.

63 V. I. Lenin, 'Telegram to S. K. Minin', vol. 44, p. 1.
64 Holquist, *Making War*, p. 184.
65 V. L. Genis, 'Raskazachivanie v Sovetskoi Rossii', *Voprosi istorii*, 1994, vol. 12, p. 42.
66 Holquist, *Making War*, pp. 180–1. Lenin did not sit on the Orgburo but close colleagues, such as Iakov Sverdlov, did.
67 See Holquist, *Making War*, p. 193; Gregory, *Terror by Quota*, p. 29.
68 For Soviet forced labour policy, including the deportation of around 45,000 Terek Cossacks in 1920, see Pavel Polian, *Ne po svoie vole ... Istoriia i geografiia prinuditel'nyikh migratsii v SSSR*, Moscow: Memorial, 2001, esp. pp. 53–4.
69 See Genis, 'Raskazachivanie', p. 44. Holquist points out that Lenin would, disingenuously, later attempt to distance the central authorities from responsibility for the policy, drawing a parallel with Stalin's attempt in 1930 to blame excessive collectivization on local officials. (Holquist, *Making War*, p. 197).
70 V. I. Lenin, 'Telegram to the Revolutionary Military Council of the Southern Front. 3 June, 1919', vol. 44, p. 2.
71 *V. I. Lenin i VChK*, Document No. 190, p. 157. By 'cunning' Lenin perhaps intended exploiting White support for the uprising to label it as a White Guard revolt.
72 *V. I. Lenin. Neizvestnyie dokumentyi*, Document No. 189, p. 297.
73 V. I. Lenin, 'First Congress of the Communist International', vol. 28, p. 13.
74 V. I. Lenin, 'Session of the Petrograd Soviet. March 12, 1919', vol. 29, p. 7.
75 *V. I. Lenin i VChK*, Document No. 159, pp. 137–8.
76 Patenaude, 'Peasants into Russians', p. 557.
77 See V. I. Lenin, 'On the Question of Relations with the Middle Peasants', vol. 42.
78 See Werth, 'A State against its People', p. 92. For discussion of the problem of desertion, see von Hagen, *Soldiers in the Proletarian Dictatorship*, pp. 67ff, and Erik C. Landis, *Bandits and Partisans: The Antonov Movement in the Russian Civil War*, Pittsburgh: University of Pittsburgh Press, 2008, Chapter 1.
79 V. I. Lenin, 'First All-Russian Congress on Adult Education. May 6–19, 1919', vol. 29, p. 5.
80 Ibid., pp. 5–7.
81 Ibid., p. 7.
82 Lenin did acknowledge that the 'treachery' of the Mensheviks and SRs was due to the fact that they did not understand the consequences of their actions. See *V. I. Lenin. Neizvestnyie dokumentyi*, Document No. 164, p. 271.
83 V. I. Lenin, 'Draft Decision of the Council of Defence on the Mobilisation of Soviet Employees', vol. 42, p. 1.
84 Lenin, 'Session of the Petrograd Soviet. March 12, 1919', p. 8.
85 Ibid., pp. 8–9.
86 See also Brovkin, *The Mensheviks after October*, p. 255.
87 V. I. Lenin, 'Plenary Meeting of the All-Russian Central Council of Trade Unions. April 11, 1919', vol. 29, p. 14
88 V. I. Lenin, 'Eighth Congress of the RCP(B)', vol. 29, Section Three, p. 13.
89 Lenin, 'Plenary Meeting of the All-Russian Central Council of Trade Unions', pp. 9–10.
90 Ibid., p. 11.
91 Ibid., p. 14.
92 *V. I. Lenin i VChK*, Document No. 188, pp. 155–6.
93 V. I. Lenin, 'Eighth Congress of the RCP(B). March 18–23, 1919. Report of the Central Committee', vol. 29, pp. 4–5.
94 Ibid., p. 10.
95 *Vos'moi s"ezd*, pp. 258–9.
96 Ibid., p. 240.
97 Ibid., pp. 240–1.

98 V. I. Lenin, 'Theses on the Central Committee of the Russian Communist Party (Bolsheviks). On the Situation on the Eastern Front', vol. 29, p. 1.
99 Lenin, 'Extraordinary Plenary Meeting of the Moscow Soviet', p. 7.
100 Ibid.
101 Lenin, 'Extraordinary Plenary Meeting of the Moscow Soviet', pp. 8–9.
102 Lenin, 'First All-Russian Congress on Adult Education', pp. 13–4.
103 V. I. Lenin, 'Achievements and Difficulties of the Soviet Government', vol. 29, p. 5.
104 V. I. Lenin, 'Draft Programme of the RCP(B)', vol. 29, Section 7, pp. 23–4.
105 Ibid., p. 24.
106 Lenin, 'Achievements and Difficulties', p. 10.
107 See Lenin, 'Extraordinary Plenary Meeting of the Moscow Soviet', p. 14.
108 'Dokladyi I. I. Vatsetisa V. I. Leninu (fevral'-mai 1919g.)', *Istoricheskii arkhiv*, 1958, 45.
109 Von Hagen, *Soldiers in the Proletarian Dictatorship*, p. 79.
110 Lenin, 'Eighth Congress. Section Two', pp. 5–6.
111 John Erickson, 'Lenin as Civil War Leader', in Leonard Schapiro and Peter Reddaway (eds.), *Lenin: The Man, the Theorist, the Leader: A Reappraisal*, New York: Praeger, 1967, p. 176.
112 See *Vos'moi s''ezd RKP(b)*, pp. 412ff. See in particular VII, p. 415; von Hagen, *Soldiers in the Proletarian Dictatorship*, pp. 57ff.
113 *V. I. Lenin i VChK*, Document No. 204, p. 168.
114 Ibid., Document No. 240, p. 197.
115 Lenin, 'Eighth Congress. Section Two', p. 13.
116 Lenin, 'Achievements and Difficulties', pp. 3–14; Lenin, 'Eighth Congress: Section Two', p. 12.
117 Lenin, 'Achievements and Difficulties', p. 15.
118 Arendt, *On Violence*, p. 56.
119 See V. I. Lenin, 'Greetings to Hungarian Workers. 27 May 1919', vol. 29, p. 4.
120 Mawdsley, *The Russian Civil War*, pp. 134; 148.
121 Lenin, 'First All-Russian Congress on Adult Education', p. 16; pp. 25–8.
122 Ibid., pp. 25–8.
123 Ibid., pp. 29–30.
124 V. I. Lenin, 'A Great Beginning. Heroism of the Workers in the Rear. "Communist Subbotniks"', vol. 29, pp. 6–7; See also Polikarpov, 'Nekotoryie voprosyi leninskoi kontseptsii istorii grazhdanskoi voinyi v rossii', in I. I. Mints and Yu. I. Korablev (eds.), *Zashchita velikogo oktiabria*, p. 91. 'Subbotniks' were days of voluntary work on Saturdays.
125 Lenin, 'First All-Russian Congress on Adult Education', p. 31.
126 Ibid., pp. 23–4.
127 *V. I. Lenin i VChK*, Document No. 208, p. 172; V. I. Lenin, 'To: M. I. Latsis, 4 June 1919', vol. 44, p. 1.
128 V. I. Lenin, 'Telegrams to S. I. Gusev and M. M. Lashevich', vol. 44, p. 1.
129 *V. I. Lenin i VChK*, Document No. 212, p. 175;
130 Ibid., pp. 174–5.
131 See *Rodina*, 2010, No. 6, pp. 70–75.
132 *V. I. Lenin i VChK*, Document No. 216, pp. 176–7.
133 Mawdsley, *The Russian Civil War*, p. 172.
134 V. I. Lenin, 'All Out for the fight against Denikin! Letter of the Central Committee of the Russian Communist Party (Bolsheviks) to Party Organisations', vol. 29, p. 2.
135 Mawdsley, *The Russian Civil War*, p. 167.
136 Lenin, 'All out for the fight against Denikin!', p. 2.
137 Ibid., p. 16.
138 Ibid., pp. 15–16.

139 V. I. Lenin, 'The Domestic and Foreign Situation of the Republic. Report Delivered to the Moscow Conference of the RCP (B)', vol. 29, pp. 2–3.

140 Lenin, 'All out for the fight against Denikin!', pp. 15–16.

141 V. I. Lenin, 'Telegram to V. A. Radus-Zenkovich', vol. 35, p. 1.

142 *V. I. Lenin i VChK*, Document No. 230, p. 188. For a discussion of the 'green' movement during the Civil War, see Erik C. Landis, 'Who Were the "Greens"? Rumour and Collective Identity in the Russian Civil War', *The Russian Review*, 2010, vol. 69, 30–46.

143 See RGASPI, f.19, op. 3, d.54, ll.76–7. The approval of this draft was raised repeatedly at subsequent Council meetings, as the Council grew irritated with the failures of the Vecheka and the RVSR leadership to reply to the draft.

144 *V. I. Lenin. Neizvestnyie dokumentyi*, Document No. 185a, pp. 294–5. Originally published in J. Meijer (ed.), *The Trotsky Papers, 1917–1922*, vol. 1, The Hague: 1964, p. 588.

145 Vladimir Burtnevskii, 'White Administration and White Terror (The Denikin Period)', *Russian Review*, 1993, vol. LII, No. 3, p. 365; Brovkin, *Behind the Front Lines*, p. 205.

146 Suny, 'Social Democrats in Power', in Diane P. Koenker, William G. Rosenberg and Ronald Grigor Suny (eds.), *Party, State, and Society*, pp. 335ff.

147 Rabinowitch, *The Bolsheviks in Power*, p. 396.

148 Brovkin, *Behind the Front Lines*, p. 190.

149 Farber, *Before Stalinism*, p. 114.

150 Lenin, 'First All-Russian Congress on Adult Education', p. 15.

151 Brovkin, *Behind the Front Lines*, pp. 189–90.

152 See RGASPI, f.5, op. 1, d.2561, ll.2 (ob.), 3.

153 See Lenin, 'Results of Party Week', p. 4; V. I. Lenin, 'Speech to Students of the Sverdlov University Leaving for the Front', vol. 30, p. 6.

154 V. I. Lenin, 'Letter to Workers and Peasants regarding victory over Kolchak', vol. 30.

155 *V. I. Lenin. Neizvestnyie dokumentyi*, Document No. 197, p. 304. In the *Collected Works* version of this document, the reference to machine guns and shootings was, not surprisingly, omitted from this work.

156 Lenin, 'Speech to Students of the Sverdlov University', p. 6.

157 V. I. Lenin, 'The Tasks of the Third International. Ramsay MacDonald on the Third International', vol. 29, pp. 2–16.

158 V. I. Lenin, 'Greetings to Italian, French and German Communists', vol. 30, p. 8.

159 Lenin, 'The State', pp. 14–5.

160 Ibid.

161 V. I. Lenin, 'Answers to an American Journalist's Questions', vol. 29, p. 2.

162 V. I. Lenin, 'Speech at the First All-Russian Congress of Workers in Education and Socialist Culture. 31 July, 1919', vol. 30, p. 5.

163 V. I. Lenin, 'The Dictatorship of the Proletariat', vol. 30, pp. 2–4; Lenin, *Polnoe Sobranie Sochinenii*, vol. 39, p. 456.

164 *V. I. Lenin i VChK*, Document Nos. 273, 275.

165 Ibid., Document No. 275, see note p. 226.

166 Ibid., Document No. 268, p. 220.

167 V. I. Lenin, 'Greetings to the Workers of Petrograd', vol. 30, p. 2.

7 War and peace: from Civil War to NEP, 1919–1921

1 V. I. Lenin, 'Speech Delivered at the Third All-Russian Congress of Economic Councils', vol. 30, pp. 1–4.

2 V. I. Lenin, 'Eighth All-Russian Conference of the RCP(B)', vol. 30, pp. 9–10.

3 Landis, *Bandits and Partisans*, p. 28.

4 V. I. Lenin, 'Seventh All-Russian Congress of Soviets', vol. 30, p. 14. For discussion of 'revolutionary subjectivity' and violent legitimation in a Marxist theoretical framework, see Christopher J. Finlay, 'Violence and Revolutionary Subjectivity: Marx and Žižek', *European Journal of Political Theory*, 2006, vol. 5, No. 4, pp. 373–97.

5 Lenin, 'Eighth All-Russian Conference', pp. 10–11.

6 V. I. Lenin, 'Speech Delivered at the First All-Russian Congress of Working Cossacks', vol. 30, p. 11.

7 Lenin, 'Seventh All-Russian Congress', p. 14.

8 Lenin, 'Eighth All-Russian Conference', p. 11.

9 Lenin, 'Seventh All-Russian Congress', p. 15.

10 Lenin, 'Eighth All-Russian Conference', p. 13.

11 Patenaude, 'Peasants into Russians', p. 560.

12 Lenin, 'Eighth All-Russian Conference', p. 13.

13 V. I. Lenin, 'Economics and Politics in the Era of the Dictatorship of the Proletariat', vol. 30, pp. 4–5.

14 Lenin, 'Seventh All-Russian Congress', pp. 25–6.

15 V. I. Lenin, 'Draft Resolution of the CC RCP(B) on Soviet Rule in the Ukraine', vol. 30, p. 2.

16 V. I. Lenin, 'Underlinings and an Instruction on S. I. Syrtsov's Telegram', vol. 44, p. 1.

17 Lenin, 'Speech Delivered at the Third All-Russian Congress of Economic Councils', pp. 1–4.

18 Brovkin, *Behind the Front Lines*, p. 274.

19 Von Hagen, *Soldiers in the Proletarian Dictatorship*, pp. 120–1; Leonov, *Rozhdenie sovetskoi imperii*, p. 241.

20 Service, *Lenin*, vol. 3, p. 107. For a contrary view, see Brovkin, *Behind the Front Lines*, p. 275.

21 See Aves, *Workers against Lenin*, p. 12.

22 V. I. Lenin, 'The Fight to Overcome the Fuel Crisis. Circular Letter to Party Organisations', vol. 30, pp. 3–4.

23 *V. I. Lenin i VChK*, Document No. 289, p. 239.

24 V. I. Lenin, 'To Members of the Council of Defence', vol. 30, p. 1.

25 E. G. Gimpel'son, "*Voennyi kommunizm": politika, ekonomika, ideologiia*, Moscow: "Myisl'", 1973, pp. 96, 191.

26 See V. I. Lenin, 'Speech at the Third All-Russia Conference of Directors of Adult Education Divisions of Gubernia Education Departments. 25 February, 1920', vol. 30, p. 2.

27 Aves, *Workers against Lenin*, p. 11.

28 See Borisova, *Voennyi kommunizm*, Chapter 3.

29 *Deviatyi s"ezd RKP(b). Mart-aprel' 1920g. Protokolyi*, Moscow: Politizdat, 1960, pp. 556–7.

30 Ibid., p. 415.

31 See for example N. F. Kuz'min et al. *Iz istorii grazhdanskoi voinyi v SSSR*, vol. 3, Moscow: Sovetskaia Rossiia, 1961, Document No. 3, pp. 10–12.

32 Andrea Graziosi, *A New, Peculiar State: Explorations in Soviet History, 1917–1937*, Connecticut: Praeger, 2000, p. 75.

33 Werth, 'A State against its People', p. 97.

34 V. I. Lenin, 'Speech Delivered at a Meeting of the Moscow Soviet of Workers' and Red Army Deputies. March 6, 1920', vol. 30, p. 3.

35 Ibid.

36 V. I. Lenin, 'Telegram to Stalin. 16 February 1920', vol. 30, p. 1.

37 V. I. Lenin, 'Ninth Congress of the RCP(B) March 29–April 5, 1920', vol. 30, p. 16.

38 See Holquist, *Making War*, esp. pp. 252–3 for a case study of the Don region and Raleigh, *Experiencing Russia's Civil War*, pp. 308–11 for a case study of Saratov on the Volga. Holquist notes that the practice of continued state food requisitioning after the end of military conflict was not a uniquely Bolshevik phenomenon. This continued in Germany, for example, until 1923. What was uniquely Bolshevik was the class rhetoric (Holquist, *Making War*, pp. 243ff.)

39 Lenin, 'Ninth Congress', p. 11.

40 V. I. Lenin, 'Speech Delivered at the Third All-Russian Trade Union Congress', vol. 30, p. 11.

41 V. I. Lenin, 'Left-Wing Communism: an Infantile Disorder: "Left-Wing" Communism in Germany', vol. 30, p. 5.

42 Lenin, 'Speech Delivered at the Third All-Russian Trade Union Congress', p. 5.

43 Ibid., pp. 7–8.

44 Lenin, 'Left-Wing Communism: "Left-Wing" Communism in Germany', pp. 2–5.

45 See Priestland, *Stalinism and the Politics of Mobilization*, pp. 97ff.

46 V. I. Lenin, 'The Trade Unions, The Present Situation and Trotsky's Mistakes', vol. 32, pp. 2ff.

47 Lenin, 'Left-Wing Communism. "Left-Wing" Communism in Germany', p. 5.

48 Karl Kautsky, 'Terrorism and Communism: A Contribution to the Natural History of Revolution', 1919, Chapter VIII: The Terror. Marxists Internet Archive. Online. Available http://www.marxists.org/archive/kautsky/1919/terrcomm/ (accessed 24 June 2011).

49 Leon Trotsky, 'Terrorism and Communism', Chapter 4, p. 5. Marxists Internet Archive. Online. Available http://www.marxists.org/archive/trotsky/1920/terrcomm/ (accessed 23 March 2009). Page numbers follow printed online version, each chapter beginning on page 1.

50 Ibid., Chapter 2, p. 1.

51 Trotsky, 'Terrorism and Communism', Chapter 4, pp. 11–12.

52 Ibid., 'The State Government and Industry', p. 6.

53 Ibid., pp. 14–15.

54 Andrea Graziosi has referred to this work as emblematic of a 'minor cult of violence'. See Graziosi, *A New, Peculiar State*, pp. 79–80.

55 Nicolai I. Bukharin, *Economics of the Transformation Period: With Lenin's Critical Remarks*, New York: Bergman Publishers, 1971, p. 151.

56 Ibid., p. 151.

57 Ibid., p. 154.

58 Ibid., p. 158.

59 Ibid., pp. 160–1.

60 *V. I. Lenin i VChK*, Document No. 314, p. 269.

61 V. I. Lenin, 'Report on the Work of the All-Russian Central Executive Committee and the Council of People's Commissars. 2 February, 1920', vol. 30, pp. 11–12.

62 Ibid., p. 12.

63 V. I. Lenin, 'Speech at the Fourth Conference of Gubernia Extraordinary Commissions', vol. 42, p. 2.

64 *F. E. Dzerzhinskii – Predsedatel' VChK-OGPU*, Document No. 259, pp. 171–2.

65 *V. I. Lenin. Neizvestnyie dokumentyi*, Document No. 218, p. 330.

66 *V. I. Lenin i VChK*, Document No. 326, pp. 283–4.

67 *F. E. Dzerzhinskii – Predsedatel' VChK-OGPU*, Document No. 251, p. 166.

68 The standard account of the Polish–Soviet War is Norman Davies, *White Eagle, Red Star: The Polish–Soviet War 1919–1920 and 'The Miracle on the Vistula'*, London: Pimlico, 2003 [1972].

69 Ibid., p. 98.

70 Norman Davies, 'The Missing Revolutionary War. The Polish Campaigns and the Retreat from Revolution in Soviet Russia, 1919–21', *Soviet Studies*, 1975, vol. XXVII, No. 2, pp. 183–4.

71 Adam Zamoyski, *Warsaw 1920: Lenin's Failed Conquest of Europe*, London: Harper Collins, 2008, p. 13.

72 *Iz istorii grazhdanskoi voinyi v SSSR*, vol. 3, Document No. 218, pp. 253–7. The author stressed the need to be ready in case the Poles struck first.

73 V. I. Lenin, 'Telegram to L. D. Trotsky', vol. 35, p. 1.

74 *V. I. Lenin. Neizvestnyie dokumentyi*, Document No. 218, p. 330.

75 Piotr S. Wandycz, *Soviet–Polish Relations 1917–1921*, Massachusetts: Harvard University Press, 1969, pp. 173ff.

76 Lenin, 'Report on the Work of the All-Russian Central Executive Committee', p. 4.

77 *V. I. Lenin. Neizvestnyie dokumentyi*, Document No. 211, p. 326; Pipes, *The Unknown Lenin*, Document No. 43, p. 78.

78 Pipes, *The Unknown Lenin*, Document No. 59, p. 96.

79 *V. I. Lenin. Neizvestnyie dokumentyi*, Document No. 219, p. 331; Pipes, *The Unknown Lenin*, Document No. 44, pp. 78–9. This document was partially published in *V. I. Lenin. Biograficheskaia khronika*, vol. 8, p. 402.

80 Davies, 'The Missing Revolutionary War', 182.

81 V. I. Lenin, 'Telephone Message to J. V. Stalin. July 12 or 13, 1920', vol. 31.

82 Robert Service, *Stalin: A Biography*, London: Macmillan, 2004, p. 177.

83 Pipes, *The Unknown Lenin*, Document No. 59, p. 95. Lenin warned that this should not be published in the press.

84 V. I. Lenin, 'Draft (or Theses) of the RCP's Reply to the Letter of the Independent Social-Democratic Party of Germany', vol. 30, p. 4.

85 V. I. Lenin, 'To: The Members of the Council of Labour and Defence', vol. 44, pp. 1–2.

86 V. I. Lenin, 'Telegram to V. P. Zatonsky', vol. 44, p. 1.

87 *V. I. Lenin. Neizvestnyie dokumentyi*, Document No. 257, pp. 399–400.

88 Ibid., Document No. 258, p. 400.

89 V. I. Lenin, 'The Second Congress of the Communist International. July 19–August 7, 1920', vol. 31, p. 26.

90 V. I. Lenin, 'Terms of Admission into Communist International', vol. 31, pp. 3–5.

91 V. I. Lenin, 'Preliminary Draft Theses on the Agrarian Question. For the Second Congress of the Communist International', vol. 31, pp. 4–5.

92 V. I. Lenin, 'Speech Delivered at an All-Russia Congress of Glass and Porcelain Workers', vol. 31, p. 2.

93 *V. I. Lenin i VChK*, Document No. 367, pp. 314–5.

94 *V. I. Lenin. Neizvestnyie dokumentyi*, Document No. 230, pp. 347–8. See also J. M. Meijer (ed.), *The Trotsky Papers, 1917–1922*, vol. 2, The Hague: 1971, pp. 210–2. Lenin knew quite well that the Poles were opposed to the Whites who, if they succeeded in overthrowing the Bolsheviks, would not accept a Polish federation in the Baltic–Belorussian–Ukrainian borderlands.

95 For a discussion of this, see Brovkin, *Behind the Front Lines*, pp. 255ff.

96 RGASPI, f.5, op. 1, d.2618, l.2. Report on period 16–30 June 1920. This report (and others) has been published, in a slightly abridged form, in A. Berelovich and V. P. Danilov (eds.), *Sovetskaia derevnia glazami VChK-OGPU-NKVD*, Document No. 158, pp. 267–76. These sources, highly valuable though they are, should be read with a certain caution in light of their tendency to draw emphasis to mass resistance and opposition to Soviet power, rather than present a comprehensive picture of the general social experience of Soviet power through the 1920s and 1930s. The purpose of surveillance was to gauge the mood of the people – as had the Tsarist police – and how this mood came about so that it could be moulded anew, becoming 'one of the essential modes of Soviet power' (see Holquist, *Making War*, pp. 236–7).

97 RGASPI, f.5, op. 1, d.2618, l.2.

98 Ibid., l.2 ob.

99 Ibid., ll.5–6 ob.

100 V. I. Lenin, 'Underlinings and an Instruction on I. N. Smirnov's Telegram', vol. 44, p. 1.

101 *V. I. Lenin i VChK*, Document No. 398, p. 340.

102 See for example RGASPI, f.5, op. 1, d.2618, l.16. The problem of peasant darkness and of the need for greater 'communist propaganda' in the countryside was a consistent theme of Bolshevik discourse. See *Vos'moi s''ezd*, p. 432.

103 V. I. Lenin, 'Speech Delivered at an All-Russia Conference of Political Education Workers of Gubernia and Uezd Education Departments. November 3, 1920', vol. 31, p. 4.

104 *V. I. Lenin i VChK*, Document No. 441, p. 372.

105 RGASPI, f.5, op. 1, d.2618, ll.7–8.

106 See von Hagen, *Soldiers in the Proletarian Dictatorship*, pp. 72–9, and *Izvestiia VTsIK*, 19 July 1920.

107 *V. I. Lenin i VChK*, Document No. 407, p. 347.

108 RGASPI, f.5, op. 1, d.2618, l.15.

109 V. I. Lenin, 'Eighth All-Russian Congress of Soviets', vol. 31, Part II, p. 13.

110 RGASPI, f.5, op. 1, d.2618, l.15 ob.

111 RGASPI, f.5, op. 1, d.2618, l.20 ob.

112 V. I. Lenin, 'Telegram to G. K. Ordzhonikidze. 9 September 1920', vol. 35, p. 1.

113 Werth, 'A State against its People', p. 107; *V. I. Lenin i VChK*, Document No. 442, p. 373.

114 V. I. Lenin, 'To: N. P. Bryukhanov. October 4, 1920', vol. 44, p. 1.

115 Lenin noted though that Ukraine could not be relied upon due to the war with Wrangel and with banditry.

116 V. I. Lenin, 'Our Foreign and Domestic Position and Party Tasks', vol. 31, p. 11.

117 V. I. Lenin, 'Draft Decision for the C.P.C. on Direct Taxes', vol. 42, p. 1.

118 V. I. Lenin, 'Tenth All-Russia Conference of the RCP(B)', vol. 32, p. 10.

119 Oliver H. Radkey, *The Unknown Civil War in Soviet Russia: A Study of the Green Movement in the Tambov Region 1920–1921*, Stanford: Hoover Institution Press, 1976, p. 205. The most definitive study of the Tambov uprising has now been written by Erik C. Landis, *Bandits and Partisans: The Antonov Movement in the Russian Civil War*, Pittsburgh: University of Pittsburgh Press, 2008.

120 V. I. Lenin, 'To: N. P. Bryukhanov. 27 September, 1920', vol. 44.

121 V. I. Lenin, 'To: E. M. Sklianskii. October 15, 1920', vol. 44; V. I. Lenin, 'To: V. S. Kornev. October 19, 1920', vol. 44.

122 RGASPI, f.5, op. 1, d.2618, l.20.

123 V. I. Lenin, 'To: E. M. Sklianskii. Late 1920/early 1921', vol. 45.

124 Delano DuGarm, 'Peasant Wars in Tambov Province', in Brovkin (ed.), *The Bolsheviks in Russian Society*, p. 189.

125 RGASPI, f.5, op. 1, d.2574, l.7. The SR slogans were the establishment of the Constituent Assembly, denationalisation of industries except railways and mines, and fixed prices for industrial goods accompanied by an end to fixed grain prices.

126 See Holquist, *Making War, Forging Revolution*, pp. 268–72 for a discussion of this in the Don.

127 RGASPI, f.5, op. 1, d.2574, l.6.

128 Radkey, *The Unknown Civil War*, p. 365.

129 *V. I. Lenin. Neizvestnyie dokumentyi*, Document No. 286, pp. 428–9; see also Meijer (ed.), *The Trotsky Papers*, vol. 2, pp. 460–1.

130 See Landis, *Bandits and Partisans*, p. 211.

131 Holquist, 'State Violence as Technique', p. 26; Landis, *Bandits and Partisans*, pp. 228ff;

132 Landis, *Bandits and Partisans*, p. 231.
133 *V. I. Lenin. Neizvestnyie dokumentyi*, Document No. 286, see note on p. 429; Radkey, *The Unknown Civil War*, pp. 326–9.
134 See Holquist, 'State Violence as Technique', p. 29.
135 Lenin, 'Eighth All-Russian Congress of Soviets. Part I', p. 6.
136 Ibid., Part II, pp. 2–6.
137 Lenin, 'Eighth All-Russian Congress of Soviets. Part III,' p. 1.
138 Ibid., Part II, p. 10.
139 Ibid.
140 Ibid., p. 8.
141 V. I. Lenin, 'The Tasks of the Youth Leagues. Speech Delivered at the Third All-Russian Congress of the Russian Congress of the Russian Young Communist League', vol. 31, pp. 7–13.
142 Lenin, 'Eighth All-Russian Congress of Soviet. Part II' p. 14.
143 See Patenaude, 'Peasants into Russians', pp. 562ff.
144 Lenin, 'Eighth All-Russian Congress of Soviets. Part II', p. 22.
145 V. I. Lenin, 'The Eighth All-Russian Congress of Soviets', vol. 42, p. 19.
146 Lenin, 'Eighth All-Russian Congress of Soviets. Part III', pp. 1–2.
147 Lenin, 'Eighth All-Russian Congress of Soviets,' vol. 42, p. 20. Raleigh, *Experiencing Russia's Civil War*, pp. 64–5.
148 See *F. E. Dzerzhinskii – Predsedatel' VChK-OGPU*, Document No. 359, p. 232.
149 RGASPI, f.76, op. 3, d.149, l.3.
150 See Ibid., l.4.
151 *V. I. Lenin i VChK*, Document No. 451, p. 381.
152 Ibid., Document Nos.451,453, pp. 381–2.

8 'We will cleanse Russia for a long time': the contradictions of NEP

1 A. N. Artizov, Z. K. Vodopianova, V. G. Makarov, V. S. Khristoforov, E. V. Domchareva (eds.), '*Ochistim rossiiu nadolgo…' Repressii protiv inakomyisliashchikh. Dokumentyi. Konets 1921–nachalo 1923g.*, Rossiia XX Vek, Moscow: Materik, 2008, Document No. 110, p. 162. Hereafter '*Ochistim rossiiu nadolgo..*'.
2 See E. B. Genkina, *Gosudarstvennaia deiatel'nost' V. I. Lenina, 1921–1923*, Moscow: Nauka, 1969, p. 146; E. B. Genkina, *Lenin – Predsedatel' Sovnarkoma i STO. Iz istorii gosudarstvennoi deiatel'nosti V. I. Lenina v 1921–1922 godakh*, Moscow: Izdatel'stvo Akademii Nauk SSSR, 1960, p. 17.
3 For an outline of these interpretations, see Cohen, 'Bolshevism and Stalinism', in Robert C. Tucker (ed.), *Stalinism: Essays in Historical Interpretation*, New York: Norton, 1977, pp. 19ff.
4 Tucker (ed.), *Stalinism*, p. 21. Not all revisionists, however, shared Cohen's interpretation. See Sheila Fitzpatrick, 'Revisionism in Retrospect,' *Slavic Review*, 2008, vol. 67, No. 3, 686–7.
5 Vladimir Brovkin, *Russia after Lenin: Politics, Culture and Society, 1921–1929*, London and New York: Routledge, 1998, p. 1.
6 Roger Pethybridge, *One Step Backwards, Two Steps Forward: Soviet Society and Politics in the New Economic Policy*, Oxford: Clarendon Press, 1990, p. 241.
7 E. G. Gimpel'son, *Novaia Ekonomicheskaia Politika Lenina-Stalina: Problemyi i uroki 20-e godyi XX veka*, Moscow: Sobranie, 2004, p. 10.
8 Priestland, *Stalinism and the Politics of Mobilization*, pp. 142–3.
9 See for example G. Bordiugov and V. Kozlov, '*K voprosu o tak nazyivaemyikh deformatsiiakh sotsializma*', in G. L. Smirnov (ed.), *Leninskaia kontseptsiia sotsializma*, Moscow: Politizdat, 1990, pp. 416ff.

10 Lars T. Lih, 'Political Testament of Lenin and Bukharin and the Meaning of NEP', *Slavic Review*, 1991, vol. 50, No. 2, pp. 248–52.

11 Halfin, *From Darkness to Light*, p. 27.

12 Service, *Lenin*, vol. 3, p. 203; 293, see especially pp. 243ff.

13 Witte, 'Violence in Lenin's Thought and Practice', pp. 168–86.

14 Moshe Lewin, *Lenin's Last Struggle*, trans. A. M. Sheridan Smith, Ann Arbor: University of Michigan Press, 2005 [1978], p. 134.

15 V. I. Lenin, 'Third Congress of the Communist International', vol. 32, p. 33.

16 V. I. Lenin, 'Speech Delivered at an Enlarged Conference of Moscow Metalworkers. February 4, 1921', vol. 32, pp. 2–3.

17 V. I. Lenin, 'Rough Draft of Theses Concerning the Peasants', vol. 32, p. 1.

18 V. I. Lenin, 'Speech at a Plenary Meeting of the Moscow Soviet of Workers' and Peasants' Deputies', vol. 32, pp. 4–5.

19 Ibid., pp. 8–9.

20 Lenin, 'Tenth Congress', Part I, vol. 2, p. 13.

21 Ibid., Part III, vol. 6, p. 11.

22 Ibid., Part I, vol. 2, p. 9.

23 Ibid., Part IV, vol. 9, p. 5. The Congress resolved to ban factions within the party.

24 Lenin, *PSS*, vol. 39, p. 452.

25 Lenin, 'Tenth Congress', Part I, vol. 2, p. 10. Lenin reasoned that it would be 'madness' to assume the imminence of revolutions in the West at that time.

26 Ibid., Part III, No. 6, p. 2. See Genkina, *Gosudarstvennaia deiatel'nost' V. I. Lenina*, p. 35.

27 V. I. Lenin, 'Tenth All-Russian Conference of the RCP (B)', vol. 32, p. 15.

28 Lenin, 'Tenth Congress', Part III, vol. 6, p. 4.

29 Ibid., pp. 1–2; 9.

30 V. I. Lenin, 'Speech Delivered at the All-Russian Congress of Transport Workers', vol. 32, p. 9.

31 Lenin, 'Third Congress of the Communist International', p. 25.

32 Ibid., p. 3.

33 V. I. Lenin, 'Eleventh Congress of the RCP(B)', vol. 33, p. 21.

34 Lenin, 'Tenth Congress', Part II, vol. 3, pp. 9–10.

35 V. I. Lenin, 'The New Economic Policy and the Tasks of the Political Education Departments. October 17, 1921', vol. 33, pp. 5–6.

36 V. I. Lenin, 'Seventh Moscow Gubernia Conference of the Russian Communist Party', vol. 33, p. 13.

37 Lenin, 'The New Economic Policy and the Tasks of the Political Education Departments', p. 10.

38 Lenin, 'Tenth Congress', Part I, vol. 2, pp. 15–6.

39 Ibid., Part II, vol. 3, p. 15.

40 See Lenin, 'Tenth Conference', p. 22; see Lenin's notes on Osinskii's speech in *V. I. Lenin. Neizvestnyie dokumentyi*, Document No. 301, p. 443.

41 See a statement of Zinoviev's in 1922, in '*Ochistim rossiiu nadolgo …*', Document No. 138, p. 237.

42 A. M. Plekhanov, *VChK-OGPU v godyi novoi ekonomicheskoi politiki 1921–1928*, Moscow: Kuchkovo Pole, 2006, p. 128.

43 Ibid.

44 See Lenin, 'Tenth Congress', Part III, vol. 6, pp. 6–7. See Holquist, *Making War*, pp. 264–70, for a description of NEP in the Don region.

45 A. Berelovich amd V. P. Danilov (eds.), *Sovetskaia derevnia glazami VChK-OGPU*, pp. 40ff.

46 Ibid., p. 51.

47 See Werth, 'A State Against its People', pp. 120–1.

48 Pipes, *The Unknown Lenin*, Document No. 70, p. 127.

49 Ibid., Document No. 73, pp. 130–1.
50 V. I. Lenin, 'To: M. I. Frumkin. 4 August, 1921', vol. 45, p. 2.
51 Plekhanov, *VChK-OGPU*, p. 349.
52 See especially V. I. Lenin, 'Fourth Anniversary of the October Revolution', vol. 33, p. 7.
53 V. I. Lenin, 'The Tax in Kind. The Significance of the New Policy and its Conditions', vol. 32, p. 13.
54 Lenin, 'Fourth Anniversary of the October Revolution', pp. 4–5.
55 Lenin, 'Eleventh Congress of the RCP(B)', p. 32.
56 Ibid.
57 V. I. Lenin, 'The Importance of Gold Now and After the Complete Victory of Socialism', vol. 33, pp. 1–3.
58 Lenin, 'Third Congress of the Communist International', p. 21.
59 For examples of such caution in practice, and illustrations of the complex nature of Soviet foreign policy during NEP, see *V. I. Lenin. Neizvestnyie dokumentyi*, Documents Nos. 306, 307 and 313, pp. 447–9, 458.
60 V. I. Lenin, 'Amendments and Remarks to the Draft Declaration of the Soviet Declaration at the Genoa Conference. March 23, 1922', vol. 42, pp. 1–2.
61 V. I. Lenin, 'Letter to G. V. Chicherin and Assignment to Secretaries. February 16, 1922', vol. 45, p. 1.
62 Plekhanov, *VChK-OGPU*, p. 100.
63 V. I. Lenin, 'On the Tasks of the People's Commissariat for Justice under the New Economic Policy', vol. 36, p. 3; L. V. Borisova, 'NEP v zerkale pokazatel'nyikh protsessov po vziatochnichestvu i khoziaistvennyim prestupleniiam', *Otechestvennaia istoriia*, 2006, vol. 1, p. 85.
64 *Leninskii sbornik*, vol. 35, p. 334; Borisova, 'NEP v zerkale', p. 85.
65 Lenin, 'On the Tasks of the People's Commissariat of Justice', p. 3.
66 *V. I. Lenin i VChK*, Document No. 599, p. 487; Plekhanov, *VChK-OGPU*, p. 107; Leggett, *The Cheka*, p. 340.
67 Plekhanov, *VChK-OGPU*, p. 104.
68 Ibid. , pp. 113–4.
69 V. I. Lenin, 'Ninth All-Russian Congress of Soviets', vol. 33, pp. 26–7.
70 Leggett, *The Cheka*, pp. 341–2.
71 V. I. Lenin, 'To: L. B. Kamenev', vol. 45, pp. 1–2.
72 See *V. I. Lenin i VChK*, Document No. 651, pp. 524–6; see also Document No. 649, pp. 522–3.
73 See Plekhanov, *VChK-OGPU*, p. 480.
74 V. I. Lenin, 'From a letter to I. S. Unshlikht', vol. 45.
75 RGASPI, f.76, op. 3, d.149, l.14; 1.49.
76 Lenin, 'From a Letter to I. S. Unshlicht', p. 1.
77 See *V. I. Lenin i VChK*, Document No. 668, p. 537; *'Ochistim rossiiu nadolgo...'*, Document No. 256, pp. 377–8; Leggett, *The Cheka*, p. 348.
78 *'Ochistim rossiiu nadolgo...'*, Document No. 149, pp. 272–3.
79 RGASPI, f.76, op. 3, d.149, ll.35–7; Plekhanov, *VChK-0GPU*, pp. 114–5.
80 See Plekhanov, *VChK-0GPU*, pp. 114.
81 Lenin, 'On the Tasks of the People's Commissariat for Justice', pp. 1–3.
82 Lenin, 'Eleventh Congress of the RCP(B)', p. 17.
83 V. I. Lenin, 'Addendum to the Draft Preamble to the Criminal Code of the RSFSR and a Letter to D. I. Kursky. May 15, 1922', vol. 42, pp. 1–2.
84 V. I. Lenin, 'Letter to D. I. Kursky. 17 May, 1922', vol. 33, pp. 1–2. See also Witte, 'Violence in Lenin's Thought and Practice', p. 182.
85 Plekhanov, *VChK-OGPU*, p. 112.
86 Ibid., pp. 157–8; *V. I. Lenin i VChK*, Document No. 674, p. 545.
87 See V. I. Lenin, '"Dual" Subordination and Legality', vol. 33.

88 See for example RGASPI, f.76, op. 3, d.149, ll.37ff.
89 Finkel, *On the Ideological Front*, p. 153.
90 *F. E. Dzerzhinskii. Predsedatel' VChK-OGPU*, Document No. 805, p. 491.
91 Paul Avrich, *Kronstadt 1921*, New York: Norton, 1970, pp. 133–4.
92 Schapiro, *The Origins of the Communist Autocracy*, pp. 296–7.
93 Brovkin, *Behind the Front Lines*, p. 393.
94 Avrich, *Kronstadt 1921*, p. 182. For the text of the resolution, see Ibid., p. 73; V. P. Naumov and A. A. Kosakovskii (eds.), *Kronstadt 1921. Dokumentyi*, Rossiia XX Vek, Moscow: 1997, Document No. 7, pp. 4–5. Hereafter *Kronstadt 1921. Dokumentyi*.
95 Avrich, *Kronstadt 1921*, pp. 167–71.
96 *Kronstadt 1921. Dokumentyi*, Document No. 2, p. 19.
97 Lenin, 'Tenth Congress', Part I, vol. 2, p. 13.
98 Ibid., Part III, vol. 6, p. 11.
99 Avrich, *Kronstadt 1921*, pp. 102–10.
100 *V. I. Lenin i VChK*, Document No. 475, pp. 401–2.
101 Ibid., p. 401.
102 Ibid., Document No. 491, p. 411.
103 Ibid., Document No. 485, p. 408. The suggestion came from a Vecheka representative, I. V. Vardin (Mgeladze).
104 *Kronstadt 1921. Dokumentyi*, Document No. 12, pp. 307–8.
105 Ibid., pp. 307–8, p. 313. One sailor was sentenced to a year's labour for simply discussing the events with Red Army soldiers in Petrograd. See Ibid., p. 323.
106 Ibid., p. 15
107 Ibid., Document No. 38, p. 361.
108 See for example E. A. Ambartsymov, 'Analiz V. I. Leninyim prichin krizisa 1921g. i putei vyikhoda iz nego', *Voprosi istorii*, 1984, No. 4, 23.
109 *V. I. Lenin i VChK*, Document No. 521, p. 431.
110 *Kronstadt 1921: Dokumentyi*, Document No. 36, pp. 355–6; '*Ochistim rossiiu nadolgo...*', Document No. 4, p. 21.
111 *Iz istorii VChK*, Document No. 333, pp. 455–8.
112 V. I. Lenin, 'The International and Domestic Situation of the Soviet Republic. 6 March 1922', vol. 33, pp. 8–12.
113 '*Ochistim rossiiu nadolgo...*', Document No. 138, pp. 233–4.
114 See Stuart Finkel, *On the Ideological Front: The Russian Intelligentsia and the Making of the Soviet Public Sphere*, New Haven and London: Yale University Press, 2007. See also Chamberlain, *The Philosophy Steamer* and Christopher Read, *Culture and Power in Revolutionary Russia: The Intelligentsia and the Transition from Tsarism to Communism*, London: Macmillan, 1990.
115 See in particular A. M. Gak, A. S. Masal'skaia and I. N. Selezneva, 'Deportatsiia inakomyisliashchikh v 1922g: (Pozitsiia V. I. Lenina)', *Kentavr*, 1993, vol. 5, pp. 75–89.
116 Lih, *Lenin*, p. 164.
117 Lenin, 'The Tax in Kind', p. 28.
118 '*Ochistim rossiiu nadolgo...*', Document No. 75, p. 118. See also Document No. 70, pp. 110–1.
119 Ibid., Document No. 75, p. 121.
120 This interview is re-produced in *Filosofskii parokhod'*, *Federal'naia Arkhivnaia Sluzhba Rossii*, 2003, 5.
121 See Sheila Fitzpatrick, 'The "Soft" Line on Culture and Its Enemies: Soviet Cultural Policy, 1922–1927', *Slavic Review*, 1974, vol. 33, No. 2, pp. 267–87.
122 '*Ochistim rossiiu nadolgo...*', Document No. 254, pp. 375–6.
123 Finkel, *On the Ideological Front*, pp. 3, 116.
124 Read, *Culture and Power*, p. 194.
125 Lenin, 'Tenth All-Russian Conference of the RCP(B)', pp. 7–8.

126 The letter was occasioned by Dzerzhinskii's request to find a basis for definitively expelling Mensheviks from the soviets, after he had read a Menshevik paper and concluded that they were the inspiration behind Kronstadt. See '*Ochistim rossiiu nadolgo...*', note 110, p. 555.

127 Ibid., Document No. 127, pp. 178–9.

128 Ibid., Document No. 176, p. 296.

129 Ibid., Document No. 138, pp. 255.

130 Ibid.

131 Ibid., Document No. 37, p. 52. See also Finkel, *On the Ideological Front*, p. 160.

132 See Marc Jansen, *A Show Trial Under Lenin: The Trial of the Socialist Revolutionaries, Moscow 1922*, trans. Jean Sanders, The Hague: Martinus Nijhoff, 1982, pp. 15–6.

133 See Evgenii Preobrazhenskii's letter to the Politburo in July in '*Ochistim rossiiu nadolgo...*', Document No. 125, p. 177.

134 '*Ochistim rossiiu nadolgo...*', Document No. 92, pp. 145–9; footnote 66, pp. 550–1. Riazanov also attacked the public prosecutor Nikolai Krylenko for making a mockery of the law.

135 '*Ochistim rossiiu nadolgo...*', Document No. 144, pp. 266–8.

136 Jansen, *A Show Trial under Lenin*, pp. 138–9.

137 See Finkel, *On the Ideological Front*, pp. 17–8. It is not clear whether this group intended to initiate an uprising or act in case of another Kronstadt-like event.

138 See Ibid., pp. 19ff.

139 For Vecheka reports sent to Lenin warning of potential dangers posed by this committee, see *V. I. Lenin i VChK*, Documents Nos. 576 and 577, pp. 470–2.

140 V. I. Lenin, 'To: F. E. Dzerzhinskii', vol. 45, p. 2.

141 See John Gonzalez, 'The Bolshevik Leadership and the Rozhkov Affair: *Inakomysliachie* and the Politics of Persecution, 1921–22', *Revolutionary Russia*, 2010, vol. 23, No. 1, pp. 67–91.

142 In fact, due to ill health, Rozhkov under Lenin's recommendation was sent to Pskov.

143 '*Ochistim rossiiu nadolgo...*', Document No. 110, pp. 162–3.

144 Ibid., Document No. 213, pp. 331–2. See also Document No. 377, pp. 519–20.

145 Finkel, *On the Ideological Front*, p. 10.

146 See in particular Arto Luukkanen, *The Party of Unbelief: The Religious Policy of the Bolshevik Party 1917–1929*, Helsinki: Studia Historika, 1994; Jonathan W. Daly, '"Storming the Last Citadel": The Bolshevik Assault on the Church, 1922', in Brovkin (ed.), *The Bolsheviks in Russian Society*, pp. 235–68; and Natal'ia Krivova, *Vlast' i tserkov' v 1922–1925 gg. Politbiuro i GPU v bor'be za tserkovnyie tsennosti i politicheskoe podchinenie dukhovenstva*, Moscow: AIRO-XX, 1997.

147 Daly, '"Storming the Last Citadel"', p. 235.

148 See Paul Gabel, *And God Created Lenin: Marxism vs. Religion in Russia, 1917–1929*, New York: Prometheus Books, 2005, p. 135.

149 See Curtiss, *The Russian Church*, pp. 90–101.

150 See for example RGASPI, f.5, op. 1, d.2618, ll.29–30ob.

151 *Leninskii sbornik*, vol. 35, p. 233; V. I. Lenin, 'To: V. M. Molotov. Between April 9 and 21 1921', vol. 45, p. 1.

152 See *Kronstadt 1921: Dokumentyi*, Document No. 36, p. 356.

153 See Daly, '"Storming the Last Citadel"', pp. 237–8.

154 See '*Ochistim rossiiu nadolgo...*', Document No. 27, pp. 37–8.

155 See this appeal in N. N. Pokrovskii and S. G. Petrov (eds.), *Arkhivyi Kremlia: Politbiuro i tserkov', 1922–1925*, Novosibirsk: Rosspen, 1997–98, vol. 1, Document No. 23–1, p. 114.

156 Quoted in Krivova, *Vlast' i tserkov'*, p. 40.

157 *Arkhivyi Kremlia*, vol. 2, Document No. P–87, p. 145.

158 Ibid., vol. 2, Document No. P–22, p. 32.

159 Ibid., vol. 1, Document No. 23–2, pp. 115–6.

160 See *V. I. Lenin. Neizvestnyie dokumentyi*, Document No. 370, pp. 519–20; *Arkhivyi Kremlia*, Document No. 23–13, pp. 132–3. For a detailed treatment of the events at Shuia in March 1922, see Natal'ia Krivova, 'The Events in Shuia: A Turning Point in the Assault on the Church', *Russian Studies in History*, 2007, vol. 46, No. 2, pp. 8–38.
161 See *Arkhivyi Kremlia*, vol. 2, Document No. P–49, pp. 73–5.
162 Ibid., vol. 1, Document No. 23–15, p. 139.
163 The letter is available in full in '*Ochistim rossiiu nadolgo...*', Document No. 45, pp. 70–3; *Arkhivyi Kremlia*, vol. 1, Document No. 23–16, pp. 140–4.
164 *Arkhivyi Kremlia*, vol. 2, Document No. P–51, p. 77.
165 Ibid., vol. 1, Document No. 23–16, p. 144; '*Ochistim rossiiu nadolgo...*', Document No. 45, p. 73.
166 See also S. G. Petrov, *Dokumentyi deloproizvodstva politbiuro TsK RKP(b) kak istochnik po istorii russkoi tserkvi (1921–1925)*, Moscow: Rosspen, 2004, p. 133.
167 '*Ochistim rossiu nadolgo...*', Document No. 52, pp. 78–80.
168 *Arkhivyi Kremlia*, vol. 1, Document No. 23–30, pp. 164–5.
169 Krivova, *Vlast' i tserkov' v 1922–1925 gg.*, p. 79.
170 *Izvestiia VTsIK*, 24 March 1922.
171 Daly, '"Storming the Last Citadel"', p. 257.
172 See *Arkhivyi Kremlia*, vol. 1, Documents No. 24:1 and 24:2, pp. 197–9.
173 Ibid., vol. 1, Document No. 24–4, p. 199.
174 *Izvestiia VTsIK*, 6 May 1922.
175 *Izvestiia VTsIK*, 6 May 1922.
176 Ibid.
177 *Pravda*, 9 May 1922.
178 Ibid.
179 See *Arkhivyi Kremlia*, vol. 1, Documents No. 24–6, 24–8 and 24–20, pp. 209–14; 223.
180 See here Holquist, 'State Violence as Technique', p. 38.
181 *Arkhivyi Kremlia*, vol. 1, Document No. 24–32, p. 236.
182 Ibid.
183 Ibid., vol. 1, Document No. 24–34, p. 241.
184 See Ibid., vol. 1, Document No. 24–36, p. 243.
185 State Archive of the Russian Federation (GARF), f.A353, op. 6, d.11, ll.131–6.
186 See for example *Arkhivyi Kremlia*, vol. 1, Document No. 24–6.
187 See Daly, '"Storming the Last Citadel"', p. 250.
188 V. I. Lenin, 'On Cooperation', vol. 33, p. 6. See especially V. I. Lenin, 'Our Revolution (Apropos of N. Sukhanov's Notes)', vol. 33.
189 See Lenin, 'On Cooperation'.
190 Erik van Ree, '"Lenin's Last Struggle" Revisited', *Revolutionary Russia*, 2001, vol. 14, No. 2, 98–100.
191 See Orlando Figes, *A People's Tragedy: The Russian Revolution, 1891–1924*, London: Pimlico, 1996, pp. 792–3.

Conclusion: Lenin's terror

1 Maksim Gorky, *Lenin: A Biographical Essay*, London: Morrison and Gibb, 1967, p. 32, quoted in Courtois (ed.), *The Black Book*, p. 756.
2 Sanborn, *Drafting the Russian Nation*, p. 176. Lenin's conception of violence was more instrumental than, for example, Georges Sorel, though the comparison with Sorel is rendered difficult by the fact that the latter's conception of 'violence' revolved around the idea of a general strike. Sorel urged this proletarian 'violence' to incite the ruling classes to abandon the pretence of philanthropy towards the working classes, to restore the 'warlike qualities' of the ruling classes and thereby to provoke sharp class struggle, to make the future revolution certain. 'Thus', he believed, 'proletarian

violence has become an essential factor of Marxism.' See Georges Sorel, *Reflections on Violence*, trans. T. E. Hulme and J. Roth, New York: Dover, 2004, p. 92. Originally published in 1906.

3 For an enlightening discussion of Marxism and morality, see Nicholas Churchich, *Marxism and Morality: A Critical Examination of Marxist Ethics*, Cambridge: James Clarke and Co., 1994. See also Eugene Kamenka, *Marxism and Ethics*, London: Macmillan, 1969.

4 See in particular here Sanborn, *Drafting the Russian Nation*, p. 167.

5 See also A. A. Strokov, *V. I. Lenin o voine i voennom isskustve*, Moscow: Nauka, 1971, pp. 15–6.

6 A. S. Shliapochnikov. 'V. I. Lenin o printsipakh sovetskoi ugolovnoi politiki', in *V. I. Lenin o zakonnosti i pravosudii, Voprosyi bor'byi s prestupnost'iu. Vyipusk 11*, Moscow: Iuridicheskaia literatura, 1970, p. 80. For a recent example of this argument from a Russian scholar and former *Pravda* columnist, see B. F. Slavin, *Lenin protiv Stalina: Poslednii boi revoliutsionera*, Moscow: URSS, 2010, p. 8.

7 See in particular Iu. I. Korablev, *V. I. Lenin i zashchita zavoevanii velikogo oktiabria*, Second Edition, Moscow: Nauka, 1979, and Shliapochnikov. 'V. I. Lenin o printsipakh', pp. 73–92.

8 See Cooper, *Merleau-Ponty and Marxism*, p. 45.

9 Martin Malia, *The Soviet Tragedy: A History of Socialism in Russia, 1917–1991*, New York: The Free Press, 1994, p. 16.

10 Ibid., pp. 77; 15.

11 Smith, 'Two Cheers', 123.

12 Mayer, *The Furies*, p. 10.

13 Ibid., p. 35.

14 Malia, *The Soviet Tragedy*, p. 124.

15 For a discussion of this, see Marcus C. Levitt, 'Introduction: The Consciousness of Violence in Russian History and Culture', in Marcus C. Levitt and Tatyana Novikov (eds.), *Times of Trouble: Violence in Russian Literature and Culture*, Madison: University of Wisconsin Press, 2007, pp. 6–7.

16 Levitt and Nokikov (eds.), *Times of Trouble*, p. 7.

17 Kevin M. Platt, 'On Blood, Scandal, Renunciation, and Russian History: Il'ia Repin's *Ivan the Terrible and His Son Ivan*', in Ibid., pp. 119–20.

18 See Bloxham and Gerwarth (eds.), *Political Violence in Twentieth-Century Europe*, p. 1.

19 Holquist, *Making War, Forging Revolution*, p. 2

20 Peter Holquist, 'Violent Russia, Deadly Marxism? Russia in the Epoch of Violence, 1905–21', *Kritika*, 2003, vol. 4, No. 3, 627.

21 For a different approach to Holquist's that stresses the violence inscribed into imperialist Russian society and the Hobbesian idea of the unleashing of human 'barbarism' during the revolutionary crisis and associated breakdown in order, see Vladimir P. Buldakov, *Krasnaia smuta: Priroda i posledstviia revolutsionnogo nasiliia*, Moscow: Rosspen, 1997, pp. 5–8.

22 Ian Kershaw, 'War and Political Violence in Twentieth-Century Europe', *Contemporary European History*, 2005, vol. 14, No. 1, 111.

23 Holquist, 'Violent Russia, Deadly Marxism?', 645.

24 William Rosenberg has also discussed this in a stimulating essay, 'Beheading the Revolution: Arno Mayer's "Furies"', *The Journal of Modern History*, 2001, vol. 73, No. 4, 917.

25 Holquist, *Making War, Forging Revolution*, pp. 285ff.

26 See David L. Hoffmann, *Stalinist Values: The Cultural Norms of Soviet Modernity, 1917–1941*, Ithaca: Cornell University Press, 2003, pp. 7–10; Beer, *Renovating Russia*; Scott, *Seeing Like a State*, pp. 100–79, and especially the introduction to Weiner (ed.), *Landscaping the Human Garden*.

27 Holquist, 'State Violence as Technique', pp. 19–45. See also Roger Griffin, *Modernism and Fascism: The Sense of a Beginning under Mussolini and Hitler*, Hampshire: Palgrave, 2007, p. 174.
28 See Hagenloh, *Stalin's Police*, pp. 11–12.
29 Beer, *Renovating Russia*, pp. 4–23.
30 For a discussion of Nietzsche's influence on Soviet culture, see Bernice Glatzer Rosenthal, *New Myth, New World: From Nietzsche to Stalinism*, University Park, PA: University of Pennsylvania Press, 2002.
31 Griffin, *Modernism and Fascism*, p. 4.
32 See Beer, *Renovating Russia*, p. 4, and Holquist, 'State Violence as Technique', pp. 21–2.
33 See also Priestland, *Stalinism and the Politics of Mobilization*, p. 14, note 48.
34 J. L. Talmon, *The Origins of Totalitarian Democracy*, London: Secker and Warburg, 1952, p. 1.
35 Ibid., pp. 1–5.
36 Halfin, *From Darkness to Light*, pp. 1–5.
37 Ibid., p. 9.
38 Halfin, *From Darkness to Light*, p. 3. Aleksei Anikin has also been impressed with the 'converted religious character' of the Russian revolutionary tradition in general. See A. V. Anikin, 'Elementyi sakral'nogo v russkikh revolutsionnikh teoriiakh (K istorii formirovaniia sovetskoi ideologii)', 1995, *Otechestvennaia istoriia*, 1, p. 90.
39 Halfin, *From Darkness to Light*, pp. 72–6.
40 Ibid., pp. 8–9.
41 Sanborn, *Drafting the Russian Nation*, p. 16.
42 I am grateful to Christopher Read for this thought.
43 See Priestland, *Stalinism and the Politics of Mobilization*, pp. 18ff.
44 Gregor, *Marxism, Fascism, and Totalitarianism*, p. 270.
45 Interestingly Steven Rosefielde, in his study of '*high* crimes against humanity', does not argue that pre-Stalinist Soviet repressions constitute such crimes, evidently because he focuses on peacetime killings. See S. Rosefielde, *Red Holocaust*, Oxford and New York: Routledge, 2010, p. 254, note 4.
46 V. I. Lenin, 'Our Revolution (Apropos of N. Sukhanov's Notes)', vol. 33, p. 4.
47 Paul Le Blanc, *Marx, Lenin, and the Revolutionary Experience: Studies of Communism and Radicalism in the Age of Globalization*, Routledge: New York and Oxon, 2006, p. 139.
48 Geoffrey Roberts, *Stalin's Wars: From World War to Cold War, 1939–1953*, New Haven: Yale University Press, 2006, pp. xii, 374.
49 David Andress, *The Terror: Civil War in the French Revolution*, London: Little, Brown, 2005, p. 7.

Bibliography

Primary sources

Archival

Russian State Archive for Social-Political History (RGASPI):
  Fond 5 (Lenin's Secretariat), opis' 1, dela: 2574, 2618, 2561, 2592.
  Fond 17, op. 2 (Plenums of the RCP (b) Central Committee, 1918–1941).
  Fond 19, op. 3 (Council of Labour and Defence, 1918–1922).
  Fond 76 (Felix Dzerzhinskii), op. 3, d.149.
State Archive of the Russian Federation (GARF):
  Fond A353 (Justice Commissariat of the RSFSR), op. 6, d.11.

Lenin

Adibekova, G. and Pirozhkov, V. P. (eds.), *V. I. Lenin i VChK: sbornik dokumentov (1917–1922)*, 2nd Edition, Moscow: Politizdat, 1987.

Amiantov, Iu. N. and Akhapkin, Yu. A. (eds.), *V. I. Lenin. Neizvestnyie dokumentyi, 1891–1922*, Moscow: Rosspen, 1999.

Lenin, Vladimir Il'ich, *Collected Works*, 45 volumes. Lenin Internet Archive. Online. Available www.marxists.org/archive/lenin/works/.

—— *Leninskii sbornik*, 50 volumes, Moscow and Leningrad, 1924–85.

—— *Sochinenii*, 3rd Edition, 30 volumes, Moscow: Partizdat TsK VKP(b), 1935–7.

—— *Polnoe Sobranie Sochinenii*, 5th Edition, 55 volumes, Moscow: Institute of Marxism–Leninism, 1958–1965.

—— *Biograficheskaia khronika*, 12 volumes, Moscow: Politizdat, 1970–82.

—— *Marxism on the State: Preparatory Material for the Book* The State and Revolution, Moscow: Progress Publishers, 1972.

—— *Selected Works*, 3 volumes, Progress Publishers, Moscow, Revised Edition, 1977.

—— *Teoriia Nasiliia*, Moscow: Algoritm, 2007.

Pipes, Richard, *The Unknown Lenin: From the Secret Archive*, Yale University Press, New Haven, 1999.

Marx and Engels

Marx, Karl and Engels, Frederick, *The Communist Manifesto*, with an Introduction and Notes by Gareth Stedman Jones, London: Penguin Classics, 2002.

—— *Collected Works*, London: Lawrence and Wishart, 1975–2004.
McLellan, David (ed.), *Karl Marx: Selected Writings*, Oxford: Oxford University Press, 1977.

Other socialist theorists/documents

Bukharin, Nicolai I., *Economics of the Transformation Period: With Lenin's Critical Remarks*, New York: Bergman Publishers, 1971.
Kautsky, Karl, *The Dictatorship of the Proletariat*, Introduction by John H. Kautsky, Ann Arbor: University of Michigan Press, 1971.
Karl Kautsky Internet Archive. Online. Available http://www.marxists.org/archive/kautsky/works/.
Kuz'min V. L., Tsipkin Iu. N. *Men'sheviki v 1917 gody. Ot iiul'skikh sobyitii do kornilovskogo miatezha*, vol. 2, Moscow: Progress-Akademia, 1995.
Josef Stalin Internet Archive. Online. Available http://www.marxists.org/reference/archive/stalin/works/.
Leon Trotsky Internet Archive. Online. Available http://www.marxists.org/archive/trotsky/works/.
Volobuiev, O. V. and Shelokhaev, V. V. (eds.), *Men'sheviki. Dokymentyi i materialyi, 1903–fevral' 1917 gg*, Moscow: Rosspen, 1996.

Party congress protocols (RSDRP, RSDLP(B) and RKP(B))

Chetvertyi (Ob'edinitel'nyi) s''ezd RSDRP. Aprel'–mai 1906 goda. Protokolyi, Moscow: Gospolitizdat, 1959.
Deviatyi s''ezd RKP(b). Mart-aprel' 1920 goda. Protokolyi, Moscow: Politizdat, 1960.
Piatyi (londonskii) s''ezd RSDRP. Aprel'-mai 1907 goda. Protokolyi, Moscow: Gosizdat, 1963.
Shestoi s''ezd RSDRP (bol'shevikov). Avgust 1917 goda: Protokolyi, Moscow: Politizdat, 1958.
Vos'moi s''ezd RKP(b). Mart 1919 goda. Protokolyi, Moscow: Politizdat, 1959.

Newspapers/periodicals

Ezhenedel'nik VChK
Filosofskii parokhod', Federal'naia Arkhivnaia sluzhba Rossii, 2003.
Izvestiia VTsIK
Pravda

Published documents

Amiantov, Yu. and Lavrov, V. (eds.), *Protokolyi zasedanii soveta narodnyikh komissarov RSFSR. Noiabr' 1917–mart 1918gg.*, Moscow: Rosspen, 2006.
Artizov, A. N., Vodopianova, Z. K., Makarov, V. G., Khristoforov, V. S. and Domchareva, E. V. (eds.), *'Ochistim rossiiu nadolgo...' Repressii protiv inakomyisliashchikh. Dokumentyi. Konets 1921–nachalo 1923g.*, Rossiia XX Vek, Moscow: Materik, 2008.

Belov, G. A., Kurenkov, A. N., Loginov, A. E., Pletnev, Ya. A. and Tikunov, V. S. (eds.), *Iz istorii vserossiiskoi chrezvyichainoi komissii, 1917–1921gg: sbornik dokumentov*, Moscow: Gospolitizdat, 1958.

Berelovich, A. and Danilov, V. P. (eds.), *Sovetskaia derevnia glazami VChK-OGPU-NKVD. Dokumentyi i mateialyi*, vol. 1 (1918–1922), Moscow: Rosspen, 2005.

Chistiakov, O. I., *Konstitutsiia R.S.F.S.R. 1918 goda*, 2nd Edition, Moscow: Zertsalo, 2003.

'Dokladyi I. I. Vatsetisa V. I. Leninu (fevral'-mai 1919g.)', *Istoricheskii arkhiv*, 1958, 41–75.

Kokurin, A. I. and Petrov, N. V., *Gulag 1917–1960*, Rossiia XX vek, Moscow: Materik, 2000.

Kuz'min, N. F. et al. (eds.), *Iz istorii grazhdanskoi voinyi v SSSR*, vol. 3, Moscow: Sovetskaia Rossiia, 1961.

Kudriavtsev, F. N. *Vospominania o Vladimire Il'iche Lenine*, vol. 2, Moscow: Gospolitizdat, 1957.

Naumov, V. P. and Kochakovskii, A. A. (eds.), *Kronstadt 1921. Dokumentyi*, Rossiia XX Vek, Moscow: 1997.

Plekhanov, A. A. and Plekhanov, A. M. (eds.), *F.E. Dzerzhinskii-Predsedatel' VChK-OGPU 1917–1926. Dokumentyi*, Rossiya XX Vek, Moscow: Materik, 2007.

Pokrovskii, N. N. and Petrov, S. G., *Arkhivyi Kremlia. Politbiuro i tserkov', 1922–1925*, Two Volumes, Novosibirsk: Rosspen, 1997–8.

Vinogradov, V., Litvin, A. and Khristoforov, V (eds.), *Arkhiv VChK: sbornik dokumentov*, Moscow: Kuchkovo Pole, 2007.

Vinogradov, V. K. (ed.), *VChK upolnomochena soobshchit'...1918g*, Moscow: Kuchkovo pole, 2004.

Secondary Sources

Alexopoulos, Golfo, *Stalin's Outcasts: Aliens, Citizens, and the Soviet State, 1926–1936*, Ithaca and London: Cornell University Press, 2003.

Ambartsymov, 'Analiz V. I. Leninyim prichin krizisa 1921g.', *Voprosi istorii*, 1984, No. 4, 15–29.

Anderson, Kevin B., *Lenin, Hegel, and Western Marxism: A Critical Study*, Chicago: University of Illinois Press, 1995.

Andics, Hellmut, *Rule of Terror: Russia under Lenin and Stalin*, New York: Holt, 1969.

Anikin, A. V., 'Elementyi sakral'nogo v russkikh revolutsionnikh teoriiakh (K istorii formirovaniia sovetskoi ideologii)', *Otechestvennaia istoriia*, 1995 (1), 78–92.

Arendt, Hannah, *On Violence*, Orlando: Harcourt, 1970.

Ascher, Abraham, *The Revolution of 1905: Russia in Disarray* (vol. 1), Stanford: Stanford University Press, 1988.

—— *P. A. Stolypin: The Search for Stability in Late Imperial Russia*, Stanford: Stanford University Press, 2001.

—— *The Revolution of 1905: A Short History*, Stanford: Stanford University Press, 2004.

Aves, Jonathan, *Workers Against Lenin: Labour Protest and the Bolshevik Dictatorship*, International Library of Historical Studies, New York: Tauris, 1996.

Avrich, Paul, *Kronstadt 1921*, New York: Norton, 1970.

Barfield, Rodney, 'Lenin's Utopianism: State and Revolution', *Slavic Review*, 1971, vol. 30, No. 1, 45–56.

Baron, Samuel, *Plekhanov: The Father of Russian Marxism*, Stanford: Stanford University Press, 1963.

Beer, Daniel, *Renovating Russia: The Human Sciences and the Fate of Liberal Modernity, 1880–1930*, Ithaca and London: Cornell University Press, 2008.

Beirne, Piers (ed.), *Revolution in Law: Contributions to the Development of Soviet Legal Theory, 1917–1938*, New York and London: M. E. Sharpe, 1990.

Benvenuti, Francesco, *The Bolsheviks and the Red Army, 1918–1922*, trans. Christopher Woodall, Cambridge: Cambridge University Press, 1988.

Besançon, Alain, *The Intellectual Origins of Leninism*, trans. Sarah Matthews, Oxford: Blackwell, 1981.

Bloxham, Donald and Gerwarth, Robert (eds.), *Political Violence in Twentieth-Century Europe*, Cambridge: Cambridge University Press, 2011.

Bolsinger, Eckard, *The Autonomy of the Political: Carl Schmitt's and Lenin's Political Realism*, Connecticut: Greenwood Press, 2001.

Borisova, L. V., *Voennyi kommunizm: Nasilie kak element khoziaistvennnogo mekhanizma*, Moscow: INION RAN, 2001.

—— 'NEP v zerkale pokazatel'nyikh protsessov po vziatochnichestvu i khoziaistvennyim prestupleniiam', *Otechestvennaia istoriia*, 2006, vol. 1, 84–97.

Brinkley, George, 'Review: Leninism: What it Was and What it Was Not', *The Review of Politics*, 1998, vol. 60, No. 1, 151–64.

Broido, Vera, *Lenin and the Mensheviks: The Persecution of Socialists under Bolshevism*, Aldershot: Gower/Temple Smith, 1987.

Brovkin, Vladimir, *The Mensheviks after October: Socialist Opposition and the Rise of the Bolshevik Dictatorship*, Ithaca: Cornell University Press, 1987.

—— *Behind the Front Lines of the Civil War: Political Parties and Social Movements in Russia, 1918–1922*, New Jersey: Princeton University Press, 1994.

—— *Russia After Lenin: Politics, Culture and Society, 1921–1929*, London and New York: Routledge, 1998.

Brovkin, Vladimir (ed.), *The Bolsheviks in Russian Society: The Revolution and Civil Wars*, New Haven: Yale University Press, 1997.

Budgen, Sebastian, Kouvelakis, Stathis and Žižek, Slavoj (eds.), *Lenin Reloaded: Towards a Politics of Truth*, Durham: Duke University Press, 2007.

Budnitskii, O. V., *Terrorizm v Rossiiskom Osvoboditel'nom Dvizhenii: ideologiia, etika, psikhologiia (vtoraia polovina XIX-nachalo XX v.)*, Moscow: Rosspen, 2000.

Buldakov, Vladimir P., *Krasnaia smyta: Priroda i posledstviia revolutsionnogo nasiliia*, Moscow: Rosspen, 1997.

Burbank, Jane, 'Lenin and the Law in Revolutionary Russia', *Slavic Review*, 1995, vol. 54, No. 1, 23–44.

Burtnevskii, Vladimir, 'White Administration and White Terror (The Denikin Period)', *Russian Review*, 1993, vol. LII, No. 3, 355–66.

Chamberlain, Lesley, *The Philosophy Steamer: Lenin and the Exile of the Intelligentsia*, London: Atlantic Books, 2006.

Chamberlin, William Henry, *The Russian Revolution 1917–1921*, vol. 1, New Jersey: Princeton University Press, 1987.

Churchich, Nicholas, *Marxism and Morality: A Critical Examination of Marxist Ethics*, Cambridge: James Clarke, 1994.

Cohen-Almagor, Raphael, 'Foundations of Violence, Terror, and War in the Writings of Marx, Engels and Lenin', *Terrorism and Political Violence*, 1991, vol. 3, No. 2, 1–24.

Cooper, Barry, *Merleau-Ponty and Marxism: From Terror to Reform*, Toronto: University of Toronto Press, 1979.

Courtois, Stephane (ed.), *The Black Book of Communism: Crimes, Terror, Represssion*, trans. by Jonathan Murphy and Mark Kramer, Massachusetts: Harvard University Press, 1999.

Curtiss, John Shelton, *The Russian Church and the Soviet State, 1917–1950*, Boston: Little, Brown and Co., 1953.

Daly, Jonathan, *The Watchful State: Security Police and Opposition in Russia, 1906–1917*, DeKalb, IL: Northern Illinois University Press, 2004.

Daniels, Robert V., *The Rise and Fall of Communism in Russia*, New Haven: Yale University Press, 2007.

David-Fox, Michael, 'On the Primacy of Ideology: Soviet Revisionists and Holocaust Deniers (In Response to Martin Malia)', *Kritika*, 2004, vol. 5, No. 1, 81–105.

Davies, Norman, 'The Missing Revolutionary War: The Polish Campaigns and the Retreat from Revolution in Soviet Russia, 1919–21', *Soviet Studies*, 1975, vol. XXVII, No. 2, 178–95.

—— *White Eagle, Red Star: The Polish–Soviet War 1919–1920 and 'The Miracle on the Vistula'*, London: Pimlico, 2003.

De George, Richard T., *Soviet Ethics and Morality*, Ann Arbor: University of Michigan Press, 1969.

Donald, Moira, *Marxism and Revolution: Karl Kautsky and the Russian Marxists 1900–1924*, New Haven: Yale University Press, 1993.

Draper, Hal, *Karl Marx's Theory of Revolution*, Volume III, New York: Monthly Review Press, 1986.

Duhamel, Luc, 'Lénine, la violence et l'eurocommunisme', *Revue canadienne de science politique*, 1980, vol. 13, No. 1, 97–120.

Eagleton, Terry, *Ideology: An Introduction*, London: Verso, 1991.

Erickson, John, *The Soviet High Command: A Military–Political History, 1918–1941*, 3rd Edition, London: Routledge, 2001.

Evans, Alfred B., 'Rereading Lenin's State and Revolution', *Slavic Review*, 1987, vol. 46, No. 1, 1–19.

Farber, Samuel, *Before Stalinism: The Rise and Fall of Soviet Democracy*, Cambridge: Polity Press, 1990.

Figes, Orlando, *Peasant Russia, Civil War: The Volga Countryside in Revolution, 1917–1921*, Oxford: Clarendon Press, 1989.

—— *A People's Tragedy: A History of the Russian Revolution*, New York: Viking, 1996.

—— *The Whisperers: Private Life in Stalin's Russia*, London: Allen Lane, 2007.

Finkel, Stuart, *On the Ideological Front: The Russian Intelligentsia and the Making of the Soviet Public Sphere*, New Haven: Yale University Press, 2007.

Finlay, Christopher, 'Violence and Revolutionary Subjectivity: Marx to Žižek', *European Journal of Political Theory*, 2006, vol. 5, No. 4, 373–97.

Fitzpatrick, Sheila, 'The "Soft" Line on Culture and Its Enemies: Soviet Cultural Policy, 1922–1927', *Slavic Review*, 1974, vol. 33, No. 2, 267–87.

—— 'Ascribing Class: The Construction of Social Identity in Soviet Russia', *Journal of Modern History*, 1993, vol. 65, 745–70.

—— 'The Bolsheviks' Dilemma: Class, Culture, and Politics in the Early Soviet Years', *Slavic Review*, 1998, vol. 47, No. 4, 599–613.

—— 'Politics as Practice: Thoughts on a New Soviet Political History', *Kritika: Explorations in Russian and Eurasian History*, 2004, vol. 5, No. 1, 27–54.

Fitzpatrick, Sheila, Rabinowitch, Alexander and Stites, Richard (eds.), *Russia in the Era of NEP: Explorations in Soviet Society and Culture*, Bloomington: Indiana University Press, 1991.

Freeden, Michael, *Ideologies and Political Theory: A Conceptual Approach*, Oxford: Clarendon Press, 1996.

Gabel, Paul, *And God Created Lenin: Marxism versus Religion in Russia, 1917–1929*, New York: Prometheus Books, 2005.

Gak, A. M., Masal'skaia, A. S. and Selezneva, I. N., 'Deportatsiia inakomyisliashchikh v 1922g. (Pozitsiia V. I. Lenina)', *Kentavr*, 1993, 5, 75–89

Ganor, Boaz, 'Defining Terrorism: Is One Man's Terrorist Another Man's Freedom Fighter?', *Police Practice and Research*, 2002, vol. 3, No. 4, 287–304.

Gatrell, Peter, *Russia's First World War: A Social and Economic History*, Harlow: Pearson, 2005.

Geifman, Anna, *Thou Shalt Kill: Revolutionary Terrorism in Russia, 1894–1917*, New Jersey: Princeton University Press, 1993.

Gellately, Robert, *Lenin, Stalin and Hitler: The Age of Social Catastrophe*, London: Jonathan Cape, 2007.

Genis, Vladimir, 'Raskazachivanie v Sovetskoi Rossii', *Voprosi istorii*, 1994, vol. 12, 42–55.

Genkina, E. B., *Gosudarstvennaia deiatel'nost' V. I. Lenina, 1921–1923*, Moscow: Nauka, 1969.

—— *Lenin – Predsedatel' Sovnarkoma i STO. Iz istorii gosudarstvennoi deiatel'nosti V. I. Lenina v 1921–1922 godakh*, Moscow: Izdatel'stvo Akademii Nauk SSSR, 1960.

Gerson, Lennard D., *The Secret Police in Lenin's Russia*, Philadelphia: Temple University Press, 1976.

Getzler, Israel, 'Lenin's Conception of Revolution as Civil War', *Slavonic and East European Review*, 1996, vol. 74, No. 3, 465–72.

Geyer, Michael and Fitzpatrick, Sheila (eds.), *Beyond Totalitarianism: Stalinism and Nazism Compared*, New York: Cambridge University Press, 2009.

Gimpel'son, E. G., *Novaia Ekonomicheskaia Politika Lenina–Stalina: Problemyi i uroki 20-e godyi XX veka*, Moscow: Sobranie, 2004.

—— *"Voennyi kommunizm": politika, ekonomika, ideologiia*, Moscow: "Myisl'", 1973.

Gleason, Abbott, Peter Kenez and Richard Stites (eds.), *Bolshevik Culture: Experiment and Order in the Russian Revolution*, Bloomington: Indiana University Press, 1985.

Gonzalez, John, 'N. A. Rozhkov and V. I. Lenin: The Forgotten Polemics of the Inter-Revolutionary Years, 1908–1917', *Revolutionary Russia*, 2005, vol. 18, No. 2, 169–200.

—— 'The Bolshevik Leadership and the Rozhkov Affair: *Inakomysliachie* and the Politics of Persecution, 1921–22', *Revolutionary Russia*, 2010, vol. 23, No. 1, 67–91

Gooding, John, *Socialism in Russia: Lenin and his Legacy, 1890–1991*, Hampshire: Palgrave, 2002.

Goodwin, Jeff, 'A Theory of Categorical Terrorism', *Social Forces*, 2006, vol. 84, No. 4, 2027–46.

Gray, John, *Black Mass: Apocalyptic Religion and the Death of Utopia*, London: Allen Lane, 2007.

Graziosi, Andrea, *A New, Peculiar State: Explorations in Soviet History, 1917–1937*, Connecticut: Praeger, 2000.

Gregor, A. James, *Marxism, Fascism, and Totalitarianism: Chapters in the Intellectual History of Radicalism*, Stanford: Stanford University Press, 2009.

Gregory, Paul R., *Terror by Quota: State Security from Lenin to Stalin: An Archival Study*, New Haven: Yale University Press, 2009.

Gupta, Dipak K., *Understanding Terrorism and Political Violence: The Life Cycle of Birth, Growth, Transformation and Demise*, London and New York: Routledge, 2008.

Hagenloh, Paul, *Stalin's Police: Public Order and Mass Repression in the USSR, 1926–1941*, Washington DC: Wilson Center/John Hopkins University Press, 2009.

Haimson, Leopold, (ed.), *The Mensheviks: From the Revolution of 1917 to the Second World War*, Chicago and London: Chicago University Press, 1974.

—— 'Lenin's Revolutionary Career Revisited: Some Observations on Recent Discussions', *Kritika*, 2004, vol. 5, No. 1, 55–80.

Halfin, Igal, *From Darkness to Light: Class, Consciousness, and Salvation in Revolutionary Russia*, Pittsburgh: University of Pittsburgh Press, 2000.

—— 'Between Instinct and Mind: The Bolshevik View of the Proletarian Self', *Slavic Review*, 2003, vol. 62, No. 1, 34–40.

Halfin, Igal (ed.), *Language and Revolution: Making Modern Political Identities*, London and Portland, OR: Frank Cass, 2002.

Harding, Neil, *Lenin's Political Thought: Theory and Practice in the Democratic and Socialist Revolutions*, London: Macmillan, 1984.

—— *Leninism*, London: Macmillan, 1996.

Held, Virginia, *How Terrorism is Wrong: Morality and Political Violence*, New York: Oxford University Press, 2008.

Heller, Mikhail and Nekrich, Aleksandr, *Utopia in Power: The History of the Soviet Union from 1917 to the Present*, trans. Phyllis B. Carlos, New York: Summit Books, 1986.

Heywood, Andrew, *Political Ideologies: An Introduction*, 3rd Edition, Hampshire: Palgrave Macmillan, 2003.

Hoffmann, David L., *Stalinist Values: The Cultural Norms of Soviet Modernity, 1917–1941*, Ithaca: Cornell University Press, 2003.

Holman, G. Paul, '"War Communism", or the Besieger Besieged: A Study of Lenin's Social and Political Objectives From 1918 to 1921. Parts I and II', Ph.D. Dissertation, Georgetown University, Washington, DC, 1973.

Holquist, Peter, *Making War, Forging Revolution: Russia's Continuum of Crisis, 1914–1921*, Massachusetts: Harvard University Press, 2002.

—— 'Violent Russia, Deadly Marxism? Russia in the Epoch of Violence, 1905–21', *Kritika: Explorations in Russian and Eurasian History*, 2003, vol. 4, No. 3, 627–52.

Hunt, Alan and Purvis, Trevor, 'Discourse, Ideology, Discourse, Ideology, Discourse, Ideology…', *The British Journal of Sociology*, 1993, vol. 44, No. 3, 473–99.

Iroshnikov, M. P., *Vo glave Sovnarkoma. Gosudarstvennaia deiatel'nost V. I. Lenina v 1917–1922 gg.*, Leningrad: Nauka, 1976.

Jansen, Marc, *A Show Trial Under Lenin: The Trial of the Socialist Revolutionaries, Moscow, 1922*, trans. Jean Sanders, The Hague: Martinus Nijhoff, 1982.

Jessop, Bob (ed.), *Karl Marx's Social and Political Thought: Critical Assessments*, Volume III: 'The State, Politics, and Revolution', London: Routledge, 1990.

Joll, James, *The Second International, 1889–1914*, London: Weidenfeld and Nicolson, 1974.

Jowitt, Ken, *New World Disorder: The Leninist Extinction*, Berkeley and Los Angeles: University of California Press, 1993.

Kalyvas, Stathis N., *The Logic of Violence in Civil War*, New York: Cambridge University Press, 2006.

Kamenka, Eugene, *Marxism and Ethics*, London: Macmillan, 1969.

Kautsky, John H., *Marxism and Leninism: Different Ideologies: An Essay in the Sociology of Knowledge*, New Brunswick: Transaction Publishers, 2002.

Kershaw, Ian, 'War and Political Violence in Twentieth-Century Europe', *Contemporary European History*, 2005, vol. 14, No. 1, 107–23.

Kingston-Mann, Esther, *Lenin and the Problem of Marxist Peasant Revolution*, New York: Oxford University Press, 1985.

Kipp, Jacob W., 'Lenin and Clausewitz: The Militarization of Marxism, 1914–1921', *Military Affairs*, 1985, vol. 49, No. 4, 184–191.

Koenker, Diane, Rosenberg, William G. and Suny, Ronald Grigor (eds.), *Party, State, and Society in the Russian Civil War: Explorations in Social History*, Bloomington: Indiana University Press, 1989.

Kogan, L. A., 'Voennyi kommunizm: Utopia i real'nost'', *Voprosi istorii*, 1998, vol. 2, 122–34.

Kolakowski, Leszek, *Main Currents of Marxism: Its Rise, Growth, and Dissolution*, trans. P. S. Falla, Three Volumes, Oxford: Clarendon Press, 1978.

Korablev, Iu. I., *V. I. Lenin i zashchita zavoevanii velikogo oktiabria*, 2nd Edition, Moscow: Nauka, 1979.

Kramer, Alan, *Dynamic of Destruction: Culture and Mass Killing in the First World War*, Oxford: Oxford University Press, 2007.

Krylova, Anna, 'Beyond the Spontaneity–Consciousness Paradigm: "Class Instinct" as a Promising Category of Historical Analysis', *Slavic Review*, 2003, vol. 62, No. 1, 1–23.

Landis, Erik C., *Bandits and Partisans: The Antonov Movement in the Russian Civil War*, Pittsburgh: University of Pittsburgh Press, 2008.

—— 'Who Were the "Greens"? Rumour and Collective Identity in the Russian Civil War', *The Russian Review*, 2010, vol. 69, 30–46.

Leggett, George, *The Cheka: Lenin's Political Police: The All-Russian Extraordinary Commission for Combating Counterrevolution and Sobotage, December 1917–February 1922*, Oxford: Clarendon Press, 1981.

Leonov, S. V., *Rozhdenie Sovetskoi Imperii: gosudarstvo i ideologiia 1917–1920gg*, Moscow: Dialog MGU, 1997.

Levitt, Marcus C. and Novikov, Tatyana (eds.), *Times of Trouble: Violence in Russian Literature and Culture*, Madison: University of Wisconsin Press, 2007.

Levytsky, Boris, *The Uses of Terror: The Soviet Secret Police, 1917–1970*, trans. H. A. Piehler, New York: Coward, McCann and Geoghegan, 1972.

Lewin, Moshe, *Lenin's Last Struggle*, trans. A. M. Sheridan Smith, Ann Arbor: University of Michigan Press, 2005.

Liebman, Marcel, *Leninism under Lenin*, trans. Brian Pearce, London: Jonathan Cape, 1975.

Lih, Lars T., *Bread and Authority in Russia, 1914–1921*, Berkeley: University of California Press, 1990.

—— 'Political Testament of Lenin and Bukharin and the Meaning of NEP', *Slavic Review*, 1991, vol. 50, No. 2, 241–52.

—— *Lenin Rediscovered: What is to be Done? in Context*, Leiden: Brill, 2006.

—— *Lenin*, London: Reaktion Books, 2011.

Lincoln, W. Bruce, *Red Victory: A History of the Russian Civil War*, New York: Simon and Schuster, 1989.

Litvin, A. L., 'Krasnyi i belyi terror v rossii, 1917–1922', *Otechestvennaia istoriia*, 1993, vol. 6, 46–62.

Lovell, David W., *From Marx to Lenin: An Evaluation of Marx's Responsibility for Soviet Authoritarianism*, Cambridge: Cambridge University Press, 1984.

Luukkanen, Arto, *The Party of Unbelief: The Religious Policy of the Bolshevik Party 1917–1929*, Helsinki: Studia Historika, 1994.

McLellan, David, *Marxism after Marx*, 4th Edition, London: Palgrave, 2007.

MacMillan, Margaret, *Peacemakers: The Paris Conference of 1919 and Its Attempt to End War*, London: John Murray, 2001.

Malia, Martin, *The Soviet Tragedy: A History of Socialism in Russia, 1917–1991*, New York: The Free Press, 1994.

Mayer, Arno J., *The Furies: Violence and Terror in the French and Russian Revolutions*, New Jersey: Princeton University Press, 2000.

Mayer, Robert, 'The Dictatorship of the Proletariat from Plekhanov to Lenin', *Studies in East European Thought*, 1993, vol. 45, No. 4, 255–80.

Mawdsley, Evan, *The Russian Civil War*, Boston: Allen and Unwin, 1987.

Mel'gunov, Sergei, *The Red Terror in Russia*, Connecticut: Hyperion Press, 1975.

Meyer, Alfred G., *Leninism*, Massachusetts: Harvard University Press, 1957.

Mints, I. I. and Korablev, Yu. I. (eds.), *Zashchita velikogo oktiabria*, Moscow: Nauka, 1982.

Naimark, Norman M., *Terrorists and Social Democrats: The Russian Revolutionary Movement under Alexander III*, Massachusetts: Harvard University Press, 1983

Nation, R. Craig, *War on War: Lenin, the Zimmerwald Left, and the Origins of Communist Internationalism*, Durham: Duke University Press, 1989.

Newell, David Allen, 'The Russian Marxist Response to Terrorism', Doctoral Dissertation, Stanford University, 1981.

Novopashin, Iu. N., 'Mif o diktature proletariata', *Voprosi istorii*, 2005, vol. 12, No. 1, 41–50.

Obukhov, Leonid, 'Ideia Odnorodnogo Sotsialisticheskogo Pravitel'stva i Politicheskie Partii na Urale', unpublished paper presented at the Study Group on the Russian Revolution Annual Conference, Aberdeen, January 2008.

Parry, John T. (ed.), *Evil, Law and the State: Perspectives on State Power and Violence*, Amsterdam and New York: Rodopi, 2006.

Patenaude, Bertrand M., 'Peasants into Russians: The Utopian Essence of War Communism', *Russian Review*, 1995, vol. 54, No. 4, 552–70.

Paxton, Robert O., *The Anatomy of Fascism*, London and New York: Penguin, 2005.

Pethybridge, Roger, *One Step Backwards, Two Steps Forward: Soviet Society and Politics in the New Economic Policy*, Oxford: Clarendon Press, 1990.

Petrov, S. G., *Dokumentyi deloproizvodstva politbiuro TsK RKP(b) kak istochnik po istorii russkoi tserkvi (1921–1925)*, Moscow: Rosspen, 2004.

Pipes, Richard, *The Russian Revolution, 1899–1919*, London: Collins Harvill, 1990.

—— *Russia Under the Bolshevik Regime, 1919–1924*, London: HarperCollins, 1994.

Plekhanov, A. M., *VChK-OGPU v godyi novoi ekonomicheskoi politiki 1921–1928*, Moscow: Kuchkova Pole, 2006.

Plimak, Evgenii, *Politika Perekhodnoi Epokhi. Opyit Lenina*, Moscow: Ves' Mir, 2004.

Polan, A. J., *Lenin and the End of Politics*, London: Methuen, 1984.

Polian, Pavel, *Ne po svoei vole … Istoriia i geografiia prinuditel'nyikh migratsii v SSSR*, Moscow: Memorial, 2001.

Pravda, Alex and White, Stephen (eds.), *Ideology and Soviet Politics*, Studies in Russia and East Europe, London: Macmillan SSEES, 1988.

Priestland, D., 'Marx and the Kremlin: Writing on Marxism–Leninism and Soviet Politics after the Fall of Communism', *Journal of Political Ideologies*, 2000, vol. 5, No. 3, 377–90.

—— *Stalinism and the Politics of Mobilization: Ideas, Power, and Terror in Inter-war Russia*, New York: Oxford University Press, 2007.

Rabinowitch, Alexander, *Prelude to Revolution: The Petrograd Bolsheviks and the July 1917 Uprising*, Bloomington and London: Indiana University Press, 1968.

—— *The Bolsheviks Come to Power: The Revolution of 1917 in Petrograd*, New York: W. W. Norton, 1976.

—— *The Bolsheviks in Power. The First Year of Soviet Rule in Petrograd*, Bloomington: Indiana University Press, 2007.

Radkey, Oliver H., *The Unknown Civil War in Soviet Russia: A Study of the Green Movement in the Tambov Region 1920–1921*, Stanford: Hoover Institution Press, 1976.

Raleigh, Donald J., *Experiencing Russia's Civil War: Politics, Society, and Revolutionary Culture in Saratov, 1917–1922*, Princeton: Princeton University Press, 2002.

Rat'kovskii, I. S., *Krasnyi terror i deiatel'nost VChK v 1918 gody*, St Petersburg: St Petersburg University Press, 2006.

Read, Christopher, *Religion, Revolution and the Russian Intelligentsia, 1900–1912: The 'Vekhi' Debate and its Intellectual Background*, London: Barnes and Noble, 1979.

—— *Culture and Power in Revolutionary Russia: The Intelligentsia and the Transition from Tsarism to Communism*, London: Macmillan, 1990.

—— *Lenin: A Revolutionary Life*, London: Routledge, 2005.

Rendle, Matthew, 'Revolutionary tribunals and the origins of terror in early Soviet Russia', *Historical Research*, http://onlinelibrary.wiley.com/doi/10.1111.

Reynolds, Charles, *Modes of Imperialism*, Oxford: Martin Robertson, 1981.

Rigby, T. H., *Lenin's Government: Sovnarkom 1917–1922*, Cambridge: Cambridge University Press, 1979.

Rigby, T. H., Brown, Archie and Reddaway, Peter (eds.), *Authority, Power and Policy in the USSR: Essays Dedicated to Leonard Schapiro*, London: Macmillan, 1980.

Roberts, Geoffrey, *Stalin's Wars: From World War to Cold War, 1939–1953*, New Haven: Yale University Press, 2006.

Robespierre, Maximilien, *Virtue and Terror: Introduction by Slavoj Žižek*, London: Verso, 2007.

Rockmore, Tom, *Marxism After Marx: The Philosophy of Karl Marx*, Oxford: Blackwell, 2002.

Rosenberg, Arthur, *A History of Bolshevism: From Marx to the First Five Years' Plan*, trans. Ian F. D. Morrow, London: Oxford University Press, 1934.

Rosenberg, William G., 'Beheading the Revolution: Arno Mayer's "Furies" ', *The Journal of Modern History*, 2001, vol. 73, No. 4, 908–30.

Rosefielde, *Red Holocaust*, Oxford and New York: Routledge, 2010.

Rozin, El'khon, *Leninskaia mifologiia gosudarstva*, Moscow: Iurist', 1996.

Rummel, R. J., *Lethal Politics: Soviet Genocide and Mass Murder since 1917*, New Brunswick: Transaction Publishers, 1990.

Ryan, James, 'Lenin's Terror. Violence in the Thought of V. I. Lenin and an Assessment of the Significance of Ideology in Early Soviet State Violence', Ph.D. Dissertation, University College Cork, 2009.

—— '"Revolution is War"': The Development of the Thought of V. I. Lenin on Violence, 1899–1907', *Slavonic and East European Review*, 2011, vol. 89, No. 2, 248–73.

Sanborn, Joshua A., *Drafting the Russian Nation: Military Conscription, Total War, and Mass Politics, 1905–1925*, DeKalb, IL: Northern Illinois University Press, 2003.

—— 'Unsettling the Empire: Violent Migrations and Social Disaster in Russia during World War I', *The Journal of Modern History*, 2005, vol. 77, No. 2, 290–324.

Sandle, Mark, *A Short History of Soviet Socialism*, London: UCL Press, 1999.

Sartori, Giovanni, 'Politics, Ideology, and Belief Systems', *The American Political Science Review*, 1969, vol. 63, No. 2, 398–411.

Schapiro, Leonard, *The Origin of the Communist Autocracy: Political Opposition in the Soviet State: First Phase – 1917–1922*, Massachusetts: Harvard University Press, 1966.

Schapiro, Leonard and Reddaway, Peter (eds.), *Lenin: The Man, the Theorist, the Leader: A Reappraisal*, New York: Praeger, 1967.

Schull, Joseph, 'What is Ideology? Theoretical Problems and Lessons from Soviet-Type Societies', *Political Studies*, 1992, vol. XL, No. 4, 728–741.

Scott, James C., *Seeing Like a State: How Certain Schemes to Improve the Human Condition Have Failed*, New Haven: Yale University Press, 1998.

Service, Robert, *Lenin: A Political Life*, Three Volumes, London: Macmillan; Bloomington: Indiana University Press, 1985–1995.

—— *Lenin: A Biography*, London: Pan Macmillan, 2000.

—— *A History of Modern Russia: From Nicholas II to Putin*, London: Penguin, 2003.

Shakhnovich, M. I., *Lenin i Problemyi Ateizma. Kritika Religii v trudakh V. I. Lenina*, Moscow and Leningrad: Academy of Sciences of the USSR, 1961.

Shearer, David R., 'Social Disorder, Mass Repression, and the NKVD During the 1930s', *Cahiers du Monde russe*, 2001. vol. 42, No. 2, 3–4, 505–34.

Shukman, Harold, *Lenin and the Russian Revolution*, London: Batsford, 1966.

Skocpol, Theda, 'Cultural Idioms and Political Ideologies in the Revolutionary Reconstruction of State Power: A Rejoinder to Sewell', *The Journal of Modern History*, 1985, vol. 57, No. 1, 86–96.

Simbirtsev, Igor', *VChK v leninskoi rossii, 1917–1922. V zavere revolutsii*, Moscow: Tsentrpoligraff, 2008.

Slavin, B. F., *Lenin protiv Stalina: Poslednii boi revoliutsionera*, Moscow: URSS, 2010.

Smele, Jonathan D. and Heywood, Anthony (eds.), *The Russian Revolution of 1905: Centenary Perspectives*, London: Routledge, 2005.

Smele, Jonathan D., *Civil War in Siberia: The Anti-Bolshevik Government of Admiral Kolchak, 1918–1920*, Cambridge: Cambridge University Press, 1996.

Singh, Rustam, 'Violence in the Leninist Revolution', *Economic and Political Weekly*, 1990, vol. 25, No. 52, 2843ff.

Singh, Gopal, 'Politics and Violence', *Social Scientist*, 1976, vol. 4, No. 11, 58–66.

Smirnov. G. L. (ed.), *Leninskaia kontseptsiia sotsializma*, Moscow: Politizdat, 1990.

Smith, Scott B., *Captives of Revolution: The Socialist Revolutionaries and the Bolshevik Dictatorship, 1918–1923*, Pittsburgh: University of Pittsburgh Press, 2011.

Smith, Steve, 'Two Cheers for the "Return of Ideology"', *Revolutionary Russia*, 2004, vol. 17, No. 2, 119–35.

Smith, Irving H., 'Lenin's Views on the First World War, 1914–1917', *Europa*, 1979–80, vol. 3, No. 1, 61–72.

Solzhenitsyn, Aleksandr, *The Gulag Archipelago 1918–1956: An Experiment in Literary Investigation I–II*, trans. by Thomas P. Whitney, London: Collins and Harvill Press, 1974.

Sorel, Georges, *Reflections on Violence*, trans. T. E. Hulme and J. Roth, New York: Dover, 2004.

Strokov, A. A., *V. I. Lenin o voine i voennom isskustve*, Moscow: Nauka, 1971.

Suny, Ronald Grigor, '"Breaking Eggs, Making Omelets": Explaining Terror in Lenin's and Stalin's Revolutions.' Unpublished paper.

—— 'Class and State in the Early Soviet Period: A Reply to Sheila Fitzpatrick', *Slavic Review*, 1988, vol. 47, No. 4, 614–9.

—— *The Soviet Experiment: Russia, The USSR, and The Successor States*, New York and Oxford: Oxford University Press, 1998.

Swain, Geoffrey, *The Origins of the Russian Civil War*, London: Longman, 1996.

Talmon, J. L., *The Origins of Totalitarian Democracy*, London: Secker and Warburg, 1952.

Temkin, Ia. G., 'Razvitie leninskoi programmyi mira na puti k Velikomu Oktiabriu', *Voprosi istorii KPSS*, 1977, vol. 6, 3–17.

Thatcher, Ian D. (ed.), *Reinterpreting Revolutionary Russia: Essays in Honour of James D. White*, Hampshire: Palgrave Macmillan, 2006.

Theen, Rolf H. W., 'The Idea of the Revolutionary State: Tkachev, Trotsky, and Lenin', *Russian Review*, 1972, vol. 31, No. 4, 383–97.

Tikhomirov, Ruslan Vladimirovich, 'Problema revolutsionnogo nasiliia v rossiiskoi sotsial-demokraticheskoi pechati (bol'shevikov i men'shevikov), fevral' 1917 – mart 1918 gg.', Ph.D. (candidate) Dissertation, St Petersburg: 2000.

Torrance, John, *Karl Marx's Theory of Ideas*, Cambridge: Cambridge University Press, 1995.

Tucker, Robert C. (ed.), *Stalinism: Essays in Historical Interpretation*, New York: Norton, 1977.

Urilov, I., *Istoriia rossiiskoi sotsial-demokratii (men'shevizma): Chast' chetvertaia: stanovlenie partii*, Moscow: Sobranie, 2008.

Van der Linden, Marcel, *Western Marxism and the Soviet Union: A Survey of Critical Theories and Debates Since 1917*, trans. Jurriaan Bendien, Historical Materialism Book Series, Chicago: Haymarket, 2009.

Van Ree, Erik, '"Lenin's Last Struggle" Revisited', *Revolutionary Russia*, 2001, vol. 14, No. 2, 85–122.

—— 'Reluctant Terrorists? Transcaucasian Social-Democracy, 1901–1909', *Europe–Asia Studies*, 2008, vol. 60, No. 1, (January 2008), 127–54.

—— 'Lenin's Conception of Socialism in One Country, 1915–17', *Revolutionary Russia*, 2010, vol. 23, No. 2, 159–181.

Varhall, Gregory, 'The Development of Lenin's Conception of the Dictatorship of the Proletariat', Ph.D. Dissertation, University of Notre Dame, 1982.

Velidov, A.S, 'Na puti k terroru', *Voprosi istorii*, 2002, 87–118.

V. I. Lenin o zakonnosti i pravosudii, Voprosyi bor'byi s prestupnost'iu. Vyipusk 11, Moscow: Iuridicheskaia literatura, 1970.

Volkogonov, Dmitri, *Lenin: A New Biography*, New York: The Free Press, 1994.

Von Hagen, Mark, *Soldiers in the Proletarian Revolution: The Red Army and the Soviet Socialist State, 1917–1930*, Ithaca: Cornell University Press, 1990.

Vourkoutiotis, Vasilis, *Reform in Revolutionary Times: The Civil–Military Relationship in Early Soviet Russia*, New York: Peter Lang, 2009.

Wade, Francis C., 'On Violence', *The Journal of Philosophy*, 1971, vol. 68, No. 12, 369–77.

Wade, Rex A., *The Bolshevik Revolution and Russian Civil War*, Connecticut: Greenwood Press, 2001.

Wandycz, Piotr S., *Soviet–Polish Relations 1917–1921*, Massachusetts: Harvard University Press, 1969.

Weiner, Amir (ed.), *Landscaping the Human Garden: Twentieth-Century Population Management in a Comparative Framework*, Stanford: Stanford University Press, 2003.

White, James D., *Lenin: The Practice and Theory of Revolution*, Hampshire: Palgrave, 2001.

White, Stephen, *Political Culture and Soviet Politics*, London: Macmillan, 1979.

White, Stephen and Pravda, Alex (eds.), *Ideology and Soviet Politics*, London: Macmillan/ SSEES, 1988.

Whittaker, David J. (ed.), *The Terrorism Reader*, 2nd Edition, London and New York: Routledge, 2003.

Williams, Beryl, *Lenin*, Profiles in Power Series, London: Longman, 2001.

Witte, Joan, 'Violence in Lenin's Thought and Practice: The Spark and the Conflagration', *Terrorism and Political Violence*, 1993, vol. 5, No. 3, 135–203.

Yakovlev, Alexander N., *A Century of Violence in Soviet Russia*, trans. Anthony Austin, New Haven: Yale University Press, 2002.

Zamoyski, Adam, *Warsaw 1920: Lenin's Failed Conquest of Europe*, London: Harper Collins, 2008.

Žižek, Slavoj, *Violence*, London: Profile Books, 2008.

Index

Printed in Great Britain
by Amazon